New Approaches to Greek and Roman Warfare

New Approaches to Greek and Roman Warfare

Edited by Lee L. Brice

WILEY Blackwell

Registered Office
John Wiley & Sons, Inc., 111 River Street, Hoboken, NJ 07030, USA

Editorial Office
111 River Street, Hoboken, NJ 07030, USA

For details of our global editorial offices, customer services, and more information about Wiley products visit us at www.wiley.com.

Wiley also publishes its books in a variety of electronic formats and by print-on-demand. Some content that appears in standard print versions of this book may not be available in other formats.

Library of Congress Cataloging-in-Publication Data

Name: Brice, Lee L., editor.
Title: New approaches to Greek and Roman warfare / edited by Lee L. Brice.
Description: Hoboken, NJ : Wiley-Blackwell, 2020. | Includes
    bibliographical references and index.
Identifiers: LCCN 2019034363 (print) | LCCN 2019034364 (ebook) | ISBN
    9781118273333 (paperback) | ISBN 9781118338780 (adobe pdf) | ISBN
    9781118340547 (epub)
Subjects: LCSH: Military art and science–Greece–History–To 500. |
    Military art and science–Rome–History. | Greece–History, Military–To
    146 B.C. | Rome–History, Military.
Classification: LCC U33 .N49 2020 (print) | LCC U33 (ebook) | DDC
    355.00938–dc23
LC record available at https://lccn.loc.gov/2019034363
LC ebook record available at https://lccn.loc.gov/2019034364

Cover Design: Wiley
Cover Images: Trajan column in Rome © boggy22/Getty Images, Chironeia Skull Courtesy of Maria A. Liston

Set in 9.5/12.5pt STIXTwoText by SPi Global, Pondicherry, India
Printed and bound in Singapore by Markono Print Media Pte Ltd

10 9 8 7 6 5 4 3 2 1

ΓΕΩΡΓΙΑΙ,
 ΑΡΙΣΤΗΙ.

Contents

Notes on Contributors *ix*
Preface *xiii*
List of Abbreviations *xv*
List of Illustrations *xvii*

1 **Ancient Warfare and Moving Beyond "New Military History"** *1*
Lee L. Brice

Part I   Greece *13*

2 **Wealth and the Logistics of Greek Warfare: Food, Pay, and Plunder** *17*
Matthew Trundle

3 **Early Greek Siege Warfare** *29*
Michael G. Seaman

4 **Daily Life in Classical Greek Armies, c. 500–330 BCE** *39*
John W.I. Lee

5 **Soldiers' Home: Life After Battle** *53*
Lawrence A. Tritle

6 **Greek Cavalry in the Hellenistic World: Review and Reappraisal** *65*
Glenn R. Bugh

7 **Skeletal Evidence for the Impact of Battle on Soldiers and Non-Combatants** *81*
Maria A. Liston

Part II   Rome *95*

8 **Financing Imperialism in the Middle Roman Republic** *99*
Nathan Rosenstein

9 **Indiscipline in the Roman Army of the Late Republic and Principate** *113*
   Lee L. Brice

10 **The Neurophysiology of Panic on the Ancient Battlefield** *127*
   Susan M. Heidenreich and Jonathan P. Roth

11 **Roman Siege Warfare: Moral and Morale** *139*
   Josh Levithan

12 **Roman Military Communities and the Families of Auxiliary Soldiers** *149*
   Elizabeth M. Greene

13 **Approaching "Ethnic" Communities in the Roman Auxilia** *161*
   Alexander Meyer

14 **Health, Wounds, and Medicine in the Late Roman Army (250–600 CE)** *173*
   Philip Rance

   Index *187*

Notes on Contributors

Lee L. Brice is Professor of History and Distinguished Lecturer at Western Illinois University. He has published numerous books on military history including most recently *Insurgency and Terrorism in the Ancient Mediterranean World* (co-edited with T. Howe), as well as articles and chapters on Greek numismatics, Greek and Roman military history, the Roman army on film, and pedagogy. He is series editor of *Warfare in the Ancient Mediterranean World* (Brill) and senior editor of the journal *Research Perspectives in Ancient History*.

Glenn R. Bugh is Associate Professor of Classical and Byzantine Studies at Virginia Tech. He holds a PhD from the University of Maryland and has been a research fellow at the American School of Classical Studies at Athens; the Institute for Advanced Study in Princeton; the Center for Hellenic Studies in Washington, DC; and the Hellenic Institute for Byzantine and Post-Byzantine Studies in Venice, Italy. He has published many articles and three books: *The Horsemen of Athens*; *The Cambridge Companion to the Hellenistic World*; and a revised edition of Kevin Andrews,' *Castles of the Morea* (2007).

Elizabeth M. Greene is Associate Professor in the Department of Classics at the University of Western Ontario. She is a Roman archaeologist focusing primarily on the western provinces and life in the frontier regions of the Roman empire. She has excavated at the military fort and settlement at Vindolanda in the Hadrian's Wall corridor since 2002. Her research explores the role of women and families in the communities of the Roman army through investigation of archeological and historical sources.

Susan M. Heidenreich is Professor Emerita of Psychology at the University of San Francisco. She received her PhD in Experimental Psychology from the University of Wisconsin at Madison. She is the author of dozens of articles and abstracts on perception and the visual system. Her work with Dr. Kathy Turano on eye movements for pictures is featured in the *Oxford Companion to the Mind*.

John W.I. Lee is Associate Professor of History at UC Santa Barbara. His research interests include Greek and Achaemenid history, ancient warfare, and the development of classics and archaeology in the nineteenth century. Lee is the author of *A Greek Army on the March: Soldiers and Survival in Xenophon's Anabasis* (2008). He is writing a book on John Wesley Gilbert (1863–1923), the first African American scholar to attend the American School of Classical Studies at Athens.

Josh Levithan is the author of *Roman Siege Warfare* (2013) and the blog *A Century Back*.

Maria A. Liston is an Associate Professor and former Chair of the Anthropology Department at the University of Waterloo, Ontario. Her research focuses on skeletal biology, paleopathology, cremation burials, skeletal remains found in wells, and military burials. She has conducted research at numerous Greek sites. In addition, she has studied military burials in the United States and Canada. She has recently co-authored *The Agora Bone Well*, a study of over 450 infant and fetal remains found in a well in the Athenian Agora.

Alexander Meyer is an Associate Professor of Classical Studies at the University of Western Ontario. He has published books and articles about the evolution of Roman auxiliary units, ancient time-keeping devices, and excavations at the Vindolanda Roman fort. His specialties are in Latin epigraphy, mobility in the ancient world, and conceptions of time and space.

Philip Rance is a Research Fellow at the Centre for Advanced Study in Sofia and a Visiting Scholar at the Free University Berlin. He has taught ancient and medieval history and Greek language and literature at universities in the United Kingdom, Germany, and Belgium, and has held senior research fellowships at the Ludwig-Maximilian University, Munich (Humboldt Foundation Senior Fellowship); Koç University, Istanbul (for research in the Topkapı Palace Library); and the Herzog August Bibliothek, Wolfenbüttel. He has published widely on military culture in Late Antiquity, and Greek, Roman, and Byzantine technical-scientific writing, its manuscript tradition, and its reception.

Nathan Rosenstein is Professor Emeritus in the Department of History at The Ohio State University. His research focuses on the social, political, and economic aspects of Republican warfare. He is the author or co-editor of several books, most recently *Rome and the Mediterranean 290–146 BC: The Imperial Republic*. He is currently co-editor of *The Oxford History of the Roman World*.

Jonathan P. Roth is Professor of History at San Jose State University. He received his PhD in Ancient History from Columbia University. Dr. Roth is the author of *Logistics of the Roman Army at War, 264 B.C. to A.D. 235* and *Roman Warfare*, as well as chapters in *The Cambridge History of Greek and Roman Warfare, Representations of War in Ancient Rome*, and *The Roman Army and The Economy*.

Michael G. Seaman received his PhD in ancient history from UCLA. He is Assistant Professor of Classical Studies, DePauw University. His main area of research is ancient Greek warfare. His studies of ancient warfare have appeared in the journal *Historia*, as well as in edited volumes published by Oxford University Press and Wiley Blackwell. He is currently finishing a book entitled *Ancient Greek Siege Warfare from Homer to Alexander* and is editing a book forthcoming from Brill on asymmetric warfare in the ancient world.

Lawrence A. Tritle is Professor Emeritus of History at Loyola Marymount University, Los Angeles, California. In 2012 he was selected as Daum Research Professor of History and in 2014 received the Rains Award for Distinguished Research and Scholarship. An ancient historian by training, his publications include *From Melos to My Lai: War and Survival*; *A New History of the Peloponnesian War*; *The Oxford Handbook of Warfare in the Classical World* (edited with B. Campbell); and most recently, *The Many Faces of War* (edited with J.W. Warren). His research focuses on comparative war and violence and his investigations center on the experience of war, investigating war's impact on the individuals who fight and the wider consequences of violence on culture and society. A combat veteran of the Vietnam War, Tritle supported South Vietnamese forces in ground operations. His decorations include the Combat Infantrymen's Badge, Bronze Star, and Vietnamese Cross of Gallantry.

Matthew Trundle moved to New Zealand in 1999 as Lecturer in Classics at Victoria University of Wellington, becoming Senior Lecturer and Associate Professor before moving to the University of Auckland to become Chair and Professor of Classics and Ancient History in 2012. His research interests are primarily in ancient Greek history, and his publications focus on the social and economic aspects of the classical Greek world. He is the author of *Greek Mercenaries from the Late Archaic Period to Alexander*, and has edited volumes entitled *New Perspectives on Ancient Warfare, Beyond the Gates of Fire: New Perspectives on the Battle of Thermopylae*, and most recently, *Brill's Companion to Sieges in the Ancient Mediterranean*. He has also published numerous articles and chapters.

Preface

This volume began life, like so many projects, at a meeting of the Association of Ancient Historians. The original idea was a project called "Before, During, and After Battle." It was intended to evoke both the core of most military history – the battle as crucible – and the disconnect between student expectations based on traditional military history and the opportunities provided by the newer approaches. I see it as an effort to get through to colleagues in history departments who still think of military history as "drums and trumpets" and see it as obsolete. Modern military history recognizes that while battle and warfare are processes that can and should be studied in both their macro- and micro-dimensions, they are not ends in themselves. The overall goal is to better understand the past, and thus the human condition. Warfare and military history is one path for getting there. In the process of the project I hoped readers might better understand military history and its place in the meta tent of history.

I want to include here a brief mention about new and recent work and about topics in need of attention. There is too much new work coming out to recognize it all; it suffices to assert here that there is a great deal of splendid work recently completed and in progress. Here's a "shout out" to watch for work by Doug Lee, Elizabeth M. Greene, Philip Rance, Sylvian Fachard, Alex Nodell, Daniëlle Slootjes, Jeremy Armstrong, Matthew Trundle, Saskia Roselaar, John Donahue, Michael Taylor, Lynne Kvapil, Matt Sears, Jake Butera, Frank Russell, Brian Turner, Kathryn Milne, Dominic Machado, Bill Murray, and Wayne E. Lee. As far as areas needing work, much more research and publishing need to be done on warfare/militaries and the groups that have been overlooked in the past – women, metics, and slaves – not only as victims but in all capacities related to military institutions, preparedness for conflict, in war, and afterwards. The environment as it connects to warfare and militaries is an area in need of investigation. A recent conference in Athens highlighted the need for much more work on post-siege sacks, destructions, and the abandonment of settlements and cities. Ancient navies need more attention too, as the Egadi Islands Project (https://rpmnautical.org/projects) and related efforts all over the Mediterranean demonstrate. Finally, more needs to be done on integrating the use of digital tools into the work on military history of the ancient world. Archaeological teams are increasingly relying on many digital tools to augment their investigations; it is time for more studies of ancient warfare to embrace these tools and bring them to the classroom.

An axiom in military studies is that no plan survives contact with an enemy. In the case of this project it was chronic diseases that visited their wrath upon the project leader. But I smote the foul pestilences and left their ruin behind. I am grateful to my medical specialists for their assistance. As a result, this project has been delayed unavoidably. I owe my fellow contributors an immense, sincere apology and even greater gratitude for their generous patience. All but three of the chapters in this volume (Chapters 1, 9, and 13) were completed by the end of 2013. Most of those authors' chapters did not have the benefit of research published since 2012. Despite that, their work is thorough and where appropriate they have addressed the issue of later research in the "Further Reading" that follows each chapter's Reference list. Before the volume could be completed one of our contributors, Matthew Trundle, passed away 12 July 2019 after a long battle with Acute Lymphoid Leukemia. He is missed by all of us.

Now the project comes to its close I have a number of other institutions and individuals to thank for their help in bringing this volume to completion. Thanks to Jad Abumrad, Robert Krulwich, and the whole *Radiolab* podcast team for explaining in clear terms some neurological puzzlers relevant to this project and for inspiring me during long commutes. Part of the research for Chapter 9 was made possible with a Summer Stipend from the Western Illinois University Foundation and Office of Sponsored Projects. I am extremely grateful to Jennifer of WIU InterLibrary Loan and Ashley and Greg of the Circulation department at Malpass Library for their generous help in acquiring materials. I am also indebted and thankful to Wiley Blackwell, especially Todd Green and Ajith Kumar for supporting the project and for their patience. Special thanks to Michael Seaman and Larry Tritle who have been there since the project started and have stuck with it. The American School of Classical Studies in Athens has been invaluable, providing a Whitehead Distinguished Scholar fellowship that gave me time to work in a fabulous library and visit relevant sites. Thanks to the 2018 ASCSA Summer Seminar students with whom we traveled to battlefields in Greece and explored ancient warfare and culture. I am also grateful to Cheryl Golden, Paul Johstono, Brian Turner, and the anonymous peer reviewers who read the volume and improved it; any mistakes that remain are my own. The most important debt of gratitude goes to Georgia Tsouvala who helped smite pestilences, provided advice, and read the volume repeatedly. This volume would not have been completed without her support and so I dedicate it to her, with great appreciation and affection.

2019

Lee L. Brice
Athens, Greece

List of Abbreviations

In the discussion an effort has been made to transliterate Greek place names following the Greek, except in cases (e.g., Plataea) of sites more well known by their Latinized transliteration. Authors' references to chapters are to this volume. Abbreviations of ancient history works employed in this book are those from the *Oxford Classical Dictionary, 4th ed.*, in addition to the following:

CHGRW   Sabin, Philip, Michael Whitby, and Hans van Wees (eds.) *Cambridge History of Greek and Roman Warfare*, 2 vols. Cambridge: Cambridge University Press, 2007.

GSW   Pritchett, W. Kendrick. *Greek State at War*, 5 vols. Berkeley: University of California Press, 1971–1991.

RIB   Collingwood, R.P. and J.P. Wright. *Roman Inscriptions of Britain I.* Oxford: University Press, 1965.

RMD   Roxan, M.M. ed. *Roman Military Diplomas*, vols. 1–4. London: Institute of Archaeology, 1978–1993.

Tab.Vindol   Bowman, Alan K., and J. David Thomas. 2003. *The Vindolanda Writing-Tablets: Tabulae Vindolandenses.* 3 vols. London: The British Museum Press, 1974, 1994, and 2003.

TRAC   *Theoretical Roman Archaeology Conference* Proceedings, Oxford: Oxbow Books, 1993–2016.

List of Illustrations

Map Pt.1   Ancient Greece. *Source:* Ancient World Mapping Center © 2015
(awmc.unc.edu). Used by permission.   14–15

Figure 6.1   Cavalry tablet; inscription #17587. *Source:* American School of
Classical Studies, Agora Excavations; Used with permission.   66

Figure 6.2   Cavalry tablet drawing; inscription #17551. *Source:* American School
of Classical Studies, Agora Excavations; Used with permission.   66

Figure 6.3   Pheidon, hipparch to Lemnos, clay tokens. *Source:* American School of
Classical Studies, Agora Excavations; Used with permission.   66

Figure 6.4   Cavalry inscription. *Source:* American School of Classical Studies, Agora
Excavations; Used with permission.   72

Figure 6.5   The *Alexander Mosaic*, filling the floor of a room in the House of the Faun in
Pompeii. Naples Archaeological Museum. *Source:* D-DAI-ROM #58.1447,
Photographer, Bartl. Used by permission.   75

Figure 7.1   Superior view of a skull from Chaironeia, showing blade wound
(right arrow) and wound from a spear butt spike (left arrow).
Source: Author. Used by permission.   86

Figure 7.2   Skull from Chaironeia with the upper face removed by a blade.
The upper arrow shows the point of impact, and the lower arrow
indicates the portion of the forehead removed by the blade.
Source: Author. Used by permission.   86

Figure 7.3   Anterior tibia (shin bone) from Charioneia. Arrows indicate location
of three blade wounds striking near the same point. *Source:* Author.
Used by permission.   87

Figure 7.4   Right ulna (lower arm bone) of an adult male killed in the Herulian
sack of Athens. Arrow indicates a partially healed blade wound.
Source: Author. Used by permission.   88

Figure 7.5   Skull of a woman killed in the Herulian sack of Athens, showing
primary blows (black arrows) to the head with a bladed weapon such
as an axe, and a secondary wound (white arrow) caused by the blade
bouncing off the head. *Source:* Author. Used by permission.   90

Map Pt.2   Ancient Roman Empire. *Source:* Ancient World Mapping Center © 2015
(awmc.unc.edu). Used by permission.   96–97

Figure 10.1   Image of normal brain physiology. *Source:* National Institute of
Health, Public Domain.   135

1

Ancient Warfare and Moving Beyond "New Military History"

Lee L. Brice

Introduction

The Greek philosopher Heraclitus once remarked, "War is the father of all things." Since our earliest Greek historians, Herodotus and Thucydides, both wrote on war then perhaps it follows that history of warfare is the father of all historical study. That is an overstatement, but there is no denying the importance of warfare and military-related topics in early historiography. These Greek authors did not invent military history. Earlier societies and states in Egypt, the ancient Near East, and throughout the Mediterranean basin preserved accounts of warfare and military preparation in songs, texts, and art. As has been noted elsewhere, warfare was a fundamental occupation and concern of all ancient societies around the Mediterranean Sea (Fagan and Trundle 2010). No wonder there are so many texts and images dealing with it. The topic's importance to historical understanding is clear so it should not be surprising that military history remained for ages one of the dominant fields of history.

Regardless of whether it is actually the "father" of any field, military history has remained important and popular over the centuries. The popularity is grounded in the fact that military history has served numerous purposes including entertainment, explanation of the past and present (incorporating propaganda), leadership skills, criticism of leaders and peers, demonstration of authors' knowledge of history and writers, civic training, antiquarianism, and displays of literary or rhetorical (and often both) skills, among other things. Readers have similarly drawn on military history for entertainment, education and training, decision-making, career preparation, and leadership skills, among other things. In bookstores, visual media, video games, and in the classroom military history enjoys a level of popularity with readers common to few other historical fields (Biddell and Citino 2014; Armstrong 2016, pp. 1–2; Morillo and Pavkovic 2017, pp. 1–9).

But as Biddell and Citino have pointed out, such popularity has been a double-edged sword (2014, pp. 2–3). It provides interest and demand but also provides works of extremely mixed quality on popular topics. This popularity has led some potential readers and scholars to dismiss the field as too popular, while others see it as obsolete (Citino 2007; Hanson 2007, pp. 10–14). Such readers are often unaware that military history is more than arms and armor; it is an interdisciplinary field that has grown and changed much since the Second World War.[1]

New Approaches to Greek and Roman Warfare, First Edition. Edited by Lee L. Brice.
© 2020 John Wiley & Sons, Inc. Published 2020 by John Wiley & Sons, Inc.

Approaches to Military History

Traditional military history has primarily focused on operational history (including battle narratives, tactics, strategy, and operations) and consideration of famous personalities. Battlefield narratives date back to New Kingdom Egypt and have long been a staple in military history. They fill educational and training roles for students and officers as well as providing entertainment for diverse audiences. Operational histories in particular have carried the negative label "drums and trumpets" because of the focus on battle narratives and a tendency at times toward nationalism. The focus on military personalities like Alexander or Julius Caesar has similarly fulfilled a desire to explain and educate readers about military success and failure as well as entertain. When most military history was written by military men for military-minded readers, as was long the case, these were the topics on which they focused as most useful. Criticism of both these topics focuses on how little they actually tell us about warfare, its history, and its place in culture (Chambers 1991, pp. 397–398, citing Kohn and Paret; Rosenstein 2009; contra Hanson 2007; Loreto 2015). These criticisms are fair of much traditional work, but it is important to acknowledge also that these topics remain a key component of military history. Besides their popularity, these kinds of work require a great deal of skill to complete well and can be outstanding treatments that can be extremely informative of not only their primary focus but also contextualizing their topic historically and culturally (Showalter 1975; Biddle and Citino 2014, pp. 3–4). This traditional fodder of military history dominates public perceptions of military history.

A third subject common in traditional military history has been the study of the various parts and minute pieces of warfare and military institutions such as arms, armor, ranks, insignia, and similar particulars. Obsession with labeling and describing these kinds of details and other minutiae has not become less antiquarian with time (Spiller 2006). While much of ancient history has moved on from antiquarianism, these kinds of military works remain popular with numerous readers, not limited to gamers and modelers (Bishop and Coulston 2006) and they can be useful for understanding the material culture of an army, such as what was recovered at the 9 CE battlefield of Kalkriese (Berger et al. 1996–2013). Until recently, however, these works seldom led to broader examinations of the infrastructure that created and distributed such items or of their cultural implications (James 2011).

New Military History, as it came to be known, emerged in publications from the late 1960s as a product of the changes that swept through all fields of history after the two world wars. Just as historians in other specializations drew on methods and approaches new to them, like anthropology and sociology, to engage in more social and cultural history after 1945, so did military historians. It had actually begun in Europe during the interwar period, but it took until the early 1970s for the "new" military history approaches to become the dominant wave among academic historians. New Military History is sometimes referred to as the "war and society school" of history because of its explicit turn away from operational histories, military principles, and command instruction to examine the impact of war on the larger society and, later, the impact of broader society and culture on warfare and military institutions (Bourke 2006; Spiller 2006). The new methods brought in more modeling and theory. These trends affected ancient history as much as modern military history (Hanson 2007; Fagan and Trundle 2010, pp. 1–19; Brice and Roberts 2011). New Military History was not a new field and it did not obliterate traditional military history, even if it felt that way to some people (Loreto 2015). It was another school of thought in the military history tent, and the name did not age well.

John Keegan in 1976 introduced in the midst of the New Military History a new approach to grasping soldiers' experience in combat. His seminal work, *Face of Battle* (1976), attempted to provide a soldier's perspective approach to the sharp end of battle. He complained that the war and society trend had, among other issues, "lost sight of what armies were for" (Keegan 1976, p. 28 quoting M. Howard). In its focus on battles it was traditional, but his attempt to examine battle from the soldiers' point of view reflected the social history approach (history from the bottom up) of which he was critical. Critics noted that Keegan's book was imperfect, but it captured readers' attention. It spawned a new "school" of military history as it inspired historians to apply Keegan's methods to other armies including those in the ancient world. Victor Hanson applied it to hoplite armies in 1989 (new edition 2009) and there have been a number of related studies on Roman armies (Goldsworthy 1996; Sabin 2000; Daly 2001). The new works have been popular and stimulated much discussion about the strengths and weaknesses of the approach (Wheeler 2011, pp. 64–75). The methods of the "face of battle school" may be imperfect, but the "school" did much to reinvigorate military history and contributed to the growth of the field in the decades that followed.

Another approach to military history that has become increasingly popular among scholars and students of history is grounded in a technocentric focus of analysis and explanation of war in history. In such works authors tend to treat technology – its adoption, development, impact, or failure to be open to it – as the key to the history of warfare. In a way, this trend is related closely to the antiquarian fascination discussed previously. This tech approach is as popular in visual media, such as television and video games, as it is in published works on warfare. Works in this vein tend to take a deterministically progressive view of history as if all innovation was leading to the present. Such works tend to privilege weapons over the individuals who develop, distribute, and employ them. Given the role of technology in our daily lives, such a connection in history may seem natural. Also, because it is (or it seems) newer than "drums and trumpets" it has been popular among academic as well as non-academic authors and analysts. This approach is also common in works written by members of the strategic studies community who may be trying to influence defense policy and appropriations (e.g. Revolutions in Military Affairs, see Brice 2011, pp. 138– 142). While the ancient world may be said by some to have been less technological than the modern world, it has been subject to this technocentric approach (Matthew 2011). However, the problem with the technocentric approach is that because it ignores much of the society that creates and uses such technology, authors in this school tend to present history in deterministic and monocausal terms (Black 2004; Spiller 2006; Lendon 2005; Rey 2010). The popularity of this technocentric school ensures that it will not be diminishing any time soon, so readers need to be careful consumers. This school also did not obliterate drums and trumpets military history.

Traditional military history topics continue to be researched and published along with New Military History. Some authors have seemed to chaff at the trend of drawing on these increasingly technical specializations and the apparent absence of operational studies (Wheeler 2011; Loreto 2015). But operational studies and military biographies centered in the ancient world have not disappeared. There are numerous battlefield books appearing annually. Some of these works are sloppy or superficial. However, the best work combines the ancient sources with new approaches to illuminate the conflicts, such as Seth Kendall's history of the Social Wars (2013) or Peter Krentz's analysis of the Battle of Marathon (2011) or the study of the Battle of Philippi by Jacob Butera and Matthew Sears, who employed satellite imaging, geographic information system (GIS), path-finding analysis, and first-hand topographical autopsy of the site in their revealing reexamination of this famous battle (2017). Similar work, drawing on the same mix of technology and methods led the same two authors to develop a modern guidebook to ancient battlefields (Butera and Sears 2019). Recently, the sources for the battles of Thermopylae and Cannae were examined in light of narrative analysis (Gils et al. 2019). Alexander the Great and Julius Caesar continue to provide topics for military biographies long after one would think every facet of their military careers had been the subject of intense analysis. New histories of Alexander, in particular, have studied anew his military career with the explicit goal of revealing new insights to educate as well as entertain readers (Lonsdale 2007; Heckel and Tritle 2009).

Military history has grown and matured as the next generations of scholars and students seek additional tools to understand and explain the past. In addition to the "New" or "war and society" school and technocentric approaches, there has been a blossoming of interdisciplinary activity as military historians have drawn methodologies from an array of fields well beyond the origins of New Military History. Comparative military history has recently grown, as a result of the recognition that the field has been too Eurocentric, and coupled with an acceptance of global approaches in other fields of history. Such examinations have been especially necessary as new models, such as the Revolution in Military Affairs (RMA), have required a better understanding of military institutions outside Europe (Black 2004). Generalist approaches in anthropology, archaeology, economics, and sociology have been augmented by focusing on more specialized sub-fields like military sociology and organizational behavior. Conflict archaeology, crowd psychology, forensic anthropology, gender studies, game theory, environmental studies, and human physiology are among the numerous specialized fields that have provided conceptual tools with which historians have tried to find ways to better understand warfare (Morillo and Pavkovic 2017; Biddle and Citino 2014). This new wave of military history reflects changes in the broader discipline.

The methodological changes are just as true of military historians of ancient Greek and Roman warfare as of modern warfare. In addition to changes in the field of military history, there have been similar developments in ancient history and classical studies that have changed the way we look at Greek and Roman warfare. Archaeologists, for example, uncover new artifacts, sites, and sources, such as new inscriptions, that illustrate features of the Athenian cavalry or daily life in the Roman camp. Specialists in various fields using laboratory sciences reveal previously unavailable data including the ways in which particular weapon-use can appear on the skeletal remains of users and victims (e.g. James 2011). Historians employ new ways of looking at old and new evidence to reveal information that was overlooked earlier. We also ask new kinds of questions of our evidence to examine previously neglected or unimagined topics, like the presence of women and children in military camps (e.g. Allison 2013; Greene 2016). Many of the gains that have been made are based on research and topical refinement initiated decades ago and reinforced by subsequent studies. But until recently, it was beyond the ken of ancient historians. As a result of these and similar efforts, the field of ancient history and ancient military history is far from being static. The field has immense vitality, methodological diversity, and depth.

The Chapters in this Volume

The studies collected here are from an array of specialists in ancient history, not all of whom would characterize themselves as military historians. They each bring their particular specialization to bear on distinct topics. Their discussions are specifically intended to illustrate: (i) how we are improving our understanding of ancient warfare and militaries by using contemporary approaches and tools, combined with traditional methodologies, to reveal new or overlooked evidence and (ii) how we reexamine old evidence in light of recent documentary and archaeological discoveries and ask new questions of it. In the process of exploring these discussions, readers will also encounter the results of these studies into warfare. In this way the book provides a good supplement to prior knowledge about the ancient world or to students taking a course in ancient warfare.

Any collection of essays may be organized in a variety of ways and this volume is no different. In order to facilitate use of this book with broader chronological surveys of military history the chapters are arranged chronologically into two parts, Greece and Rome. Chapters 2 and 8 examine the close connection between cash and conflict. Instead of battles, sieges figure in the discussions of Chapters 3 and 11, so that reader get a better sense of the importance of this brutal and expensive element of warfare. The personal experience of military service and its society is emphasized in Chapters 2, 4, 5, 9 12, and 13. Case studies in Chapters 5, 10, 11, and 14 examine psychological components of military service in terms of morale, panic, recovery, and psychological trauma. Hard science approaches grounded in human physiology and anatomy are the topics of Chapters 7 and 10 as they reveal some of warfare's biological impacts on individuals. A number of the chapters, including 3, 5, 7, and 11, consider aspects of the victims of warfare, reminding us that war is more than what happens to soldiers. Two chapters engage new evidence about components of ancient militaries: Chapter 6 on Greek cavalry, and Chapter 14 on Roman medical professionals. Lastly, although traditional military history tends to ignore the role of women in families and as victims, four Chapters (3, 5, 7, 11, and 13) address issues connected with women and war. Each chapter is self-contained; readers may read them in any order they like. Continuous narratives of the events discussed in the chapters and further reading opportunities can be found in the bibliographies and further readings.

Since the early twentieth century, the economics of warfare and the capacity of states and societies to wage war have been topics of interest. But these economic analyses have not always paid attention to the ways in which wealth, especially coinage, greased the wheels of warfare. Thucydides noted that wars in the past were smaller not due to lack of manpower as to lack of money (*chremata*, 1.11). By his day, coinage made possible larger fleets and larger armies because it enabled more efficient coordination of the resources required to supply armies in sieges and campaigns. In this book's second chapter, Matthew Trundle discusses the economic basis of ancient Greek warfare by analyzing the truth of Thucydides' statements. Trundle's discussion focuses on the need, use, and redistribution of resources, provisions, coins, and booty by Greek commanders in the classical age. Commanders needed resources at all stages. Given that coinage still required conversion into food and other logistically useful supplies, this chapter assesses the way that coinage especially assisted (and hampered) Greek communities in their ability to prosecute warfare on a grander scale in the classical world. The chapter and its parallel in the Roman section reexamine old evidence in our ancient sources to reveal new ways of understanding aspects of the role of wealth in warfare.

Roman finances related to war have also received much attention from economic historians, but less so from military historians. Although Cato the Elder coined the famous dictum *bellum se aluet* (war will feed itself) both he and his contemporaries knew that this could be true only to a limited extent. A few rich conquests during the second century BCE yielded enough spoils to offset the costs involved; otherwise Roman warfare operated at a loss. Yet financing was key to the Republic's military effectiveness. In Chapter 8, Nathan Rosenstein examines the means by which the Roman Republic financed its wars in the third and second centuries BCE. Because Rome paid its own soldiers and supplied grain to its allied contingents, armies were able to remain in the field for months and even years on end. Their long service together, and the training they underwent during that time, enabled Roman armies to develop a skill at arms, cohesion, and ability to maneuver that made them far superior to their opponents. Money made that superiority possible, and that money came principally from the *tributum*, the tax that Roman citizens paid to support the Republic's military endeavors. Regular payment of the *tributum* in turn depended on the existence of a robust class of moderately prosperous citizens who could afford to shoulder most of the burden of financing the

Republic's military expansion, a body of taxpayers that the Roman leadership took pains to create and sustain.

Modern historians generally believe that the hoplite battle was the preferred and dominant form of warfare among Greeks in the Archaic (800–480 BCE) and Classical periods (480–323 BCE) and that sieges were rare and infrequent occurrences. A further principle is that when Greeks did undertake sieges, a number of conventions or unwritten laws in warfare kept them from committing wholesale destruction of towns and cities until the mid or late fifth century BCE. A closer look at Greek warfare in the Archaic period, however, suggests that there were a significant number of sieges, followed by uncommonly violent sacks of the fallen cities. Michael Seaman in Chapter 3 provides a new consideration of our evidence for early Greek siege warfare. His analysis of early siege techniques reveals that the small number of sieges in the Archaic period was due not to "traditional cultural restraints" but rather to the inability of attacking armies to carry out successful sieges. He argues that the increase in siege warfare and the resulting violence in the fifth century BCE is in part a result of the increased number of classical sources and of the Greeks', primarily the Athenians', ability to overcome some of the difficulties inherent in besieging an enemy polis.

While Roman historians have tended to focus on battles, sieges – always monumental occasions – are uncommon but better-represented (in both senses) in the histories. Chapter 11 by Josh Levithan provides a Roman companion to Chapter 3. Sieges are a special case because the ordinary "rules" of war – moral and ethical expectations, the relationship of command to the common soldiers, the expectation of tactical discipline – are in abeyance, and the whole jostling, semi-tactical heart of battle is gone. Instead, siege warfare is a war of extremes: slow, highly technical siegecraft punctuated by short bursts of desperate fighting between small groups. Both of these situations present a motivational challenge very different from that of marshaling troops for decisive battle. While Seaman's chapter is generally asking new questions of old and overlooked evidence to draw new conclusions and illuminate Greek sieges, Levithan brings a new approach, addressing questions of morale, culture, and moral pressure in the process of examining and explaining Roman sieges and the sack that followed. He starts with a consideration of military narratives and then draws on a handful of siege narratives, including Caesar's sieges in Gaul and the siege of Jerusalem in 70 CE. Together these narratives demonstrate the themes Levithan develops and provide a better way to consider Roman sieges.

It has been typical for military historians to focus on the bigger picture of armies rather than on the soldiers. Victor Hanson tried to bring a more soldier-centered focus to his discussion of early Greek hoplite warfare (2009) by drawing on the "face of battle school." Despite much initial buzz, Hanson's account suffered from difficulties inherent in the limited sources for early warfare. In Chapter 4, John W. I. Lee seeks to understand the Greek soldier's experience as a whole in the late fifth through the fourth centuries BCE. Topics Lee treats include practical issues like cooking, eating, clothing, wealth, and training as well as social and communal aspects of Greek military life. What emerges is that while war-making changed dramatically during the fourth century BCE, soldiers' experiences are not so different in many respects from what they had been in earlier periods; rather, what changed was the potential scale of their experience, with opportunities for fighting all over the Hellenistic world and unprecedented enrichment. Lee demonstrates how cultural and social history continue to help us reveal soldiers' experiences.

Eventually, when the fighting was completed soldiers returned from service. Lawrence A. Tritle uses Athenian drama to address the topics of veterans returning home from war and the way their combat experience affected them and the society to which they return in Chapter 5. Euripides (c.424–418), for example, in staging his play of the homecoming of Heracles, tinkered with the traditional storyline and made it clear that Heracles was not returning from his labors, but "from the war." Thoughtful members of the audience would have picked up that Euripides was speaking to them of their own homecoming from far-off campaigns and war-related traumas. Tritle points out that among the other war plays of Euripides – *Andromache, Hecuba,* and *Trojan Women* – we find themes that would resonate with contemporary veterans. In addition to the violence of the returning soldier and the issue of suicide, he comments also on the varied impact of war on women. Additionally, Tritle uses the plays of Euripides and Sophocles to explore issues of interest to veterans and their families: Why war? What drives men to fight and die? The result is a significant discussion of combat trauma, violence, the plight of the war-wounded, and survivors' guilt in the context of veterans returning home.

Although there has been renewed interest in the study of Greek cavalry in the last 25 years, most scholarship on the subject has focused on the Archaic and Classical periods where the literary and artistic evidence is plentiful. Glenn R. Bugh uses new approaches and asks new questions of his materials as he examines evidence for Greek cavalry of the Hellenistic period in Chapter 6. Since the 1960s, excavations in Athens and Attica have generated a fresh archive of cavalry-related material including lead tablets, clay seals, cavalry equipment, and decrees by, and for, the cavalry. Using Athens as a case study, Bugh reviews and reappraises the impact of archaeology, epigraphy, and prosopography on Hellenistic cavalry studies in the last 50 years. His particular interests are in the effectiveness of Hellenistic cavalry as defined by ethnicity and technique, the dichotomy between citizen and mercenary cavalries, and the status of *hippeis* within the political and social life of Hellenistic city-states and kingdoms. Bugh's chapter contextualizes the Athenian evidence within the broader Hellenistic world and explores promising new cavalry scholarship made possible through new evidence and methodologies.

Military history has long been an important element of classical studies; literature, battlefield archaeology, and topography contribute to our analysis and understanding of battles. However, until recently most examinations of ancient combat lacked explicit consideration of the impact of battle on the bodies of the participants. Skeletal remains of soldiers and non-combatant victims who died in battle offer unique contributions as physical witnesses to the tactile reality of ancient warfare. In Chapter 7, Maria A. Liston applies recent developments in physical anthropology to examine the evidence for ancient combat found on the skeletons buried under the Theban monument after the Battle of Chaironeia in 338 BCE, and the victims of the Herulian Sack of Athens in 267 CE. Comparisons with prehistoric and historic combat-related trauma from other sites in Europe and North America provide additional data on the practice of hand-to-hand combat and the fate of victims unable to defend themselves. Demography, ante-mortem health, and perimortem trauma all contribute to our understanding of who died, why, and how. Liston's analysis sheds light on not only combat wounds, but also the kinds of injuries weapons inflicted, the ways some weapons were employed, and the mutilation of the dead.

Roman military discipline was a key component of the military's success. It was a regular part of soldiers' daily life in the army. It is unrealistic, however, to expect soldiers to be automata who never break ranks or participate in military disobedience or indiscipline. In Chapter 9, Lee L. Brice explores indiscipline in the Roman military. He argues that examinations of indiscipline have been hamstrung by a focus on large-scale mutinies that ignores the numerous other incidents that appear in our sources. Considering all these episodes provides a better sense of the scale and variety of discipline problems in the Roman army. A bigger problem in trying to study indiscipline is in our tools for analyzing military disobedience. We can hardly blame historians for previously focusing exclusively on mutiny – their toolbox for analyzing disorder contained only a hammer, so every incident looked like a nail. However, good analytical and explanatory tools are available from other fields such as sociology. Military sociology, collective action, and organizational behavior studies provide definitions, models, and vocabulary that, coupled with careful historical analysis, permit us to examine and discuss mutinies and other forms of indiscipline with more precision and authority. Brice shows how careful reading of the ancient sources with an awareness of these new approaches reveals specific details about indiscipline that permit us to discuss episodes with more certainty and clarity.

Panic was a key issue in ancient battles. Numerous battles turned on part of one side or the other panicking. The Greeks recognized the *strophe*, the spot on the battlefield where the defeated army turned and ran. Roman soldiers who panicked in combat could face severe punishment. There has not, however, been much study of the phenomenon of panic in ancient history, and none that has taken into consideration recent advances in our understanding of behavior and correlated brain functions. Susan M. Heidenreich and Jonathan P. Roth collaborate in Chapter 10, bringing together physiological and historical approaches. They combine descriptions of Roman battles and the role of panic in ancient training and combat, with a discussion of the underlying neurophysiological processes. Heidenreich and Roth point out that the neurophysiology of the ancient Roman is the same as that of the modern person and, therefore, it is possible to consider physiological responses and understand the biological process of the ancient soldier. Given that panic and fear can be described as normative responses to stress, understanding the biology of panic provides insight into how ancient combat functioned and how it was experienced by the ancient soldier. The authors are able to make clearer why some soldiers panicked and others did not, under the same conditions. Their examination contributes to understanding of the physical battle experience of ancient soldiers and highlights physiological approaches to understanding ancient warfare.

The men who served in the Roman imperial army were generally professional soldiers who committed many years to military service. The non-citizen auxilia, for example, could expect no discharge for 25 or so years. These were prime years when non-soldiers would start families, but Roman soldiers were not legally allowed to marry during their service. Historians, therefore, have assumed the role of family in the lives of soldiers was minor. However, recent research has made it clear that the ban on marriage did not stop soldiers from forming de facto marriages while serving. In Chapter 12, Elizabeth M. Greene takes a closer look at these auxilia soldiers and their families in Roman camps by focusing on documentary sources and material culture. Greene points out that some families clearly lived within the fort itself, while thriving settlements that were dependent on the fort often housed the family members of the soldiers of the garrison. The presence in and around camps of a significant population with familial ties to soldiers has broader implications for our understanding of military supply, use of the landscape, movement of units, and the daily life of soldiers in the first and second centuries CE. Her chapter provides readers with a better sense of the life of Roman soldiers and a clearer picture of the communities on the frontiers of the empire. The improved understanding of the military family in the first two centuries of the principate that she provides helps to better contextualize some of the changes in military life and organization in the later Roman Empire.

As noted, auxilia were an important component of the Imperial Roman army. These units were originally recruited from subject peoples within the empire to fulfill specialized roles like cavalry, and under Augustus came to include infantry that supplemented the legions. Auxilia units were often posted far from the areas in which they were originally recruited. As they needed to enlist replacements, they often recruited soldiers locally, near the base where they were stationed. Auxilia were the non-citizen "ethnic" units of the army. But "ethnicity" is a complicated and, at times, fraught term that has only recently reemerged as a topic scholars are examining. Alexander Meyer investigates the topic of ethnicity in the military in Chapter 13, by focusing on the identification of ethnic communities in the epigraphic record of the auxilia and on the treatment of these groups by their commanding officers and the military administration. He explains what is meant by ethnicity and why it has sometimes been a taboo category. Meyer draws heavily on documentary evidence, asking new questions of it in a successful effort to reveal how regular soldiers were self-identifying. Traditionally, historians have argued that auxilia units lost their initial ethnic character by the end of the first century CE, as local recruitment became the norm. However, Meyer's detailed examination argues that tribally and geographically based groups persisted. Additionally, he found that the military command structure maintained these groups as distinct elements of the Roman army, perhaps indicating that officers perceived them as ethnically distinct. Meyer's conclusions contribute to a better understanding of the auxilia and the topic of ethnicity in the Roman empire.

An important criterion for judging the sophistication and effectiveness of an army is the degree to which it cares for its sick and wounded. The shifting focus of military historiography brings the book to its fourteenth chapter and Philip Rance's discussion of the military medical services of the late Imperial period or Late Antiquity, 250–600 CE. The Roman army created the largest and most sophisticated military medical services in the pre-industrial age. Rome recognized trained soldiers as a hard-to-replace resource in an age when minor ailments, if left untreated, could become debilitating or fatal, especially when exacerbated by the inhospitable frontier environments in which Roman forces typically served. Rance explores the extensive evidence for medical services and demonstrates that during this crucial period of political, social, and religious transformation, the Roman army was still concerned about successfully providing for the health of its soldiers. In the process of investigating medical personnel, facilities, and practices both on and off the battlefield, Rance employs the full range of available sources including historical narratives, military handbooks, medical treatises, law codes, inscriptions, papyri, and comparative evidence from other periods. His chapter illustrates the differing methodologies with which ancient historians approach diverse source-materials. The result is a reconstruction of institutions, personnel, and practices that were key to the successful maintenance of the army and that impacted the lives of numerous soldiers, not only during the period he covers, but also earlier. More broadly, the evidence provides insights into contemporary attitudes to health, sanitation, disease, wounds, class, and military service.

Future Directions

What should be clear from the previous discussion is that the field of military history has matured beyond the so-called New Military History. Joanne Bourke observed in 2006, "The term 'New Military History' is a misnomer. Judged by its chronological birth during the social, political, and intellectual upheavals of the 1960s, it is distinctly middle-aged" (p. 258). It has been more than a decade since Bourke's characterization. Even the alternative name, "war and society school," is no longer accurate, as the school has diversified and grown immensely. It is time to retire the phrase New Military History in favor of something more accurate.

Before inventing a new label, however, let us take stock of where we stand in the methodological tent. Military history has not abandoned traditional topics. Indeed, an array of approaches breathe new life into drums and trumpets history. The "face of battle school" may have lost its initial luster, but it remains present and popular. The technocentric school looks beyond some of the traditional antiquarianism that remains popular and there are new projects expanding what arms, armor, and military material culture reveal. There is also much new work being completed that employs methods and tools unavailable a generation ago. The result of the field's growth and methodological expansion is renewed vitality. Rather than providing a name to these new directions and vitality such as the "New" New Military History, which sounds trite, it is more accurate to recognize that it is all, the traditional and the contemporary, simply part of the course of scholarship in military history. This seems to be a good place to conclude.

Despite more than two centuries of work on warfare and military institutions in the Greek and Roman worlds there is much good work presented and published annually and there remains much to be done. The study of ancient warfare is not going away any time soon.

Note

1 Rather than provide a lengthy history for the field, since that has been done elsewhere, a brief sketch of the changes the field has undergone will suffice here and readers may consult other works, e.g. Citino 2007; Morillo and Pavkovic 2017.

References

Allison, P. (2013). *People and Spaces in Military Bases*. Cambridge: Cambridge University Press.

Armstrong, J. (2016). "War and society in the ancient world: an introduction." In: Circum Mare: *Themes in Ancient Warfare* (ed. J. Armstrong), 1–9. Leiden: Brill.

Berger, F. et al. (1996–2013). *Kalkriese*, 6 vols. Mainz am Rhein: P. von Zabern.

Biddle, T. and Citino, R. (2014). "The role of military history in the contemporary academy." Society for Military History White Paper. Accessed May 25, 2019. http://www.smh-hq.org/whitepaper.html.

Bishop, M.C. and Coulston, J.C.N. (2006). *Roman Military Equipment, from the Punic Wars to the Fall of Rome*, 2e. Oxford: Oxbow.

Black, J. (2004). *Rethinking Military History*. London: Routledge.

Bourke, J. (2006). "The new military history." In: *Palgrave Advances in Modern Military History* (eds. M. Hughes and W.J. Philpott), 258–280. New York: Palgrave Macmillan.

Brice, L.L. (2011). "Philip II, Alexander the great, and the question of a Macedonian revolution in military affairs (RMA)." *Ancient World* 42 (2): 137–147.

Brice, L.L. and Roberts, J.T. (eds.) (2011). *Recent Directions in the Military History of the Ancient World*. Claremont, CA: Regina.

Butera, C.J. and Sears, M. (2017). "The camps of Brutus and Cassius at Philippi, 42 B.C." *Hesperia* 86 (2): 359–377.

Butera, C.J. and Sears, M. (2019). *Battles and Battlefields of Ancient Greece: A Guide to the History, Topography and Archaeology*. Havertown, PA: Pen and Sword Military.

Chambers, J. (1991). "The new military history: myth and reality." *Journal of Military History* 55 (3): 395–406.

Citino, R. (2007). "Military histories old and new: a reintroduction." *American Historical Review* 112 (4): 1070–1090.

Daly, G. (2001). *Cannae: The Experience of Battle in the Second Punic War*. New York: Routledge.

Fagan, G. and Trundle, M. (2010). "Introduction." In: *New Perspectives on Ancient Warfare* (eds. G. Fagan and M. Trundle), 1–19. Leiden: Brill.

van Gils, L., de Jong, I., and Kroon, C. (eds.) (2019). *Textual Strategies in Ancient War Narrative: Thermopylae, Cannae, and Beyond*. Leiden: Brill.

Goldsworthy, A. (1996). *The Army at War, 100 B.C.–A.D.200*. Oxford: Clarendon Press.

Greene, E.M. (2016). "Identities and social roles of women in military communities of the Roman west." In: *Women in Antiquity: Real Women Across the Ancient World* (eds. S. Budin and J. Turfa), 942–953. New York: Routledge.

Hanson, V. (2007). "The modern historiography of ancient warfare." In: *CHGRW*, vol. 1, 325–357.

Hanson, V. (2009). *The Western Way of War: Infantry Battle in Classical Greece*, 3e. Berkeley: University of California Press.

Heckel, W. and Tritle, L. (eds.) (2009). *Alexander the Great: A New History*. Malden, MA: Wiley Blackwell.

James, S. (2011). *Rome and the Sword: How Warriors and Weapons Shaped Roman History*. London: Thames and Hudson.

Keegan, J. (1976). *The Face of Battle*. New York: Penguin Books.

Kendall, S. (2013). *The Struggle for Roman Citizenship: Romans, Allies, and the Wars of 91–77 BCE*. Piscataway, NJ: Gorgias Press.

Krentz, P. (2011). *The Battle of Marathon*. New Haven, CT: Yale University Press.

Lendon, J.E. (2005). *Soldiers and Ghosts: A History of Battle in Classical Antiquity*. New Haven, CT: Yale University Press.

Lonsdale, D. (2007). *Alexander the Great: Lessons in Strategy*. New York: Routledge.

Loreto, L. (2015). "Military history, Roman: Modern." In: *The Encyclopaedia of the Roman Army* (ed. Y. Le Bohec), 654–655. Malden, MA: Wiley.

Matthew, C. (2011). *A Storm of Spears*. Havertown, PA: Pen & Sword Military.

Morillo, S. and Pavkovic, M. (2017). *What Is Military History?* 3e. Malden, MA: Polity.

Rey, F.E. (2010). "Weapons, technological determinism, and ancient warfare." In: *New Perspectives on Ancient Warfare* (eds. G. Fagan and M. Trundle), 21–56. Leiden: Brill.

Rosenstein, N. (2009). "New approaches to Roman military history." Presented as part of the panel "New Approaches to the Political and Military History of the Greek, Roman, and Late Roman Worlds." Sponsored by the APA Committee on Ancient History. https://classicalstudies.org/sites/default/files/documents/RosensteinAPA2009.pdf (accessed May 15, 2019).

Sabin, P. (2000). "The face of Roman battle." *The Journal of Roman Studies* 90: 1–17.

Showalter, D. (1975). "A modest plea for drums and trumpets." *Military Affairs* 39 (2): 71–74.

Spiller, R. (2006). "Military history and its fictions." *Journal of Military History* 70 (4): 1081–1097.

Wheeler, E. (2011). "Greece: mad hatters and march hares." In: *Recent Directions in the Military History of the Ancient World* (eds. L.L. Brice and J.T. Roberts), 53–104. Claremont, CA: Regina.

Further Reading

Armstrong, J. and Fronda, M.P. (2020). *Romans at War: Soldiers, Citizens, and Society in the Roman Republic*. New York: Routledge.

Konijnendijk, R. (2017). *Classical Greek Tactics: A Cultural History*. Leiden: Brill.

Morillo, S. and Pavkovic, M. (2017). *What Is Military History?* 3e. Malden, MA: Polity.

Paret, P. (1992). "The history of war and the new military history." In: *Understanding War: Essays on Clausewitz and the History of Military Power* (ed. P. Paret), 209–226. Princeton: Princeton University Press.

Paret, P. (2009). "The annales school and the history of war." *Journal of Military History* 73: 1289–1294.

Reid, B. (2009). "Michael Howard and the evolution of modern war studies." *Journal of Military History* 73: 869–904.

Sears, M. (2019). *Understanding Greek Warfare*. New York: Routledge.

Part I

Greece

Map Pt.1. Ancient Greece. *Source:* Ancient World Mapping Center © 2015 (awmc.unc.edu). Used by permission.

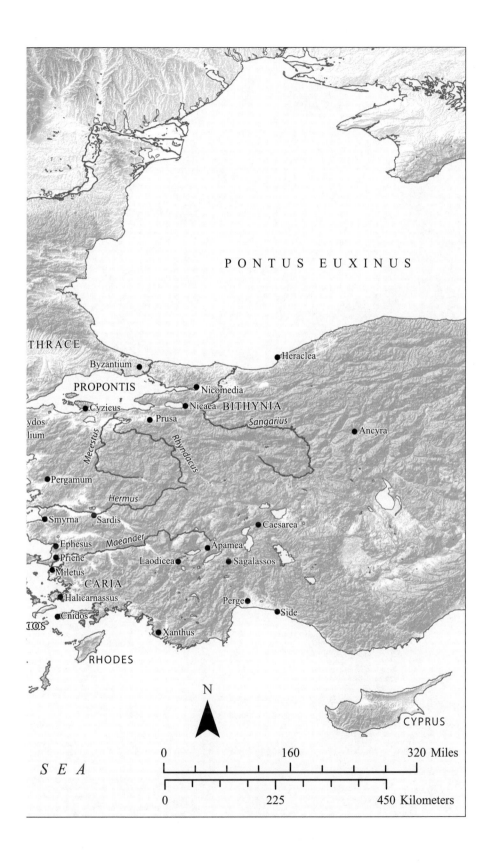

PONTUS EUXINUS

THRACE

Byzantium ●

PROPONTIS

●Cyzicus

ydos
lium

Mecestus

Pergamum ●

Hermus

Smyrna ● ● Sardis

Ephesus ●
Priene ●
Miletus ●

CARIA

Halicarnassus ●

Cnidos ●

IOS

RHODES

● Heraclea

● Nicomedia
● Nicaea BITHYNIA
● Prusa

Sangarius

Rhyndacus

● Ancyra

● Caesarea

Maeander ● Apamea
Laodicea ● ● Sagalassos

Perge ●
● Side

● Xanthus

N

S E A

CYPRUS

0   160   320 Miles

0   225   450 Kilometers

2

Wealth and the Logistics of Greek Warfare

Food, Pay, and Plunder

Matthew Trundle[†]

Introduction

Thucydides (1.11.1–2) noted that wars before his own day were smaller not due to lack of manpower as much to lack of *chrêmata*. *Chrêmata* in earlier sources referred generally to wealth, but by Thucydides' day the word specifically meant coined money. He suggests that soldiers in previous wars (his example is the Trojan War), had to spend much time gathering provisions, farming the Chersonesus and plundering rather than prosecuting the siege itself. Thucydides thought that Troy would have fallen far more quickly and easily if the men had spent all their time prosecuting the war. The role of coinage and its coordination in Greek military engagements with feeding, paying, and redistributing resources in the Classical period remains central to understanding how Greek warfare changed from small-scale raids and border skirmishes to the great wars of the later fifth and fourth century.[1] Thucydidean *chrêmata* provides the answer, in that *chrêmata* represents coined money, through which sold-plunder produced coins that facilitated the payment of the troops. In turn, the coinage then enabled the soldiers and their commanders to purchase food and other supplies and so centralized the operations of the army as a whole. Coins therefore transformed the ways and means that the Greeks waged warfare.

By Thucydides' day greater resources made possible larger fleets and armies. Surplus wealth in any form enabled better coordination of military resources in general. Wealth in the form of coinage, however, facilitated more efficient coordination of the resources required to supply armies in sieges and campaigns. Coinage did not relieve any army of its logistical problems, for coins cannot be consumed. They needed conversion into the raw materials of life, food, and equipment. So what did Thucydides actually mean when he stated that coinage facilitated larger armies, longer wars, and their more efficient prosecution?

Logistics

We possess limited information about the logistics of warfare prior to the Persian Wars. Scholars like Hanson (2009) describe Archaic Age hoplite encounters as short and sharp with minimal long-term consequences, fought between amateur soldiers intent on returning to their farms. Hoplites

---

† Deceased

New Approaches to Greek and Roman Warfare, First Edition. Edited by Lee L. Brice.
© 2020 John Wiley & Sons, Inc. Published 2020 by John Wiley & Sons, Inc.

carried their own provisions. Fifth and fourth century images of how wars had become profession-alized, less honorable, and nastier affairs reflect a long tradition of Greek reminiscence about their past as the good old days. Pericles triumphs the new campaign warfare that the Athenians employ in sustained warfare by land and sea, something the old-fashioned Peloponnesians cannot do. As he states (Thuc. 1.141.4–5), "A surplus supports a war more than forced contributions. Farmers are the type of men more prepared to serve with their bodies than with their money. Having trust that they will overcome the dangers, they are by no means so sure that the latter will not be prematurely exhausted, especially if the war last longer than they expect, which it very likely will."

On the one hand, the farmer-hoplites of the Peloponnese fight pitched battles in person, which Pericles himself admits they will most likely win. On the other, he doubts their ability to sustain wars of any duration and, therefore, questions their overall effectiveness.

To begin a campaign, the call-up went out (Christ 2001; Krentz 2007, pp. 148–150). This announced the length and nature of the coming campaign. Three days' rations were standard (Ar. *Ach.* 197, *Pax* 311–12; Eub. fr. 19.3 K-A). Even naval call-up demanded troops bring rations. Thucydides (1.48.1) reports that three days of grain went with Corinthian ships to fight Corcyra. Three days cannot have given commanders much flexibility. The Spartan invasions of Attica at the start of the Peloponnesian War lasted between three and 40 days. Of the first and longest invasion, Thucydides (2.23.2) states that the Spartans stayed in Attica as long as their supplies lasted. Armies struggled to feed themselves.

Aristophanes' *Acharnians* refers to the organization of both naval (1071–1142) and land (545–556) campaigns. Navies involved complex arrangements from loading and preparing ships to enlist-ing and training oarsmen. Infantry needed supplies at a more private level. Hoplites carried their own provisions. Lamachus commanded his slave to collect salt, thyme, onions, and some salt-meat wrapped in a fig leaf for his knapsack or bag (*gylios*). Even as late as the 420s many hoplites must still have traveled to battle carrying meager provisions with their attendant slaves. Aristophanes envisaged a campaign within Attica against invading Boeotians. The Athenians were off to one of the Attic frontiers in their country's defense. Such an operation presented limited necessity for coinage or opportunities for living off the land beyond hunting wild game – for which soldiers often took metal spits to roast meat – or plundering wild fruits in the countryside. Military operations often lay further afield than a three-day campaign on the frontier, and on occasion well beyond home or allied territories. These at least provided some opportunity for stealing food from others.

The sources referred to provisions generically as *epitêdeia* – literally, necessary things. Provisions were so necessary that Lysander waited for the besieged Athenians to run out of them at the end of the Peloponnesian War – and then they would, as they did, surrender (Xen. *Hell.* 2.2.2). When the Spartans invaded Attica for the first time in the Peloponnesian war they stayed for only as long as their provisions lasted (Thuc. 2.23).

Campaigns that went longer than a few days in territory that could not be plundered made cen-trally organized provisioning necessary. Seasonal conditions and previously harvested or denuded lands provided few options for feeding invading armies. Without supplies armies required access to markets (Xen. *An.* 1.4.19, 5.10; Diod. Sic. 16.13.3). Commanders might arrange a market them-selves from which the men could buy food. Cyrus seems to have done this for the Ten Thousand (Xen. *An.* 1.3.14, 1.5.6, *Hell.* 3.4.11). If they had it commanders also might sell food directly to their men, even at a profit (Andoc. *De Redit.* 14.2–4; Dem. 50.17.2–4; Diod. Sic. 17.94.4).

A commander's responsibilities included arranging provisions for his army. Thucydides (5.47.6) describes the alliance between Athens, Argos, Mantineia, and Elis in 420. The city that sent troops to assist the other must supply grain for 30 days from the time of an ally's arrival in their city as well as for their return journey, but that after 30 days the other city became responsible for its ally's men. It was not uncommon for allies to make such agreements. Agyris provided food to the entire army of his ally Dionysius against the invading Carthaginians (Diod. Sic. 14.95.7). Less generously, commanders sometimes provided grain (*sitos*) to the men in lieu of wages (see Aristotle, *Oec.* 1350a32, 1350b7). A commander's responsibilities ran only as far as ensuring that grain was available. Aristotle (*Oec.* 1351a) implies that Timotheus normally charged his men for grain. When the general faced a potential mutiny over lack of pay, he calmed the men by saying that he would not charge anything for the three months of grain he had already provided. Several stories in Aristotle's *Economics* (1350a–1351b) illustrate how tightly commanders controlled military provisioning.

Athens organized all manner of provisions and supplies during the Sicilian campaign, which was itself a unique affair in its scale. Nicias outlined the logistics necessary for such a complex campaign (Thuc. 6.22). He told his fellow Athenians they could not rely on allied cities in Sicily to feed such a large force. They needed to transport both wheat and roasted barley along with bakers and had to ensure these men would be paid. The Athenians were unmoved by Nicias' arguments so that presumably the Athenian war fund paid for the provisions and the men to bake them. The sanctuaries throughout Attica, but most notably on the Acropolis, stored enormous wealth. Thucydides refers to money in the treasury put aside for the war effort (Thuc. 6.22.1, 2.24.1–2, 7.16.2). At the start of the war, Pericles reminded the Athenians of their wealth: 600 talents of tribute a year, 6000 talents in coin on the Acropolis and 500 uncoined talents of gold and silver along with "not a little" across Attica (Thuc. 2.13.3–4). These funds made Athens different from Sparta. Significantly, the commanders who went to Sicily took much of this money with them. We are told that the second expedition took more of it. A fragment of an inscription (Meiggs and Lewis 78 = *IG* 1³ 93 = Fornara 146) states that the Athenians had put aside 3000 talents for the Sicilian expedition in 416/5 and a further 500 talents went to the island after the initial invasion (Thuc. 6.94.4, 7.16.2; *IG* 1³ 370, 371) and then an unspecified amount (*IG* 1³ 371). The money served many purposes: purchasing food, paying wages, and buying alliances.

By the turn of the fifth century commanders provided cash-payments specifically for the men to buy their own food supplies in advance of campaigning. *Sitêresion* was grain money (Harp. *Lex.* 273.11–12). It appears first in Xenophon's *Anabasis* (6.2.4). By the fourth century Demosthenes (4.28–29) confirms its common use. He hoped to send mercenaries to Thrace and pay them with grain money with which they would sustain themselves, while plunder would provide a decent income. Demosthenes distinguished full pay (*misthon enteles*) from pay without *sitêresion*. In another speech (Dem. 50.10), Apollodorus states that the Athenian commanders provided grain money to his naval crew, but expected him to make up the remainder of their wages. Clearly both wages and food represented full-payment by the mid-fourth century. Demosthenes (4.28.1–29, 50.10.4–6) and Xenophon (*An.* 6.2.4) illustrate that employers had responsibilities for providing grain money and that the army expected it. *Sitêresion* had a specific purpose: to buy the food for the campaign. In the Apollodoran speech Demosthenes (50.24.10–12) explicitly confirms this. Grain money would only serve its purpose if paid up-front to sustain a campaign rather than at its conclusion.

Some later fifth and fourth century commanders provided traveling expenses (*ephodia*) to help soldiers get to a campaign.[2] Thus, Callicratidas gave five drachmas worth of traveling expenses for his soldiers to get to him (Xen. *Hell.* 1.6.12–3). Traveling expenses were usually calculated in terms of days (e.g. Dem. 23.209.8–10) or even months (Dem. 19.158.3–5; Epicharm. 4.85.5; Xen. *Hell.* 1.1.24). There is never any suggestion that it might be a cash payment for food, like the grain money payments. Demosthenes explicitly used the word for traveling expenses and not grain money in certain passages, implying they were not the same thing (see Dem. 19.158.3–5, 25.56.6–8, 53.8.8–9; Plut. *Ages.* 10.5.4–5). As rations traveling expenses (*ephodia*) have much in common with generic terms for food (*trophê*) and provisions (*epitêdeia*) (Dem. 23.209.8; Plut. *Mor.* 79.160.B.2), but had no relationship to wages (Dem. 25.56.6–8, 50.19.5–6; see also Lys. 12.11.3–4). In sum, there were two types of non-wage cash payments soldiers might receive before combat: grain money and traveling expenses. The latter were given as an advance for travel to an army (Xen. *Hell.* 1.6.12–13).

Wages

In addition to sustenance, ideally, troops in the later fifth century received wages while on campaign (*GSW* 1.3–29; Loomis 1998, pp. 266–271; Trundle 2004, pp. 80–103). Unlike provisions or money for purchasing provisions, commanders paid wages at the end of a period of service (e.g. Xen. *An.* 1.3.21, 5.6.23, 7.2.36, 6.1). They usually paid wages monthly, despite the amount recorded as a daily rate. Pay differed from plunder redistribution. The sale of plunder had often provided the means by which armies might be sustained in the field or paid, but by the later fifth century cash had largely replaced the redistribution of plunder for wage payments. Such wages represented something entirely new to Greek warfare.

The first known payments for military service, rather than plunder redistribution, emerged late in the Archaic period alongside the introduction of coinage. Coins entered the Greek world from the east c. 540. Coinage transformed the ways and means by which remuneration occurred (Trundle 2010). The earliest evidence of payment for military service appears in naval contexts. Naval service lent itself to the introduction of payment alongside centralized provisioning and logistics more than military service on land. Ships required larger numbers of men than their land-based counterparts; poorer men played significant roles in rowing and crewing, and unlike their wealthier hoplite counterparts, required payment for their services; specialists (*hyperesiai*) piloted, navigated, and rigged vessels adding an element of professionalism to naval warfare; and ships engaged in longer ranging military expeditions than land-based armies.

As always the evidence prior to the Persian Wars for logistics of any kind is sparse (Raaflaub 1999, pp. 134–138; van Wees 2004, pp. 28–30; Pritchard 2010, pp. 7–15). Sixth-century military ventures are obscure. The Athenians undertook perhaps only 10 campaigns prior to the fall of the tyranny (Pritchard 2010, p. 8). Warfare was not a public affair, but limited to winning new agricultural land on the borders of Attica or private individuals establishing colonies overseas. Solon's campaign against Salamis promised land to those who joined the venture (Plut. *Sol.* 9.2) and Miltiades undertook to fight for Thracians in the Chersonese without any reference to the Polemarch, Council, or Areopagus (Hdt. 6.34–7; Pritchard 2010, p. 9). Vincent Gabrielsen (1994, pp. 24–26, 2008, p. 57) and others (Haas 1985; Morrison and Williams 1968, pp. 73–117) have concluded that private vessels for raiding and trading made up the early Athenian navy.

An inscription from Eretria dated 550–525 illustrates the use of wages to pay sailors who traveled beyond specified coastal locations (*IG* XII.91273.1274, lines 10–16 = *SEG* 41.725; van Wees 2010; Cairns 1984, pp. 147–148). Wages represent a change in the relationship between crew and captain. Pay replaced a previously ad hoc system of redistributing resources and so presents a more centralized approach to resource redistribution. In this inscription, contributions are stipulated communally and reward probably distributed on the same principle. State navies emerged in this context and had to have centralized, coordinated management. The evolution of the Athenian navy in the sixth and early fifth century represents a further transformation in a process toward centralized resource management made possible with city coinage.

The silver found at Laurion and its potential economic redistribution made possible the dominant Athenian navy in c.482 (Hdt. 7.144; *Ath. Pol.* 22.7; Plut. *Them.* 4.1). Despite some historians' view of the private nature of Athenian naval activity prior to this investment, sixth century Athens had connections overseas. The Peisistratids and other families had interests in the Hellespont and the mines of Maroneia, and, as we have seen, even Solon had fought over the island of Salamis. Such interests required ships of some kind. Cleisthenes' late sixth century revolution did not ignore the navy. According to the fourth-century author Cleidemus, Cleisthenes created 50 naval magistrates or ship captaincies (Cleidemus *FGrH* 323 F 8; *Ath. Pol.* 21.5). His naval magistrates were part of the evolutionary development toward the fifth century state navy. Hans van Wees points out that a new publicly funded navy, even of only 50 ships, would require new means of management and financing. He argues that through reforms Cleisthenes created a publicly owned navy. This reorganization would have centralized this part of the Athenian navy and required new means to pay for it.[3] The navy, therefore, became an integral part of state mechanisms and of resource redistribution. We should also note that coins played a significant role in financing the fleet (Humphreys 1970; Trundle 2004, pp. 92–93). Plunder and the profits of empire – the tribute – were not redistributed amongst the citizens who had secured it, nor the specific members of the military involved in the operation by which it was taken, but the state as a whole received and oversaw it. Aristophanes parodied this situation in the *Wasps* in which poor men lament how little they get in payment from the wealth of empire (672–679, 684–685, 1099–1101, 1114–1121). The wage, therefore, replaced the traditional Homeric style redistribution of spoils.

Wages are hardly known in Athens prior to the mid-fifth century. Plutarch (*Them.* 10.6–7; also Cleidemus 323 *FGrH* 21; *Ath. Pol.* 23.1) records that in 480 each Athenian family received two obols a day from the people of Troezen, while the Areopagus gave each soldier an advance of eight drachmas (*Ath. Pol.* 23.1). He also (*Pericles* 11.4; *GSW* 1.8) shows that one and a half drachma a day were paid to citizens training on triremes by the 450s. Pritchett concluded that regular payment was introduced between 460 and 450 (*GSW* 1.11). It is conceivable that pay emerged in the later 460s for the context of the first regular payments for state service is the rivalry between Pericles and Cimon. Pericles' payment of wages to the poor occurred prior to Cimon's ostracism in 462/1 (*Ath. Pol.* 27.3–4; Plut. *Cim.* 10.1–7, *Per.* 11; Theopompus *FGrH* 115 F 89).

Thucydides provides nine instances of the amount of wages paid to soldiers and sailors serving in the Peloponnesian War. One drachma a day was the common rate for the fifth century (Dover *HCT* 4.293; Andrewes *HCT* 5.97–8; Rhodes 1981, 306; Loomis 1998, p. 55; Trundle 2004, pp. 80–103). Payment varied depending on circumstances. Aristophanes (*Ach.* 159) has one drachma for service in the year 425, but he (*Wasps* 682–685, 1188–1189) notes only three and two obols a day in the following year. In 412 sailors in the fleet received three obols a day (Thuc. 3.17.4, 6.8.1, 6.31.3, 7.27.2, 8.29, 8.45.2, 8.101.13) and again in 408 (Plutarch, *Alc.* 35.4). The Persians paid four obols a day toward the end of the War (Xen. *Hell.* 1.5.7). Two obols per day became a minimum wage.

Campaigns also yielded spoils and plunder. Plundered property came in different forms, from the enemy's arms to their movable property and, of course, enslaved inhabitants (see *GSW* 1.55–56 and 5.58–152). Selling captured civilians into slavery was generally the most lucrative aspect of military ventures in the Classical period (*GSW* 1.82). Ransoming prisoners back to their families remained common throughout antiquity (Bielman 1994, pp. 13–18). In early Greek history, plunder redistribution reflected a culture of gifts and reciprocity in which status determined reward, rather than payment of any kind. Individuals reciprocated alliances, friendships, and service, most commonly military service, with such gifts. Alcaeus' brother Antimenides received a fine sword when he left the service of an eastern king in return for his military services (Bowra 1936, p. 160).

Even in the fourth century commanders still gave bounties for victory in epic tradition. The Syracusans thus gave to Dion's mercenaries 100 *minae* for overthrowing the Dionysian tyranny in 357 (Plut. *Dion*, 31); Alexander gave his mercenaries two months' pay along with large bounties to his regular troops after the Battle of Gaugamela in 331 (Diod. Sic. 17.64.6). Some commanders gave awards and gifts for bravery and heroism (e.g. Diod. Sic. 14.53.4). Jason of Pherae gave generously to the men who loved hard work and danger (Xen. *Hell.* 6.1.6). Cyrus the Younger promised five *minae* to each mercenary should he become Great King (Xen. *An.* 1.4.13).

Plunder

Homer's heroes distributed plundered goods according to status. The chieftains received the pick of the booty, but the men received the leftovers. By the Classical period a series of rules governed booty-division. Pritchett (*GSW* 2.365–433) discusses booty and its distribution in detail. The victorious side owned all the captured property of a campaign. This was a rule of war (Andoc. 1.507; *On The Peace* 11; Xen. *Cyr.* 7.1.44). Dedications of the *akrothinia*, or first fruits, the best arms and armor captured in battle went to the gods (Hdt. 1.86.5, 8.122; Pindar, *Ol.* 2.4). Some went to great Panhellenic sanctuaries, like Olympia or Delphi, others went more locally near the battlesite and to those associated closely with the victorious community like the Athenian Acropolis or Argive Heraeon (Jackson 1991). By the later Archaic and Classical period, the increased power of the state meant that it, rather than any individuals, controlled the prizes of war and with them state sanctuaries bristled with military spoils. This was true in Athens at least as early as 507/6. The Athenians captured an unstated number of Chalcidians and 700 Thebans whom they ransomed back for 200 drachmas each (Hdt. 5.77). There appears no suggestion of redistribution among the victorious soldiers and the state seems to control all the resources.

Herodotus confirms a similar pattern (8.122–124) of booty redistribution after Salamis. The contingent that provided the most men received the most reward (Hdt. 8.123). Dedications of the first fruits went to three major sanctuaries: the Isthmus, Sounion, and Ajax at Salamis. Delphi received offerings from each of the Greek cities present at the battle. The commanders then met at the altar of Poseidon at the Isthmus to vote for the man they thought deserved the prize of valor. They each voted for themselves first, but second for Themistocles. The prize went unawarded, despite Themistocles' obvious claim (Hdt. 8.123). The valor-prize remained a part of Greek warfare at least until the Persian Wars. Significantly, Thucydides makes no mention of it, but then Thucydides hardly mentions redistribution of spoils at all.

After Plataea, Herodotus (9.85) briefly mentions spoil distribution before the burial of the dead. He (9.70.3) states that the Greeks had a common pool of captured objects, though whether he meant for individuals or states (most likely) remains unclear. The common pool is mentioned in connection with how the Tegeans came to acquire the feeding trough of Mardonius' horses that they dedicated to the temple of Athena Alea. Diodorus (11.33) reports that the Greeks distributed Plataean booty to states by the number of soldiers who fought. He also stated (11.33) that the Spartan King, Pausanias, received the award of the valor prize at Plataea, though Herodotus (9.81.1–2) claims to have no knowledge of such honors. Herodotus does say that Pausanias received 10 of everything. He then notes that each of those who fought received spoils according to their worth. This could have been receipt by contingent or by individual – the Greek is ambiguous. The booty included concubines, gold, silver, other wealth, and animals. Some individuals received prizes from Persian War battles. These recipients dedicated their booty at local sanctuaries. Lykomedes presented the *parasema* of the Persian ship he had captured at Artemision to a sanctuary in his own Deme at Phyle (Hdt. 8.11; Plut. *Them.* 15.2).

The division of spoils and its proper disposal was a serious matter. Herodotus (8.122) noted how the Aeginetans had not dedicated enough to Delphi, which they rectified forthwith; and Xenophon (*Hell.* 3.5.5) records how Theban appropriation of Apollo's tenth from Deceleia gave the Spartans justification to start the Corinthian War. Equal division occurred only occasionally, as when the Argives, Thebans, Messenians, and Arcadians took Cromnus and divided the booty equally by state (Xen. *Hell.* 7.4.27) or when Knossos and Tylissos may have divided spoils according to the numbers each committed to joint action. (*Incr. Cret.* 1.56–57; *GSW* 2.365; Garlan 1976, p. 76). The erection of the trophy or wooden *tropaion* upon which arms of the defeated were heaped represented the last act of the engagement, recognition of victory and of defeat (Janssen 1957; Vanderpool 1966, pp. 93–106; *GSW* 2 and 5; Krentz 2002, pp. 23–39).

Post-battle practices changed dramatically from Herodotus to Thucydides. State control of plunder increased through the fifth century. Thucydides never refers to the distribution of plunder, the dedication of first fruits, or the award of a valor prize. Later fifth century Spartans and Athenians approached booty in different ways. Like any army, the Spartans needed resources to feed and sustain themselves on campaign. As such, Spartans plundered grain in specially designated wagons as they did before First Mantineia in 418 (Thuc. 5.64.5) and in Argive territory in 416/5 (Thuc. 6.7.1). Plundered grain was always useful (e.g. Thuc. 5.47.6; Xen. *An.* 1.2.19; Diod. Sic. 12.63.1, 14.95.6, 16.13.3, 56.2). Pritchett suggested (*GSW* 5.403–16) that as a rule the Spartans sold their booty in the field on the spot. The Spartans had officials who oversaw this sale. They called them *laphuropoloi* or plunder-sellers. Pritchett (*GSW* 5.403) described them as officers attached to the king's staff (Xen. *Hell.* 1.6.15, 4.5.8, 6.6, *Lac.* 13.11, *Ages.* 1.18.4). He notes their connection to the army treasurers and the secretary. They first appear at the start of the fourth century. Pritchett (*GSW* 1.87–91) proposed such booty-sellers were new, created to avoid corrupting Spartan austerity by bringing plunder home. Earlier armies attracted such salesmen on the make. Mercenary armies regularly sold booty while on campaign, though the crucial distinction is to whom and where they sold (*GSW* 1.425). The Spartans' booty-sellers of the early fourth century were classic middlemen. The Spartans rarely recompensed service or even valor, though the soldier who killed Epaminondas received honor and gifts (Plut. *Ages.* 35.1–2; *GSW* 5.407 n. 590). Despite the Spartan practice of selling booty in the field we know little of its redistribution. Certainly, traditional, conservative Spartan society brooked no consideration of payment or wages for military service since these represented base professionalism at its worst.

The demos at Athens controlled booty closely and carefully from a distance (*GSW* 5.424). Commanders often sought instructions from the assembly regarding booty. Thus, Iphicrates wrote to ask what to do with captured statues from Syracusan vessels bound for Olympia and Delphi, only to receive the reply, "let the men eat well" (Diod. Sic. 16.57.2; but see Diod. Sic. 15.47.7; Xen. *Hell.* 6.2.33–39). Such Athenian public control of plunder comes as no surprise in the wake of the Persian War not to mention the coordination of Athenian military affairs since the Cleisthenic reforms and the Themistoclean state navy. Thus, the communal use of war spoils became common. Athenians had pitched in to rebuild Athens' outer walls following the Persian sack (Thuc. 1.90–92). After the Battle of the Eurymedon River the Athenians completed extensive public works including the south wall of the Acropolis and the foundations of the Long Walls (Plut. *Cim.* 13.5; Paus. 10.15.4; Diod. Sic. 11.62.3). Pritchett (*GSW* 5.371) associated the victory at Oenophyta of 457 with the completion of those walls. Thucydides (1.108.3) mentions the victory and the walls contiguously, but Pritchett notes that Diodorus (11.82.5) claims that Myronides divided the spoils among his soldiers. If he did so, then one has to add that this is a rare moment of sharing among Athenian troops. This said, Athenian commanders regularly converted booty into money and food for the soldiers' pay and sustenance (*GSW* 5.416–425).

Fifth-century Athenians like other states regularly captured plunder, but there is little to suggest its redistribution to particular individuals within the army (e.g. Thuc. 5.115.1). Commanders sold booty at cities or markets or sent them home. Demosthenes in Aitolia sent the booty to Eupalion in Locris for sale (Thuc. 3.96.3). The Athenians took what they could from Hikkara and then sold it at Catane (Thuc. 6.62.1), probably for redistribution as provisions, grain money, and wages. At Iasus in 411 the army received coinage (Thuc. 8.28.3) from the plunder; indeed Thucydides (8.36.1) states great amounts of money were distributed. Here, typically, plunder became converted into money rather than redistributed as spoil.

The state played the central role in the appropriation and disposal of plunder in the Classical period. The Athenians and their navy produced an extensive mechanism of resource acquisition and redistribution. Coins replaced plunder as the means by which individuals received recognition and reward. A daily wage supplanted division of spoils. Every man in the fleet and the army received a share of the profits of empire, but one predetermined as a wage. Thus in many instances extortion had replaced appropriation to achieve remuneration from defeated or disempowered civilian populations. The fifth-century Athenian fleet threatened annihilation to encourage payment of the tribute. We may note that such extortion appears even in Herodotus prior to Aristeides' assessments of 478/7. Themistocles threatened islands with blockade. He invested Andros thus causing Carystus and Paros to pay up (Hdt. 8.112). The threat of siege and destruction underpinned payment of silver to the Athenian empire. We can even see extreme need directing Athenian aggression against compliant allies. In 406 sailors and soldiers in need of pay and food forced their commander Eteonicus to threaten the Chians with destruction if they did not provide money for their pay (Xen. *Hell.* 2.1.1–5). This activity was not uncommon.

Despite the importance of regular pay to poor men in military service, like the rowers of the Athenian fleet (Gabrielsen 1994, p. 124), plunder represented real opportunities for wealth acquisition. Pritchett (*GSW* 2.102) noted that in the fourth century men entered service knowing that their commanders had little pay to give them and that booty would make up the major part of their remuneration. We have already seen that plunder played a key role in provisioning armies and fleets away from the city. We have also mentioned Demosthenes' plan to send mercenaries to Thrace with money to pay for provisions, but whose income would come from plunder (Dem. 5.28). Seuthes planned to use plunder that Xenophon's men captured to pay their wages (Xen. *An.* 7.3.10–11), which he then did at Byzantium (Xen. *An.* 7.4.2). Dionysius I of Syracuse regularly financed wars and paid men from booty (Diod. Sic. 14.111.4, 15.14.3–4; Justin 20.5). The Phocian commanders minted coins from the dedications of the sanctuary at Delphi to pay soldiers in the Third Sacred War (Diod. Sic. 16.25.1, 30.1, 36.1, 60.1; Aesch. 2.130–131; Plut. *Mor.* 249F, 401F; Athenaeus, 6.231D; Polyaenus *Strat.* 5.45).

Many soldiers joined armies in hopes of plunder. Arcadians went to Sicily with the Athenians with such gain in mind (Thuc. 7.57.9–10). Arcadians and Achaeans followed Agis for booty as he marched on Elis (Xen. *Hell.* 3.2.26). Non-combatants aplenty followed armies to war with hopes of profit from the fighting. Thirty merchantmen followed the Athenians to Sicily (Thuc. 6.44.1). A crowd of market-traders numbering as many as the armed forces followed Agesilaos from Ephesus into Asia Minor in 396 (Diod. Sic. 14.79.2). Epaminondas' invasion of the Peloponnese attracted a similarly large band of non-combatants intent on plunder (Plut. *Ages.* 22). Booty quality varied (*GSW* 1.53–92 and 5.68–203; Krasilnikoff 1992, 1993; Trundle 2004, pp. 99–101). Some soldiers did well from plunder. Xenophon took enough from the *Anabasis* to dedicate to Apollo at Delphi, buy land, build a temple and altar for the goddess Artemis at Scylla in the Peloponnese, and host festivals (Xen. *An.* 5.3.6–10). Later he received the pick of the plunder taken from Asidates (Xen. *An.* 7.8.23). As an aristocrat and commander he took the best of the plunder. The medium he used to transport his wealth and pay for his dedications at Scylla must have been coins, which he gave to his agent for safekeeping and transported back to Greece.

Plunder alleviated payment responsibilities, but it came at a price. It weighed armies down with baggage trains of captured goods and potentially dangerous slaves. To solve the problem booty-sellers readily converted plunder into coinage or grain. Naturally, quick sales in the field yielded less than in a picked urban marketplace (*GSW* 1.77, 5.434–435). The army of the *Anabasis* made good money selling booty at the city of Cerasus (Xen. *An.* 5.3.1–6) as did Seuthes at Perinthus to pay the soldiers through his agent Heracleides (Xen. *An.* 7.5.1). The advantages of such on campaign sales were obvious, with armies not distracted from their military objectives and ready to move on, fed, paid, and content. Coins provided a medium of exchange by which armies could buy food and pay men, literally redistributing resources easily.

Conclusion

In conclusion, by the latter part of the fifth century, coinage had transformed the way in which many soldiers received remuneration instead of redistributed plunder. Booty remained prized, but coins substituted for the redistribution of cumbersome slaves, animals, and metals. Coins became the mechanism to centralize the logistics of warfare. Thucydides referred to the lack of coinage making wars smaller and less efficient in the past. The introduction of a means of exchange, like coinage, gave military organization flexibility. Commanders captured goods, all of which they could now sell in return for a coin. They could then do with that whatever they wished. They could keep it secure for long periods of time, leave it at a designated place, or carry it with them more easily than wagon loads of plunder. They might pay men their wages, or their ration money or even buy them their food. With their wages the men could buy from the commander himself in a neat cycle of money distribution. In the fifth century, traders came to and from the army. Some came to buy plundered goods with coins, while others came to sell food and services for coins. The army became a focal point of exchange. In the past, as Thucydides said, in a world before coinage, men had to spend their time in the countryside gathering food, now the food came to them. In short, money enabled the efficient centralization of economic exchange for armies and navies in the field. Hence wars became greater and campaigns longer in the Classical period.

Notes

1 All dates BCE. On the culture of early land warfare see (Hanson 1995; van Wees 2004, pp. 26–30; Whitby 2007; Pritchard 2010, pp. 7–15; and Kagan and Viggiano 2013). On naval raiding prior to the Persian Wars see (Haas 1985 pp. 29–46; Howgego 1993, 2000; Tandy 1997; and de Souza 1998).

2 The term does not appear only in military contexts. See Aesch. 1.172.2–3; Andoc. *Alc.* 30.3–5; and Ar. *Ach.* 53–4.

3 For the debate and references see (Gabrielsen 1985, 1994, pp. 19–26; Haas 1985; Rhodes 1993, pp. 151–153; and van Wees 2010). See Androtion *FGrH* 324 F 4 for *theoroi* paid from naukleric silver.

References

Bielman, A. (1994). *Retour à la liberté: libération et sauvetage des prisonniers en Grèce ancienne. Etudes Epigraphiques 1*. Athens: University of Lausanne.

Bowra C. M. (1936). *Greek Lyric Poetry from Alcman to Simonides*. Oxford: Oxford University Press.

Cairns, F. (1984). "*Chrêmata Dokima: IG* XII, 9, 1273 and 1274 and the early coinage of Eretria." *Zeitschrift für Papyrologie und Epigraphik* 54: 145–155.

Christ, M. (2001). "Conscription of hoplites in Classical Athens." *The Classical Quarterly* 51 (2): 398–422.

Gabrielsen, V. (1985). "The Naukrariai and the Athenian navy." *Classica et Mediaevalia* 1985, 36: 21–51.

Gabrielsen, V. (1994). *Financing the Athenian Fleet*. Baltimore: Johns Hopkins University Press.

Gabrielsen, V. (2008). "Die Kosten der athenischen Flotte in klassicher Zeit." In: *Kriegskosten und Kriegsfinanzierung in der Antike* (eds. F. Burrer and H. Muller), 46–73. Darmstaadt: Wissenschaftliche Buchgesellschaft.

Garlan, Y. (1976). *La Guerre dans l'Antiquité*. London: Norton.

Haas, C. (1985). "Athenian naval power before Themistocles." *Historia* 34: 29–46.

Hanson, V. (1995). *The Other Greeks: The Family Farm and the Agrarian Roots of Western Civilization*. New York: The Free Press.

Hanson, V. (2009). *Western Way of War: Infantry Battle in Classical Greece*, 2e. Berkeley: University of California Press.

Howgego, C. (1993). "Wars and raids for booty in the world of Odysseus." In: *War and Society in the Greek World* (eds. J. Rich and G. Shipley), 64–76. London: Routledge.

Howgego, C. (2000). "Sea-raiding in Archaic Greece with special attention to Samos." In: *The Sea in Antiquity* (eds. R. Brock, T.J. Cornell, S. Hodkinson and G.J. Oliver), 133–144. Oxford: BAR.

Humphreys, S.C. (1970). "Economy and society in Classical Athens." *Annali della Scuola Normale Superiore di Pisa, Classe di Lettere e Filosofia* 39: 1–26.

Jackson, A.H. (1991). "Hoplites and the gods. The dedication of captured arms and armour." In: *Hoplites: The Classical Greek Battle Experience* (ed. V.D. Hanson), 228–249. London: Routledge.

Janssen, A. (1957). *Het antieke Tropaion*. Brussels: Paleis der Acad.

Kagan, D. and Viggiano, G.F. (2013). *Men of Bronze: Hoplite Warfare in Ancient Greece*. Princeton: Princeton University Press.

Krasilnikoff, J.A. (1992). "Aegean mercenaries in the fourth to second centuries B.C.: a study in payment, plunder and logistics of ancient Greek armies." *Classica et Mediaevalia* 43: 23–36.

Krasilnikoff, J.A. (1993). "The regular payment of Aegean mercenaries in the Classical period." *Classica et Mediaevalia* 44: 77–95.

Krentz, P. (2002). "Fighting by the rules: the invention of the hoplite *Agôn*." *Hesperia* 71: 23–39.

Krentz, P. (2007). "War." In: *CHGRW*, vol. 1, 147–185.

Loomis, W. (1998). *Wages, Welfare, Costs and Inflation in Classical Athens*. Ann Arbor: Michigan University Press.

Morrison, J. and Williams, R.T. (1968). *Greek Oared Ships 900–322 BC*. Cambridge: Cambridge University Press.

Pritchard, D. (2010). "The symbiosis between democracy and war." In: *War, Democracy and Culture in Classical Athens* (ed. D. Pritchard), 1–62. Cambridge: Cambridge University Press.

Raaflaub, K. (1999). "Archaic and Classical Greece." In: *War and Society in the Ancient and Medieval Worlds* (eds. K. Raaflaub and N. Rosenstein), 129–162. Cambridge, MA: Harvard University Press.

Rhodes, P.J. (1993). *A Commentary on the Aristotelian Athenaion Politeia*. Oxford: Clarendon Press.

de Souza, P. (1998). "Towards thalassocracy? Archaic Greek naval developments." In: *Archaic Greece: New Approaches and New Evidence* (eds. N. Fisher and H. van Wees), 271–294. London: Duckworth.

Tandy, D. (1997). *Warriors into Traders: The Power of the Market in Ancient Greece*. Berkeley: University of California Press.

Trundle, M. (2004). *Greek Mercenaries from the Late Archaic Age to Alexander*. London: Routledge.

Trundle, M. (2010). "Coinage and the transformation of Greek warfare." In: *New Perspectives on Ancient Warfare* (eds. G. Fagan and M. Trundle), 227–253. Leiden: Brill.

Vanderpool, E. (1966). "A monument to the battle of Marathon." *Hesperia* 35: 93–106.

van Wees, H. (2004). *Greek Warfare, Myths and Realities*. London: Duckworth.

van Wees, H. (2010). "Those who sail shall receive a wage." In: *New Perspectives on Ancient Warfare* (eds. G. Fagan and M. Trundle), 205–226. Leiden: Brill.

Whitby, M. (2007). "Reconstructing ancient warfare." In: *CHGRW*, vol. 1, 54–81.

Further Reading

Jeremy, A. (ed.) (2016). Circum Mare: *Themes in Ancient Warfare*. Leiden: Brill, 2016. Bresson, Alain. 2015. In: *The Making of the Ancient Greek Economy: Institutions, Markets, and Growth in the City-States*. Princeton: Princeton University Press.

Fawcett, P. (2016). "When I squeeze you with Eisphorai': taxes and tax policy in Classical Athens." *Hesperia* 851: 153–199. https://doi.org/10.2972/hesperia.85.1.0153.

Pritchard, D. (2016). "Public spending and democracy." In: *Classical Athens*. Austin: University of Texas Press.

3

Early Greek Siege Warfare

Michael G. Seaman

Despite its continuous presence in Greek warfare, the topic of Greek siege warfare has been neglected by ancient military historians. Certainly, the Greeks were active in sieges in the Hellenistic period and Thucydides mentions no fewer than 100 sieges undertaken in the Peloponnesian War (Seaman 2013, pp. 653–655). In his five-volume history of Greek warfare, W. K. Pritchett devoted a mere two pages to siege operations, when discussing slingers, while Victor Davis Hanson treats siege warfare in less than a paragraph in his landmark volume *The Western Way of War* (*GSW* 5.57–58; Hanson 2009, p. 32). It is commonly thought that, because sieges were expensive and siege techniques were not well understood, the Greeks rarely undertook them until the mid-fifth century.[1] A number of ancient historians today have argued that during the Peloponnesian War, the Athenians "reintroduced into Greek warfare the 'Homeric' custom of destroying a captured city, killing the men, and selling the women and children into slavery" (Raaflaub 1999, p. 142; cf. also Hanson 1996, p. 606, 2000, p. 206; Ober 1994, pp. 12–26; *GSW* 2.173, 2.251–252; Connor 1988, pp. 3–28; Strauss 2007, p. 240). While Thucydides states that the Peloponnesian War saw an increase in the number of cities taken and Greeks killed or exiled because the war was fought over many years and involved a great number of poleis (Thuc. 1.23.1–2), the historian does not state or imply that this behavior was a recent phenomenon, only that it was on an unprecedented scale. If the many sieges and wanton destruction of poleis that Thucydides' narrative bears out were a new development, we might have expected the historian to state as much. In fact, besieging and destroying towns were prevalent in Greek warfare long before the mid or late fifth century. This chapter argues three main points: first, that sieges were always essential to Greek warfare and that Greeks undertook them and captured and destroyed poleis from the earliest periods; second, that we see an increase in the number of attempted sieges in the Archaic period with the advent of interstate coalitions; and third, that with the rise of the Athenian empire, we see a further increase in attempted sieges, along with a shift to a preference for circumvallation, which led to sieges that were far costlier and much longer in duration.

The Archaic Period

Ancient Greek siege warfare required the attacking army to surround the enemy polis in order to prevent the escape of the inhabitants, the importing of provisions, or securing of reinforcements. A besieging army normally tried to capture a polis by storm through penetrating the fortifications,

New Approaches to Greek and Roman Warfare, First Edition. Edited by Lee L. Brice.
© 2020 John Wiley & Sons, Inc. Published 2020 by John Wiley & Sons, Inc.

mining under them, or crossing over them. If these efforts failed, the attackers used the alternative method of circumvallation – they built a wall around the city, creating in effect a blockade, in order to starve the citizens into surrender. Direct attack, however, was the preferred method in the Archaic period since encirclement took much longer and proved far costlier, particularly if those undergoing the siege had prepared well for it. The Greeks of the Archaic period lagged behind the Assyrians and Persians in siege technique. These monarchies, rulers of large empires, could marshal the resources necessary for effective sieges. The independent Greek city-states, however, with their limited resources and manpower, and their reluctance to incur high rates of casualties, were slow to develop effective methods of siege warfare. Nevertheless, we should not equate rudimentary siegecraft with an unwillingness to attack an enemy polis.

Evidence both from the archaeological record and from early Greek literature suggests that the Greeks of the Archaic period, and perhaps even earlier, sought the conquest of cities, even without weaponry specifically designed for such use. The widespread destruction of the Mycenaean palaces and the subsequent abandonment of some of the sites are two indications that Greek cities in the Bronze Age did not coexist peacefully. The causes of what has been termed "the end of the Bronze Age" are debated; however, the architecture of the citadels themselves – with their massive walls of Cyclopean masonry, towering bastions to the right of the approach to the gates, designed to take advantage of an advancing enemy's exposed right – and great efforts to secure access within the walls to subterranean springs, like those at Mycenae and Athens, not to mention the destruction and burning of the citadels, suggest that the fortified Mycenaean centers undertook preparations for sieges. The fact that nearly all of the Mycenaean citadels were attacked and burned at the close of the Bronze Age also strongly suggests that they were subject to sieges.

The earliest Greek literature relates the struggle to capture and destroy an enemy city and to kill or enslave its inhabitants. The characters of the *Iliad* foretell more than once how the walls of Troy will someday fall, and they relate in some detail what the victors will do to the defeated when that day arrives. Homer makes no mention of specific siege techniques but he does speak of the capture of walled cities (cf. e.g. *Il.* 6.414–427, 16.56–59; *Od.* 9.39.61, 14.211–275). The poet includes on the shield of Achilles an army encamped near a walled town contemplating whether to storm and sack it or accept an offer to share half the possessions of the besieged, a proposal Hector later contemplates making to Achilles (*Il.* 18.509–512, 22.117–121). Frequent references to the two celebrated campaigns against "seven-gated" Thebes, that of the Seven and a decade later of their sons, the *Epigoni*, serve as evidence for early Greek sieges (cf., e.g. *Il.* 4.376–381, 4.406–410). In Hesiod's sobering critique of the present "fifth age," he decries that "one man will sack (*exalapaxei*) another one's city [...] for might will make right and reverence will cease to be" (Hes. *Op.* 189, 192; cf. also 245). Archaic poets mention warfare frequently, sometimes lamenting the destruction of a polis. Fragments of Tyrtaeus mention the Messenian Wars, the first of which apparently concluded about 715 with the destruction of Ithome "to its foundations" and the taking of the other Messenian cities (cf. Paus. 4.14.2).

Later Greek writers also relate early Spartan aggression in the Peloponnese, particularly in Arcadia (cf. Hdt. 1.66-68). In his discussion of Arcadia, Pausanias mentions the Spartan siege of the Arcadian town Phigalia (Paus. 8.39.3-5). The Phigalians stoutly resisted the invasion and gave battle to the Spartans, who, however, quickly defeated them and "settled down to besiege the city" (*epoliorkoun proskathezomenoi*), which they soon captured. Pausanias also recounts early Spartan conquests in Laconia and even claims to have been shown a trophy that the Spartans raised over the Laconian city Amyklai after it fell to a Spartan siege (Paus. 3.2.6). Details of these early wars are lacking, but if we accept these two Spartan sieges of the seventh century, they are the earliest reliable evidence that Greeks of the Archaic period followed up victories on the battlefield with conquests of towns.

Thucydides argued that Greek warfare in earlier periods remained on a relatively small scale, consisting mostly of border disputes between neighboring states:

> But there were no land wars by which power was amassed; all wars that did occur were individual conflicts over boundaries and the Greeks did not undertake foreign expeditions to subject others. For they did not yet unite around the greatest cities, subjecting themselves to them, nor did they undertake campaigns jointly as equal partners, but rather individually made war against neighboring states (Thuc. 1.15.2).

It is tempting to read the above passage and conclude that Thucydides described Archaic Greek warfare as relatively minor hoplite battles between poleis over borders, but this is not what he says. His main point is to state that in this early period, no one state was able to acquire great power through land warfare. This began to change, he explains, when alliances between poleis emerged. Thucydides believed that the first such conflict which can be described as a general Greek war was the so-called Lelantine War, between Eretria and Chalcis, as many cities joined either side (Thuc. 1.15.3). The date and nature of this war are obscure but Theognis preserves the tradition that, in the course of the fighting, the town of Cerinthos in northeast Euboea was destroyed (*ololen*), probably in the seventh century (Thgn. 891–894; cf. also Hdt. 5.99; Strabo 10.1.12; Plut. *Mor.* 760e–761b).

The first well-attested conquest of a fortified Greek town in the historical period is another example of a siege undertaken by an alliance – the capture and destruction of Cirrha at the conclusion of the First Sacred War in the late seventh century (Isoc. 14.31; *FGrHist* 124 F 1; Aeschin. 3.107–112; *FGrHist* 239; Diod. Sic. 9.16.1; Strabo 9.3.1, 9.3.4; Plut. *Sol.* 11; Paus. 2.9.6, 10.37.5–8; Polyaenus *Strat.* 3.5, 6.13). The conflict arose when Cirrha, situated on the north shore of the Corinthian Gulf and controlling one of the main routes to Delphi, was accused of interference with the oracle. The Amphictyonic League, a coalition of forces from Thessaly, Sicyon, and Athens, declared war, ostensibly on the grounds of sacrilege against Apollo, and besieged the town. A detailed account of its fall has not survived but two relatively late sources recount how the city was taken after the attackers discovered a hidden water pipe leading from a spring into the city and contaminated it with the roots of the poisonous herb hellebore (Paus. 10.37.7; Polyaenus *Strat.* 6.13). Aeschines (3.109), our earliest source that treats the First Sacred War in any detail, reports that the victors enslaved the Cirrhans. As for the town, all the sources agree: Cirrha was destroyed and its fertile land given over to the sanctuary of Apollo. Aeschines relates that, after razing the city, members of the Amphictyonic League swore an oath never to lay siege to or raze the cities of fellow members (Aeschin. 2.115). If the oath was genuine, it suggests that Greek city-states were already engaged in sieges and were likely to be so in the future. This is made clear in the closing line of the oath: "if anyone should violate this oath [league members] would march against him and raze his cities." No doubt there was some realization that the siege had been successful at least in part because it was carried out by a large coalition of cities. Such an oath would therefore provide some assurance to the league members who swore it that a powerful coalition, one capable of bringing a siege to a successful conclusion, would not attack an allied polis. The advent of alliances led to large-scale wars involving many city-states, as noted by Thucydides, which in turn fueled an increase in sieges.

Not all early sieges ended with the capture of the town. The combined Spartan and Corinthian force that besieged Samos circa 525, ostensibly to remove the tyrant Polycrates, ended in failure. After winning a land battle, the invaders shut the Samians up in their principal city and attacked it both by sea and by land. But the townspeople resisted and after 40 days the siege was abandoned, perhaps because the besiegers' supplies ran out. The Spartans may also have reasoned that after 40 days there was less hope for a betrayal from an anti-tyrannical faction within the town and that their victory in battle and ravaging Samian land were sufficient punishment. The Athenians had mixed results in their sieges in the early fifth century. Miltiades captured Lemnos for the Athenians, probably while acting as tyrant in the Chersonese in the 490s. Of its two towns, Hephaestia, the more vulnerable of the two, submitted, while Myrina gave in only after it was put under siege (Hdt. 6.140; Diod. Sic. 10.19.5; Nep. *Milt.* 2.4). However, less than a decade later, Miltiades led a similar expedition that ended in failure and brought about his condemnation. After the Battle of Marathon, the Athenians called on Miltiades to expand their influence in the Cyclades, perhaps with the pretext of punishing those islands that had in some way assisted the Persians on their expedition of 490 (Hdt. 6.133; Ephorus fr. 107, *FGrHist* I.263; Nep. *Milt.* 7.1). He sailed first to the prosperous island of Paros and demanded 100 talents, threatening to destroy the city if the inhabitants resisted (Hdt. 6.133). The ensuing siege lasted 26 days and may have been broken off either out of fear that the Persian fleet was approaching or because Miltiades himself was seriously injured. It may be that Miltiades was not prepared logistically for a long siege but had expected that a strong show of force coupled with threats of destruction would prompt the Parians to negotiate, as had happened earlier on Lemnos. Similarly, the Athenian siege of Andros by Themistocles seems to have been short-lived and ended in failure probably because the campaign was really intended as an attempt at extortion (Hdt. 8.111–112; Plut. *Them.* 21.1).

We know of sieges of Western Greek cities in the Archaic period. Some time between 550 and 510, Siris, a Greek polis in southern Italy, was destroyed by coalition of Metapontines, Sybarites, and Crotoniates (Justin 20.2; cf. also Lycoph. *Alex.* 978–985; Strabo 6.1.14). Perhaps the most notorious destruction of a city in the Archaic period was that of Sybaris by its neighbor Croton about 510. In this war, the two most celebrated citizens of Croton took active roles: the philosopher Pythagoras is said to have urged his fellow Crotoniates, who were disinclined to fight, to undertake the war; and Milo, six times victor in wrestling at Olympia, regarded by many modern scholars as the greatest athlete of Antiquity, led his countrymen to battle sporting his Olympian crowns (cf. Diod. Sic. 12.9-4-5). According to Diodorus and Strabo, Sybaris was the most prosperous Greek polis in Italy, with an enormous population and resources (Diod. Sic. 10.23.1, 12.92; Strabo 6.1.13). Both sources, as well as Herodotus, relate how Sybaris was besieged and captured by Croton, which razed the city to the ground (Hdt. 6.21; Diod. Sic. 10.23.1, 11.48.4, 12.9–10; Strabo 6.1.14). Strabo reports how the attackers diverted a river to submerge the town and that the siege lasted 70 days.

Elsewhere in the West, from Herodotus we learn that when a number of Samians along with some Melesians, who had recently escaped the Persian destruction, accepted the invitation of Zancle (i.e. Messana) to sail west to found a colony in Sicily, the tyrant of Rhegium persuaded the Ionians instead to seize Zancle, which was at that time deserted since the Zanclaeans were "besieging a Sicilian town desiring to capture it" (Hdt. 6.22–23; Thuc. 6.4.5). Thucydides adds that some Samians had joined the Ionians in seizing Zancle but that together they were themselves driven out not long afterward by Anaxilas, tyrant of Rhegium, who recolonized the polis and changed the name to Messana (Thuc. 6.4.5-6). Lastly, Hippocrates, tyrant of Gela, carved out an empire in Sicily in the 490s, besieging Callipolis, Sicilian Naxos, Zancle, and Leontini, and he would have taken Syracuse too if it had not been for the intervention of the Corinthians and Corcyraeans (Hdt. 7.154; cf. also Thuc. 6.4.2).

Our knowledge of wars waged by Greek poleis in the Archaic period is fragmentary. However, the evidence permits several observations about early Greek siege warfare. Apart from the poorly attested sieges undertaken by Sparta and those in Sicily, of the Greek sieges in the Archaic period mentioned by our sources, two ended in failure (Samos, Paros), while five were brought to successful conclusion (Cerinthos on Euboea, Cyrrha, Myrina on Lemnos, Siris, and Sybaris). It is telling that of this latter group, three (Cerinthos, Cyrrha, Siris) fell to coalitions of cities. Herodotus reminds us that when a polis sends its infantry abroad on campaign, it leaves its own city vulnerable to attack, a lesson learned by the Zancleans (Hdt. 6.23). Forming a coalition to besiege a town not only added military strength to a polis but also secured the dual benefits of not leaving your own city overly exposed and of sharing the costs of what might prove to be an expensive campaign.

While the lengths of these early sieges varied, the sources preserve a fixed number of days of duration in three cases. We are told that the sieges of Paros, Samos, and Sybaris lasted 26, 40, and 70 days, respectively, while only the last of these ended in the capture of the city. We might infer that a siege undertaken by Greeks in the Archaic period might last a few months at most. This would change in the Classical period when sieges would go on and on, sometimes for years, costing exorbitant amounts of money. Already in 479, when Xanthippos led the Athenians and their allies in the siege of Sestos, which probably began in early autumn (Hdt. 9.117) and continued perhaps through the entire winter (cf. Thuc. 1.89.2), i.e. upwards of four to five months, the Athenians grew impatient and begged the commanders to break off the siege. Xanthippos persevered and insisted that the siege continue until either Sestos was taken or the Athenians were recalled (Hdt. 9.117). He no doubt had in mind the fate of his nemesis Miltiades, whom he had prosecuted a decade earlier for having broken off the siege of Paros prematurely.

What changed to allow this? As we shall see, it is the advent of the Athenian empire in the early fifth century and the rise of a powerful and wealthy interstate coalition, the point made by Thucydides above in 1.15.2 (cf. Trundle, chapter 2).

It is difficult to say just how frequent siege warfare was among Greeks in the Archaic period. Not many wars among Greeks of that age are known, so the relatively small number of sieges reported by the sources cannot be taken as evidence that sieges were rare. We cannot infer, for example, that, because our sources mention only a handful of wars fought among the Greeks in the Archaic period, warfare was less frequent than in later periods of Greek history. Further, our best source for the period is Herodotus, though his purpose is really to relate the conflict between the Persians and Greeks and therefore he only mentions the sieges insofar as they relate tangentially to the larger conflict. Nowhere does he or Thucydides indicate that sieges were rare or that Greeks reluctantly undertook them. It may be that sieges were more frequent in the Archaic age than can be gathered from the literary sources. Little is certain of early hoplite warfare but we should not conclude that just because wars "were fought between neighboring states" (Thuc. 1.15.2) that these wars did not involve sieges and the capture of cities. Despite the limitations of our sources, there is enough evidence to suggest that the Greeks were engaging in sieges from as far back as we can examine. Moreover, it is clear that when the Greeks began in the Archaic period to form alliances and have at their disposal increased resources to carry out effective sieges, the result was that larger poleis were now at risk and cities were attacked and destroyed with greater frequency, even if the methods of the siege were rudimentary compared with those of their neighbors to the East or with the large besieging armies of the fourth and later centuries.

The Early Fifth Century

As we have seen, the Greeks of the Archaic period were prepared to undertake sieges and, though they may not have employed sophisticated siege techniques, they nonetheless captured towns. In the early fifth century, the number of attempted sieges in the Greek world mentioned by the ancient sources increases dramatically. In the roughly 50 years between the Persian and Peloponnesian Wars, we know of at least 30 sieges undertaken by Greek poleis, twenty seven of which ended successfully in the sense that the polis being attacked either surrendered on terms or was captured and destroyed (Seaman 2013, p. 653). It is significant that Athens, or the Athenians leading the combined forces of the Delian League, were the aggressors in all but four of these 30 sieges, the vast majority. Thucydides tells us that by about 465, when the Spartans encountered difficulty in besieging the helots in revolt on Mt. Ithome, Athens already enjoyed a reputation for siege warfare (Thuc. 1.102.2). One scholar famously commented that this reputation was akin to "the one-eyed among the blind" (Grundy 1898, p. 220). But this view perhaps interjects a mistaken notion that taking a city by circumvallation is somehow less effective than taking it by storm. Both methods were considered "siege warfare" by the Greeks and their goal was the same: capitulation of the city. In fact the Athenians leading the Delian League had just prior to the helot revolt besieged Sestos, Eion, an unknown number of cities in Caria, Phaselis, and perhaps other poleis in Lycia, Scyros, Byzantium, Carystos, Naxos and, most recently, Thasos, bringing all operations to a successful conclusion. The only other attack on a city mentioned in the sources over the years from approximately 479 to 465, successful or otherwise, is the capture and destruction of Mycenae by the Argives about 468 (cf. Diod. Sic. 11.65; Paus. 2.16.4). Of the sieges in the early fifth century found worthy of mention by the historians, the Athenians undertook all but one and were always successful.[2] On the surface, it might appear that Athens was acting more aggressively than was the norm in Greek warfare. However, a closer analysis of these sieges reveals other reasons for the apparent rise in this type of warfare.

The increase in the number of sieges reported in the fifth century should be seen, at least in part, as a result of the growth of historical writing, which develops later in the century. We can draw on a greater number of literary sources for our information, sources that provide a clearer picture of interstate relations and greater details in their narratives of the wars among Greek city-states. Second, the best source for the period between the Persian and Peloponnesian Wars is the Athenian Thucydides. But the general-turned-historian, who laments that his predecessors have neglected this period in their histories (1.97.2), admits that he includes a narrative of these years because he wishes to show the growth of Athenian power (1.89.1). We would do well to recall that Thucydides is not writing a universal history of the Greek world of the sort that Ephorus, Timaeus, and Diodorus would later compose. We might, therefore, expect Thucydides to relate in the *Pentecontaetia* only those sieges that have a bearing on the increase in Athenian power. When covering the wars in Sicily in 426 waged between Greeks and Siceliots, Thucydides admits that he will confine himself "to the actions in which the Athenians took part, choosing the most important" (3.90.1). In fact, Thucydides leaves out of his narrative not only the sieges of Greek towns in the west but also the capture of Oeniadae in Acarnania by the Messenians settled at Naupactos (Paus. 4.25.1–2), a feat that eluded Pericles (Thuc. 1.111.3; Diod. Sic. 11.85.2), as well as the previously mentioned Argive annihilation of Mycenae, which took place about 465 (Diod. Sic. 11.65; Paus. 2.16.4). Thucydides undoubtedly knew of the destruction of Mycenae but deemed it unworthy of inclusion in his history. Diodorus states that the Argives waited for an opportune moment to attack Mycenae, and made their move when the Spartans were occupied with the helot revolt. After the successful siege, they razed the city and sold the inhabitants into slavery. Both Diodorus and Pausanias relate the end of the storied city and so we might well wonder how many sieges have gone unreported by Herodotus, Thucydides, and others, particularly those that were unsuccessful, because they had no bearing on the overall narrative or purpose of their history.

Thucydides makes it clear that it did not take an enormous force to capture a relatively small Greek polis. In 432, it took only 1000 Athenian hoplites a few months to capture Thermae in the Chalcidice and begin the siege of Pydna in Macedon (Thuc. 1.57.6, 1.61.2). It is also evident that a city under siege stood a better chance for survival if it could depend on allies or friendly neighboring states. About 453, Pericles led the Athenians to victory in battle against Sicyon in the First Peloponnesian War (Thuc. 1.111.2; Diod. Sic. 11.88.1–2). Diodorus says that Pericles "shut them up in their city" and laid siege to it but was forced to retire after help sent by the Spartans arrived. If the besieged were colonists, assistance might be sent by the mother city, as when the Corinthians sent 1600 hoplites and 400 light-armed troops to aid their colonists, the Potidaians (Thuc. 1.160.1). Diodorus underlines the vulnerability of a smaller polis that might not receive the necessary assistance in its hour of need when he gives the chief reason why Mycenae fell to the Argives: the Spartans were too busy with the helot revolt to assist them and, "since there were no other allies, [the Mycenaeans] were taken by storm because they lacked allied support" (Diod. Sic. 11.65.4).

It is noteworthy that, of the four known cities besieged by non-Athenian Greeks in this period – Mycenae, Sybaris, Trinacie, and Oiniadai – at least three fell by being stormed, not through starvation by circumvallation. This contrasts sharply with the sieges undertaken by the Athenians in the same period, where circumvallation was the preferred method of laying siege. Given our relative dependence on Thucydides as a source for the early fifth century, and given his stated purpose of relating events pertaining to the growth of Athenian power, we might conclude that the data are somewhat skewed toward showing a Greek preference for siege by circumvallation. In his Sather lectures at Berkeley, Frank Adcock held that "until the last decade of the fifth century no Greek city of any size was taken by assault" (Adcock 1957, p. 58). One presumes he meant to say that no Greek city of any *significant* size was taken by assault until late in the fifth century, but even this is somewhat misleading since many Greek cities, even some big ones (e.g. Thebes; cf. Hdt 9.86–87), capitulated after being put under continuous siege. Other large cities or island-states captured by siege earlier than the close of the fifth century include Sybaris, Naxos, Thasos, Aegina, and Samos.[3] From this pattern, we might infer that the cities that surrendered on terms did so out of fear that they would have fallen and received worse conditions had they not capitulated. Further, we should not conclude that since no major Greek city was taken by assault, sieges were not common. Estimates for the number of Greek cities, not all of which were necessarily a polis, range from about 1000 to 1500 (Ruschenbusch 1985, pp. 253–263; Hansen 2006, p. 1). The fact that none of the 10 largest Greek cities fell by assault before the late fifth century reflects more on the *abilities* of the Greeks in siege warfare than on their *habits*. In other words, we might rephrase Adcock's observation by noting that before the late fifth century, nearly all Greek cities were vulnerable to siege by assault or circumvallation, especially if the invading force was large and strong (i.e. a coalition of poleis) and that by the late fifth century, when Athens could draw on enormous resources, the figure increases to 100%. Therefore, even before the late fifth century, Greeks attacked cities, taking some quickly by storm and others more patiently by starving them into surrender.

What stands out immediately in warfare of the early fifth century is the surge in sieges undertaken by Athens: over the approximately 50 years before the outbreak of the Peloponnesian War, Athens undertook twenty five sieges of varying lengths and was successful in all but three.[4] The reason for such success is that Athens could now command a large coalition of allied states and had, with the annual tribute of the Delian League, the resources to undertake extended and costly sieges, some of which (e.g. those of Thasos and Potidaia) lasted over two years. Not surprisingly, it is in this period that we begin to get specific information about the costs of protracted sieges, presumably because they were so expensive. Herodotus, Nepos, and Plutarch all report that Miltiades was fined 50 talents for his unsuccessful siege at Paros in 489 but the Roman biographer adds that the amount was set at "the cost of the fleet" of the failed expedition (*quantus in classem sumptus factus erat*), a believable amount given the brevity of the war and the nature of Athenian *eisangelia*, which would have seen Miltiades tried and found guilty by the Assembly (Hdt. 6.136.3; Nep. *Milt.*

7.6; Plut. *Cim.* 4.3). The Athenian siege of Samos in 440 lasted nine months and cost over 1400 talents (*IG* I^3 363 = ML 113). This is double the total cost of the Parthenon's construction, a 10-year project (cf. Buford 1965, p. 25). Less than a decade later, the Athenians would spend 2000 talents over almost three years to seize Potidaia. Thucydides informs us that the Athenians never employed fewer than 3000 hoplites in the siege, not including another 1600 hoplites under the command of Phormio who departed before it was over. All were paid a wage of two drachmas a day, one for the hoplite and another for his servant (see Trundle, Chapter 2), a massive expense that drained Athenian revenue (Thuc. 3.17.3–4). Thucydides realized the importance of money in siege warfare (Thuc. 1.11) and it is clearly Athens' ability to draw on the League's funds that fueled its ability to wage an extraordinary number of successful sieges throughout the fifth century.

Already in the Archaic period, we had heard of the unfortunate fate that awaited the successfully besieged: their city was usually destroyed and they themselves were killed or enslaved (e.g. Messene, Cerinthos, Cirrha, Siris, Sybaris). But it is not until the early fifth century, with improved literary sources, that we begin to learn some details of the horrors experienced by the starving inhabitants of a city under siege or blockade. When the grain ran out at Sestos, besieged by Xanthippos, the townspeople purportedly boiled the leather straps of their beds for food until even these ran out (Hdt. 9.118.1). And at Potidaia, after more than two years of the Athenian blockade, the civilians were said, in the end, to have resorted to cannibalism before surrendering (Thuc. 2.70.1). The Athenian preference for circumvallation brought with it a new form of suffering for the besieged: slow starvation and untold suffering as they strove to outlast the resources and patience of the besieging army.

Conclusion

As we have seen, a careful survey of Greek siege warfare in this early period suggests more continuity with the later periods than is commonly thought. There is no compelling reason to assume that at the time of the Peloponnesian War the Athenians or others reintroduced into Greek warfare the idea of capturing or destroying cities. Already in the Archaic period, when our sources are weaker, we nonetheless hear of successful sieges. At the same time, we detect an increase in attempted sieges when city-states begin to avail themselves of the military advantages gained by joining an interstate coalition. In the early fifth century, we begin to see a dramatic rise in the number of sieges due in part to an improvement in our sources but also to the fact that the Greeks, namely the Athenians, were able to draw on the extensive resources of the Delian League. This wealth afforded them the luxury of engaging in circumvallation, which was less risky than assault but was very time-consuming and expensive. Consequently, from the fifth century on, sieges could become terribly long affairs and extremely costly. However, though the cost, duration, and techniques changed over time, we may conclude that siege warfare, the capture and destruction of cities and the enslavement or capture of the inhabitants, was from the earliest period an essential part of Greek warfare.

Notes

1 All dates in this chapter are BCE.
2 As noted in the section "The Archaic Period," circumvallation was normally preceded with assaults on the city, which would have given the Athenians ample experience in this method of siege warfare. The Athenians may have gained notoriety at sieges following the Battle of Plataea when they successfully assaulted the Persian stockade (Hdt. 9.70.1–2; Plut. *Arist.* 19.3). Thucydides noted

the astonishment of the Syracusans at how rapidly the Athenians could build the large wall of circumvallation around their polis (Thuc. 6.98.2).

3 The successful sieges of large city-states prior to the late fifth century were those of Sybaris (Hdt. 6.21; Diod. Sic. 10.23.1, 11.48.4, 12.9–10; Strabo 6.1.14), Naxos (Thuc. 1.98.4, 1.137.2), Thasos (Thuc. 1.100.2–101.3; Diod. Sic. 11.70; Plut. *Cim.* 14.2), Aegina (Thuc. 1.105.2, 1.108.4; Diod. Sic. 11.70.2–4; cf. also Thuc. 2.27.1–2; Diod. Sic. 12.44.2–3; Plut. *Per.* 34.1), and Samos (*IG* I³ 363 = ML 55; Thuc. 1.116–117; Diod. Sic. 12.27.2–28; Plut. *Per.* 26–28; Nep. *Timoth.* 1.2).

4 The three failures: Pericles at Oeniadae in c. 454 (Thuc. 1.111.2–3; Diod. Sic. 11.85.2; Plut. *Per.* 19.4) and at Sicyon the following year (Diod. Sic. 11.88.1–2; cf. also Thuc. 1.111.2); and Callias and others at Strepsa in 432 (Thuc. 1.61.2–4).

References

Adcock, F. (1957). *The Greek and Macedonian Art of War*. Berkeley: University of California Press.

Buford, A.M. (1965). "The economics of Greek temple building." *Proceedings of the Cambridge Philological Society* 11: 21–34.

Connor, W.R. (1988). "Early Greek land warfare as symbolic expression." *Past & Present* 119: 3–28.

Grundy, G. B. (1898). "A suggested characteristic in Thukydides' work." *Journal of Hellenic Studies* 18: 218–231.

Hansen, M. (2006). *An Introduction to the Ancient Greek City-State*. Oxford: Oxford University Press.

Hanson, V. (1996). "Land warfare in Thucydides, as Appendix F." In: *The Landmark Thucydides: A Comprehensive Guide to the Peloponnesian War* (translated and edited by R.B. Strassler), 603–607. New York: The Free Press.

Hanson, V. (2000). "Hoplite battle as ancient Greek warfare: when, where, and why?" In: *War and Violence in Ancient Greece* (ed. H. van Wees), 201–232. London: Duckworth.

Hanson, V. (2009). *Western Way of War: Infantry Battle in Classical Greece*, 3e. Berkeley: University of California Press.

Ober, J. (1994). "Classical Greek times." In: *The Laws of War: Constraints on Warfare in the Western World* (eds. M. Howard, G.J. Andreopoulos and M.R. Schulman), 12–26. New Haven, CT: Yale University Press.

Raaflaub, K. (1999). "Archaic and Classical Greece." In: *War and Society in the Ancient and Medieval Worlds* (eds. K. Raaflaub and N. Rosenstein), 129–141. Washington, D. C.: Center for Hellenic Studies.

Ruschenbusch, E. (1985). "Die Zahl der griechischen Staaten und Arealgrösse und Bürgerzahl der 'Normalpolis'." *Zeitschrift für Papyrologie und Epigraphik* 59: 253–263.

Seaman, M.G. (2013). "The Peloponnesian war and its sieges." In: *The Oxford Handbook of Warfare in the Classical World* (eds. B. Campbell and L. Tritle), 642–656. Oxford: Oxford University Press.

Strauss, B. (2007). "Naval battles and sieges." In: *CHGRW*, vol. 1, 223–247.

Further Reading

Armstrong, J. and Trundle, M. (eds.) (2019). *Brill's Companion to Sieges in the Ancient Mediterranean*. Leiden: Brill.

Ballmer, A., Fernandez-Götz, M., and Mielke, D. (eds.) (2016). *Understanding Ancient Fortifications: Between Regionality and Connectivity*. Oxford: Oxbow Books.

Frederikson, R. (2016). "Fortifications and the Archaic city in the Greek world." In: *Le fortificazioni arcaiche del Latium vetus e dell'Etrurie meridionale (IX-VI sec. a.C.) Stratigrafia, cronologia e urbanizzazione* (eds. P. Fontaine and S. Helas), 252–266. Rome: Academia Belgica Giornate di studio.

Frederiksen, R., Müth, S., Schneider, P., and Schnelle, M. (eds.) (2016). *Focus on Fortifications: New Research on Fortifications in the Ancient Mediterranean and the Near East.* Oxford: Oxbow Books.

Lendon, J.E. (2017). "Battle descriptions in the ancient historians, 2 Pts." *Greece & Rome* 64: 39–64 and 145-67. https://doi.org/10.1017/S0017383516000231. https://doi.org/10.1017/S0017383517000067.

Sears, M. (2019). *Understanding Greek Warfare.* New York: Routledge.

4

Daily Life in Classical Greek Armies, c. 500–330 BCE

John W.I. Lee

The study of daily life in Classical armies encompasses topics such as soldiers' social organization, their cooking, eating, and sanitation practices, sexual behavior, relationships with slaves and camp followers, and much else besides. Examining these diverse aspects of the Classical soldier's experience takes the history of warfare beyond the battlefield, from purely military concerns into the realm of social, cultural, and economic history.

While some might be tempted to dismiss soldiers' everyday experiences as "boring" or "trivial" compared to battle, studying daily life is essential to understanding war in the Classical world. To begin with, the study of daily life forcefully reminds us how much more difficult basic survival was in the ancient world. It could cost Classical warriors great time and effort to do things most of us take for granted – get a drink of water, cook a meal, stay warm and dry. Moreover, many Classical soldiers possessed few if any of the institutional structures and support services that soldiers in modern armies enjoy.

Studying daily life also reminds us that armies are not just military machines; they are social organisms. An army is a particular type of community, with its own demography, institutions, social structures, and values. Its members must constantly interact among themselves and with those they meet on campaign or in garrison. In their quest for food, water, and firewood, soldiers can reshape the economy and environment of the lands they encounter.

Even those who prefer traditional battle-focused history can still profit from learning about the ordinary soldier's experience. Appreciating Classical soldiers' everyday challenges helps explain why their needs sometimes got in the way of generals' plans, causing confusion, delay, and even disaster. The soldier's viewpoint on daily life, then, is an essential complement to the commander's perspective on strategy and tactics.

In this chapter, we begin by considering the approaches and methods scholars have used in recent years to study the Classical military experience. From there, we examine the institutions and social structures that shaped soldiers' worlds. After that, we survey some of the daily routines of campaign and garrison. While most discussions of Classical warfare focus on the Greeks alone, we will consider not only Greek armies but also the armies of Achaemenid Persia, in order to get a broader perspective on the varieties of Classical military life.

New Approaches and Methods

Classical military life can be approached from several interlinked perspectives, starting with logistics or military supply. For ancient historians, Donald Engel's 1978 book *Alexander the Great and the Logistics of the Macedonian Army* has long provided a model for studying logistics. While his

New Approaches to Greek and Roman Warfare, First Edition. Edited by Lee L. Brice.

work remains a valuable reference, Engels very much takes the commander's perspective on logistics and some details of his analysis have not stood up over time. Other studies too have contributed greatly to our knowledge of ancient logistics, again often from the commander's point of view (Young 1980; Lazenby 1994; O'Connor 2011).

One way to escape the commander's eye view of logistics is to foreground the soldier's viewpoint in what has been called the "face of battle" approach, after the title of John Keegan's influential 1976 book. Instead of emphasizing generals, strategy, and tactics, Keegan focused on the ordinary soldier's physical and emotional experience of combat. In doing so, he created a vivid new style of military history that has been widely emulated. As early as 1989, Victor Hanson's *Western Way of War* applied Keegan's method to Classical Greek battle, and today it could fairly be said that the "face of battle" is standard practice for historians of both ancient and modern warfare.

Both Keegan and Hanson noted the importance of small group loyalties to soldiers' experience of battle (Keegan 1976, pp. 52–53; Hanson 2009, pp. 117–125). Interest in small military communities, or "primary groups" as they are sometimes called, goes back to the nineteenth century. After the Second World War, military scholars sought to explain why armies fought and to improve unit cohesion by studying the nature and effectiveness of small group bonds. During the last few decades, the debate over gay and lesbian service people serving openly in the United States military – ending in the repeal of "Don't Ask Don't Tell" – fostered continued interest in issues of small group cohesion. And, the idea that soldiers fight for their comrades or buddies has become widespread in popular culture through movies and books.

Despite the cliché that soldiers form "bands of brothers," scholars now recognize how misleading it is to use an unchanging idealized model of small group behavior to analyze modern armies (Hamner 2011). Changes in weapons, tactics, and culture all have to be taken into account, along with the composition, situation, and norms of military small groups. In contrast to the romantic stereotype of military comradeship, research is also showing how small groups can harm rather than enhance unit cohesion and combat effectiveness.

Conclusions drawn from studying modern military group behavior cannot, of course, simply be transferred wholesale to the ancient world (Wheeler 2007, p. 213; cf. Wheeler 2011). Even so, analysis of Classical soldiers' small groups and social relationships offers another promising way to understand their daily experiences. Used judiciously, comparisons with modern armies can provide the basis for asking new questions about the ancient evidence, as long as we keep in mind the specific factors that influenced the behavior of Classical warriors, such as weak unit structures, the explicit desire for booty and plunder, sexual relationships between soldiers, and the desire to emulate Homeric ideals (Lendon 2005; on comparing see also Tritle, Chapter 5, on cohesion see Brice, Chapter 9). Indeed, such comparisons are sometimes most valuable for the ways in which they highlight the differences between our modern assumptions and the realities of ancient military life.

In recent years, historians have combined the logistical, face of battle, and small group approaches to study modern armies as diverse as the Confederates in the US Civil War (Glatthaar 2008), the Soviets in the Second World War (Merridale 2006), and the South Vietnamese in the 1960s and 1970s (Brigham 2006). Classical warfare scholars, likewise, have increasingly focused on Greek soldiers' daily lives and the social dynamics of Greek armies (Trundle 2004; Krentz 2007; Lee 2007).

While traditional military history is often largely text-based, reconstructing the patterns of life in Classical armies requires investigating both written and archaeological sources. Most ancient authors do not focus at length on daily life, but many offer incidental or offhand comments about military behavior that, even if embedded in otherwise biased or selective accounts, reflect ancient realities. Excavated remains of Classical barracks are rare, but can reveal much about soldiers' eating, drinking, and sleeping practices (Coulton 1996; Sapouna Sakellaraki et al. 2002). Since there were few specifically "military" utensils in the ancient world, excavated material from domestic contexts can also be useful. For perishable items such as clothing and tents, though, we must rely on images from terracotta figurines or painted pottery. Skeletal evidence can provide clues about soldiers' nutrition, lifestyle, and overall health, as Maria Liston explains in Chapter 7 of this volume (Vassallo 2010).

A variety of other analytical approaches have been fruitfully employed in recent years. While scholars are wary of unscientific amateur reenactors, textual, and archaeological analysis combined with controlled reconstruction and reenactment can produce significant new insights. One study, for example, reveals that ancient linen armor may have been lighter, tougher, and more cost-effective than previously imagined (Griffiths 2000; Aldrete et al. 2013). Topographical and environmental analysis of weather, settlement patterns, resource availability, and other factors can clarify fragmentary or obscure textual evidence. And, since certain physical factors such as human nutritional needs and waste output have remained roughly constant over the ages, we can sometimes employ modern comparative data to help understand ancient soldiers' everyday requirements even when ancient evidence is lacking.

Institutional Frameworks

Now that we have examined the methods and approaches scholars have used to study Classical armies in recent years, let us turn to consider the armies themselves. Formal institutions and hierarchies define the modern military: think officers and sergeants, platoons and squads, mess halls and supply depots. In the Classical period, only the Persian and Spartan armies had anything similar. The Achaemenid Persians had standard-sized units, extensive bureaucracy, and efficient support services. The Spartans had supply officers, formal subunit organization, and famously strict discipline: "Every Spartan an officer" was basically how Thucydides put it (Thuc. 5.66).

Most Classical Greek armies, though, had weak formal structures. Citizen militias typically formed in tribal regiments of a 1000 or so, sometimes divided in companies of a few hundred men. Subunits and subofficers were rare. In mainland Greece, men often brought their own equipment and rations, while medical care and transport were not centrally organized. In citizen armies with elected leaders, discipline could be limited, hierarchy vague, and authority weak (*GSW* 2.232-45; van Wees 2004, pp. 108–113; Hunt 2007, pp. 127–132). Soldiers talked back to their commanders and occasionally threw stones at them. Sometimes generals could control their troops only by making a game or contest of the behavior they wanted (Xen. *Hell.* 6.2.28). Often armies relied on communal pressure and mutual exhortation to keep order.

Social Structures

The weak institutions of most Classical Greek armies left soldiers on their own when it came to the necessities of life in the field. In response, men borrowed from the patterns of home. Informal clubs, eating groups, and social associations were common in Classical Greek society, so it is no surprise informal eating and tent groups also became central to daily military life. These groups went by various names, most commonly "tent group" (*suskenia*) and "common mess" (*sussitia*), and the soldiers who belonged to them called each other "tent-mates" (*suskenoi*), "mess-mates" (*sussitoi*), or other similar terms. The Spartans and Cretans were exceptional in having formally regulated mess groups.

Tent and mess groups made daily survival practicable. Nobody could cut his own wood, draw his own water, light his own fire, bake his own bread, build his own shelter, and so on, all while keeping on guard against attack. Grouping together allowed soldiers to share the necessary labor and get mutual protection. As Plato put it, "when men go into the field as soldiers they are compelled by circumstance to mess together for the sake of their own security" (Pl. *Leges* 625e).

Small groups also offered friendship and solidarity. Belonging to a group helped men find a place in the crowd, gave them aid against rivals, and might even make them fight better (Xen. *Cyr.* 2.1.25–28). Soldiers' groups could also play a role in religious practice, and groups sometimes helped bring dead comrades home for burial (Isae. 9.4). In the Athenian military, being a messmate was the closest of a gradually expanding set of relationships, as a courtroom speaker revealed by claiming that two men were "neither messmates nor friends nor members of the same unit" (Isae. 4.18). Xenophon said it plainly: "Messmates are closer than those who quarter apart" (Xen. *Cyr.* 8.7.14). In desperate straits, men called out to their closest comrades: their relatives and tent-mates (Thuc. 7.75.4). On the other hand, not being accepted by a mess or tent group was to be shunned as if ritually polluted (Lys. 13.79).

Mess or tent groups in both citizen and mercenary forces often carried on ties from home, as friends, relatives, or neighbors banded together (Dem. 54.3; Isae. 2.6; Lys. 16.14–16; Xen. *An.* 5.7.15, 5.8.6, 6.4.8). On short campaigns or during sieges, men from different formal units could still tent together. The most famous examples are Socrates and Alcibiades, who were tent-mates at Potidaea in 432 BCE, despite being in different tribal regiments (Pl. *Symp.* 219e). There was more regulation in the Spartan army, where men lived as part of the same formal mess group they belonged to back home in Sparta.

Classical Greek soldiers are sometimes criticized for indiscipline, but the reality is that the absence of formal support mechanisms gave soldiers little choice but to attend to their own daily needs first. Because soldiers had to rely on each other, their loyalties could become more focused on their small group than on the army as a whole. In this way, small group cohesion sometimes put Classical Greek soldiers at odds with their leaders, hindering rather than promoting military effectiveness.

Xenophon provides a particularly vivid example of small group loyalty in action (Xen. *An.* 5.8.1–11). During the Cyrean retreat to the sea, Xenophon forced a soldier leading a mule to carry a sick stranger, but soon after found the mule driver trying to bury his charge alive. Later, the soldier complained that Xenophon had scattered his tent-mates' baggage and compelled him to carry a stranger. As Xenophon the general spins the story, the mule driver comes off as callous and unreasonable. But, think of it from the mule-driver's perspective: would you rather save the precious gear that you and your comrades needed to survive, or be stuck with some dying stranger? Elsewhere, Xenophon records some soldiers left ranks temporarily in battle to look after the needs of their small group; others plotted desertion with their mess-mates (Xen. *An.* 4.3.30, 5.7.14–16).

Non-Combatants

Now, the Cyreans had few slave attendants at the start of their campaign, although they picked up both male and female companions along the way (Lee 2007, pp. 255–275). Indeed, mercenary forces in general may have had fewer slaves and servants. In Greek citizen armies, though, attendants were common (van Wees 2004, pp. 68–71). Spartan soldiers had at least one helot servant apiece, while many Athenian citizen hoplites had personal slaves (Hdt. 7.229, 9.29; Thuc. 3.17.3, 4.16, 7.75.5; Dem. 54.4). In one case, an Athenian hoplite allegedly used an impoverished free relative as a personal servant (Isae. 5.11).

Modern commentators tend to see attendants as markers of laziness. Again, though, it helps to consider matters from an ordinary citizen-soldier's viewpoint: servants were essential to carry the baggage and do the chores so that soldiers could focus on fighting. That said, over-reliance on slave attendants could cause problems if the slaves deserted (Thuc. 7.75.5). Soldiers without slaves might also resent the easier camp life that men with attendants enjoyed. In one Athenian court case, a group of tent-mates harassed another group's slaves as a way of picking a fight (Dem. 54.4–5). In armies with fewer servants, men had to work together to accomplish daily tasks like foraging and cooking. Communal labor of this sort could increase group cohesion, but there was always the possibility of the lazy mess-mate who did not pull his weight (Xen. *Cyr.* 2.2.22–25).

Family members or other non-combatants may also have accompanied Greek armies in the field, as was the case in many armies before the nineteenth century (Hacker 1981; Mayer 1996). Most of the women Xenophon mentions in his *Anabasis*, though, were captives taken en route, not family members who began the march with the army. Indeed, mercenaries going on campaign may typically have left their families behind (Plut. *Pel.* 27.4; Xen. *An.* 1.4.8). Women sometimes cooked and carried supplies for the defenders of besieged cities (Diod. Sic. 13.55.4; Thuc. 2.78.3).

Sexuality

Popular books and movies often misrepresent or elide the place of sexuality in ancient armies (Bridges et al. 2007). Ancient evidence, however, clearly shows homoerotic ties were important to Classical Greek militaries (Ogden 1996). In the Spartan army institutionalized pederasty encouraged bonds between soldiers and helped strengthen unit cohesion, while at Athens same-sex ties were widely accepted. Pairs of lovers formed the elite Sacred Band of Thebes (Leitao 2002; Davidson 2007). Xenophon mentions a mercenary captain who once raised a picked company of beautiful recruits (Xen. *An.* 7.4.7–9). Plato, reflecting widespread Greek attitudes, wrote that a small band of lovers and their beloveds could defeat a much larger force, for a lover would rather die many times over rather than have his beloved see him leaving his post or throwing away his arms (Pl. *Symp.* 178e–197b).

Our ancient sources tend to emphasize emotional and affective ties as features of same-sex military relationships. Little evidence exists for casual sexual hookups amongst soldiers, though they may well have occurred. Since Greek soldiers often had easy access to female and male prostitutes or slaves, though, it is not unlikely that at least some men strictly followed the ideals of Greek pederastic behavior.

In some cases soldiers formed sexual and emotional relationships with captives. For example, the mercenaries of Cyrus kept desirable male and female captives despite being ordered to abandon them (Xen. *An.* 4.1.14–15). Some of the troops even got into fights over attractive boy captives (Xen. *An.* 5.8.4). For Xenophon, same-sex ties became a problem only when they distracted commanders and troops from their duties (Xen. *Hell.* 4.8.18, 5.4.57). At other times he speaks positively about homoerotic attachments, especially if they fostered bravery (Xen. *Hell.* 4.8.39, 5.4.33).

Daily Routines

Weak institutional structures, strong social groups, and the presence of non-combatants all influenced daily life in Greek armies, especially in camp. A commander might specify the general location of a camp, but within that area officers apparently imposed little order. Small groups often competed to stake out the best ground (Polyaenus *Strat.* 2.3.11), probably resulting in a jumble of tents and pathways. In summertime, soldiers could simply spread out their bedding in the open, but some troops carried tents when they expected wet or cold conditions (Xen. *An.* 1.1.11). Most Classical Greek camps were not fortified (*GSW* 2. 133–146; Krentz 2007, pp. 162–165; Lee 2007, pp. 173–180), although sentries were sometimes stationed (Russell 1999, pp. 27–37). The Spartans, once again, were exceptional for their highly organized camps (Xen. *Lak. Pol.* 12).

Once they had set up camp, men needed to find food and water. On short campaigns soldiers or their servants could carry rations from home. In some cases, generals provided supply trains or markets (Diod. Sic. 11.80.2–4, 14.55.5–6; Hdt. 9.39), and mess groups might pool their money to shop at markets (Arist. *Vesp.* 557). Otherwise men foraged for supplies with their mess-mates (Thuc. 3.111; Xen. *An.* 4.3.11). Depending on the situation, troops might take grain and livestock from the locals, plunder farms and fields, and even gather vegetables.

Soldiers in the field probably exploited every water source they could find, reserving the best water for drinking. Brackish or salt water was still useful for bathing or laundry. In Greek towns water came readily from cisterns, wells, and fountain houses, while basins, drains, and pipes helped people save and recycle water. Troops on campaign had no such infrastructure unless they camped near a town or sanctuary. That meant soldiers often had to go further to find water and wasted more of it. Lack of official supervision increased the chances of illness or disease, for example if men drank from a stream while others upstream were using it for laundry or a toilet (Crouch 1993, pp. 314–315; Krentz 2007, pp. 162–163).

Foragers looked for fuel as well as food and water. Greeks at home preferred charcoal and soldiers could have brought some on short expeditions, but foraging for wood was more common (Thuc. 3.111, 7.13.2; Xen. *An.* 4.3.11, *Hell.* 2.4.25). Comparative data suggest troops perhaps burned 1 kg (2.2 lb) of wood per person per day. Some commanders sought out wooded bivouacs so their men would not have to go far for wood (Xen. *An.* 1.4.10–11; Diod. Sic. 13.73.1). Battlefield debris like arrows, shields, and wagons could also be burned (Xen. *An.* 2.1.6–7; Olson 1991; Lee 2007, pp. 212–214).

The longer an army stayed in one place, the further from camp soldiers had to go in search of supplies. Properly supervised slaves could help in foraging, but soldiers might hesitate to send even trusted slaves out alone lest the slaves desert. Enemy cavalry could be a serious threat to scattered foragers (Thuc. 7.13.2; Diod. Sic. 13.88.1). Generals tried to control foragers, but even the battle-hardened mercenaries of Cyrus had to pass a special resolution to go foraging in organized parties rather than in small groups (Xen. *An.* 5.1.6–7). Ranging ever farther afield in search of supplies without taking precautions against surprise attack could end in disaster (Xen. *Hell.* 2.1.27; Diod. Sic. 13.105.2).

Back in camp, men had to build fires. Xenophon claims the Spartans on campaign carried a pure sacrificial flame that was never extinguished (Xen. *Lac.* 13.2–3). This flame may also have provided a source for camp fires. Indeed, the Spartan king Agesilaos once sent "fire in cooking pots" – probably charcoal or embers – to troops stationed on a cold, rainy ridge (Xen. *Hell.* 4.5.3–4). Armies without sacred flames could get fire from nearby settlements or sanctuaries, but troops stuck in open country had to kindle fire with friction drills or flint and iron pyrites. Some of Cyrus' mercenaries learned to make fire even in deep snow, possibly by building fire platforms of green wood (Xen. *An.* 4.5.5–6).

Fires were normally kindled in the evening and kept burning all night. Not building an evening fire could be considered a mark of despondency (Xen. *An.* 3.1.3). In good weather an army wishing to hide its position might extinguish its fires at night (Xen. *An.* 6.3.20–21). Some armies set watch fires at the edges of camp to provide light for sentries (Xen. *An.* 7.2.18, *Cyr.* 3.3.25).

Fire had major implications for camp life. Because only so many people can gather around a fire, campfires split an army into disparate small groups that literally turned their backs on each other.

Having to build and maintain fires highlighted inequalities amongst groups or individuals: soldiers with slave servants could relax, while those without had to do these chores themselves. The smoke from cooking fires could cause friction with neighboring groups (Dem. 54.4). In extreme situations, things could get even worse. At one point in the snows of Anatolia, the mercenaries of Cyrus reached a stopping place with plentiful wood, which the first troops to arrive immediately grabbed. Those who came later were without wood, and could only find spaces at a fire by paying in food (Xen. *An.* 4.5.5).

In at least one case, a cooking fire changed the course of an entire campaign. In summer 425 BCE, troops from the Athenian naval force blockading the Spartans on Sphacteria island landed on the island to cook a meal. Their fire accidentally spread into a blaze that denuded Sphacteria of vegetation, exposing how few defenders there were and encouraging the Athenians to make a successful assault (Thuc. 4.30).

Once they found food, water, and fuel, soldiers could move on to cooking and eating. Classical Greek armies normally seem to have eaten two meals a day: a mid-morning breakfast and a late afternoon dinner. The usual staple of both meals was grain. Unmilled grain could be parched or roasted, while flour could be boiled as porridge or baked into bread. Porridge required no more than a pot, water, and fire. Bread, baked over a fire or in a makeshift oven, took more time. Given enough time, a mess or tent group might bake several days' of bread in advance (Lee 2007, pp. 208–231).

How Classical soldiers milled grain in the field remains a puzzle. The stone querns used in Greek households weighed up to 20 kg (44 lb), too heavy for carrying on the march. Xenophon mentions light "hand-mills" for grinding grain (*Cyr.* 6.2.31), but although light rotary hand-mills were used in the western Mediterranean as early as the fifth century BCE, so far no eastern Mediterranean examples are known until the later Hellenistic period (Frankel 2003).

Commander-centered logistical studies often focus on the quantities of rations that soldiers consumed, but taking the ordinary soldier's perspective foregrounds other aspects of mealtime. Cooking and eating together helped reinforce feelings of small-group solidarity, both through the experience of shared labor and the opportunity it provided men to relax and talk. Telling stories of recent battles or challenges overcome helped soldiers cope with the stress of life on campaign (Xen. *An.* 4.3.2). Modern research even suggests troops tend to eat more and digest better when they eat as a group. Some men were content to let their personal attendants handle the cooking, but for others the communal experience of mealtimes had heroic echoes going back to the *Iliad* (Hom. *Il.* 9.205–220).

Drinking could take place along with a meal or as a separate activity. Scholars have long focused on the ritualized aristocratic symposium as the model for Greek drinking but recent research suggests other, less formalized forms of drinking were more common (Kelly-Blazeby 2006). Wine, typically mixed with water, was the preferred beverage. When wine was unobtainable troops found other ways to get drunk. The Cyrean mercenaries, for example, sampled beer and intoxicating honey during their retreat (Xen. *An.* 4.5.26, 4.8.20–21).

Eating and drinking leads inevitably to sanitation. Modern flush toiletry makes it easy to forget the major challenge that sanitation posed in the ancient world. Each day the average person produces 0.2 kg (about 0.5 pounds) of feces and 0.6–1.1 l (0.16–0.3 gal) of urine, while baggage animals might produce 10 kg (22 pounds) of manure apiece (Lee 2007, p. 236). An army had to cope with tons of waste daily.

While some Classical houses had indoor plumbing and cities did have waste disposal services, defecating and urinating in the street or on others' property remained commonplace in Classical Greece. Likewise, Greek armies in the field apparently did not usually dig latrines. Some citizen hoplites relied on chamber pots emptied by their personal servants (Dem. 54.4). Otherwise, men went wherever they could find a spot. Ideally, that meant outside camp, but cold weather or enemy activity might keep them somewhere in camp. Privacy may not have been a major concern anyway, in contrast to the Persians, who allegedly made a point of not passing waste in front of others (Xen. *Cyr.* 8.8.11).

Even the otherwise well-organized Spartans did little to organize sanitation, aside from requiring soldiers not to stray any further away from camp than necessary (Xen. *Lac.* 12.4). Xenophon notes the Spartans changed camps frequently to harm the enemy and help their friends, which may be a polite way of saying armies moved on when they had fouled their surroundings (Onas. 9.1). Local farmers perhaps appreciated the bounty of manure an army left behind, although the gift of fertilizer had to be balanced against the damage done by foragers and grazing animals.

Understanding the bodily needs of soldiers and the casual nature of camps helps explain the tactics used to attack camps. Encamped armies were vulnerable in the morning, as troops moved away from quarters to defecate (Xen. *Cyr.* 1.6.36). At Phyle in 403 BCE, the Athenian democrats launched a morning surprise attack when the enemy had gone off "wherever he had to go" (Xen. *Hell.* 2.4.6). The Thebans did likewise in 369, catching the Spartans by surprise at dawn (Xen. *Hell.* 7.1.16; *GSW* 2. 156–176).

Each day in camp brought with it a whole host of other chores. Troops had to make sure their baggage animals were fed and watered, and cavalry horses had to be groomed in the morning and evening (Xen. *Hell.* 2.4.6; see also Bugh, Chapter 6). Mule drivers had to pack and unpack their loads each day (Xen. *Hell.* 5.4.42; Pl. *Lysis* 208b). And on top of all that, soldiers had to bathe, clean equipment, sharpen weapons, mend clothes, and so on (Xen. *Hell.* 7.2.22). If time permitted, they might exercise, as Spartan soldiers did twice a day (*Lak. Pol.* 12.6).

As we end this section, it is worth noting that sailors and marines in Classical navies had similar daily routines. Modern warships can stay at sea for months on end, but Classical navies relied on triremes or war galleys with no room on board for cooking or sleeping. Triremes had to find a beach or port at the end of each sailing day so their crews could rest. Only in exceptional circumstances did trireme crews eat and sleep aboard ship (Thuc. 3.49).

Once ashore, the rowers, sailors, and marines of a trireme faced the same challenges of finding water, food, and firewood. Although the Athenians sometimes used slave rowers and others, such as the Chians, used them regularly, triremes had no space for personal attendants. Even so, social divisions could develop between the rowers and deck crew, who came from the lower strata of society, and the usually more prosperous marines.

While navies made it possible to carry troops, supplies, and support personnel such as bakers over long distances, the limited sea-keeping capability of triremes made Classical fleets extremely vulnerable when caught on shore. Perhaps the most famous example is the disaster at Aegospotami, which sealed Athens' defeat in the Peloponnesian War (Xen. *Hell.* 2.1.22–28).

Garrison Life

Being stationed in a garrison was less arduous than active campaigning, but had its own set of challenges. Troops in rural outposts or forts could face boredom, excessive drinking, and petty squabbles (Dem. 54.4). Centralized supply may have been more common for garrisons, although archaeological evidence from a fort on the island of Euboea suggests that men there continued to cook and eat in small groups (Sapouna Sakellaraki et al. 2002, pp. 97–98).

In urban settings, citizen soldiers went back to their homes, while mercenaries quartered in barracks or local houses. Armies also took up temporary winter quarters in or near settlements (Xen. *An.* 7.2.1–6; Diod. Sic. 13.91.1, 14.17.11–12). Urban garrisons could have a love-hate relationship with the local population. On the one hand, tavern keepers, prostitutes, and other merchants ben-efited economically from the presence of troops with money to spend. On the other hand, local women and youths might face assault or rape, and locals were sometimes forced to quarter soldiers in their homes. As Aeneas Tacticus' manual on city defense reveals, urban populations often eyed mercenary garrisons – even those they had hired themselves – with suspicion (Whitehead 2002).

Daily Life in Achaemenid Armies

No picture of Classical military life would be complete without considering the armies of Achaemenid Persia. Achaemenid armed forces were diverse and multicultural, drawn from all over the vast empire. Their ranks included men from Central Asia, Egypt, Babylonia, Greece, and elsewhere. The Persians themselves were a minority of perhaps only a million or so in an empire of 20 million or more people (Briant 1999, 2002).

Achaemenid armies had stronger institutional frameworks than those of the Classical Greeks. Persian units had squads of 10, companies of 100, regiments of a 1000, and brigades of 10,000 (Hdt. 3.25, 7.81). Many mercenary units in Persian service also used companies of 100. Officers had more authority than in Greek armies and soldiers who disobeyed orders or shirked duty could face severe punishment. Garrison troops were issued rations, while armies on campaign had access to a network of supply depots. Soldiers could also buy food from the traveling markets that regularly accompanied Achaemenid armies (Hdt. 7.23; Xen. *An*. 1.3.14; Ps.-Arist. *Oec*. 2.1350b). Imperial scribes tracked troop movements and supply distributions.

Professional soldiers, including thousands of Greek mercenaries, were posted in cities and strong-points across the empire (Tuplin 1987). Other professional forces, including Persian cavalry, were based in rural settlements. In many places the Persians relied on a land grant system under which groups of farmer-soldiers received the use of land in return for serving as archers, horsemen, or charioteers (Kuhrt 2007, pp. 669–672). In theory these troops were subject to yearly inspections. This system facilitated local defense and gave the empire a ready source of manpower, but call-ups could cause difficulties. Cuneiform documents from Babylonia reveal that men had to bring their own arms, armor, food, and pack animals. Some rich men hired substitutes to do their military service, but poor farmers had to take out loans to pay for equipment (Kuhrt 2007, pp. 715–716, 722–723).

The empire's military sophistication greatly influenced the campaign experiences of its soldiers. If Xenophon's description of Cyrus the Great's ideal army has any basis in reality, Persian camps may have been neater, cleaner, and better-smelling than any Greek bivouac, with tents pitched in orderly rows and flags indicating officers' quarters; at the least it seems the Persians organized their camps better than the Greeks (Xen. *Cyr*. 2.1.25–28, 8.5.1–16). Some Persian units may even have had company cooks (Xen. *Cyr*. 2.2.2–5). Mercenaries may have adopted some Persian prac-tices, but the Persians do not seem to have imposed uniform military customs on all their forces.

Noble Persians went through a strenuous physical and mental upbringing that has been compared to that of Sparta (Strabo 15.13.18). On campaign, though, some Persian nobles lived luxuriously, bringing along womenfolk and banqueting gear (Hdt. 9.76–80; Xen. *An*. 4.4.21). Ordinary troopers on the other hand do not seem to have had personal servants, despite the exaggerated claims of Herodotus (8.186–187). Menial laborers sometimes followed imperial armies in hopes of finding work (Plut. *Artax*. 11.5). Most imperial soldiers carried their own weapons and equipment, or shared the use of a pack animal brought from home (Plut. *Artax*. 24.6; Kuhrt 2007, pp. 715–716). Thanks to their efficient supply service, imperial soldiers probably did not have to forage for food as much as their Greek counterparts, although they still had to gather firewood (Xen. *An*. 2.4.11).

Defined unit structures, a stronger sense of hierarchy and discipline, and less accessible leaders made the Persian military experience in some ways more akin to a modern soldier's. Interestingly, then, modern models of small-group cohesion may be more helpful in understanding Persian rather than Greek military behavior. In fact, Herodotus in his narrative of the battle of Plataea mentions Persian soldiers dashing out individually or in groups of ten before charging the Greek lines (Hdt. 9.62.3). And, just as modern armies that are suddenly cut off from supplies sometimes shrink into confusion, Achaemenid troops may have been less able to cope when their supply system broke down, because they were less accustomed to fending for themselves (Hdt. 8.115; Plut. *Artax.* 24.2; Diod. Sic. 15.3.2–3).

We saw earlier that same-sex relations played an important role in the daily lives of Classical Greek soldiers. The same was true for Greek mercenaries in Persian service. Some elite Persians may also have practiced military same-sex relations. Herodotus alleges that the Persians adopted pederasty from the Greeks and Xenophon describes a local Achaemenid noble involved in pederastic courtship with Greeks (Hdt. 1.135; Xen. *Hell.* 4.1.39–40). Probably, though, same-sex attachments did not play a major role in the daily lives of most ordinary soldiers in Achaemenid armies.

Garrison life provided opportunities for intercultural contact. Documents from Achaemenid-period Egypt, for example, show Bactrians, Carians, Greeks, Jews, and others serving together in imperial garrisons. These soldiers became familiar with each other's languages, religion, and customs, and sometimes married across ethnic lines. Other soldiers took local wives and adopted Egyptian culture (Kaplan 2003). Even so, these connections did not erase Egyptian resentment against Achaemenid occupation, and Egypt repeatedly rebelled against Persian power during the Classical period (Ruzicka 2012).

From Classical to Hellenistic

The Achaemenid Empire came to an end with the campaigns of Alexander, and the rise of his successors would herald a new era in the history of warfare. Yet daily life in Greek armies had already begun changing in the early fourth century as commanders from Sicily to the Aegean took steps to centralize logistics and formalize small unit organization. In the mid-fourth century, Philip II of Macedon remade his army: he limited the number of personal attendants, trained soldiers to carry more gear, and gave them defined unit identities (Diod. Sic. 16.3; Polyaenus *Strat.* 4.2.10; Front. *Str.* 4.1.6; Anaximenes *FGrH* 72 F4). From Philip's reforms ultimately came the professional armies of the Hellenistic kings.

While Greek city-state militias survived into the Hellenistic period, the daily experience of many Hellenistic soldiers arguably became more like that of Achaemenid troops and less like that of Classical Greek citizen soldiers. The Hellenistic kings employed military settlers and urban mercenary garrisons, and borrowed or adapted other aspects of Achaemenid administration. Hellenistic armies had formal military subunits and, as inscriptions reveal, soldiers also joined formal religious, civic, and social associations (Chaniotis 2005). As in the Achaemenid military, the multi-ethnic composition of Hellenistic armies fostered intercultural contacts. Greek soldiers posted in far-flung garrisons built up ties with the surrounding community and some married native women. And, as in the Persian Empire, foreign garrisons could still cause resentment or unrest amongst the locals (Chaniotis 2002; Ma 2002). At the same time, Hellenistic soldiers still faced the daily garrison tedium and campaign stresses that their Classical predecessors had.

Studying daily life in Classical armies can be frustrating. The lack of evidence means that sometimes the best we can do is offer a range of possibilities or make informed conjectures about how soldiers might have done things. Yet, even if we cannot always give definite answers, exploring the possibilities is far better than dismissing or neglecting the subject. By asking new questions about the ancient evidence, we become better able to understand the realities of ancient life and the daily struggles for survival that underlay the dramas of battle and command. At the same time, the study of daily life should not be seen as a replacement for, or alternative to, other ways of studying Classical armies. Rather, our goal should always be to draw together the insights of many different approaches, so that we can shed the fullest possible light on the history of ancient warfare.

References

Aldrete, G., Bartell, S., and Aldrete, A. (2013). *Ancient Linen Body Armor: Unraveling the Linothorax Mystery*. Baltimore: Johns Hopkins University Press.

Briant, P. (1999). "The Achaemenid Empire." In: *War and Society in the Ancient and Medieval Worlds* (eds. K. Raaflaub and N. Rosenstein), 105–128. Cambridge, MA: Harvard University Press.

Briant, P. (2002). *From Cyrus to Alexander: A History of the Persian Empire*. Winona Lake, IN: Eisenbrauns.

Bridges, E., Hall, E., and Rhodes, P.J. (2007). *Cultural Responses to the Persian Wars: Antiquity to the Third Millennium*. Oxford: Oxford University Press.

Brigham, R. (2006). *ARVN: Life and Death in the South Vietnamese Army*. Lawrence, KS: University Press of Kansas.

Chaniotis, A. (2002). "Foreign soldiers - native girls? Constructing and crossing boundaries in Hellenistic cities with foreign garrisons." In: *Army and Power in the Ancient World* (eds. A. Chaniotis and P. Ducrey), 99–113. Stuttgart: Franz Steiner Verlag.

Chaniotis, A. (2005). *War in the Hellenistic World: A Social and Cultural History*. Malden, MA: Blackwell Publishing.

Coulton, J.J. (1996). "Euboean Phylla and Greek barracks." In: *Minotaur and Centaur: Studies in the Archaeology of Crete and Euboea Presented to Mervyn Popham* (eds. D. Evely, I. Lemos and S. Sherratt), 161–165. Oxford: Tempus Reparatum.

Crouch, D.P. (1993). *Water Management in Ancient Greek Cities*. Oxford: Oxford University Press.

Davidson, J. (2007). *The Greeks and Greek Love: A Radical Reappraisal of Homosexuality in Ancient Greece*. London: Weidenfeld & Nicolson.

Engels, D. (1978). *Alexander the Great and the Logistics of the Macedonian Army*. Berkeley: University of California Press.

Frankel, R. (2003). "The Olynthus mill, its origin, and diffusion: typology and distribution." *American Journal of Archaeology* 107 (1): 1–21.

Glatthaar, J. (2008). *General Lee's Army: From Victory to Collapse*. New York: Free Press.

Griffiths, W.B. (2000). "Re-enactment as research: towards a set of guidelines for re-enactors and academics." *Journal of Roman Military Equipment Studies* 11: 135–139.

Hacker, B. (1981). "Women and military institutions in early modern Europe: a reconnaissance." *Signs: Journal of Women in Culture and Society* 6 (4): 643–671.

Hamner, C. (2011). *Enduring Battle: American Soldiers in Three Wars, 1776–1945*. Lawrence KS: University Press of Kansas.

Hanson, V. (2009). *Western Way of War: Infantry Battle in Classical Greece*, 2e. Berkeley: University of California Press.

Hunt, P. (2007). "Military forces." In: *CHGRW*, vol. 1, 108–146.

Kaplan, P. (2003). "Cross-cultural contacts among mercenary communities in Saite and Persian Egypt." *Mediterranean Historical Review* 18 (1): 1–31.

Keegan, J. (1976). *The Face of Battle*. New York: The Viking Press.

Kelly-Blazeby, C. (2006). "Kapeleion: casual and commercial wine consumption in Classical Greece." PhD dissertation. University of Leicester.

Krentz, P. (2007). "Archaic and Classical Greece: war." *CHGRW* 1: 147–185.

Kuhrt, A. (2007). *The Persian Empire: A Corpus of Sources from the Achaemenid Period*. London: Routledge.

Lazenby, J.F. (1994). "Logistics in Classical Greek warfare." *War in History* 1 (1): 3–18.

Lee, J.W.I. (2007). *A Greek Army on the March: Soldiers and Survival in Xenophon's Anabasis*. Cambridge: Cambridge University Press.

Leitao, D. (2002). "The legend of the Sacred Band." In: *The Sleep of Reason: Erotic Experience and Sexual Ethics in Ancient Greece and Rome* (eds. M.C. Nussbaum and J. Shivola), 143–169. Chicago: University of Chicago Press.

Lendon, J.E. (2005). *Soldiers and Ghosts: A History of Battle in Classical Antiquity*. New Haven, CT: Yale University Press.

Ma, J. (2002). "'Oversexed, overpaid, over here': a response to Angelos Chaniotis." In: *Army and Power in the Ancient World* (eds. A. Chaniotis and P. Ducrey), 115–122. Stuttgart: Franz Steiner Verlag.

Mayer, H. (1996). *Belonging to the Army: Camp Followers and Community During the American Revolution*. Columbia SC: University of South Carolina Press.

Merridale, C. (2006). *Ivan's War: Life and Death in the Red Army, 1939–1945*. New York: Metropolitan Books.

O'Connor, S. (2011). "Armies, navies and economies in the Greek World in the fifth and fourth centuries BCE." PhD dissertation. Columbia University.

Ogden, D. (1996). "Homosexuality and warfare in ancient Greece." In: *Battle in Antiquity* (ed. A. Lloyd), 107–168. Swansea: The Classical Press of Wales.

Olson, S.D. (1991). "Firewood and charcoal in Classical Athens." *Hesperia* 60 (3): 411–420.

Russell, F. (1999). *Information Gathering in Classical Greece*. Ann Arbor: University of Michigan Press.

Ruzicka, S. (2012). *Trouble in the West: Egypt and the Persian Empire, 525–332 BC*. Oxford: Oxford University Press.

Sapouna Sakellaraki, E., Coulton, J.J., and Metzger, I.R. (2002). *The Fort at Phylla, Vrachos: Excavations and Researches at a Late Archaic Fort in Central Euboea*. London: British School at Athens.

Trundle, M. (2004). *Greek Mercenaries: From the Late Archaic Period to Alexander*. London: Routledge.

Tuplin, C. (1987). "Xenophon and the garrisons of the Achaemenid Empire." *Archäologische Mitteilungen aus Iran* 20: 167–245.

Vassallo, S. (2010). "Le battaglie di Himera alla luce degli scavi nella necropoli occidentale e alle fortificazioni. I luoghi, i protagonisti." *Sicilia Antiqua* 7: 17–38.

van Wees, H. (2004). *Greek Warfare: Myths and Realities*. London: Duckworth.

Wheeler, E. (2007). "Archaic and Classical Greece: battle." In: *CHGRW*, vol. 1, 186–247.

Wheeler, E. (2011). "Greece: mad hatters and march hares." In: *Recent Directions in the Military History of the Ancient World* (eds. L.L. Brice and J.T. Roberts), 53–102. Claremont, CA: Regina Books.

Whitehead, D. (2002). *Aineias the Tactician: How to Survive Under Siege*, 2e. London: Bristol Classical Press.

Young, T.C. (1980). "480/479 B.C.– a Persian perspective." *Iranica Antiqua* 15: 213–239.

Further Reading

Campbell, B. and Tritle, L. (eds.) (2013). *The Oxford Handbook of Warfare in the Classical World*. Oxford: Oxford University Press.

Käihkö, I. and Haldén, P. (2019). "Full-spectrum social science for a broader view on cohesion." *Armed Forces & Society* https://doi.org/10.1177/0095327X19841669.

Pretzler, M. and Barley, N. (eds.) (2017). *Brill's Companion to Aineias Tacticus*. Leiden: Brill.

Sears, M. (2019). *Understanding Greek Warfare*. New York: Routledge.

5

Soldiers' Home

Life After Battle

Lawrence A. Tritle

> In memoriam, *Commander Eugene Zeiner, (1930–2011), United States Navy Fleet Air, Korea (1952–1953), Vietnam (1965, 1967)*

Introduction

News of a great defeat and the destruction of a mighty army descends upon the city like a shroud. Hearing someone at the door, the broken-hearted mother goes, only to see the son feared dead standing very much alive, who then watches his mother collapse and die (Livy 22.7.13). Other soldiers return home but not well. In his "Spartan Sayings," Plutarch tells of brave but crippled Spartans, limping home barely able to walk (Plut. *Mor.* 241E–F). Other men, like the Athenian Epizelus, return home blind with an amazing story of battlefield survival that would be retold for generations (Hdt. 6.117.2–3). Some, seemingly whole, are so shaken by battlefield experiences that resuming a "normal" life becomes nearly impossible (Gorg. *Hel.* 16–17).

As philosopher George Santayana remarked of World War I survivors at Oxford in the 1920s, "only the dead have seen the end to war" (attributed to Plato, Palaima 2012, pp. 734–735, traces it to Santayana). Life after battle is seldom easy and usually hard. While art and literature memorialize the "heroic dead," by far the greater number of soldiers resume a quiet life of labor: Athenian citizen soldiers and pensioned-off veterans across the provinces of imperial Rome alike, living as they can, remembering the experience, the fallen, and, in some extraordinary cases, writing about the beast called War.

Western literature begins with the story of the returning warrior and the very name Odysseus and his return home to the woman he left behind has become a byword for a long and arduous journey. Two millennia later Odysseus' story became a metaphor for another generation of soldiers, those who survived "the Nam" and whose "homecoming" was no less difficult than that of Odysseus, as revealed in Jonathan Shay's *Odysseus in America* (2002). Since Homer, others have embraced the tale of the returning or wandering warrior: Euripides' Heracles and Vergil's Aeneas find their modern day counterparts in Honoré de Balzac's *Colonel Chabert* (1832), Erich Remarque's *The Road Back* (1931), and Larry Heinemann's *Paco's Story* (1986) – these are but a few of the many such stories that could be cited.[1]

While accounts of the returning warrior abound in literature and poetry, historians have been less interested in the plight of those who return home from war. The suffering that war causes its

New Approaches to Greek and Roman Warfare, First Edition. Edited by Lee L. Brice.
© 2020 John Wiley & Sons, Inc. Published 2020 by John Wiley & Sons, Inc.

combatants too often remains the domain of psychologists as historians regard wartime traumas and the study of violence as too irrational a subject for inquiry. Stéphane Audoin-Rouzeau and Annette Becker, two of the founders of the Historial de la Grande Guerre, a First World War study center, have commented on this in regard to French historians. I agree with this assessment and support their view that too many in the modern day academy are "unconcerned with the violence of the battlefield, the men in the arena, the suffering they endure, the perceptions of the men who try to survive and, in a nutshell, the immense stakes that are crystallised in the combat zone" (Audoin-Rouzeau and Becker 2002, pp. 15–16).

Such attitudes may apply more to ancient historians than modern, as the evidence is scattered and fragmentary; there are also depressing and ugly dimensions to war and the conduct of war that discourage scholarly study of the returning soldier and lives complicated by physical and psychic trauma (see further, e.g. Cohen 2001). This chapter investigates the realities of soldiers' homecomings not only in the ancient world but more broadly, looking at the experiences of modern conflicts from the American Civil War to Afghanistan for comparative guidance in understanding the past.

The Warrior Returns

Soldiers often return home to a question that some at least would prefer not to answer: "What was it like," sometimes accompanied by the still harder: "Did you kill anyone"? Plato brings this scene to life in his dialogue *Charmides* (153b–c), where he tells of Socrates' return from northern battlefields (Plato probably refers to the Potidaia campaign early in the Peloponnesian War; see Thuc. 2.79). Socrates' old friend Chaerephon asks, "Socrates, how did you survive the battle?" Socrates says only, "In the condition you see me." Not to be put off, Chaerephon continues, saying that reports told of a sharp fight in which a number of their friends were lost, to which Socrates replies only, "The report's about right." When Chaerephon then asks, "You were present then?," Socrates answers as tersely, "I was." After this laconic exchange, Plato adds that Socrates and Chaerephon joined others and Socrates discussed the affair further.

How do we understand Socrates' pointed responses to Chaerephon's questions? Do we simply accept the conversation at face value? I would suggest that a way to deconstruct Socrates' responses may be found in a similar response to a similar question put to Praxiteles Swan, former captain in the army of the Confederacy. When asked about Gettysburg, Swan replied: "We all went up to Gettysburg, the summer of '63: and some of us came back from there: and that's all except the details. I wouldn't bother you with the details" (Thomason 1941, p. 132). John Thomason was a decorated Marine of the First World War and the story told here is a slightly fictionalized account of his grandfather, little different in tone from Michael Herr's cryptic Vietnam era story of a lost patrol (1977, p. 6).

Socrates' clipped replies reflect the lasting impressions of wartime violence. Of these Plato had no personal knowledge and he has created the scene from sketches belonging to the Socratic legend. Yet he makes clear that Socrates was brave in battle – saving the life of Alcibiades (Pl. *Symp.* 220d–221b) and demonstrating unquestioned courage on the battlefield. But courage, as Socrates seemingly recognized (suggested in Plato's *Laches*), is a sometime thing and even the brave can be cowardly. This aspect the poet Archilochus had long before made clear, scandalizing some with his nonchalant admission of throwing away a shield so that he might live, while grimly noting too the killing that was done (Davenport 1964, frs. 79, p. 184).

Even the famed Spartans sometimes succumbed to their fears and ran for dear life, as most famously in the case of Aristodemus at Thermopylae who later found a hero's death at Plataea (Hdt. 7.231 with How and Wells 1912, 2.231). Labeled *tresas* (pl. *tresantes*) "coward" or "runaway," the Spartans gradually increased the penalties for such conduct, forcing the cowardly to shave half their distinctive beards and making marriage all but impossible (related forms of *tresas* in Tyr. 11.14; Plut. *Ages.* 30.2; Ehrenberg 1937, pp. 2293–2297 explores more fully; cf. Tritle 2010, pp. 163–164, n. 38). Yet there were occasions when these penalties were ignored: the survivors of Sphacteria (425) were later rehabilitated out of fear they might engage in revolutionary activities (Thuc. 5.34.2), while those of Leuctra (371) suffered no punishment, other than the presumed contempt of the families of the dead (Plut. *Ages.* 30).[2]

Battle is stressful and often a mystery even to those who experience it. Socrates saw this feature as did Archilochus and the Spartans. While they may not have understood how and why men fight, one thing they did recognize was courage – who shows it, who does not, what it might be. Plato's *Laches* attempted to unravel its mysteries and so have many since then, e.g. Stephen Crane's *The Red Badge of Courage* (1895) and Lord Moran's *The Anatomy of Courage* (1945).

The Wounds of War

The photograph of a Theban soldier – now called Gamma 16 – killed at Chaironeia in 338/7 BCE reminds us graphically that the dead truly see the end of war (fig. 2 in Liston, chapter 7; Ma 2008). The wounds of war come in many forms and leave a lifetime of memory and suffering. Just as Homer relates the first homecoming tale in western literature, he also reveals for the first time the fear closest to any soldier's mind, that of being wounded, of being abandoned. Homer tells of Ares' complaint to Zeus that in risking battle he narrowly avoided lying in pain among the dead or "living without strength because of the strokes of the bronze spear" (*Il.* 5. 886–887). The hero Eurpylos retires from battle, limping with a wound to his thigh (*Il.* 11. 809–811), an injury similar to what later killed Miltiades, the hero of Marathon (Hdt. 6.134-6).

There can be no question that Socrates witnessed terrible sights at Potidaia and even worse at Delium, a battle that claimed the lives of nearly 1000 Athenians in a day. An early example of this suffering appears in Herodotus' account of the battle of Marathon and the story of the Athenian soldier Epizelus, the son of Couphagoras. Herodotus reports how in the midst of the fighting, Epizelus caught sight of a giant of a warrior – so big that his beard covered his shield – who passed him by and struck down the man next to him – a neighbor or kinsman in all likelihood – and with that he became instantly blind (Hdt. 6.117.2-3; cf. Tritle 2000, pp. 63–65; similar conclusions reached independently by Louis Crocq 1999, p. 33). Such psychic wounds are known from other times and places: in his account of the D-Day invasion, Stephen Ambrose (1992, p. 98) tells a similar story of airborne trooper Albert Blithe who became temporarily blind in the early morning hours of June 6, 1944 (depicted in the HBO–Tom Hanks–Steven Spielberg production *Band of Brothers*, 2000), but once rested recovered his sight.

Until recently scholars have not associated Epizelus' experience with combat trauma let alone attempted to account for his survival. The pre-World War I commentary on Herodotus published by W.W. How and J. Wells (1912, ii, p. 114) attempted to explain Epizelus' "vision" as a Pauline-like experience citing *Acts* (9:1–9); one cannot help but wonder what they might have said only a few years later when stories of hysterical blindness, mutism, and paralysis became commonplace in the war-torn countries of Europe. More recent explanations have ranged from the influence of hero cults (Bowden 1993, p. 55) to the stuff of legends (Lazenby 1993, pp. 12, 80). Moreover, little has been said of Epizelus' survival, blind and in the midst of a raging fight, and how he might have gotten safely off the battlefield. In fact his survival argues for a more open battle order within the phalanx, as only in such a situation could he have survived, presumably led away by others who saw him become disabled (cf. Tritle 2009).

What happened to Epizelus at Marathon is not an isolated instance of ancient battle trauma. Similar cases appear in the surviving body of testimonies known as the Epidaurian miracle inscriptions. One text records how a former soldier, Anticrates of Cnidus, slept in the sacred precinct so that the god Asclepius might heal him:

> This man had been struck with a spear through both his eyes in some battle, and he became blind and carried around the spearhead with him, inside his face. Sleeping here, he saw a vision. It seemed to him the god pulled the dart and fitted the so-called girls (i.e., the pupils of the eyes) back into his eyelids. When day came he left well. (LiDonnici 1995, p. 109)

While the point may be superfluous, it is unlikely that anyone could live with a spearhead (some 12–18 inches in length) "inside his face" and what has clearly been preserved here is a case of psychic trauma. Other texts relate stories of men appealing to the god for help with spearheads embedded in their jaws, hysterical paralysis, and blindness (LiDonnici 1995, pp. 95, 109, 113, 115). Plutarch's collection of "Spartan Sayings" refers several times to men who survived battle but returned home with debilitating foot and leg injuries (Plut. *Mor.* 241E–F). One of these men, Androcleidas, attempted to enlist for a campaign in spite of his crippled leg which other Spartans believed debarred him from service: he defended his petition on the grounds that what was needed were men who stood their ground, not those who would run away (Plut. *Mor.* 217C).

The wounds described in these literary texts are in fact accurate. The leg wounds that Plutarch relates could easily be inflicted by weapons such as the *kopis* or "cleaver," a sword with a curved blade that could reach over a man's back or side, severing leg tendons and muscles (depicted on a cup of the Triptolemus Painter, c. 470, Bridges et al. 2007, p. 11). Such a wound would leave a man crippled just as Plutarch tells of Androcleidas and reported as well by Livy (22.51.7), describing wounds inflicted on Roman soldiers at Cannae. Broken bones could result just as easily from weapons such as sling-stones or a simple mishap such as a fall from a horse.

Wounds often kill – sometimes in days or weeks and even years later – and were surely dreaded no less then as today. The Hippocratic writer of *On Fractures* remarks on the problems of treating broken bones, whether the result of weapons or injury, and how even if treated successfully would result in atrophied limbs or infections that could kill just as easily (Edwards 2015, pp. 61–63). Such medical realities explain the crooked legs and feet that Plutarch reports in his "Spartan Sayings."

Surviving sources rarely tell much about how the battle-injured survivor coped with such life-changing injuries. In a relatively affluent community like classical Athens, modest payments (ranging from one to two obols, a sum less than an unskilled worker's daily wage) were distributed in the later fifth and fourth centuries (*Ath. Pol.* 49.4; cf. Rhodes 1981, pp. 570–571). Frequently, however, crippled soldiers had to fight for these modest payments as seen in a speech delivered before an Athenian court (Lys. 24), a scene little different in modern America and the complaints brought by veterans against the Veterans Administration. During the campaigns of Alexander the Great, many sick and injured soldiers were left behind in garrisons (e.g. Arr. *Anab.* 4.16.6, 5.8.3; see further commentary in Bosworth 1980–1995 on these passages) while lingering injuries and illnesses became an issue that threatened army morale and even challenged Alexander's leadership in the months before his death (Arr. *Anab.* 7.12.1). Diodorus (18.7.2) reports the mass uprising of Greek mercenaries after Alexander's death – a number of whom might have been invalids, now recovered. In the Hellenistic era, disabled mercenaries often became dependent on their families (who often accompanied them) for support, while in other situations, local citizens were charged with caring for invalided soldiers (cf. Chaniotis 2005, pp. 96–97). In the Roman empire, beginning with Augustus and until discontinued (evidently) in the early third century CE, disabled legionaries received the same benefits (e.g. legal marriage, citizenship, land or donation of money, and tax exemption) as those who completed a full enlistment (see further Van Lommel 2013, pp. 65–74)

Herodotus states that he had learned of Epizelus' story (*logos*) as he was researching and writing his Persian War account in the decades of the 430s and 420s and against the backdrop of the great Peloponnesian War between Athens and Sparta. This notice points to an oral tradition that spanned decades, the existence of which is confirmed too by Aristophanes' references to the "Marathon-fighters" of Periclean Athens (Ar. *Ach.* 181, *Nub.* 986). Old soldiers gathering to reminisce is a timeless phenomenon: informal gatherings of veterans in my ancestral village in Germany today find parallels in nineteenth century America with the organization of the Grand Army of the Republic, followed in the twentieth by the American Legion and Veterans of Foreign Wars. One can almost imagine Epizelus visiting the *agora*, making the rounds with a slave in hand, or accompanied by old comrades in arms, asking passersby if they had heard how at Marathon he had caught sight of a fearsome warrior and how that experience had ever after left him blind.

There are many ways to die in war, or suffer lifelong debilitating injury. While the dead have seen the end of war, the survivors remember both those who are no more and that their achievements were remarkable. Aristophanes' "Marathon-fighters" demonstrate a camaraderie that bears comparison not only with veterans' organizations generally, but with the spirit of that Second World War generation recognized today as "The Greatest."

Psychic Trauma in the Ancient World

In his 1937 article discussing Spartan "cowards" – men like Aristodemus the survivor of Thermopylae – World War I combat soldier and veteran Victor Ehrenberg called them "shakers" (*gezittert*), applying contemporary Weimar era terms of German veterans of the Great War (1937, p. 2292). While acknowledging the traumatic effects of war on veterans, the very idea of posttraumatic stress disorder or PTSD continues to be challenged in some circles (cf. Young 1995; Fassin and Rechtman 2009). For such critics the notion of PTSD in the ancient world is even more remote and questionable.

Full discussion of the realities of PTSD exceeds what can be reviewed here and would require a separate treatment (see Heidenreich and Roth, Chapter 10 in this volume). Additionally, arguments of mine made previously identifying psychic trauma in the ancient world have been criticized, though this is hardly proof of error (Couvenhes 2005, p. 431; Wheeler 2011, p. 73, n. 72, with "editor's dissent"). In brief response to critics and to provide context to what follows, some rationale for psychic trauma in the ancient world seems useful. In short, ongoing medical and scientific research shows that traumatic stressors – especially the biochemical reactions of cortisol (generically the glucocorticoids) – hyperstimulate the brain's hippocampus and amygdala obstructing bodily homeostasis, disrupting the memory process, and otherwise producing symptoms consistent with combat stress reactions. The realities, then, of the evolution of humankind and advancements made in the late twentieth and twenty-first centuries in neuroscience and evolutionary biology, should render the debate otiose, though probably not in the view of philologists and positivist historians (see further Wilson 2004, pp. x–xvii; Eagleman 2011, pp. 126, 153; Chapters 7 and 10 in this volume).

That objections to the reality of PTSD in the ancient world are idle seems clear in an oblique reference to the horrors of war found in an unlikely place, the *Encomium of Helen* of the philosopher and rhetorician Gorgias of Leontini. Composed midway through the Peloponnesian War

(Tritle 2010, pp. 158–160), Gorgias wrote this speech as an exhibition piece designed to absolve Helen of blame in abandoning Menelaus for Paris. In arguing for Helen's innocence, Gorgias observes that

> when warriors put on their armor and weapons, some for defense others for offense, the mere sight of these terrifies the souls of some, who flee panic-stricken even from anticipated dangers as if these were really present. ... And [later] some of these [men] lose presence of mind, and others become unable to work, suffering terrible diseases or incurable madness. (MacDowell 1982, pp. 16–17, adapted by the author)

Today instances of hysterical blindness and other psychic trauma are easy enough for us to diagnose. In the fifth-century Greek world, however, contemporaries of these men would not have known or understood the physiology that induced these reactions. External explanations such as divine intervention would have been the only way to explain unusual or otherwise strange human responses to violence and the whole range of human emotions. Herein lies the value of Gorgias' testimony. He actually senses a connection, though he could not have explained it, between the effects of going into battle, seeing horrific things, and how these affect the mind and change the man. Again his words are worth reviewing – "many have become unable to work, suffering terrible diseases or incurable madness" – in short, experiencing war's violence breaks some who give up on life, becoming unable to function in a meaningful way; others suffer breakdowns of the psyche that manifest themselves differently too. Essentially, Gorgias' description refers to the change of character, and if put alongside psychiatrist and author Jonathan Shay's list of symptoms of PTSD, would compare favorably in many respects (Shay 1994, p. xx).

Essentially, Greeks and Romans were physiologically like us, which means that their responses to stress would differ little from ours. This chapter began with the Roman mother who dropped dead on seeing her supposedly dead son alive. This is a typical human response to stress and a phenomenon that could easily find parallels in current newspapers or the nightly news.

Theater of War

There would seem to be little question that Gorgias' defense of Helen influenced his contemporaries. Within a few years, probably in 412, the Athenian dramatist Euripides presented his drama of *Helen*. Melodramatic and even funny at times – Helen complains that her beauty was the source of all her troubles – Euripides staged a blameless victim whose divine-made phantom Paris took to Troy while the real Helen sat out the war in Egypt. Greeks and Trojans then slaughter each other to recover, or protect, a phantom – in other words, good men die in vain: the greatest war of them was all fought for nothing (see further Allan 2008, p. 28, n. 132, p. 46, n. 204).

Not long before (c. 424–418), Euripides had staged his play of the homecoming of the greatest of Greek heroes, Heracles (Papadopoulou 2005, p. 141, n. 42; cf. Croally 1994). Again the playwright adapted the traditional storyline and made it clear that Heracles was not returning from his famous labors, but rather "from the war" (Eur. *HF* 1133–1134, cf. 198–202; cf. Bond 1981, pp. 354–355, 119–120). Thoughtful members of the audience would have picked up at once that Euripides was speaking to them of their own homecoming from far-off campaigns – that the issues being explored before them were real and were as much about their own lives and war-related traumas as any hero's. Euripides expresses this theme with dramatic clarity. Finding his family in mortal danger, threatened by Lycus, the local tyrant, Heracles intervenes quickly and brutally, killing

Lycus before he can act. But the violence pushes Heracles over the edge – he loses control and kills as quickly those dearest to him, his wife and children (Eur. *HF* 821–874; cf. Bond 1981, pp. 279–280; Tritle 2010).

We often think of Euripides as the "poet of war," but his older and more successful contemporary Sophocles had explored similar and related themes. In the *Ajax*, performed c. 440, Sophocles relates the readiness with which an angry and battle-hardened soldier could explode in a paroxysm of violence, as Ajax slaughters herds of animals imagining them to be his enemies Agamemnon and Odysseus. As the *Ajax* explores issues of shame and suicide, it also touches on the constant potential for violence among veterans, themes which movie-goers have seen recently in such Iraq War films as *In the Valley of Elah* (2008) and *Stop-Loss* (2008). In the same vein his play *Philoctetes*, performed some 30 years later amid the ongoing trauma of the Peloponnesian War (409), reveals soldiers' perennial fear of abandonment and living in pain with a crippling wound (Edwards 2015, pp. 55–69). Just as striking is the burden of guilt, the emotional baggage of survival, when friends, always better men, have died. As the Iraq War dragged on, this play was frequently staged before audiences ranging from West Point cadets to multiple generations of combat veterans, each time eliciting empathetic reactions (see articles in the *Los Angeles Times* [August 15, 2008] and *New York Times* [September 19, 2008]).

Euripides picks up on these Sophoclean themes, not only in *Heracles* but in an earlier drama *Andromache* (c. 430–424). Here in the fierce rage of battle Achilles' son Neoptolemus is not only slain by his enemies, but like Hector suffers worse, namely vicious mutilation (cf. Hom. *Il.* 22. 369–371; Eur. *Andr.* 1149–1155).

Murdered Children and Mutilated Warriors

Today there may remain a few critics such as Denys Page who imagine that acts of extreme violence like Medea's killing of her children are beyond not only our experience but that of contemporary Athenians as well. Such criticisms do not take the time to connect the violence staged in *Medea* or *Andromache* or *Heracles* to the ongoing trauma and terror of Athens and Greece through most of the fifth century.[3] In his 1954 study of Sophocles, Victor Ehrenberg reminds us that the poet is not only an artist but also a contemporary voice (Ehrenberg 1954, pp. 6–7). While both wartime violence and poetical truth could be demonstrated many times over, the Ft. Bragg murders of June and July 2002, in which four Army wives were killed by their husbands returning "from the war" (in this case Afghanistan), provides but one real-life tragic counterpart to Euripides' story of Heracles' homecoming (see further Biank 2006, especially 207, pp. 240–242, 254).

The war plays of Euripides then – *Hecuba* (c. 425/4), *Trojan Women* (c. 416/5), as well as *Andromache* and *Heracles* – offer themes that would have surely resonated with contemporary audiences and especially members of the veteran population. Not only do we see the violence of the returning soldier and the issue of suicide (*Heracles*), but also the extremes of violence carried out on women. In his *Andromache*, Euripides explores the plight of the widow who becomes the property of another, while in *Hecuba* the suffering mother who has lost her children to violence dominates the action, and in *Trojan Women* echoes of all these themes may be found. This explains the number of times Euripides explores the fundamental question: Why war? What drives men to fight and die? Not long before abandoning Athens for Macedonia, he presented the *Orestes* (408): here Orestes and Pylades seek vengeance on Helen, the symbol of war, whom they seek to kill. In other words, kill Helen, kill "War."

Stories such as these emerging from a society at war should not seem surprising. No one thinks more about war than veterans. Vietnam veteran and novelist Tim O'Brien writes that "the bad stuff never stops happening: it lives in its own dimension, replaying itself over and over" (O'Brien 1990, p. 32). Aeschylus, the founding father of Greek drama, was no less obsessed with the "bad stuff," though he remembered it a little differently. Sometime after staging the *Oresteia* (458), Aeschylus accepted an invitation to Sicily where not long after he died. An epitaph has survived which most authorities accept as authentic, in part as it omits any reference to his dramatic accomplishments. Instead, the epitaph recounts his Persian War service, an experience that claimed his brother at Marathon (Paus. 1.14.5; Aeschylus' *Vita* 11 preserves the epitaph; on authenticity, Sommerstein 1996, p. 24):

At Gela, rich in wheat, he died, and lies beneath this stone:
Aeschylus the Athenian, son of Euphorion.
His valour, tried and proved, the mead of Marathon can tell,
The long-haired Persian also, who knows it all too well.

Aeschylus remembers war but contextualizes it naturally in heroic terms couched in the cultural values of manliness inspired by Homer. But there is something else present. The battles fought by Aeschylus and that generation of "Marathon-fighters" were, like those of our own "Greatest Generation," victorious. On the other hand, Tim O'Brien's much harder memory of "bad stuff" is contextualized not just by the horrors of a vicious war, but by a lack of success, defeat. In short, winning does help a little in remembering the bad stuff, yet both Aeschylus and O'Brien live with the same "happening bad stuff" right to the end.

Memorials – Remembering the Fallen, Remembering War

As Euripides and Sophocles and their many modern counterparts have observed, the dead have a powerful grip on the psyches of the living. While it has been human custom for millennia to bury the dead and set up some sort of remembrance over them, the practice became ritualized and even formalized in both the Greek and Roman worlds. In the middle years of the fifth century, for example, the Athenians began a spring ritual that would be followed like a film script for well over a century: the public laying-out of biers containing the cremated remains of the previous year's dead where they could be mourned and then interred in a public cemetery called the Kerameikos, followed by an inspiring speech for the grieving families that would conclude the period of public mourning and memorializing (Tritle 2000, pp. 168–172). Broadly speaking, this annual ritual is little different from the public gathering and ceremony that occurred at Gettysburg after the great 1863 battle and the occasion of Abraham Lincoln's famous address.

Athens, however, was not the only city in the Greek world that conducted such rituals. After their victory over the Athenians at Delium (424) the people of Thebes built a memorial park called the Delia where they set up engraved *stelae* of their fallen; the Thespians, Theban neighbors, also set up a memorial precinct to honor their fallen, again recording the names (Low 2003, pp. 98–111 for discussion and images).

Memorial precincts in Thebes and Thespiae suggest that in the fifth-century Greek world such memorializing was not unique to Athens, though how widespread the practice was is unclear. Steps to remember the fallen were also taken by the Romans, though perhaps not in the same way or to the same degree. Writers of war in the Republic, for example, the comics Plautus and Terence, did recycle Hellenistic era stories of soldiers and their rough and tumble ways, but these are a far cry from the introspection of Euripides or Sophocles, though Vergil, particularly in the *Aeneid*, reveals a compassion and understanding of war's violence (e.g. 1.464–178, Aeneas remembering battle at Troy, and weeping; 12.938–952, Aeneas, about to spare Turnus, kills him on finding him wearing armor taken from his dead friend Pallas). Just as Roman literature differs from Greek drama in exploring war's effects, so, too, do Roman monuments take a different and more communal approach to commemorating the experience of war.

A striking example of a Roman memorial is to be found today in modern Romania. At Adamklissi a large memorial known as the *Tropaeum Traiani* was set up to remember the many who fell fighting in this region of the Roman world in the early second century CE. Some 3800 names were listed here, including not only the names of officers, but also citizen legionaries and foreign auxiliaries. Just how representative the *Tropaeum Traiani* is of Roman memorials is unclear, as the Adamklissi monument is the only surviving example of a commemorative monument of this sort. Allison Cooley suggests that "it was not usual to commemorate the human cost of war through memorials," as the Romans evidently preferred to remember defeat by incorporating it into ritual (cf. the Day of Allia which commemorated the Gallic occupation of Rome, 387/6 BCE), an effort, perhaps, to win back divine favor (Cooley 2012, p. 85).

There can be little question that the memorials and the rituals of commemoration created and followed by the Greeks and Romans alike produced an emotional response similar to what is known in the modern world, whether it be the various national memorials of twentieth-century World Wars or the "Wall," the Vietnam Veterans Memorial in Washington, DC. An example of the emotional response can be seen in Athenians' decision, following the failed expedition to Sicily in 413, to exclude Nicias from the memorial to the campaign dead because there was such grief over the loss (Thuc. 7.87-8.1). This commemoration may also be seen in the objects left behind at the Athenian Kerameikos by the grieving families of the dead, just as may be seen on any given day now at the "Wall" (Tritle 2000, pp. 171–172, 2012).

Restless Soldiers

The experience of battle produces many responses and emotions. Tim O'Brien perhaps said it best: "War is hell, but that's not the half of it, because ...war is nasty; war is fun; war is thrilling; war is drudgery. War makes you a man; war makes you dead" (O'Brien 1990, p. 80). Perhaps because of this it is no surprise that some soldiers, finding peace elusive are driven to return to the soldier's life. After the Civil War many veterans went west where they contributed to a culture of mayhem that remains part of the American psyche today. Others went farther, entering the service of Isma'il Pasha, Khedive of Egypt, the subject of a 1961 study, *The Blue and the Gray on the Nile*.

The Spartan soldier and commander Clearchus exemplifies the soldier who keeps soldiering despite advancing age. Xenophon, the Athenian soldier of fortune, author, and one-time companion, reports that the 50-year-old Clearchus could have lived a life of peace and ease, but chose war, lived for it, and became excited when battle began (Xen. *An.* 2.6.6, 7, 10). Among the "10,000" other Greeks who accompanied Clearchus east with the Persian prince Cyrus were surely others driven by the same emotions. These men had become hooked on the violence of war and, as noted above, researchers today understand this lust for battle far better than at any time previously. It is the result of neurologic changes in the brain, the result of hormones that enable every human to withstand that basic dilemma – fight or flight. Without these chemicals in our bodies we could not survive: on the other hand, in excessive amounts, and in war they are produced to excess, they have a severe and negative impact, often producing the actions of a Heracles or Clearchus, or so many among the US veteran population today (see further Bremner 2002, pp. 108–220; Heidenriech and Roth, Chapter 10).

A powerful chemical need for excitement, an adrenaline rush, drives some to return to battle; so, too, do poverty and need. Among Xenophon's Ten Thousand a large number, perhaps as high as 40%, came from Arcadia and Achaea, poor lands in the Peloponnese of Greece rich only in their manpower (Lee 2007, p. 65). With few economic prospects at home, many Arcadians and Achaeans turned to mercenary service as a means to survive. A recent study of modern America at war, Kriner and Shen's *The Casualty Gap* (2010), demonstrates how increasingly since 1945 the absence of economic and educational opportunities drives many young Americans into military service. Like their Arcadian counterparts in the late fifth century, they, too, fight in order to survive.

Conclusions

The Greek philosopher Heraclitus once remarked that "war is the father of all things," a sentiment later elaborated by Winston Churchill: "The story of the human race is War" (Winter and Prost 2005, p. 175). It is this universal experience of war that allows for dramas produced in democratic Athens to reach out and speak to audiences in another democratic society 2500 years later. No less important is the universal experience of the returning soldier, and how the realities he or she faces on returning to the "World" are little different over the millennia and across culture.

Notes

1 An abbreviated version of this chapter, "Soldiers Home," first appeared in 2009 as part of the National Endowment for the Humanities sponsored program "Ancient Greeks/Modern Lives" organized and directed by Peter Meineck of New York University.
2 All ancient events are BCE unless otherwise indicated.
3 Page 1938, p. xiv, with Palaima 2012, pp. 32–37 on the intersection of war and violence. Sources seldom refer to acts of homicide (or manslaughter), but Dracon's seventh-century laws on homicide continued to be observed into the fourth (*Ath. Pol.* 7.1; with Gagarin 1981, pp. 167–168; Rhodes 1981, pp. 130–135), surely attesting ongoing acts of violence.

References

Allan, W. (ed.) (2008). *Euripides' Helen*. Cambridge: Cambridge University Press.

Ambrose, S. (1992). *A Band of Brothers*. New York: Simon and Schuster.

Archilochus and Davenport, G. (1964). *Carmina Archilochi* (trans. G. Davenport; foreword by H. Kenner). Berkeley: University of California Press.

Audoin-Rouzeau, S. and Becker, A. (2002). *14–18: Understanding the Great War* (trans. C. Termerson). New York: Hill and Wang.

de Balzac, H. (1832/2003). *Colonel Chabert* (trans. A. Brown). London: Hesperus Press.

Biank, T. (2006). *Army Wives: The Unwritten Code of Military Marriage*. New York: St. Martin's.

Bond, G. (ed.) (1981). *Euripides' Heracles*. Oxford: Clarendon Press.

Bosworth, B. (1980–1995). *Commentary on Arrian's History of Alexander*. 2 vols. Oxford: Clarendon Press.

Bowden, H. (1993). "Hoplites and Homer: warfare, hero cult and the ideology of the polis." In: *War and Society in Ancient Greece* (eds. J. Rich and G. Shipley), 45–63. London: Routledge.

Bremner, J.D. (2002). *Does Stress Damage the Brain? Understanding Trauma-Related Disorders from a Mind-Body Perspective*. New York: W.W. Norton & Co.

Bridges, E., Hall, E., and Rhodes, P.J. (eds.) (2007). *Cultural Responses to the Persian Wars*. Oxford: Oxford University Press.

Chaniotis, A. (2005). *War in the Hellenistic World*. Oxford: Blackwell Publishing.

Cohen, D. (2001). *The War Come Home: Disabled Veterans in Britain and Germany, 1914–1939*. Berkeley: University of California Press.

Cooley, A. (2012). "Commemorating the war dead of the Roman world." In: *Cultures of Commemoration: War Memorials, Ancient and Modern* (eds. P. Low, G. Oliver and P.J. Rhodes), 61–88. Oxford: Oxford University Press for the British Academy.

Couvenhes, J.-C. (2005). "*De disciplina Graecorum*: les relations de violence entre les chefs militaries grecs et leur soldats." In: *La violence dans les mondes grec et romain* (ed. J.-M. Bertrand), 431–454. Paris: Publications de la Sorbonne.

Crane, S. (1895). *The Red Badge of Courage*. New York: D. Appleton & Company.

Croally, N.T. (1994). *Euripidean Polemic. The Trojan Women and the Function of Tragedy*. Cambridge: Cambridge University Press.

Crocq, L. (1999). *Les traumatismes psychiques de guerre*. Paris: Editions Odile Jacob.

Eagleman, D. (2011). *Incognito: The Secret Lives of the Brain*. New York: Pantheon Books.

Edwards, M. (2015). "*Philoctetes* in historical context." In: *Disabled Veterans in History*, rev. ed. (ed. D.A. Gerber), 55–69. Ann Arbor: University of Michigan Press.

Ehrenberg, V. (1937). "Tresantes." *RE* 6A: 2292–2297.

Ehrenberg, V. (1954). *Sophocles and Pericles*. Oxford: Blackwell.

Fassin, D. and Rechtman, R. (2009). *The Empire of Trauma: An Inquiry into the Condition of Victimhood*. Princeton: Princeton University Press.

Gagarin, M. (1981). *Drakon and Early Athenian Homicide Law*. New Haven, CT: Yale University Press.

Heinemann, L. (1986). *Paco's Story*. New York: Farrar Straus and Giroux.

Herr, M. (1977). *Dispatches*. New York: Alfred A. Knopf.

Hesseltine, W. and Wolf, H. (1961). *The Blue and the Gray on the Nile*. Chicago: University of Chicago Press.

How, W.W. and Wells, J. (1912). *A Commentary on Herodotus*. 2 vols. Oxford: Clarendon Press.

Kriner, D. and Shen, F. (2010). *The Casualty Gap: The Causes and Consequences of American Wartime Inequities*. Oxford: Oxford University Press.

Lazenby, J.F. (1993). *The Defence of Greece, 490–478 B.C.* Warminster: Aris and Phillips.

Lee, J.W.I. (2007). *A Greek Army on the March*. Cambridge: Cambridge University Press.

LiDonnici, L. (ed.) (1995). *The Epidaurian Miracle Inscriptions*. Atlanta: Scholar's Press.

Low, P. (2003). "Remembering war in fifth-century Greece: ideologies, societies, and commemoration beyond democratic Athens." *World Archaeology* 35: 98–111.

Ma, J. (2008). "Chaironeia 338: topographies of commemoration." *The Journal of Hellenic Studies* 128: 72–91.

MacDowell, D. (ed. and trans.) (1982). *Gorgias: Encomium of Helen*. Bristol: Bristol Classical Press.

Moran, L. (1945). *The Anatomy of Courage*. London: Constable.

O'Brien, T. (1990). *The Things They Carried*. New York: Penguin Books.

Page, D.L. (ed.) (1938). *Euripides, Medea*. Oxford: Clarendon Press.

Palaima, T. (2012). "The first casualty." *Times Higher Education Supplement* 20/27 December: 32–37.

Papadopoulou, T. (2005). *Heracles and Euripidean Tragedy*. Cambridge: Cambridge University Press.

Remarque, E.M. (1931). *The Road Back* (trans. A.W. Wheen). Boston: Little, Brown and Co. (= *Der Weg zurück*. Frankfurt: Verlag Ullstein, 1931/1984).

Rhodes, P.J. (1981). *A Commentary on the Aristotelian Athenaion Politeia*. Oxford: Clarendon Press.

Shay, J. (1994). *Achilles in Vietnam: Combat Trauma and the Undoing of Character*. New York: Atheneum.

Shay, J. (2002). *Odysseus in America: Combat Trauma and the Trials of Homecoming*. New York: Scribner.

Sommerstein, A. (1996). *Aeschylean Tragedy*. Bari: Levante Editori.

Thomason, J. (1941). *Lone Star Preacher. Being a Chronicle of the Acts of Praxiteles Swan, M.E. Church South, Sometime Captain, 5th Texas Regiment Confederate States Provisional Army*. New York: Scribner's Sons.

Tritle, L.A. (2000). *From Melos to My Lai: War and Survival*. London: Routledge.

Tritle, L.A. (2009). "Inside the hoplite agony." *Ancient History Bulletin* 23: 50–68.

Tritle, L.A. (2010). *A New History of the Peloponnesian War*. Oxford: Wiley Blackwell.

Tritle, L.A. (2012). "Monument to defeat: the Vietnam Veterans Memorial in American culture and society." In: *Cultures of Commemoration: War Memorials, Ancient and Modern* (eds. P. Low, G. Oliver and P.J. Rhodes), 159–179. Oxford: Oxford University Press for the British Academy.

Van Lommel, K. (2013). "The terminology of the medical discharge and an identity shift among the Roman disabled veterans." *Ancient History Bulletin* 27: 65–74.

Wheeler, E. (2011). "Greece: mad hatters and march hares." In: *Recent Directions in the Military History of the Ancient World* (eds. L.L. Brice and J.T. Roberts), 53–104. Claremont: Regina Books.

Wilson, E.O. (2004). *On Human Nature*, rev. ed. Cambridge, MA: Harvard University Press.

Winter, J. and Prost, A. (2005). *The Great War in History: Debates and Controversies, 1914 to the Present*. Cambridge: Cambridge University Press.

Young, A. (1995). *The Harmony of Illusions: Inventing Post-Traumatic Stress Disorder*. Princeton: Princeton University Press.

Further Reading

Horwitz, A. (2019). *PTSD: A Short History*. Baltimore, MD: Johns Hopkins University Press.

Konstan, D. (2010). "Anger, hatred and genocide in ancient Greece." *Genocide* 2: 151–170.

Meineck, P. and Konstan, D. (eds.) (2016). *Combat Trauma and the Ancient Greeks*. New York: Palgrave Macmillan.

Palaima, T. (2013). "Epilogue: the legacy of war in the Classical world." In: *The Oxford Handbook of Warfare in the Classical World* (eds. B. Campbell and L.A. Tritle), 726–736. New York: Oxford University Press.

Shay, J. (2015). "Afterword: a challenge to historians." In: *Disabled Veterans in History*, rev. ed. (ed. D.A. Gerber), 375–382. Ann Arbor: University of Michigan Press.

6

Greek Cavalry in the Hellenistic World

Review and Reappraisal
Glenn R. Bugh

Introduction

Publication of J.K. Anderson's *Ancient Greek Horsemanship* in 1961 resulted in a proliferation of studies on the Greek cavalry, but from the mid-1960s archaeology took center stage, due to excavations in Athens at the ancient Kerameikos cemetery and the Agora. The Agora had already produced thousands of inscriptions since the 1930s, but in 1962 in the area near the Theseion, a cavalry inscription dated to 282/1 BCE (all ancient dates BCE) was uncovered. This inscription revealed that the Athenian cavalry had fallen to 200 troopers, and that the hipparchs and phylarchs were being honored for increasing it to 300 (Threpsiades and Vanderpool 1963). This dramatic reduction of cavalry forces from the canonical 1000 to a modest 200 was completely unrecorded in literary sources. But this was just the beginning of the impact of material culture. In 1965, German archaeologists uncovered 574 inscribed lead tablets dated to the mid-third century from a well near the Dipylon Gate (Braun 1970; Posner 1974), and in 1971, the Americans found 111 more lead tablets from a well in the northwest corner of the Agora, 26 dated to the fourth century and 85 to the third century (see Figures 6.1 and 6.2; Camp 1998, pp. 35–38). In addition, archaeologists recovered 25 clay tokens inscribed with the name of Pheidon, hipparch to Lemnos (see Figure 6.3; Bugh 1988, pp. 209–218) and 9 lead armor tokens (Kroll 1977a).

The lead tablets provided specific information: the name of the owner of the horse, the horse's color and brand, and its value in drachmas, up to 1200. It became readily apparent that these records must have come from the archives of the cavalry headquarters, the *Hipparcheion* (Habicht 1961; Bugh 1988, pp. 219–220), and that they were part of the state's inspection process (*dokimasia*) to determine the value of the mount by an annual evaluation (*timesis*). Not only did these inform us about Greek horses, but they also provided intimate details about the administration of the Athenian cavalry in the fourth and third centuries, information unparalleled in the rest of the Greek world. They also added many new persons to, or supplemented known ones in, Attic prosopography. As Launey (1987) and Chaniotis (2005) have shown, inscriptions provide important information about war and society, particularly when literary sources are lacking – especially important in the Hellenistic period where no complete narrative history exists.

The importance of these archives cannot be overstated for our understanding of the Athenian cavalry in the Classical and Hellenistic periods. In a moment, earlier exhaustive studies of the Athenian cavalry seemed dated. Synthetic studies on the Athenian cavalry appeared in rapid

New Approaches to Greek and Roman Warfare, First Edition. Edited by Lee L. Brice.
© 2020 John Wiley & Sons, Inc. Published 2020 by John Wiley & Sons, Inc.

Figure 6.1 Cavalry tablet; inscription #17587. *Source:* American School of Classical Studies, Agora Excavations; Used with permission.

Figure 6.2 Cavalry tablet drawing; inscription #17551. *Source:* American School of Classical Studies, Agora Excavations; Used with permission.

Figure 6.3 Pheidon, hipparch to Lemnos, clay tokens. *Source:* American School of Classical Studies, Agora Excavations; Used with permission.

succession (Bugh 1988; Spence 1993). Soon, examinations of Greek and Macedonian cavalry (Worley 1994; Gaebel 2002; Corrigan 2004) drew heavily on material culture. Archaeology and material culture have assumed full partnership with the ancient authors in any discussion of ancient military studies, in all its aspects. Snodgrass (1999) and Sekunda (1994, 1998, 2010, 2012) have shown how successful this integrated and interdisciplinary approach can be. The splendid color illustrations of arms and armor published by the Osprey military series are all based on ancient pictorial representations or contemporary descriptions. Recent debates over the material culture of cavalry require the careful, combined use of literary, artistic, and material culture sources. It is a given that cavalry studies in the Hellenistic period cannot be written without considerations of material culture. This chapter provides a review and reappraisal of this new approach to ancient warfare.

Classical and Hellenistic Greek Cavalry: A Brief Survey

The importance of Greek cavalry in the Archaic Greek world was eclipsed by the rise of hoplite armies in the seventh century, and the infantry reigned supreme on the battlefield in the Classical period. The Thessalians, Boeotians, Greeks of Magna Graecia, and eventually the Athenians could field respectable cavalry forces by the mid-fifth century, but the cities of the Peloponnese fielded none at all. The Spartans did not even organize a cavalry until 424 (Thuc. 4.55.2) and even then, it numbered only 400 and was not highly regarded.

In the Classical period, the cavalry was intended to support the hoplite phalanx, much like other light-armed troops (Spence 1993, pp. 121–163). They could soften up a compact and serried line of hoplites with javelins or attack individual soldiers with the long spear (*kamax*), but they dared not charge into a phalanx. Since they lacked stirrups and saddles for support, the horsemen would do well just to stay mounted. The equestrian skills and training needed for cavalry service were not inconsiderable, as Xenophon, himself once a member of the Athenian cavalry, details in his two military treatises, *The Cavalry Commander* and *On Horsemanship* (Anderson 1961).

Positioned on the flanks of the infantry, the cavalries of the Classical period engaged and neutralized their opposing counterparts, then withdrew to watch the "real men" go at it. They reentered the battle to provide cover for their defeated infantry comrades, or, if victorious, to pursue and cut down the fleeing soldiers of the enemy. The horsemen of Classical Greece cut a dashing image, as visually demonstrated by the youthful and energetic Athenian troopers sculpted on the Panathenaic frieze of the Parthenon or the Dexileos monument in the Kerameikos (Bugh 1988, Figures 3–4, 9, 12), but on the battlefield their role remained secondary to infantry. Only in Thessaly, the preeminent cavalry power in Greece, was the horse elevated to primary importance in the military forces (Worley 1994, pp. 28–32).

Philip II and his son, Alexander III, changed the role of cavalry. Philip of Macedon reformed his armies, consolidated and expanded his power in the north, and began to exercise hegemonial designs on southern Greece. We do not know all the details, but it appears that Philip created a professional army that was more than a match for the seasonal armies of the Greek cities. Inspired perhaps by the brilliant tacticians Epaminondas and Pelopidas, Philip grasped the importance of a coordinated deployment of infantry, cavalry, and auxiliary troops, and he reformed the hoplite phalanx by equipping each soldier with a *sarissa*, a long spear of 15–18 ft, to be held by both hands, which extended feet beyond the front ranks (Sekunda 2010). This hedgehog effect of protruding spears must have presented a terrifying sight to armies still equipped with shields and shorter spears (Plut. *Aem.* 19). He made his point on the plains of Chaironeia in 338.

This is not the place to detail Alexander's Persian campaigns, but simply to note that Alexander elevated the Macedonian Companion cavalry to a level that only his Thessalian allies could match in terms of equestrian skill and military effectiveness (Tarn 1930, pp. 55–57). The most reliable primary sources calculate that Alexander crossed over into Asia with slightly more than 30,000 infantry and 5000 horse (Arr. *Anab.* 1.11.3; Diod. Sic. 17.17.3-5), the latter divided up between 1800 Macedonians, 1800 Thessalians, 600 allied Greeks, and 900 Thracians, *prodromoi*, and Paeonians. The proportion of cavalry to infantry would never approach this ratio again, save perhaps in the armies of the first generation of the Successors, and over the course of the next 1000 years it would gradually drop from 1:6 to 1:10, and by so doing, would return to Classical norms (Snodgrass 1999, p. 122). No one disputes Alexander's brilliance at the tactical coordination of infantry and cavalry, but his place in the army was always on the right flank at the head of the Companion cavalry. This became the strike force of his armies and it represented a radical departure from Classical military practice. Alexander's success would rarely be duplicated, even by the most capable cavalry commanders in Hellenistic military history.

This is not to suggest that cavalry diminished into insignificance during the third century; on the contrary, it still played an important role in every major battle from the late fourth century to the early second century. But there is some truth to the axiom that Hellenistic cavalry never won a battle (as it had done in Alexander's campaigns), but the misuse of it by commanders could, and did, contribute to defeat.

A brief survey of some of the major battles of the Hellenistic period can serve to illustrate this point. At the battle of Ipsos in 301, Demetrius Poliorcetes, son of Antigonus the One-Eyed, commanded the Macedonian cavalry on the right wing. He led a charge against the cavalry of Antiochus, son of Seleucus, and swept them from the field. However, his pursuit led him too far from his father's phalanx, and when he realized his tactical error and tried to return, he was blocked by a screen of elephants hastily positioned by Seleucus. As a result, his father's phalanx was compromised, attacked by light infantry and horse, and he died fighting, still waiting for his reckless son to return and save the day (Plut. *Dem.* 28–29; Diod. Sic. 21.1.2; Waterfield 2011, pp. 151–154).

In the battles of Raphia (217) and Magnesia (189), we observe similar mishandling of cavalry, this time by the same king, Antiochus III (the Great) of the Seleucid kingdom. At Raphia, in Egypt, Antiochus led a furious cavalry charge around his elephants and swept away Ptolemy IV's heavy cavalry on the left wing, but pursuing too far, he lost contact with the rest of his army. By the time Antiochus was persuaded to return, his army has been defeated on other fronts (Polyb. 5.79-86.7; Roberts and Bennett 2012, pp. 80–100). Antiochus made the same mistake at the battle of Magnesia in 190/189 against Rome and its ally, king Eumenes II of Pergamum. Antiochus III personally commanded 3000 armored cavalry called cataphracts along with 1000 heavy cavalry on the right wing. He led a charge that scattered the Roman cavalry and forced some of the infantry to flee to their camp, but they rallied, stalled Antiochus' progress, and allowed Eumenes, to bring reinforcements. Antiochus fled the field, ending the battle with huge Seleucid losses (Livy 37. 37–44; App. *Syr.* 11.6.30-37; Gaebel 2002, pp. 250–254; Sidnell 2006, pp. 143–148). Yet again, Antiochus' impetuous cavalry charge removed him from close coordination with his main army.

New Cavalry in the Third Century

In the third century, in the face of the overwhelming military power of the Hellenistic kings, particularly the Antigonids, a number of Greek states banded together for mutual protection. This is a Hellenistic phenomenon. The two most famous leagues of this period were the Achaean and the

Aitolian. The former became a formidable power in the Peloponnese, the latter in central Greece, and they rarely found common cause, even against the Antigonids of Macedon. Cavalry figures prominently in the success of both alliances, in ways that were not evident in the Classical period.

Achaean League

The Achaean League had become an important regional power under the leadership of Aratus in the middle of the third century. Facing a resurgence of Spartan power in the late third century, the Achaean League found it expedient to ally with Macedon and fought with Antigonus Doson at the battle of Sellasia in 222. Philopoemen was appointed in 211 as hipparch of the Achaean League, the second highest military office, for 210/09 (Plut. *Phil.* 6; Polyb. 10.22.5–24; Errington 1969, pp. 49–54). What he found was a cavalry in disarray, dispirited and ineffective militarily. According to Polybius, some who had served as cavalry commanders were unskilled in horsemanship or were using the office simply as a stepping-stone to the generalship of the league (Polyb. 10.22.6). Philopoemen immediately set about instituting cavalry reforms, imposing discipline, introducing a rigorous training regimen, and instilling an *esprit du corps* among the Achaean horsemen. His training regimen could have been lifted from the pages of Xenophon's cavalry treatises. For example, Philopoemen demanded rapid turning and wheeling movements in squadron formations and mock cavalry battles that involved charging and withdrawing in formation, a practice that was called *anthippasia* in Classical and Hellenistic Athens. This cavalry practice is amply attested in literature and art (Bugh 1988, pp. 59–60). These reforms would bear fruit in the battle of Mantineia in 207 (Polyb. 11.11–18; Gaebel 2002, pp. 243–244; Roberts and Bennett 2012, pp. 135–144) when Philopoemen defeated the armies of the Spartan tyrant Machanidas, even killing him in single-handed combat (Polyb. 11.18.4). The Achaean League would be the last Greek state to resist Roman domination in 145.

Aitolian League

The Aitolian League was a major player in the third century (Head 1982, pp. 8–9). It had been instrumental in protecting the sanctuary of Apollo at Delphi from Galatian invaders in 279 and it had expanded rapidly in central Greece, even to the point of invading southern Thessaly and thereby defying Antigonid hegemony. The Aitolian League was the principal Greek ally of the Romans in the First Macedonian War, effectively pinning down Philip V in the Balkans while Rome dealt with Hannibal. During this rise to regional power, the Aitolians had created a small – never more than 500 troopers in our sources (Grainger 1999, pp. 213–214; Nefedkin 2009) – but highly respected cavalry force that drew the praise of Polybius, no fan of the Aitolian League. They appear in the battles of the Social War (220–217), contesting Philip V's designs on southern Greece (Scholten 2000, pp. 200–228); as mercenaries in the army of Ptolemy V under the command of Scopas in the battle of Paneion (Syria) in 200 against Antiochus III (Polyb. 17.18–19; Livy 31.43.5; Grainger 1999, p. 212; Roberts and Bennett 2012, pp. 145–156); and most famously, in the battle of Cynoscephalae (197) between Philip V and the Roman consul T. Quinctius Flamininus. Polybius offers up praise for the vigorous military actions of the Eupolemos and his Aitolian cavalry during the preliminaries (Polyb. 18.19.9–12), and later, Eupolemos and Archedamos were sent by Flamininus to relieve Roman units being overwhelmed by Macedonian forces (Polyb. 18.21.5–8); and finally, turning the tide of the battle by their bravery under fire, "so much is their cavalry superior to that of the other Greeks in detached and single combats" (Polyb. 18. 22.4–6, Loeb translation; Gaebel 2002, pp. 247–250; Grainger 1999, p. 210; Hammond 1988, pp. 71–73). Tarn (1930, pp. 55–57) suggested that this cavalry success should be attributed to the presence of Thessalians recruited from their annexed territories. There is no proof to this claim. More likely, the Aitolians had made a conscious effort to elevate their cavalry to match their regional ambitions (as Athens had done in the mid-fifth century to match its imperial aspirations).

Unfortunately for the Aitolians, their dissatisfaction with Roman compensation for military services rendered during the Second Macedonian War would lead them into the arms of Antiochus III, whose international fortunes would soon unravel at the battle of Magnesia. The Aitolian cavalry would fight on the side of the Romans in the Third and Fourth Macedonia Wars and then fade into obscurity.

New Forces: Tarantines, *Prodromoi*, Cataphracts

Tarantines

The Tarantine cavalry, originating in the Greek city of Taras (Tarentum) in south Italy, was a light cavalry, famed as skirmishers, known to carry several throwing javelins, and protected by a large round shield (Griffith 1935, pp. 246–251; Launey 1987, pp. 601–604; Snodgrass 1999, pp. 128–129; Bugh 2006, p. 273; Sekunda 2007, p. 346; Fields 2008). This image is well documented by the striking coinage of Taras in the fourth and third centuries (Vlasto 1947: Inv. Nos. 790–801, pp. 877–904; Brauer 1986; Bugh 2011a, p. 294, Illus; Head 1982, pp. 115–116, no. 44; Fields 2008, Pls. C, D). The military manuals suggest that the *true* Tarantine horseman threw his spears from a distance, whereas "light" (*elaphroi*) cavalry threw their spears and then engaged the enemy at close quarters (Asclep. *Tact.* 1.3; Aelian *Tact.* 7.10; Arr. *Tact.* 4.5–6). This may be either overly semantic or reflect practices in two different historical periods, but I see no reason why the Tarantine horsemen could not do both, particularly in light of the defensive functionality of the shield, a piece of equipment not used in the cavalries of mainland Greece until the third century, but well attested among the south Italians (Launey 1987, p. 603; Brauer 1986, p. 176). The shield would also give the Tarantine horsemen the option of dismounting to fight on foot if the circumstances called for it or in the event of the loss of his mount in battle. The multiple spears and the shield are the most distinguishing features of a Tarantine horseman on the coins of Taras. Strabo (6.3.4) tells us that in the 360s Taras could field 3000 horsemen and 1000 hipparchs (this term cannot mean "cavalry commanders" in the usual sense: Fields 2008, p. 9). When we consider that Athens could only field a cavalry force of 1000 (along with 200 mounted archers) at the height of its imperial power, it affirms Taras' status as a major cavalry power in the larger Greek world. Our first literary reference to the use of Tarantine cavalry in the Greek East appears in Diodorus' account of the campaigns of Antigonus the One-Eyed against Eumenes in 317–316. Diodorus (19.29.2) reports that Antigonus had in his army, "2200 Tarantines who had come with him from the sea, men skilled in ambush and loyal to him." This piece of information has generated some debate: 2200 is a ginormous number for a single city-state, even one as cavalry-rich as Taras. Nefedkin (2006, pp. 111–112) has suggested that Tarantine citizens were augmented by mercenaries from south Italy, fighting in the same style, but I am persuaded by Ueda-Sarson's suggestion that the figure 2200 in fact represents the combined force of Tarantine horse and Median lancers, 2000 of which were Medes – as Diodorus seems to enumerate at 19.39.2 (Ueda-Sarson 2004, p. 21; Bugh 2011a, pp. 287–288). Tarantine mercenaries appear in the armies of Demetrius Poliorcetes in subsequent campaigns (Diod. Sic. 19.42.2; 19.82.2; Polyaenus *Strat.* 3.7.1: Athens).

A new cavalry inscription from the Athenian Agora documents their service as mercenaries alongside the citizen cavalry in 282/281 (Camp 2006, pp. 252–261; Camp 1998, p. 31). After this date there is a gap in our literary sources until the late third century when they appear in the armies of Elis (Polyb. 4.77.7), the Achaean League (Polyb. 11.12.4–7), Sparta (Polyb. 11.12.4–7; Livy 35.37.8, 39.1–2), and Antiochus III (Polyb. 16.18.7; Livy 37.40.12–15.). Because of the ubiquity of Tarantines in the armies of the late third to second century, most scholars have concluded that during the course of the third century, the term Tarantine came to mean a particular style of cavalry fighting, not actual citizen mercenaries from Taras. While this is certainly the case in the second century, e.g. the Tarantines and their commanders (Tarantinarchs), recorded in Athenian inscriptions, are Athenian citizens (Martin 1887, pp. 418–423; Bugh 1988, pp. 197–198), and for Boiotia (Nefedkin 2006, pp. 116–117) and for Thessaly (Larissa: *IG* IX.2. 509, lines 5–7), I have argued that ethnic Tarantine mercenary cavalry probably continued to offer their military services into the early second century, all the while Greek city-states, Greek leagues, and Hellenistic kings were recruiting and training foreign recruits in the Tarantine fighting style. When the Romans sacked Taras in 209, sold 30,000 inhabitants into slavery, and distributed their (horse-breeding) lands as *ager publicus* (Livy 27.16.1–9; Brauer 1986, pp. 202–203) they also brought to a close the rich numismatic tradition of Tarantine horsemen. It would not be surprising to see a sizeable number of exiles seek their fortunes as mercenary cavalry or as instructors of mercenaries in the Greek East, as they had done for over 100 years (Brauer 1986, p. 204; Bugh 2011a, pp. 291–292). The fact that Tarantines fought on opposing sides at the battle of Mantineia in 207, might hint at their recently disenfranchised and stateless status. We should note, however, that Aitolian mercenaries also served in opposing armies in this period (Head 1982, pp. 8–9).

Prodromoi

The term *prodromoi* literally means "front-runners." As a javelin-throwing light cavalry, they operated as an advance force, as skirmishers, scouts, or couriers. *Prodromoi* are first mentioned in Athens by Xenophon in his *Hipparchikos* (1.25). They probably replaced the *hippotoxotai*, a force of 200 mounted archers adjoined to the regular 1000 man Athenian cavalry in the fifth and early fourth centuries. Athens seems to have introduced this new arm sometime between the 390s and 360s (Sekunda and McBride 1986, 54 argues for 395/394). By the 330s, the *prodromoi* were included in the annual evaluation (*dokimasia*) of the Athenian cavalry by the Council of 500 (Arist.[*Ath. Pol.*] 49.1). Those judged unfit for service, were dismissed. For comparison, we have an inscription found near ancient Potidaia from the reign of Philip V that seems to describe a similar form of *dokimasia* (Hatzopoulos 2001, p. 157, lines 2–3; Sekunda 2012, p. 10).

The Athenian *prodromoi* are attested epigraphically as late as the mid-third century on several lead tablets associated with the state evaluation of Athenian cavalry mounts (Kroll 1977a, pp. 124–127, no. 62; Braun 1970, p. 234, no. 565; Bugh 1988, pp. 221–224, 1998, p. 88). Important new information came to light in 1982 from the excavations of the Athenian Agora. An inscription, dated to 330–285, records a decree by the *prodromoi* honoring the secretaries (*grammateis*) of the cavalry for their good service to the cavalrymen with respect to the distribution of grain for the horses (Bugh 1998, pp. 83–90; see Figure 6.4). This is the first reference to *prodromoi* in an Attic decree and the first occurrence of the secretaries of the cavalry as honorands. This inscription may suggest a greater civic and social prominence for the *prodromoi* than is usually assumed (Russell 2013, p. 479). They disappear in the second century, presumably to be replaced by a citizen body of Tarantines (see the section above), just as the *prodromoi* themselves had replaced the mounted archers in the fourth century (Bugh 1998, pp. 88–89). It is worth noting that Alexander the Great deployed *prodromoi*, also described as *sarissophoroi*, in a reconnaissance capacity (Arr. *Anab.* 3.7.7) as well as an advance strike force in his early campaigns (Arr. *Anab.* 1.14.5–7, 2.9.2, 3.8.1–2, 3.12.3; Gaebel 2002, pp. 172–179). Although there is no evidence that Athenian *prodromoi* carried the cavalry lance (*sarissa*), they

Figure 6.4 Cavalry inscription. *Source:* American School of Classical Studies, Agora Excavations; Used with permission.

functioned in the same capacity on the battlefield. Analogously, Philopoemen used his Tarantine mercenaries as an attacking force to initiate the battle of Mantineia in 207 (Livy 35.28.8, 29.1–2).

Cataphracts

The Greek term *kataphraktos* means "fully armored," and it could be applied to heavy cavalry as well as to ships. The cataphract marks the heaviest form of defensive armor for Hellenistic cavalries, with the horse protected by scale or lamellar armor (small rectangular iron or bronze plates laced together in horizontal rows) and the rider by chain mail (Mielczarek 1993; Bugh 2006, pp. 272–273; Sekunda 2007, p. 345). In the Hellenistic period, the unshielded cataphract carried a huge *kontos* (literally, "barge pole") or lance (*sarissa*). This type of heavy cavalry was borrowed from the eastern provinces of Alexander's empire. Among the Successor kingdoms of the Hellenistic world, only the Seleucids incorporated cataphracts into their armies (Serrati 2013, p. 189). After the successful eastern campaigns of Antiochus III in the last decade of the third century, he seems to have borrowed this style of Asian cavalry. There are no cataphracts mentioned at the battle of Raphia

(217), but they are present at Paneion in 200 (Polyb. 16.18.6–8). In fact, his son Antiochus defeated the stout Aitolian mercenary cavalry with cataphracts.

In 192, the Seleucid envoy to Flamininus boasted of them (Livy 35.48.3), and they were present at the battle of Magnesia (Livy 27.40.5, 11). Numerically, with 3000 cataphracts stationed on each wing, they represented the largest single cavalry unit on the field. Cataphract armor from this battle (and other battles) is depicted as spoils of war on the second-story balustrade marble reliefs of the Sanctuary of Athena at Pergamon (Webb 1998, pp. 241–243, fig. 25.2; Sidnell 2006, p. 143, Plate). Antiochus' defeat at Magnesia, however, did not discourage their use by his Seleucid successors: 1500 of them marched in Antiochus IV's grand parade at Daphne in Syria in 166. Later in the same century, the Hellenized king Mithridates VI of Pontus, whose family had marriage connections with the Seleucid dynasty since the third century, deployed cataphracts during his wars with Rome, and there may have been cataphracts stationed in Athens and the Piraeus during the First Mithridatic War (Bugh 1992b, pp. 114–119). The military experiment with cataphracts failed to attract takers in the Hellenistic Greek world, but in the east, among the Parthians, Armenians, Sassanids, and others, it would remain a formidable strike force for centuries to come, and serve as the prototype for the knights of Medieval Europe.

Cavalry Controversies: Spears and Shields

Cavalry Spears

One of the most hotly debated issues in cavalry studies in the late Classical and Hellenistic worlds was the nature and length of the cavalry spear, a debate in which material culture has played a key role. This lance was cut from the cornel-wood tree and was equipped with a spear tip on either end, thereby doing double-duty as a spear if broken in combat. Customarily called a *sarissa*, this word does not actually appear in our sources as the spear regularly used by the Alexander's Companion cavalry (Arr. *Anab.* 1.14.1, 6, 3.12.2; Curt. 4.15.13). During the late Classical and Hellenistic periods, the cavalry spear was called a *xyston* ("whittled" spear), but no length is specified in our sources (Gaebel 2002, p. 162 with references). A whole class of Hellenistic cavalry thus became known as *xystophoroi*, often translated as "lancers," from this style of long spear (Sekunda 2012, p. 9). It is usually thought to be longer than a traditional hoplite spear, but shorter than its famous namesake wielded with two hands by the infantry of the Macedonian phalanx. The infantry *sarissa* has itself generated a modern debate because our ancient sources list its length as varying from 10 to 12 cubits (15–18 ft) in the fourth century (Theophr. *Hist. Pl.* 3.12.2) to 14–16 cubits (21–24 ft) in the second century (Polyb. 18.29.2–4). Other ancient military writers put the length of the infantry *sarissa* within these parameters (Arr. *Tact.* 12.7; Asclep. *Tact.* 5.1; Aelian *Tact.* 14; and Polyaenus *Strat.* 2.29.2). The usual explanation is that in Theophrastus' time, that is, Alexander's time, the *sarissa* measured 18 ft at its longest, but by Polybius' time in the second century, it had increased to 24 ft. This proved unwieldy, and forced a reduction to a 21-footer. The debate is further complicated by the fact that the standard of measure, the cubit, has no secure and precise length. Moreover, it has been suggested recently that Philip II should not get the credit for introducing the long pike for infantry, that in fact, the Athenian commander Iphicrates who lead a mercenary force of peltasts in the early fourth century, had armed his men with a hoplite spear doubled to 16 ft, effectively creating the prototype for the Macedonian *sarissa* (Sekunda 2007, p. 329; Matthew 2012, pp. 94–97).

This debate about the precise length of the infantry *sarissa* has carried over to the cavalry, and has proved no less heated. The most creative solutions have incorporated "experimental history," i.e. building replicas for thesis-testing on unsuspecting horses. Some of these tests appear rather comical, inasmuch as they cannot possibly recreate the actual conditions of war (Brice and Catania 2012, pp. 68–70).

In any event, Minor Markle reconstructed a *sarissa* of 18 ft and published his results in 1977 and 1978 (Markle 1977, 1978). In a subsequent article, he "downsized" his lance, reducing the cavalry *sarissa* to about 15 ft (Markle 1982, pp. 104–111). In this, he found some support from Connolly (2000, pp. 107–109) and Corrigan (2004, pp. 440–531). Both replicated and tested 15-ft *sarissas* of their own. Connolly recruited a "very accomplished horseman" to charge a dummy target, experimenting with the overhand and underhand techniques (108, photos; Sidnell 2006, p. 82). Corrigan, an accomplished equestrian and horse owner, wielded her *sarissa* in simulated cavalry charges and took a series of positional photos. Markle's thesis, however, was attacked by Peter Manti who argued for a cavalry lance of 9 ft (Manti 1983, 1994). The 9-ft *sarissa* has persuaded a number of scholars who simply cannot believe that cavalry can be effective in battle with anything longer (Worley 1994, p. 156; Gaebel 2002, p. 168 (7–10 ft); Tarn 1930, p. 71). What now seems to be emerging as a compromise is a lance of 12 ft. This length finds its strongest support in the pictorial evidence (Mixter 1992; Sidnell 2006, pp. 80–84).

Experimental history relies in part on pictorial representations, and for the *sarissa* the most commonly cited are: the *Alexander Sarcophagus*, the *Alexander Mosaic*; and *Kinch Tomb*. Coins also depict cavalry spears, e.g. the Elephant Medallions depicting Alexander spearing the war elephant of Porus (Holt 2003) or the coins of Eukratides, king of Greco-Bactria from around 160 (Tarn 1951, pp. 196–219). In the latter case, the horsemen are clearly carrying long spears that could be classified as a *sarissa* (Markle 1982, pp. 90–91, fig. 6; Gaebel 2002, p. 171).

The *Alexander Sarcophagus* in the Istanbul Archaeological Museum does not belong to Alexander the Great. It bears this name because there is a magnificent sculptured relief on its sides depicting Alexander the Great in battle. The date for the sarcophagus is usually around 300; therefore, only a few decades after the death of the conqueror. A mounted Alexander is shown spearing (with an overhand thrust) a Persian enemy, but his spear, originally of bronze, has not been preserved. Only the holes that once anchored the *sarissa* to the relief can be used to calculate its length. Based on these, Alexander's lance should measure between 11 and 12 ft (Sidnell 2006, p. 83).

The *Alexander Mosaic* (see Figure 6.5), filling the floor of a room in the House of the Faun in Pompeii (second century), but believed to have been inspired by an original painting of Philoxenos near the time of Alexander's death (323), depicts Alexander spearing (with underhand style) a Persian horseman in front of the panicked eyes of the Persian king, Darius III at the turning moment in the battle of Issus (or no specific battle: Cohen 1997, p. 130). The spearhead has penetrated completely through the victim and is clearly visible. Although the mosaic section that would have shown the end of Alexander's lance has not survived, the best calculations project a length of 12–15 ft (Markle 1982, p. 105; Sidnell 2006, p. 83; Cohen 1997, pp. 86–93, figures 51–57). Since Gaebel has argued for a standard cavalry *sarissa* of 7–10 ft and yet agrees with Markle and Sidnell on the lance length depicted in the mosaic, he must explain away the discrepancy as a case of "artistic license," i.e. the painter of the original intended the elongated lance to be symbolic, linking Alexander as conqueror with Persia as a "spear-won land." "In the scene, the cavalryman receiving the spear thrust represents Persia" (Gaebel 2002, p. 171). This argument is pure speculation.

The *Kinch Tomb* was discovered in the late nineteenth century near the town of Naoussa in Macedonia, by a Danish archaeologist whose name now identifies the vaulted tomb. The date is uncertain, but probably mid to late third century (Cohen 1997, p. 54). On the back wall was a painting (now lost, but preserved in a color drawing) depicting a Macedonian horseman charging a foot

Figure 6.5 The *Alexander Mosaic*, filling the floor of a room in the House of the Faun in Pompeii. Naples Archaeological Museum. *Source:* D-DAI-ROM #58.1447, Photographer, Bartl. Used by permission.

soldier with a lance. The length is problematic: Gaebel calculates the spear at between 8 and 9 ft (2002, p. 170); Sidnell argues for about 12 ft (2006, p. 83). The aft spear point is clearly visible, but the fore spear point is obscured by the soldier's shield and a lost section of painting (Cohen 1997, pp. 54–57, Fig. 32; Miller 1993: Plate 8a).

The Macedonian cavalry appear to have also wielded traditional javelins and shorter spears when on reconnaissance and pursuit. The debate over the spear has for now compromised on the 12 ft *sarissa,* which still found utility in direct assaults (Markle 1982, pp. 104–105).

Cavalry Shields

If there are any surprises to match the Greek failure to develop stirrups or saddles, it is the fact that cavalry in mainland Greece carried no shields until the Hellenistic period. When men on horses carry round shields in vase paintings of the Archaic period they were probably serving as mounted hoplites (Greenhalgh 1973, pp. 122, 131; Anderson 1961, pp. 146–147; Worley 1994, p. 48, fig. 3.3: Thasos). Xenophon never suggests using a shield to protect the left arm of a horseman holding the reins, but rather proposes a *cheira* ("hand"), a piece of armor to protect shoulder, arm, elbow, and fingers (Xen. *Eq.* 12.5; Anderson 1961, p. 142). This is all extremely curious. It is not as if there were not shields being used by other cavalry states, including the Greeks of Magna Graecia, most notably the horsemen of Taras.

Most scholars believe that the cavalry shield was adopted in mainland Greece in the first third of the third century, in the 270s. That may answer the "when," but not the "why." Two theories have won support: Pyrrhus, the king of Epirus and mercenary captain, was invited by the Tarantines to protect them from Roman expansion in southern Italy (280–275). During his campaigns, he observed that they and other Italian states carried shields into battle and performed well. Thus, he adopted the shield and brought the idea back with him to Greece in 273. His reputed brilliance as a field tactician may have convinced other Greeks of the usefulness of his reforms. The second theory is grounded on the Galatians who, in 280–279 descended upon Greece and Macedonia bringing great devastation. I have already mentioned that the Aitolians were lifted to regional prominence by their successful defense of Delphi. The Galatians were eventually expelled from the Balkans by Antigonus Gonatus, but a large group ended up in Asia Minor. These invaders carried a large (over a meter in diameter), round, wooden cavalry shield. To the Galatians, some argue, goes the introduction of the cavalry shield into Greece (Sekunda 2012, p. 9; Sidnell 2006, pp. 139–140). They may also have been responsible for introducing the *thureos*, a tall oblong shield similar to the Roman *scutum*, which was adopted by both infantry and cavalry in the later Hellenistic period in both military and quasi-military activities (Sekunda 2006, pp. 9–17, with photos; Bugh 1992a). There is evidence that Thracians also adopted the round shield from the Greeks and later served as *thureophoros* cavalry in Hellenistic armies (Sekunda 2006, pp. 15–16; Webber 2003, pp. 540–545).

Both of these theories are reasonable, and they do agree on the approximate date of introduction; however, it has been suggested that the impact of the Tarantines need not have waited for the arrival of Pyrrhus. Head comments: "It is likely that Tarantine influence was responsible for the spread of shields to other Hellenistic cavalry" (Head 1982, p. 116, no. 44). I would go further by noting that Spartan mercenary captains, sometimes kings, had campaigned on behalf of Taras in the 330s and Antigonus employed Tarantines as mercenaries. They continued to serve his son and the city of Athens into the 280s. After nearly 50 years of direct contact with the widely praised Tarantine cavalry, it defies logic to think that this would not have had an effect on the military strategists of the Greek world. The Galatian success may have reinforced a confidence in the utility of the cavalry shield in the hands of confident skirmishers. Head also suggests that units that adopted shields seem to have reverted to multiple javelins as their main offensive weapon. He argues that cavalry who still wielded the *xyston* would have found it difficult to handle both shield and lance, necessitating a choice of one or the other, but not both. And it has been observed that true lancers are not often shown carrying a shield (Head 1982, p. 117). A conversion to a "Tarantine" style of fighting allowed for both shield and javelin to operate without conflict. Hatzopoulos has suggested on the basis of inscriptions that the *sarissophoroi* of Alexander the Great had been replaced by Philip V with shield-bearing javelin throwers, much like Tarantines (Hatzopoulos 2001). In response, Sidnell has added that this does not mean a wholesale conversion to light cavalry, only that starting in the third century Macedonians deployed "several specialized types of cavalry": light, heavy, and lancer (Sidnell 2006, p. 142).

Furthermore, it appears that by the time of Philip V, cavalry shields were being provided by the state. We may have a parallel with Macedonian state support at Athens where nine lead tokens stamped with images of cavalry armor, including shields, were excavated in context with the mid-third century cavalry tablets. These tokens have been thought to indicate the state supplied the gear on the token (above and Kroll 1977b, pp. 145–146).

Sidnell also offers a new intriguing proposal: the spread of cavalry shields may be connected with the development of the saddle by the Scythians, either directly or mediated by the Thracians (Webber 2003, p. 536) or by the Galatians. "These early saddles may have offered riders enough extra security to tip the cost/benefit analysis in favour of carrying a shield" (Sidnell 2006, p. 140).

One of the most illustrative examples of the round cavalry shield carried by the Macedonians (or Thracians: Webber 2003, p. 541) can be found on the famous victory monument of L. Aemilius Paullus erected at Delphi after his victory against Perseus of Macedon in 168 (Plut. *Aem.* 13–21). We see on the monument episodes of the battle between cavalry and infantry, with precise images of the weapons used by both sides (Kähler 1965, esp. Plate 18; Sekunda 2012, p. 14). The Romans were armed with oblong shields and the Macedonian cavalry carry round shields.

Recently, a revision to the standard chronology for the introduction of the cavalry shield in the 270s has been proposed. On a funerary stele from Gephyra, Macedonia, dated by the authors to around 300, a Macedonian horseman named Nikanor, son of Herakleides, is said to be carrying a shield (Hatzopoulos and Juhel 2009, pp. 428–433). If this is true, the chronology needs to be back-dated by about 30 years and would represent the earliest example of a shielded cavalryman in the Hellenistic period. However, the faint line behind the rider that is confidently interpreted as the rim of a round shield by the authors is not so obvious, and could be the rider's upper left arm (Sekunda 2012, p. 11, with photo). There is nothing intrinsically impossible about an early example of the cavalry shield in the Greek world, but it is, for the moment, an exceptional case, even if the shield can be verified on the stone. Future cavalry studies of the Hellenistic period will depend on finding other such stelae in Macedonia or depictions of cavalry weapons in wall paintings in Macedonian tombs yet undiscovered (Miller 1993: the Tomb of Lyson and Kallikles). It is no exaggeration to claim that the most exciting archaeological discoveries in the Greek world over the past 30 years have been in Macedonia.

Concluding Remarks

Diversification and specialization of arms and armor are the hallmark of the Hellenistic period. Battles of the Classical period seem simple by comparison. What Classical Greek army ever faced the diverse array of elephants, chariots, cataphracts, and war camels in a single battle? Mercenaries, both cavalry and infantry, served in every army fielded by the Hellenistic kings, the leagues, and the old Greek cities, yet citizen cavalry (as in Athens) continued also in the Greek cities to the end of the Hellenistic period. While the corpus of ancient authors has remained relatively static into the modern age, archaeology continues to generate fresh material, whether it be inscriptions, coins, sculpture, and paintings, or military material culture. The sands of Egypt may yet reveal more details about the cavalry cleruchies established under the Ptolemies (Sidnell 2006, pp. 131–132; Sekunda 1998) on some unexamined papyrus fragment in the British Museum. Cavalry studies in the Hellenistic period stand to be one of the beneficiaries of these discoveries. Perhaps, the hunt for the *Hipparcheion* of Athens will lead to new revelations about the Athenian cavalry in the Hellenistic period. We know it was located in the northwest corner of the Agora, an inscription refers to it, and it may be just beyond the current American excavations in the area of the Stoa Poikile. The cavalry tablets were once stored there and cavalry inscriptions were set up nearby. The young horsemen of Athens are just waiting for our arrival.

References

Anderson, J. (1961). *Ancient Greek Horsemanship*. Berkeley: University of California Press.

Brauer, G. (1986). *Taras: Its History and Coinage*. New Rochelle, NY: Aristide D. Caratzas.

Braun, K. (1970). "Der Dipylon-Brunnen B1: Die Funde." *Mitteilungen des Deutschen Archäologischen Instituts, Athenische Abteilung* 85: 197–269.

Brice, L.L. and Catania, S. (2012). "A pedagogical trebuchet: a case study in experimental history and history pedagogy." *The History Teacher* 46 (1): 67–84.

Bugh, G. (1988). *The Horsemen of Athens*. Princeton: Princeton University Press.

Bugh, G. (1992a). "The Theseia in Late Hellenistic Athens." *Zeitschrift für Papyrologie und Epigraphik* 83: 20–37.

Bugh, G. (1992b). "Athenion and Aristion of Athens." *Phoenix* 46: 108–123.

Bugh, G. (1998). "Cavalry inscriptions from the Athenian Agora." *Hesperia* 67: 81–90.

Bugh, G. (2006). "Hellenistic military developments." In: *Cambridge Companion to the Hellenistic World* (ed. G. Bugh), 265–294. Cambridge: Cambridge University Press.

Bugh, G. (2011a). "The Tarantine cavalry in the Hellenistic period: ethnic or technic?" In: *Pratiques et identités culturelles des armées hellénistiques du monde méditerranéen: Hellenistic Warfare*, vol. 3 (eds. J.-C. Couvenhes, S. Crouzet and S. Péré-Noguès), 285–294. Bordeaux: De Boccard.

Camp, J.M.K. (1998). *Horses and Horsemanship in the Athenian Agora*. Princeton: American School of Classical Studies at Athens.

Camp, J.M.K. (2006). "Excavations in the Athenian Agora: 1994 and 1995." *Hesperia* 65: 231–261.

Chaniotis, A. (2005). *War in the Hellenistic World: A Social and Cultural History*. Oxford: Oxford University Press.

Cohen, A. (1997). *The Alexander Mosaic: Stories of Victory and Defeat*. Cambridge: Cambridge University Press.

Connolly, P. (2000). "Experiments with the sarissa – the Macedonian pike and cavalry lance: a functional view." *Journal of Roman Military Equipment Studies* 11: 79–88.

Corrigan, D. (2004). "Riders on high: an interdisciplinary study of the Macedonian cavalry of Alexander the Great." PhD dissertation. University of Texas at Austin.

Errington, R. (1969). *Philopoemen*. Oxford: Clarendon Press.

Fields, N. (2008). *Tarentine Horseman of Magna Graecia: 430–190 BC*. Oxford: Osprey Publishing.

Gaebel, R. (2002). *Cavalry Operations in the Ancient Greek World*. Norman, OK: University of Oklahoma Press.

Grainger, J. (1999). *The League of the Aitolians*. Leiden: Brill.

Greenhalgh, P.A.L. (1973). *Early Greek Warfare: Horsemen and Chariots in the Homeric and Archaic Ages*. Cambridge: Cambridge University Press.

Griffith, G.T. (1935). *The Mercenaries of the Hellenistic World*. Cambridge: Cambridge University Press.

Habicht, C. (1961). "Neue Inscriften aus dem Kerameikos." *Mitteilungen des Deutschen Archäologischen Instituts, Athenische Abteilung* 76: 127–143.

Hammond, N.G.L. (1988). "The campaign and the Battle of Cynoscephalae in 197 BC." *Journal of Hellenic Studies* 108: 60–82.

Hatzopoulos, M. (2001). *L'organisation de l'armée macedoine sous les Antigonides*. Paris: De Boccard.

Hatzopoulos, M. and Juhel, P. (2009). "Four Hellenistic Funerary Stelae from Gephrya, Macedonia." *American Journal of Archaeology* 113: 423–437.

Head, D. (1982). *Armies of the Macedonian and Punic Wars 359 BC to 146 BC. Organisation, Tactics, Dress, and Weapons*. Cambridge: Wargames Research Group.

Holt, F. (2003). *Alexander the Great and the Mystery of the Elephant Medallions*. Berkeley: University of California Press.

Kähler, H. (1965). *Der Fries vom Reiterdenkmal des Aemilius Paullus in Delphi*. Berlin: Gebr. Mann Verlag.

Kroll, J. (1977a). "An archive of the Athenian cavalry." *Hesperia* 46: 83–140.

Kroll, J. (1977b). "Some Athenian armor tokens." *Hesperia* 46: 141–146.

Launey, M. (1987). *Recherches sur les armées hellénistiques*. 2 vols, reprint ed. (eds. Y. Garland, P. Gauthier and C. Orrieux). Paris: E. de Boccard.

Manti, P. (1983). "The cavalry sarissa." *Ancient World* 8: 73–80.

Manti, P. (1994). "The Macedonian sarissa, again." *Ancient World* 25: 77–91.

Markle, M. (1977). "The Macedonian sarissa, spear, and related armor." *American Journal of Archaeology* 81: 323–339.

Markle, M. (1978). "Use of the sarissa by Philip and Alexander of Macedon." *American Journal of Archaeology* 82: 483–497.

Markle, M. (1982). "Macedonian arms and tactics under Alexander the Great." *Studies in the History of Art* 10: 86–111.

Martin, A. (1887). *Les cavaliers athéniens*. Paris: E. Thorin.

Matthew, C. (2012). "The length of the sarissa." *Antichthon* 46: 79–100.

Mielczarek, M. (1993). *Cataphracti and Clibanarii: Studies on the Heavy Armoured Cavalry of the Ancient World* (trans. M. Abramowicz). Lodz: Oficyna Naukowa MS.

Miller, S. (1993). *The Tomb of Lyson and Kallikles: A Painted Macedonian Tomb*. Mainz am Rhein: Philipp von Zabern.

Mixter, J. (1992). "The length of the Macedonian sarissa during the reigns of Philip II and Alexander the Great." *Ancient World* 23 (2): 52–53.

Nefedkin, A. (2006). "Tarentine cavalry in Hellenistic armies." *Antique World and Archaeology* 12: 109–117.

Nefedkin, A. (2009). "On the origin of Greek cavalry shields in the Hellenistic period." *Klio* 91 (2): 356–366.

Posner, E. (1974). "The Athenian cavalry archives of the fourth and third centuries B.C." *The American Archivist* 37: 579–582.

Roberts, M. and Bennett, B. (2012). *Twilight of the Hellenistic World*. Barnsley, UK: Pen & Sword.

Russell, F. (2013). "Finding the enemy. Military intelligence." In: *The Oxford Handbook of Warfare in the Classical Period* (eds. B. Campbell and L. Tritle), 474–492. Oxford: Oxford University Press.

Scholten, J. (2000). *The Politics of Plunder: Aitolians and their Koinon in the Early Hellenistic Era, 279–217 B.C.* Berkeley: University of California Press.

Sekunda, N. (1994). *Seleucid and Ptolemaic Reformed Armies 168–145 BC. Vol. 1: The Seleucid Army under Antiochus IV Epiphanes*. Stockport, UK: Montvert.

Sekunda, N. (1998). *Seleucid and Ptolemaic Reformed Armies 168–145 B.C. Vol. 2: The Ptolemaic Army under Ptolemy VI Philometer*. Stockport, UK: Montvert.

Sekunda, N. (2006). "The introduction of cavalry *Thureophoroi* into Greek warfare." *Fasciculi Archaeologicae Historiae* 19: 9–17.

Sekunda, N. (2007). "Military forces. A. Land forces." In: *CHGRW*, vol. 1, 325–357.

Sekunda, N. (2010)." The Macedonian army." In: *A Companion to Ancient Macedonia* (eds. J. Roisman and I. Worthington), 446–471. Malden, MA: Wiley Blackwell.

Sekunda, N. (2012). *Macedonian Armies After Alexander 323–168 BC*. Oxford: Osprey Publishing.

Sekunda, N. and McBride, A. (1986). *The Ancient Greeks. Armies of Classical Greece 5th and 4th Centuries BC*. London: Osprey Publishing.

Serrati, J. (2013). "The Hellenistic world at war: stagnation or development." In: *The Oxford Handbook of Warfare in the Classical Period* (eds. B. Campbell and L. Tritle), 179–198. Oxford: Oxford University Press.

Sidnell, P. (2006). *Warhorse: Cavalry in Ancient Warfare*. London: Hambledon Continuum.

Snodgrass, A. (1999). *Arms and Armour of the Greeks*. Baltimore, MD: Johns Hopkins University Press [updated bibliographical commentary from 1st ed., 1967].

Spence, I.G. (1993). *The Cavalry of Classical Greece: A Social and Military History with Particular Reference to Athens*. Oxford: Clarendon Press.

Tarn, W.W. (1930). *Hellenistic Military and Naval Developments*. Cambridge: Cambridge University Press.

Tarn, W.W. (1951). *The Greeks in Bactria and India*, 2e. Cambridge: Cambridge University Press.

Threpsiades, J. and Vanderpool, E. (1963). "Pros tois Hermais." *Deltion* 18: 99–114.

Ueda-Sarson, L. (2004). "Tarantine cavalry." *Slingshot* 236: 21–25.

Vlasto, M. (1947). *Descriptive Catalogue of the Collection of Tarantine Coins*. Compiled by Oscar E. Ravel. Spink & Son [Reprint—Chicago, IL: Obol International, (1977)].

Waterfield, R. (2011). *Dividing the Spoils: The War for Alexander the Great's Empire*. Oxford: Oxford University Press.

Webb, P.A. (1998). "The functions of the Sanctuary of Athena and the Pergamon Altar (the Heroon of Telephos) in the Attalid building program." In: *Stephanos: Studies in Honor of Brunilde Sismondo Ridgway* (eds. K. Hartswick and M. Sturgeon), 241–254. Philadelphia: The University Museum.

Webber, C. (2003). "Odrysian cavalry arms, equipment, and tactics." In: *Early Symbolic Systems for Communication in Southeast Europe* (ed. L. Nikolova), 529–554. Oxford: Archaeopress.

Worley, L. (1994). *Hippeis: The Cavalry of Ancient Greece*. Boulder, CO: Westview Press.

Further Reading

Campbell, B. and Tritle, L. (eds.) (2013). *The Oxford Handbook of Warfare in the Classical World*. Oxford: Oxford University Press.

Graninger, D. (2010). "Macedonia and Thessaly." In: *A Companion to Ancient Macedonia* (eds. J. Roisman and I. Worthington), 306–325. Malden, MA: Wiley Blackwell.

Sears, M. (2019). *Understanding Greek Warfare*. New York: Routledge.

Sekunda, N. (2013). *The Antigonid Army*. Gdansk, Poland: Foundation for the Development of Gdansk University for the Department of Mediterranean Archaeology.

Willikes, C. (2016). *The Horse in the Ancient World: From Bucephalus to the Hippodrome*. London: I.B. Taurus.

7

Skeletal Evidence for the Impact of Battle on Soldiers and Non-Combatants

Maria A. Liston

Despite the variety of evidence for ancient battles from literature, art, and archaeology, the remains of the actual participants are rare. Few battle cemeteries have been excavated and those that have been were, for the most part, dug before skeletal biology was a part of Mediterranean archaeology. The skeletons were either discarded or left where they lay after the artifacts were removed from the graves or tumuli. There are a few exceptions that shed light on the impact of battle on the participants – combatants and unwilling participants, the "collateral damage" in the terminology of modern warfare. Although separated in time by over 600 years, two ancient engagements, the Battle of Chaironeia and the Herulian sack of Athens, offer extremely useful evidence on the impact of battle on soldiers and non-combatants and may also shed light on the evolution of Greek warfare.

Introduction

The Battle of Chaironeia in 338 BCE was a pitched battle, in which both hoplites and cavalry fought. The Macedonian army under Philip II and Alexander overwhelmed the forces of Athens, the Boiotian League, and their allies. Anchoring the Greek right was the Theban Sacred Band (Plut. *Pel.* 15–16, 18). It was distinguished as one of the few battle units to train extensively for combat and was recognized as one of the most effective fighting forces in the Greek world (Rahe 1981; Lendon 2005). At Chaironeia most of the Sacred Band's 300 members were killed, and the Thebans never reformed the unit.

Because the ancient historical accounts lack detail, modern historians of the battle have expended considerable effort to reconstruct the battle using topography and archaeological evidence (Pritchett 1958; Soteriades 1903; Ma 2008). Most of the landmarks mentioned by the ancient accounts of Diodorus (16.86), Pausanias (9.40.10), Plutarch (*Alex.* 9), and Polyaenus (4.2.2–7) have now been identified with some confidence, but only the skeletons can speak to the experience of battle for those who fought and died there. A sample of skeletal remains with battle injuries was preserved from the excavation of the Lion Monument at Chaironeia, the presumed burial place of the Theban Sacred Band (Pritchett 1958; Ma 2008).

A second source of skeletal information on ancient Greek battle comes from the Herulian sack of Athens in the 267 CE. The Herulians appeared suddenly in the Black Sea region, and after attacking cities in Asia Minor they entered Greece, sacked Athens and went on to attack cities in the Peloponnese (Wilson 1971). There are few historical sources for this invasion, other than P. Herennius Dexippus,

New Approaches to Greek and Roman Warfare, First Edition. Edited by Lee L. Brice.
© 2020 John Wiley & Sons, Inc. Published 2020 by John Wiley & Sons, Inc.

who was personally involved in the defense of the city. Scraps of information can be found in Syncellys (381), Zosimus (1.39), and Ammianus Marcellinus (31.5.15–17). The surviving fragments offer few details and little evidence of the true devastation. No author identifies who exactly the Herulians were, although they were said to be related to the Goths or Scythians (Franz 1988; Heather 1998).

The attack by the Herulians was long believed to be a relatively minor event, with little damage or impact on the life of the city. However, excavations in the Athenian Agora have made it clear that the sack was devastating for the city, although some parts of the city were spared (Chioti 2018). Afterwards, a new fortification wall was constructed, largely of debris from buildings and monuments damaged in the sack. The new wall encompassed a much smaller area, estimated to be approximately 1/14 of the previous walled city. Significantly, the entire ancient Agora lay outside the new fortification wall (Franz 1988).

Following the sack, the survivors cleared the Agora, dumping the debris into the wells scattered across the site. Perhaps because they now lay outside the new city walls, a number of wells were also used as burial places for five victims of the attack and an adult male who may have been one of the invaders. As with Chaironeia, their skeletons are our only testament to the human consequences of this battle.

Skeletal Trauma Studies

The study of battle-related skeletal trauma requires caution in interpretation. Depending on the history of the bone after it was buried, there may be considerable damage that has nothing to do with injuries sustained while living or shortly after death. Distinguishing between ante-mortem, perimortem (around time of death), and postmortem damage is critical to accurate analyses. In addition, it is important to keep in mind that the skeletal injuries that can be assessed in skeletal remains represent only a small portion of the injuries sustained in conflict. Analyses of modern clinical data on assaults indicate that soft tissue injuries make up the majority of the wounds resulting from conflicts, while skeletal injuries account for less than 30% of the total injuries (Judd and Redfern 2012). Regardless of how devastating the skeletal trauma we can examine today may be, the individuals who died in battle probably had a much greater number and distribution of soft tissue wounds that leave no evidence.

It is possible to determine when damage occurred to bones. Bone is a living tissue composed of flexible collagen proteins interlacing a rigid structure of calcium-salt crystals or hydroxyapatite (Galloway et al. 1999). When damaged before death, the organism responds to remove dead and damaged cells and replace them with new tissue. This healing is an indication that the injury took place before death, but these changes normally are not visible macroscopically for 10–14 days after the injury. Bone that is broken or damaged around the time of death lacks these indications of healing. Fortunately, the combination of flexible collagen and rigid mineral structure in fresh or living bone produces fractures that are recognizable as having occurred in either living or recently dead individuals. The fracture lines move through the bone at an acute angle to the bone surface, and may be beveled or follow the lines of the collagen fibers. In the absence of evidence for healing, such fractures are termed perimortem. Bone damaged long after death responds quite differently. When the collagen has dried or decayed, bone is brittle, and fractures form with crumbled edges and straight, transverse breaks that extend at a right angle from the bone's surface, indicating postmortem damage. In addition, damage sustained after removal from the ground will normally show a color difference in the break, because staining from surrounding soil does not normally penetrate through the full thickness of the bone, and recent damage appears as a different color (Galloway et al. 1999; Kanz and Grossschmidt 2006).

Battle injuries to bone in antiquity were nearly all the result of either blunt or sharp force trauma. Blunt force trauma results from a relatively low-velocity impact on bone with an object that does not cut the bone surface, but distributes the force over a wider area (Galloway et al. 1999). The array of items that can produce blunt force trauma is nearly infinite, and the skeletal evidence suggests that blunt force trauma was a significant factor in the outcome of battle. While blade injuries are often more distinctive and noticeable, blunt force trauma, particularly to the face and head, is often more immediately debilitating or even fatal. Even a survivable blow to the head or face is often disabling, leaving the recipient vulnerable to subsequent attack. In hoplite battles, blunt force trauma could commonly result from impact with shields rims, spear butts and shafts, or sword hilts, as well as blows from fists or feet.

The skeletons from the Battle of Chaironeia and the Herulian sack of Athens exhibit trauma consistent with hand-to-hand combat using both bladed and blunt weapons. Details of the injuries, both type and location, enable us to reconstruct evidence for the fighting. It is important to remember that actual battle was not the patterned, choreographed event depicted in art. Rather, it was messy, chaotic, and brutal. Desperate men would seize anything available in an attempt to continue fighting, or just to survive. In addition to the spear, sword, and shield, the potential weapons, particularly in urban battles such as the Herulian sack of Athens, included clubs, knives, broken lances, rocks, roof tiles, fists, feet, and anything else that might be available (Tritle 2009; Lee 2010).

Blade wounds, or sharp force traumas, are produced by a more narrow range of weapons. In antiquity, metal for blade weapons was expensive and relatively rare, in comparison to the ubiquity of metal blades today. Sharp force injuries are distinctive, and more reliably indicate battle injuries, since they are unlikely to be incurred accidentally (Bennike 2008). Swords, knives, daggers, spear points, and axes or hatchets were the most common bladed instruments. Swords and spears were the standard hoplite weapons, but since each soldier provided his own kit, their quality and size would have varied at Chaironeia. In the Herulian sack of Athens, the attacker's bladed weapons include axes or other chopping/hacking weapons, as the evidence on one Athenian victim's skull attests.

The third major category of weapon trauma, penetrating and projectile wounds, is more rarely seen in ancient skeletons (Roberts and Manchester 2010). Punctures result from low-velocity impact with narrow or pointed objects. Projectile wounds may be similar, but are the result of higher velocity impacts from objects moving through the air, such as arrows, sling stones or thrown spears. Both sling stones and arrows, if propelled with sufficient force, might produce projectile wounds somewhat similar to gunshot wounds today. A rare example, probably from a sling stone, is known from a Mycenaean burial in the Athenian Agora (Smith 1998; Smith and Liston 2013). However, the characteristics attributed to high velocity penetrating wounds are uncommon in antiquity because of the limited propulsive forces available in battle (Golubović et al. 2009). Low-velocity punctures or stab wounds are more common, in which a pointed object such as a spear point or butt spike, or a knife, penetrates the bone.

The Skeletons: Chaironeia

The land under the Lion Monument at Chaironeia was excavated on several occasions. Seven rows with 254 skeletons were uncovered; selected bones exhibiting significant trauma were saved. These included ten partial or complete crania, teeth, a large number of leg bones, hand bones, an isolated partial foot and a pair of feet, cut off above the ankles (Phytalis 1881). These represent a minimum of 10–12 individuals, and probably as many as 15–18. The remains excavated from the Lion Monument at Chaironeia all have features consistent with adult males, 18–40+ years old, as would be expected in a battle cemetery (Buikstra and Ubelaker 1994).

The skeletons of individuals killed in battle also can tell us about their health before death. Developmental stress lines in teeth, known as linear enamel hypoplasias (Buikstra and Ubelaker 1994), indicate that childhood was stressful for most of these men. One suffered a severe infection in the right ear, resulting in an abscess and almost certain deafness.

The Skeletons: Athenian Agora

In the Athenian Agora excavations, there are four wells in which skeletons were found clearly associated with debris from the clean-up of the city after the Herulian attack. These wells are all located on the north slopes of the Areopagus hill, although other wells with debris from the sack have been found across the site (Chioti 2018). The skeletons preserve traces of adipocere, sometimes called "grave wax" which forms from body fat in a moist, anaerobic environment, such as would be found deep in a well (Forbes et al. 2005). Once formed, adipocere is stable and resistant to decay. Together with the lack of weathering on the bones, this indicates that these bodies went into the wells in relatively fresh condition, and were not secondary deposits of bone from disturbed graves. The presence of six skeletons in these four wells, all with clear perimortem injuries typical of conflict wounds, and all deposited amidst the debris as relatively fresh bodies provides an indication of the timing of the clean-up. Despite the devastation of the city, not only were the resulting corpses quickly cleared away, which is hardly surprising, but the associated clean-up debris indicates that the effort to clear less polluting messes was also carried out shortly after the attack. While the Agora was not included in the area enclosed by the post-Herulian city walls, some effort was made to clear the area of debris quickly after the event.

Among these Agora skeletons there is a single adult male, AA 76. His skeleton exhibits both ante-mortem and perimortem blade trauma, indicating that he was in an earlier battle, two to four weeks before death, and died with multiple new wounds on his limbs. Additionally, unusual perimortem punctures suggest his body was dragged or mutilated with a multipronged instrument. Together with a physiognomy markedly different from other individuals buried in Athens, this suggests that he is a Herulian invader, wounded in an earlier battle, whose corpse was handled quite roughly before being deposited in an Agora well.

Five other skeletons, three women, all in their 30s and two young children approximately four and seven years old at death, are presumably victims of the attack. All exhibit perimortem fractures, and the adults also sustained blade wounds. All appeared to have endured considerable physical strain during their lives. Two of the women had earlier-healed fractures to their faces, one arm, and one leg prior to their deaths, and the third was dying of bone cancer when she was killed. Based on the nature of the burials, it is possible that these may all have been slaves, foreigners, or other lower-class individuals. If so, in the confusion following the sack of the city, they were informally deposited with the debris, rather than receiving a conventional burial.

Evidence for Battle Injuries: Combatants

Trauma from interpersonal violence, whether in warfare, domestic conflict, or individual fights, tends to occur in certain patterns, with some variation according to the nature of the conflict and the weapons used. The skeletons of individuals who died at Chaironeia and in the Herulian sack of Athens exhibit these patterns, with some variation due to the roles of the victims in the violence.

Craniofacial injuries are common and normally are the most frequent combat-related trauma in both battle/massacre sites and among general cemetery populations in societies with high levels of violence (Judd 2004; Williamson et al. 2003; Willey and Emerson 1993). Craniofacial injuries are often immediately debilitating, even when not necessarily fatal (Kanz and Grossschmidt 2006). In a fight, a blow to the face or cranial vault can stun the recipient, leaving him vulnerable to his opponent. Facial blows are extremely painful and tend to bleed profusely, potentially blinding the victim. But some head wounds are also fatal, either immediately or within a short period of time due to intracranial hemorrhage.

At Chaironeia all but one of the skulls sustained blunt force trauma to the face in the perimortem period. Two individuals have severe facial fractures along the lines of structural weakness in the facial skeleton. One soldier sustained a severe facial fracture that separated the face from the braincase, and a mandible fracture as well. This combination is often fatal due to associated intracranial bleeding and trauma. The soldier's injuries were produced from a blow to the face with a large blunt object such as the rim of a shield. The shift in the alignment of the facial bones suggests the force was directed upward from the right to left, in turn suggesting a blow from a facing opponent's left side, which would be appropriate for a shield impact. This same soldier also has a blunt force fracture of the cranial vault, and a small blade wound on the back of the skull which sliced off a portion of the occipital, about 1 cm in diameter.

The other facial traumas are less severe, but would have been debilitating, as any blow to the face sufficient to fracture bones will be. There are two additional individuals with perimortem mandible fractures; one of these and another individual lost teeth as a result of blows that cracked the bone in the upper jaw. A third hoplite had lost the two central incisors in his mandible at an earlier date, and the lack of wear or decay on his other teeth suggests that this, too, may have been the result of trauma which he survived, only to die in the battle of Chaironeia.

In addition to the cut on the back of the head mentioned above, three of the Chaironeia skulls exhibit severe sharp force injuries to the cranial vault, none of which are likely to have been survivable. All three appear to have been caused by a long, straight, heavy blade, such as a sword. Two individuals have deep linear cuts on the top of the skull; both cuts sliced through the bone and would have severed underlying membranes, and probably cut into the brain itself. The sharp force trauma on one individual extends across the skull at the apex, for a length of 6.7 cm. The second cut, on a fragmentary skull, is located just to the left of the midline, extending for 6.4 cm toward the back of the skull (see Figure 7.1). Both blows were delivered from above with such force that there is also a beveled fracture adjacent to the cut, producing both blunt force and sharp force trauma in a single impact.

This second individual with blunt force trauma to the face and a sword cut to the top of the head also has the only example of a penetrating wound found in the sample from Chaironeia. The posterior left parietal has been pierced with a weapon that was nearly square in cross-section, producing an opening approximately 6 × 8 mm (see Figure 7.1). The penetrating shaft was surrounded by a round collar or flange that impacted the bone, producing a round crush fracture, just over 2 cm across. The morphology of the wound suggests that it was produced by a spear butt-spike. This was attached to the back end of a spear, providing a counterbalance to the weight of the spearhead, and allowed the butt end to be used as a weapon if the other end was lost or broken (Markle 1977). It would appear that in this case, it was used in exactly this manner.[1]

The final example from Chaironeia of sharp force trauma to the skull is most remarkable. A blade, probably also a sword, delivered a blow that effectively amputated the face of one of the Theban hoplites (see Figure 7.2). The blade initially struck the frontal bone, probably near the hairline, at the top right of the forehead. The point of impact is indicated by a small semicircular fracture. The blade continued downward behind the eyes and nose to the top of the mandible, removing the front of the braincase and upper face. The force of the impact created an additional

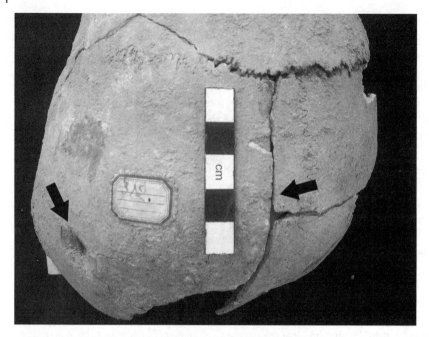

Figure 7.1 Superior view of a skull from Chaironeia, showing blade wound (right arrow) and wound from a spear butt spike (left arrow). *Source:* Author. Used by permission.

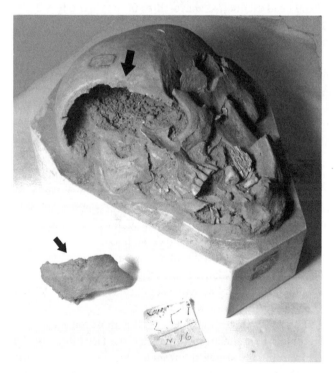

Figure 7.2 Skull from Chaironeia with the upper face removed by a blade. The upper arrow shows the point of impact, and the lower arrow indicates the portion of the forehead removed by the blade. *Source:* Author. Used by permission.

radiating fracture on the right side of the frontal bone, terminating at the coronal suture. This trauma would have been almost instantaneously fatal.

The postcranial skeletons of the Chaironeia warriors are less well represented in the collection, suggesting that there was less obvious trauma on these bones. The single femur collected from Chaironeia has a deep chop or cut on the anterior surface above the knee that is not unusual for battle-related trauma. The direction of the cut was from above, penetrating the soft tissue and ending in a hinge fracture.

The tibiae, or shinbones show a pattern of injuries that are unlikely to have occurred in battle. These bones have cuts that appear to be intended to sever the feet, and the angle and depth of the cuts suggests that the victims were lying prone at the time. Two tibiae from different individuals have single deep cuts that appear to be the result of a blow aimed at the shin. One is located on the anterior surface and nearly severed the leg. This would be difficult to accomplish unless the leg were lying on a fixed surface. Another tibia exhibits at least three chopping cuts in one location just below the midpoint of the bone that resemble an attempt to cut down a small tree (see Figure 7.3). As it is unlikely that even the most stoic of Theban hoplites would stand still while an assailant hacked away at his shin, landing three blows in the same place, this presumably took place after the victim was dead or unconscious.

From a third individual, there is a single pair of articulated feet, cleanly severed above the ankles, buried together and removed en bloc during the excavations. The description of the bones removed by Phytalis (1881) notes that these feet were found outside of the peribolos of the Lion Monument, suggesting that they had perhaps been found later and brought to the burial place. The preservation of nearly perfect anatomical order of the bones, and the clean, sharp appearance of the cuts through the tibiae and fibulae confirm that the feet were severed in the perimortem period and not as part of the excavation of the site. A third isolated partial foot may also be the result of perimortem amputation, but the evidence is not as clear.

Figure 7.3 Anterior tibia (shin bone) from Chaironeia. Arrows indicate location of three blade wounds striking near the same point. *Source:* Author. Used by permission.

The single combatant from the Athenian Agora excavations who died in the Herulian attack, AA 77, shows a slightly different pattern of injuries from those who died in hoplite and cavalry battle at Chaironeia. The evidence suggests he had previously engaged in conflict. There is an actively healing blade wound on the lateral surface of his right ulna, in a location that may be associated with an attempt to parry a blow aimed at the head. The spongy disorganized bone here is indicative of early stages of healing, suggesting a wound that was sustained perhaps two to three weeks before death (see Figure 7.4). This is a serious blade injury, probably caused by a large, heavy blade such as a sword. Before reaching Athens, the Heruli had moved down from the Black Sea, passing through the Hellespont, sacking and pillaging as they went. A healing battle wound, therefore, is more likely to be found on one of the marauders than a local Athenian.

While he survived one serious injury, it appears that in Athens this man's luck ran out. Around the time of his death, he sustained one or more blows to the face, fracturing his upper jaw and knocking out his central incisors. A blow to the right side of his nose produced fractures that extended into his right eye orbit as well, possibly causing a "blow out" of the eyeball. While devastatingly painful and bloody, none of these injuries is likely to have been immediately fatal, and there are no further injuries to his skull; most of the trauma on this skeleton is in the postcranial region.

There are at least four significant perimortem blade wounds, involving his right and left upper arms, the left lower arm and the left lower leg. In addition, there are areas of damage to the right shoulder and left elbow that also appear to be perimortem injuries. The combination of these wounds would have left him completely incapacitated and bleeding profusely. Although not one of

Figure 7.4   Right ulna (lower arm bone) of an adult male killed in the Herulian sack of Athens. Arrow indicates a partially healed blade wound. *Source:* Author. Used by permission.

these injuries would be immediately fatal, the complete lack of healing on the wounds indicates that he did not survive the attack.

Finally, there are three areas of curious puncture wounds, on his back and both knees. The clearest injury is on the right tibia, where a spike has penetrated the bone completely, passing from the medial surface just below the knee joint to the lateral surface, and pushing a fragment of the cortical bone into the interior of the bone. On the corresponding right femur, just above the knee, there is a small notch or scrape, as if a similar object damaged the anterior surface. The other knee has a pair of scrapes that appear to be caused by a similar double-pronged instrument, causing two wounds 5–6 cm apart. In two places on the vertebrae, there are also damaged areas that again appear to have been caused by a two-pronged instrument, producing punctures also 5–6 cm apart. The impact of this tool or weapon can be seen in two places on the middle of the spine, and the fifth lumbar vertebra at the base of the spine was punctured in two places.

These puncture wounds do not appear to be typical battle injuries, and may have occurred through handling the corpse in the aftermath of the attack. There are examples of Roman-era agricultural tools with a pair of prongs that could have caused this damage (Painter 1961, Fig. XLIXa). Such an instrument may have been used to roughly move the corpse from the place where he was killed to the well where he was deposited, not unlike the use of a hook to drag the corpse of a slain gladiator from the arena. The mosaic of trauma exhibited by this man presents a pattern that best fits an invading Herulian, recovering from a wound received earlier in that expedition, killed in Athens, and further mutilated after death by angry survivors, who were forced to dispose of the attacker's body.

Evidence for Battle Injuries: Non-Combatants

In any war, there are deaths among those who do not participate directly in the fighting. Non-combatants, particularly women and children, are likely to be victims in urban warfare. The bodies of five such individuals, three women and two children, were found in wells in the Athenian Agora, in association with debris from the post-sack clean-up of Athens. Although it is impossible to determine at what point during the attack of the city they were killed, there is little doubt that their deaths were grim. The patterns of trauma seen in the bodies associated with the Herulian sack of Athens show a preponderance of cranial injuries. The non-combatants all sustained significant facial fractures. The children have potentially fatal head trauma and the adults also exhibit blade trauma, although for two of them this was probably not the cause of death, which instead was probably the result of additional blunt force cranial trauma.

The three women all received blows to the left side of the face resulting in massive fracturing. In two of the women, AA 13 and AA 14, whose bodies were found together in a single well, the left cheekbones and eye sockets were fractured. AA 13's face separated along the midline, and there were fractures extending through the cranial base, possibly from a blow to the back of the head. These alone would almost certainly have proved fatal; the hemorrhaging associated with these cranial base fractures is almost certainly her cause of death. However, there also are four sharp force wounds on the top of her skull (see Figure 7.5). These cut marks were made in fresh, not dried bone, probably with an instrument similar to an axe or hatchet. The deep slice on one side of the cut, and the rough surface on the opposing edge, where a fragment of bone was levered away by the blade, is commonly seen in cranial injuries inflicted with a heavy bladed instrument, such as an axe. Shallow secondary impacts suggest the blade bounced against the skull after two of the blows.

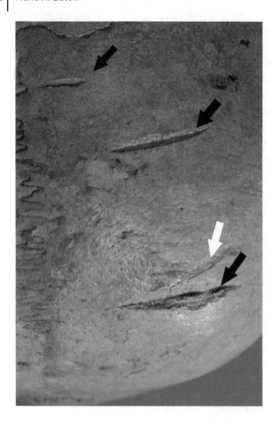

Figure 7.5 Skull of a woman killed in the Herulian sack of Athens, showing primary blows (black arrows) to the head with a bladed weapon such as an axe, and a secondary wound (white arrow) caused by the blade bouncing off the head. *Source:* Author. Used by permission.

The second adult female, AA 14, also suffered major blunt force trauma to the right side of her face. Portions of the right cheekbone, palate, nasal region, and eye orbit are all separated from the skull. However, the right nasal concha, arguably the most fragile bone in the skeleton, remains intact. This, together with the beveled fractures on bone surfaces, indicates that the damage occurred while the bone was fresh, and the nasal structures were supported and protected by soft tissue.

Like the previous victim of this attack, there is evidence of blade wounds as well as blunt trauma on this skull. A deep triangular cut on the inferior angle of the mandible is an indication that this woman's throat was cut. The pattern of a sharp clear cut on the inner surface and a more ragged outer edge is indicative of the direction of the blade's movement. The blade was drawn across the throat from left to right, angling upward toward the right, where it nicked the mandible at the end of the stroke.

The third woman, AA 20, found in another well, suffered a complete comminuted fracture (a break that produces separate fragments, or has multiple fracture lines) just left of the midline of her mandible from a blow which also fractured the temporo-mandibular joint. She also has a perimortem comminuted fracture of her right femur, just above the knee. In an adult without osteoporosis, such a fracture is almost always the result of high energy trauma (Galloway et al. 1999). She also has a single blade wound, a shallow oblique cut on her scapular spine, and a possibly associated fracture of the joint surface at the shoulder. None of these wounds would be immediately fatal, and it is not possible to determine how this woman died, but her body was placed in a well on top of a mass of destruction debris from the Herulian sack, so she presumably also died from violent trauma sustained in the attack.

In two other wells, children's skeletons were found in association with debris from the Herulian sack. Both are possibly male, one aged seven to eight years, the other four to five years at death. The older child, AA 77, suffered massive trauma to the right side of the skull. There is a concentric beveled fracture on the posterior right parietal bone, indicating a point of impact. The entire temporal bone separated from the skull. Fracture lines extend across the base of the skull along the sutures. This degree of trauma is probably not survivable, even with modern medical care.

The younger child, AA 315, exhibits blunt force trauma to the right side of the face. The zygomatic arch of the cheekbone and portions of the right maxilla separated from the skull. Fracture lines extend up to the top of the nose and across the eye orbit. There is also extensive damage to the alveolar bone in the area of the upper incisor teeth. While this level of damage is potentially survivable today, there probably was significant intracranial hemorrhage which could be fatal. There is, of course, no way to tell what additional soft tissue injuries were present in this and the other cases.

Discussion and Conclusions

The skeletal injuries seen at Chaironeia and the Herulian attack on Athens offer grim testimony to the violence of ancient warfare. Massive cranial trauma killed many, both combatants and bystanders. In many cases there is evidence of excessive violence, with multiple injuries inflicted on individuals who were probably already dead or dying. The multiple head wounds on three of the hoplites' skulls from Chaironeia and the women from the Agora attest to the ferocity of the attacks. The number of wounds inflicted on the Herulian attacker suggests the aggression of the Athenian response.

The pattern of injuries provides evidence to the conduct of battle, particularly at Chaironeia. Although Plutarch (*Pel.* 18.5) described Philip II viewing the bodies of the Sacred Band in the place where they had met with the *sarissas* of his army, it is clear that many died not in an initial clash between spear-bearing hoplites, but in the aftermath of hand-to-hand combat, facing enemies wielding swords.

Just how, and by whom, those swords were applied has been the subject of some debate. Accounts of the battle of Chaironeia indicate that the Theban Sacred Band faced the Macedonian left, anchored by Alexander and the cavalry. The degree to which these cavalry had a significant role in the defeat of the Sacred Band is the subject of some debate, generally centering on the whether or not the Macedonian cavalry carried *sarissas*, and if the cavalry was effective against the hoplite phalanx and in the destruction of the Sacred Band (Markle 1978; Rahe 1981).

The nature of the wounds on the Theban dead provides some evidence in this debate. The sharp force trauma wounds on the skulls from Chaironeia are consistently on the top of the head. Evidence from other pre-modern battles, where men armed with swords are facing each other on foot, clearly shows that most of the blows fall on the sides of the head, not the apex (Novak 2000). At Chaironeia all of the sharp force trauma on these skulls resulted from blades directed downward toward the top of the skulls with considerable force. The angle of all but one of the injuries suggests the assailants were above their victims, or at least were reaching high above their heads before inflicting the blow. There are no cranial blade wounds caused by a horizontal or upwardly angled strike. The blades sliced directly into the skull, perpendicular to the surface of the bone, and did not slide or drag downward, as might happen if the assailant were at the same level as the target. This in turn suggests that the blows could have been inflicted by mounted cavalry or the soldiers were kneeling at the time they were struck.

Likewise, there is interest among historians in the evolution of Greek warfare, from the individual combats of Homeric heroes to the emergence and use of the hoplite phalanx. The evidence of sword wounds also supports the idea that, despite the development of the organized phalanx, in the end, hoplite battle remained a series of individual encounters (Krentz 1985). It would be helpful if we had all of the skeletons from the Lion Monument to examine for wounds, but the pattern seen in the examples that are preserved indicates that the fatal wounds are blade wounds inflicted on the head from above or blunt force trauma to the face in face-to-face combat.

The apparent attempts to sever the feet of fallen hoplites also provide evidence for behavior in the aftermath of battle. Insulting a corpse or taking body parts as trophies is a practice documented in many cultures. However, the ancient literature of Greek warfare insists that mutilation of the corpses of defeated enemies was done only by barbarians. The presence of what may be incidents of mutilation by the Macedonian forces at Chaironeia may be indicative of one of the many differences that made Macedonians not-quite-Greek in the eyes of the more southern poleis. Alternatively, these severed and nearly severed feet may represent a practice intended not to mutilate a corpse for trophies, but to ensure that wounded enemies did not survive to fight again – although there are easier ways to kill a downed man.

One final aspect of hoplite battle is suggested by the wounds, and the patterns of injury may be instructive. The two areas of the body from which we have samples, the head and the lower legs, are two areas that could have been protected by sturdy armor attached to the body, namely a helmet and greaves. Yet there is evidence of significant wounds on these areas, indicating that the soldiers were not wearing helmets or greaves at the time of their deaths. There is evidence that the use of armor declined through time, and that by the time of the Battle of Chaironeia, few hoplites were wearing bronze body armor (Krentz 1985). Helmets, either of bronze or hardened leather were probably still in extensive use, but at the time of their deaths, some of the hoplites from Chaironeia were no longer wearing effective headgear. The mutilation of the legs was probably postmortem, so greaves could have been removed by the attacker.

The sample of bones available for study from these battles is small. Nevertheless, the patterns of injury in these individuals contribute to the study of ancient warfare. There is evidence for a variety of types of weapons, and indications of the patterns of how these are used. There is also evidence for the mutilation of the bodies of fallen soldiers, and brutal treatment of women and children in urban battles. The careful analysis of skeletal remains associated with battle can contribute significantly to our understanding of the conduct of ancient battles and its impact on both soldiers and non-combatants.

Note

1 Ma's (2008, p. 82) creative description of this wound as a *coup de grâce* following the cranial sword cut assigns both greater intent and a more definitive sequence of events than the skeletal evidence allows.

References

Bennike, P. (2008). "Trauma." In: *Advances in Human Paleopathology* (eds. R. Pinhasi and S. Mays), 309–328. Chichester, UK: Wiley & Sons, Ltd.

Buikstra, J. and Ubelaker, D. (eds.) (1994). *Standards for Data Collection from Human Skeletal Remains*. Fayetteville, AR: Arkansas Archeological Survey.

Chioti, L. (2018). "The Herulian invasion in Athens (A.D. 267). Contributions to the study of the invasions, implications, and the city's reconstitution until the end of the 4th century." PhD thesis. University of Athens.

Forbes, S., Stuart, B., and Dent, B. (2005). "The effect of the burial environment on Adipocere formation." *Forensic Science International* 154: 24–34.

Franz, A. (1988). *Late Antiquity: A.D. 267-700. Excavations in the Athenian Agora*, vol. XXIV. Princeton: The American School of Classical Studies at Athens.

Galloway, A., Symes, S., Haglund, W., and France, D. (1999). "The role of forensic anthropology in trauma analysis." In: *Broken Bones: Skeletal Analysis of Blunt Force Trauma* (ed. A. Galloway), 5–31. Springfield: C.C. Thomas Publisher.

Golubović, S., Mrdjić, N., and Speal, C.S. (2009). "Killed by the arrow: grave no. 152 from Viminacium." In: *Waffen in Aktion (ROMEC XVI)* (eds. A. Busch and H.-J. Schalles), 55–63. Mainz: Philipp Von Zabern.

Heather, P. (1998). "Disappearing and reappearing tribes." In: *Strategies of Distinction: The Construction of Ethnic Communities, 300–800* (eds. W. Pohl and H. Reimitz), 95–111. Leiden: Brill.

Judd, M. (2004). "Trauma in the city of Kerma: ancient versus modern injury." *International Journal of Osteoarchaeology* 14: 34–51.

Judd, M. and Redfern, R. (2012). "Trauma." In: *A Companion to Paleopathology* (ed. A.L. Grauer), 359–379. Chichester, UK: Wiley Blackwell.

Kanz, F. and Grossschmidt, K. (2006). "Head injuries of Roman gladiators." *Forensic Science International* 160: 207–216.

Krentz, P. (1985). "The nature of hoplite battle." *Classical Antiquity* 4: 50–61.

Lee, J.W.I. (2010). "Urban warfare in the Classical Greek world." In: *Makers of Ancient Strategy: From the Persian Wars to the Fall of Rome* (ed. V.D. Hanson), 139–162. Princeton: Princeton University Press.

Lendon, J.E. (2005). *Soldiers and Ghosts: A History of Battle in Classical Antiquity*. New Haven, CT: Yale University Press.

Ma, J. (2008). "Chaironeia 338: topographies of commemoration." *The Journal of Hellenic Studies* 128: 72–91.

Markle, M. (1977). "The Macedonian sarissa, spear, and related armor." *American Journal of Archaeology* 81: 323–339.

Markle, M. (1978). "The use of the sarissa by Philip and Alexander of Macedon." *American Journal of Archaeology* 81: 483–497.

Novak, S. (2000). "Battle-related trauma." In: *Blood Red Roses: The Archaeology of a Mass Grave from the Battle of Towton AD 1461* (eds. V. Fiorato, A. Boylston and C. Knüsel), 90–102. Oxford: Oxbow Books.

Painter, K. (1961). "Roman iron implements from London." *British Museum Quarterly* 23: 115–118.

Phytalis, L. (1881). "Ereunai en to Poluandrio Chaironeia." *Athenaion* 9: 347–352.

Pritchett, W.K. (1958). "Observations on Chaironeia." *American Journal of Archaeology* 61: 307–311.

Rahe, P. (1981). "The annihilation of the Sacred Band at Chaeronea." *American Journal of Archaeology* 85: 84–87.

Roberts, C. and Manchester, K. (2010). *The Archaeology of Disease*, 3e. Stroud, UK: Sutton.

Smith, S.K. (1998). "A biocultural analysis of social status in Mycenaean (late Bronze Age) Athens, Greece." PhD dissertation. Department of Anthropology, Indiana University.

Smith, S.K. and Liston, M. (2013). "Conflicting evidence of warfare in Mycenaean Athens, Greece: bodies vs. bronzes." Presented at the Annual Meeting of the American Association of Physical Anthropologists, Knoxville, TN, 12 April 2013.

Soteriades, G. (1903). "Das Schlachtfeld von Chäronea und der Grabhügel der Makedonen." *Mitteilungen des Deutschen Archäologischen Instituts, Athenische Abteilung* 28: 301–330.

Tritle, L. (2009). "Inside the hoplite agony." *Ancient History Bulletin* 23: 50–68.

Willey, P. and Emerson, T. (1993). "The osteology and archaeology of the Crow Creek massacre." *The Plains Anthropologist* 38: 227–269.

Williamson, M., Johnston, C., Symes, S., and Schultz, J. (2003). "Interpersonal violence between 18th century native Americans and Europeans in Ohio." *American Journal of Physical Anthropology* 122: 113–122.

Wilson, G.E. (1971). "The Herulian sack of Athens, A.D. 267." PhD dissertation. University of Washington.

Further Reading

Grauer, A.L. (ed.) (2012). *A Companion to Paleopathology*. Chichester, UK: Wiley Blackwell.

Katzenberg, M.A. and Saunders, S.R. (eds.) (2000). *Biological Anthropology of the Human Skeleton*. New York: Wiley-Liss.

Kimmerlee, E.H. and Baraybar, J.P. (eds.) (2008). *Skeletal Trauma: Identification of Injuries Resulting from Human Rights Abuse and Armed Conflict*. Boca Raton, FL: CRC Press.

Lovell, N.C. (1997). "Trauma analysis in paleopathology." *Yearbook of Physical Anthropology* 40: 139–170.

Martin, D.L. and Harrod, R.P. (2012). "Body parts and parts of bodies: traces of violence in past cultures." *International Journal of Paleopathology* 2 (2–3): 49–52.

Martin, D.L., Harrod, R.P., and Ventura, R. (2012). *The Bioarchaeology of Violence*. Gainesville: University Press of Florida.

Wedel, V. and Galloway, A. (eds.) (2014). *Broken Bones: Skeletal Analysis of Blunt Force Trauma*, 2e. Springfield, IL: C.C. Thomas.

Part II

Rome

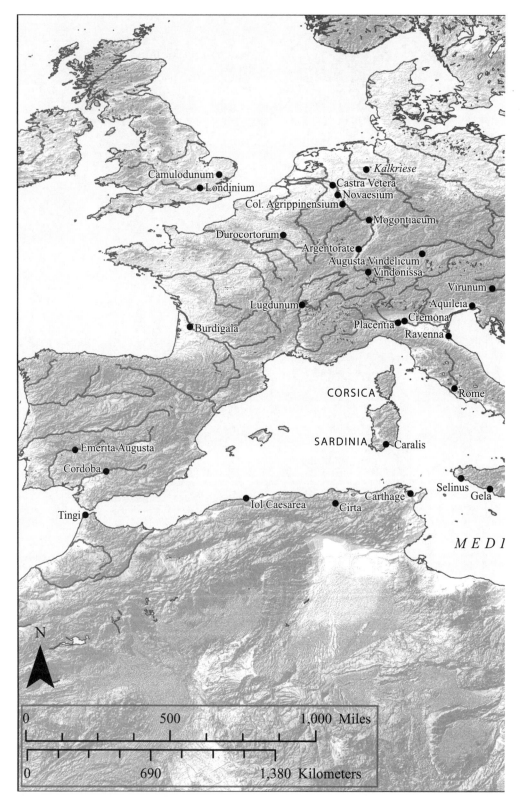

Map Pt.2 Ancient Roman Empire. *Source:* Ancient World Mapping Center © 2015 (awmc.unc.edu). Used by permission.

8

Financing Imperialism in the Middle Roman Republic
Nathan Rosenstein

Three pillars supported the armies that conquered Italy, defeated Hannibal, and extended the Republic's sway across the Mediterranean in the century and a half between c. 300 and 146.[1] These pillars were manpower, marriage patterns, and money.

Manpower

The first pillar was simply overwhelming manpower. Over the course of the late fourth and third centuries, Rome's practice of imposing its citizenship on some of its allies and requiring contingents of soldiers from the rest created a military potential unparalleled in the ancient west. The Greek historian Polybius in his account of the Gallic crisis of 225 preserves a detailed catalogue of the forces that Rome could call upon to oppose a massive raiding party from the north of Italy (2.24.1–17). Although his figures are not without problems, on the most conservative interpretation their total is breathtaking: over 600,000 Roman and allied men capable of bearing arms. Other scholars would put the figure even higher. Those numbers gave Rome the ability to absorb punishing defeats and yet continue the fight until it ultimately prevailed. And it could field multiple armies to campaign simultaneously in different theaters. These two strengths proved the key both to defeating Hannibal and then to the explosive extension of the Republic's hegemony in the Greek east, Spain, and northern Italy during the early decades of the second century.

Marriage Patterns

Yet realizing this vast military potential depended on a second factor: patterns of Italian family formation. The population from which Rome drew its soldiers was overwhelmingly rural. Recruits were members of families many of which lived on small farms and grew the food they needed primarily through their own labor. Conscripting soldiers for periods longer than the relatively brief period in the summer when the demands of agriculture slackened could have deprived those families of the men they needed to work their land and so threatened their survival. On the other hand limiting military campaigns to those few weeks in the summer would have made distant wars in Spain or Greece impossible to say nothing of the long struggle to defeat Hannibal. However, Roman

New Approaches to Greek and Roman Warfare, First Edition. Edited by Lee L. Brice.

and Italian men typically married for the first time in their late 20s or early 30s while their military service began around age 17. Therefore, during the 10–15 years before they wed and took on the responsibility for providing most of the heavy agricultural labor necessary to feed their new wives and children, young men could be drafted for long periods of military service without threatening the viability of the farms and natal families they left behind, particularly those whose fathers were still living. Yet even in families were the father had died, women and children were capable of doing field-work in a pinch should their sons go off to war. Indeed the challenge facing most families on the smallest farms was not a shortage of labor but too many mouths to feed compared to the amount of land available to support them. Conscripting a young man for several years of military service in effect brought the productive capacity of those farms into closer balance with their families' food requirements (Rosenstein 2004, pp. 63–106).

The Republic's ability to mobilize so many soldiers for months and often years at a stretch meant that its military capabilities were not only quantitatively superior to their opponents' but often qualitatively as well. The Romans could train the forces they put into the field to a much higher degree than would have been the case with armies assembled for only a few weeks during the summer. P. Cornelius Scipio (soon to be "Africanus") devoted the whole of 205 BCE to training the army he would lead to Africa in the final showdown with Carthage in the following year (Livy 29.22.2). His effort may represent an exceptional case, but his homonymous father, consul thirteen years earlier, believed that he could substantially improve the legions of recent recruits facing Hannibal in northern Italy by a winter's training (Polyb. 3.70.4). At an even more basic level, long daily marches in formation and the labor of fortifying marching camps every afternoon conditioned the soldiers to withstand the physical rigors of hand-to-hand combat and imparted the discipline, obedience to orders, and teamwork that battle would require. Africanus' grandson, likewise a P. Cornelius Scipio Africanus, imposed just these remedies when he took command of a defeated and dispirited army in Spain in 134 and transformed it into the force that would finally conquer Numantia (App. *Hisp.* 86). And that fact that the Republic's armies typically spent long years at war meant that they contained many veterans whose experience of battle and skill at arms gave them an exceptionally high degree of effectiveness in combat.

Broader advantages accrued as well. Strategy could dictate the length and timing of campaigns rather than being constrained by the requirements of the farming cycle. Agriculture then became a vulnerability that the Republic could exploit. Armies that could stay in the field for months or even years on end were able to bring intense pressure to bear on their enemies by disrupting the planting and harvesting of their crops and so threaten them with starvation. During the middle years of the Second Punic War the legions so thoroughly dominated the countryside around Hannibal's ally, Capua, defeating its forces and forcing the population to remain within the protection of its walls that by 212 they had prevented the Capuans from planting their crops and famine loomed (Livy 25.13.1–2). A Roman army's ability to deny the enemy access to its fields confronted it with a difficult choice: either march out to challenge the Romans in order to regain control of the crop land, or withstand a siege. The former course meant facing a well-trained, battle-tested, and highly effective army in combat, and the odds of prevailing were never good. Yet even in the unlikely event the enemy won a victory, a single defeat never stopped Rome for long. Its deep manpower reserves allowed it to return again and again until it finally triumphed. However, the second alternative was no better. The Republic's ability to recruit its armies from among men whose labor could be spared on their farms meant that if its forces could not storm a city, they could maintain a siege for months or even years on end if needs be until the enemy finally exhausted its food stores and was forced to capitulate. Either case typically eventuated in a brutal sack. Often, therefore, surrender before an assault began and an appeal to the victors' mercy came to seem an enemy's only viable option.

Money

Still, manpower and marriage patterns by themselves were not enough. Armies in the field for many months had to be fed, armed, and clothed, and something had to entice the men who would undertake far-off wars to leave their homes and undergo the dangers and hardships involved. Money met both needs. By the later fourth century, if not earlier, the Republic was paying its legionaries, and Rome's allies did the same for the soldiers they sent to serve alongside them. Pay, *stipendium*, enabled Roman soldiers to buy food and, for those who needed them, clothing and equipment. The same was true for allied troops, the *socii*, save that Rome supplied them with grain rations at no charge. Paying its soldiers enabled Rome to realize the potential for long military service that Italian marriage patterns created, and it provided an enticement for recruits to come forward to serve. Neither Rome nor its allies possessed the bureaucracy or police forces that would have been necessary to conscript unwilling recruits. Soldiers had to be willing to serve, and money provided a major enticement. And while the prospect of booty was the principal lure, gain from that source was never guaranteed; the *stipendium*, however, was certain. We do not know how much of his pay an average legionary might have had left once stoppages for food, clothing, and equipment had been withheld, and we have no information at all to tell us how much allied soldiers were paid. But that the soldiers who fought Rome's wars had money to spend is evident in the camp followers who regularly accompanied them on their campaigns. Sutlers sold food and other items to the troops while fortune-tellers, prostitutes, and others met additional needs in exchange for cash. And on at least one occasion soldiers with money in their purses are found traveling around the countryside apparently pursuing private trading ventures while the army was camped for the winter, suggesting that the savings they could accumulate from pay and booty were substantial (Livy 33.29.4). However, while pay for the troops and food for the allies probably represented the bulk of the Republic's military budget, other costs were not insubstantial. Tents and other equipment along with the army's food rations; a massive number of mules to carry it all; muleteers to drive the animals; and a variety of other non-combatants, including perhaps even publicly owned slaves – all had to be fed and paid for. The Republic also had to bear the cost of transporting grain and other items from their sources to the magazines whence mules took them to the army. And a variety of miscellaneous expenses required a supply of cash on hand to meet them. It is no surprise, therefore, that those in command of Rome's armies left the city with substantial war-chests. The elder P. Cornelius Scipio Africanus had arrived in Spain in 210 to take command there with 400 talents of silver – over 10 metric tons (Polyb. 10.19.2).

Given the vital importance of money in sustaining Roman military power, where did it come from? Most immediately, from the *tributum* (Nicolet 1980, pp. 149–169). This was a levy on all *assidui* – Roman citizens whose wealth qualified them for military service – who were not currently serving in the legions. The *tributum* funded the soldiers' pay and the other expenses of the Republic's wars. It was not a true tax, however, but something like a compulsory loan that could be repaid when the spoils of victory permitted, as famously happened in 187 when the riches that Manlius Vulso brought back from Asia Minor enabled the senate to order the repayment of all arrears still owing from *tributum* previously collected (Livy 39.7.4–5). Moreover the *tributum* was not fixed but variable. The sum required from each *assiduus* depended on the military expenses anticipated for that year and what proportion of them the senators believed funds already in the treasury could meet. In 167, with the spoils from Macedon safely tucked away in the treasury, the senate could suspend collection of the *tributum* indefinitely (Plin. *HN* 33.56). Presumably, therefore, in other years, when victories had left the public coffers bulging, the senate could elect to reduce or even forgo collection of the *tributum*. If so, then the question becomes to what extent

Rome's wars paid for themselves: how often, in other words, had prior victories brought so much money into the treasury that no *tributum* had to be collected for the coming year? How often could *tributum* previously collected be repaid?

Pretty regularly, one might suppose, in view of Livy's reports of the enormous wealth displayed in the triumphs of generals returning to Rome after victories in the first third of the second century. The Romans and especially their generals attached enormous importance to their spoils: they came first in the triumphal procession. They measured the magnitude of the victory and so gauged the glory accruing to the army's commander. The sums were recorded and preserved in the archives and even at times on stone, as in the inscription that trumpeted C. Duilius' victories over Carthaginian forces in 260 and the money he brought back to Rome (*CIL* I^2 25 line 17 = *Remains of Old Latin* 4.128–131). The spoils displayed in triumphs celebrated between 200 and 167 and the indemnities some of the vanquished paid in addition make it possible to calculate the value of these victories. On the basis of such evidence scholars have often assumed that Rome's acquisition of an empire in the third and second centuries naturally turned a profit. As one eminent historian puts it, "expansion before the Second Punic War had greatly increased public revenues without a comparable increase in regular liabilities. Once the war was over, the impression must have returned to senatorial minds that in general both war and expansion were profitable to the state" (Harris 1979, pp. 68–69).

War: Expenses vs Income

However, to gauge the profitability of Roman warfare, we need to know its costs, and we have no way to determine the expenses incurred in winning a victory and so no ability to decide whether it was won at a profit or a loss (Frank 1933, 1.126-46). We lack evidence for what it costs to equip and maintain Rome's armies to say nothing of the numbers and pay of the support personnel who accompanied them or the expense of transporting all this material. The costs of warships and their crews are completely unknown. And although Rome obtained much of the food for its armies and fleets after 241 through taxation in kind from Sicily, Sardinia, and eventually Spain, the amounts were never sufficient to meet all of its military's needs during the third and second centuries. In 191, as the senate prepared to embark upon its war against Antiochus the Great, it requisitioned double tithes of grain from Sicily and Sardinia for the two legions and fleet it was sending east, some 58,500 men. In addition it bought large amounts of grain from Carthage and Numidia, amounting to some 8700 metric tons (Livy 36.3.1, 4.1–10). It is unlikely, therefore, that the single tithe of their grain crop that Rome's Sicilian and Sardinian subjects normally paid as tribute came anywhere close to feeding the 104,000–117,000 legionaries and allies that the Republic normally fielded in the first third of the second century, much less the sailors in the fleets it from time to time launched, or even the four legions typically levied in the years prior to the Hannibalic war (Erdkamp 1998, pp. 89–90). In 225, the *patres* dispatched legates to Hiero, the ruler of Syracuse, to purchase grain in anticipation of its coming struggle against the Gauls (Diod. Sic. 25.14). Even Cato the Elder's famous boast in 195 that his war in Spain "will feed itself" came by way of explaining why he was sending away the merchants who had come to buy provisions for his army (*Bellum se ipsum alet*: Livy 34.9.12). Cato happened to be starting his operations when the harvest was being threshed so that his soldiers were easily able to capture enough grain to feed themselves during their campaign. But this was unusual. No army was able to "live off the land" for very long because in the Mediterranean grains like wheat and barley are ripe and therefore edible for only a few weeks in the early summer, and once their crops are harvested, farmers either hide them or store them behind city walls (Erdkamp 1998, pp. 94–102, 112–121; Roth 1999, pp. 224–232). For that reason, after Cato's campaign, the senate over the next 25 years regularly sent grain to support the troops stationed in Spain (Livy 40.35.4).

There is, however, one cost we can be relatively certain of, and that is legionary pay, the *stipendium*. Polybius reports (6.39.12) that an ordinary infantryman in the mid-second century earned two obols a day, a centurion four obols, and a cavalryman received a drachma. Conversion of this Greek currency into Roman money produces pay of three, six, and nine *asses* respectively (Crawford 1985, pp. 146–147; Rathbone 1993, pp. 151–152). These rates remained unchanged until Julius Caesar doubled army pay (Suet. *Iul.* 26.3), while the value of the legionaries' wages prior to the coinage reform of 212/211 that introduced the Polybian rates was probably about the same even though the legionaries earned fewer *asses*. This is because prior to 212 an *as* weighed ten ounces rather than two. Hence the weight of the bronze coins that a legionary received as his wage before 212 is likely to have been more or less equal to their weight subsequently. If that is so, since we know how many soldiers were in a legion and how many legions were mobilized every year, we can estimate the Republic's yearly outlay for *stipendium* during the third and second centuries. Those estimates in turn make it possible to compare at least this expense and the income Rome derived from booty and indemnities year. Even though the result will not yield the total cost of Roman warfare and so tell us whether or not Roman warfare was turning a profit, *stipendium* were undoubtedly one of the Republic's largest if not the largest military expense, certainly well over half of the cost in most years. So the degree to which income from war exceeded or fell short of it would at least serve as a very rough gauge of the profitability of conquest.

Between 200 and 167 spoils and indemnities as reported by Livy and other ancient authors amounted to over 267 million denarii. Total *stipendium* during the same period was about 171.5 million denarii, giving the Republic a net surplus of about 95.5 million denarii over *stipendium* from its wars or 56%. However, Rome deployed several armies each year during this period, and even though not all of them won victories and so produced income for the treasury they still had to be paid. Hence a mismatch between income from warfare and military expenses was a regular feature on the Republic's balance sheet, as Table 8.1 indicates. Equally important is the fact that the annual totals for profits given here include not only the money and precious metals that armies paraded in their triumphs but also the indemnities imposed on some of Rome's defeated foes. The sums involved were anything but trivial. Carthage had to pay 200 talents of silver every year (a talent weighed about 26 kg, so over five metric tons) for fifty years following its defeat in 201. After his defeat at Cynoscephalae in 197, Philip V was ordered to pay 500 talents at once and then 50 talents annually for ten years. Two years later, an indemnity of 100 talents immediately and then 50 talents a year for eight years was imposed on Nabis of Sparta as the price of peace. Likewise the Aitolians in 189 had to agree to a demand for 500 talents up front and 50 talents a year thereafter for eight years. These sums, as large as they were, pale in comparison to the whopping 3000 talents Antiochus the Great was forced to pay at once plus the additional dozen annual payments of 1000 talents each following his loss in 190 to the Scipios at Magnesia, 390 metric tons of silver in total. All of these indemnities together amounted to over 140 million denarii, that is over half of the surplus of spoils over *stipendium* that Rome's victories produced. Take them away, as in Table 8.2, and that surplus disappears, and the booty from Rome's wars falls short of the cost of *stipendium* by some 44.5 million denarii.

This fact is worth emphasizing because indemnity payments on this scale were rare before the second century. Rome made the Carthaginians pay 3200 talents over 10 years following their surrender in 241 and added another 1000 in 238 (Polyb. 1.62.9-63.3, 88.12). The ruler of Syracuse, Hiero, was mulcted 100 talents in 263, a portion of which, however, was later forgiven (Polyb. 1.16.9; Zon. 8.16). Otherwise, the record of Roman victories in the third century lacks evidence of

Table 8.1 Warfare income vs *stipendium*.

Year	NUMBER of legions	*Stipendium* (denarii)	Total income from war (denarii)
200	8	5,077,920	7,151,700
199	6	3,808,440	1,474,200
198	8	5,077,920	1,348,200
197	6	3,808,440	1,529,550
196	10	6,347,400	13,701,450
195	10	6,347,400	1,685,250
194	8	5,077,920	13,400,076
193	8	5,077,920	2,022,300
192	10	6,347,400	2,022,300
191	12	7,616,880	3,905,020
190	13	8,251,620	4,007,000
189	12	7,616,880	19,391,312
188	12	7,616,880	8,763,300
187	8	5,077,920	38,697,428
186	10	6,347,400	8,426,250
185	8	5,077,920	10,813,530
184	8	5,077,920	10,442,250
183	8	5,077,920	9,278,010
182	10	6,347,400	8,089,200
181	8	5,077,920	8,089,200
180	8	5,077,920	8,288,440
179	8	5,077,920	8,089,200
178	7	3,173,700	13,129,200
177	7	3,173,700	8,460,477
176	10	5,077,920	8,089,200
175	7	3,173,700	1,348,200
174	7	3,173,700	6,388,200
173	7	3,173,700	1,348,200
172	6	2,538,960	1,348,200
171	10	5,077,920	1,348,200
170	10	5,077,920	1,348,200
169	8	3,808,440	1,348,200
168	10	5,077,920	1,606,600
167	6	2,538,960	31,475,476
Totals		171,379,800	267,853,519

Table 8.2 Breakdown of indemnities as portion of spoils.

Year	Number of legions	*Stipendium* (denarii)	Total booty (denarii)	All indemnities (denarii)
200	8	5,077,920	5,803,500	1,348,200
199	6	3,808,440	126,000	1,348,200
198	8	5,077,920	0	1,348,200
197	6	3,808,440	181,350	1,348,200
196	10	6,347,400	12,353,250	1,348,200
195	10	6,347,400	0	1,685,250
194	8	5,077,920	11,377,776	2,022,300
193	8	5,077,920	0	2,022,300
192	10	6,347,400	0	2,022,300
191	12	7,616,880	1,882,720	2,022,300
190	13	8,251,620	1,984,700	2,022,300
189	12	7,616,880	17,706,062	1,685,250
188	12	7,616,880	0	8,763,300
187	8	5,077,920	29,934,128	8,763,300
186	10	6,347,400	0	8,426,250
185	8	5,077,920	2,387,280	8,426,250
184	8	5,077,920	2,016,000	8,426,250
183	8	5,077,920	851,760	8,426,250
182	10	6,347,400	0	8,089,200
181	8	5,077,920	0	8,089,200
180	8	5,077,920	199,240	8,089,200
179	8	5,077,920	0	8,089,200
178	7	3,173,700	5,040,000	8,089,200
177	7	3,173,700	371,277	8,089,200
176	10	5,077,920	0	8,089,200
175	7	3,173,700	0	1,348,200
174	7	3,173,700	5,040,000	1,348,200
173	7	3,173,700	0	1,348,200
172	6	2,538,960	0	1,348,200
171	10	5,077,920	0	1,348,200
170	10	5,077,920	0	1,348,200
169	8	3,808,440	0	1,348,200
168	10	5,077,920	258,400	1,348,200
167	6	2,538,960	30,127,276	1,348,200
Totals		171,379,800	127,640,719	140,212,800

big cash payments from defeated foes. More importantly, if we separate second century indemnities from the cash and precious metals that Rome's victories produced and compare the latter with the annual costs for *stipendium*, as in Table 8.2, it becomes immediately clear that only in rare instances, 8 out of 30 years, did booty apart from indemnity payments exceed the total cost of pay for all the legions in a given year. Yet even these exceptions need qualification. In 200, cash and precious metal booty in that year exceeded *stipendium* only because the total includes two triumphs. The same was true in 196 except that this year saw five triumphs celebrated. The booty that the Elder Cato displayed in his triumph in 194 did not match what Rome had spent on military pay in that year; only the enormous wealth that Flamininus brought back from Greece put the Republic's costs for *stipendium* in the black for that year. In fact, Flamininus' spoils by themselves exceeded the total cost of that year's *stipendium*, and the same was true of the other great eastern triumphs: Lucius Scipio's over Antiochus in 190; Fulvius Nobilior's over the Aitolians and Manlius Vulso's over the Gauls of Asia in 187; and of course most spectacularly Aemilius Paullus' over Perseus in 167. Otherwise, only the spoils that L. Postumius Albinus and Ap. Claudius Centho brought home in 178 and in 174 respectively from Spain exceeded the Republic's outlay for *stipendium* in these two years. Simply put, a few spectacularly rich victories in the East account for the positive balance between income and expenditure for *stipendium* in the first third of the second century, both because of the enormous wealth carried in the triumphs celebrated for them and because of the extraordinary indemnity payments they produced. Without them, Rome's acquisition of a Mediterranean-wide empire would have come at a loss, at least as far as the public treasury was concerned.

This conclusion sheds important light on the financial implications of Rome's wars prior to the second century. Between the later fourth century and the last years of the third Roman armies subjugated Italy and celebrated 89 triumphs in the process. We have no way of determining directly whether those victories between 337 and 218 produced enough booty to pay for all of the expenses Roman warfare in this period incurred, but additional evidence from the early second century triumphs is highly suggestive. As Table 8.3 indicates, only about half of all triumphs between 200 and 167 produced enough money in booty and indemnities to equal the *stipendium* of only those legions that won the victories that these triumphs celebrated (Rosenstein 2011). No Gallic victory is certain to have done so, and the same is definitely true of victories over the Ligurians. To be sure, the riches that Rome's eastern victories produced paid the future *stipendia* of many legions levied subsequently that failed to win any victory, but the same cannot be said of others, not even those won in Spain. The seven victories there between 200 and 178, when Tiberius Gracchus' settlement made the provinces self-supporting in terms of the Republic's military outlays, produced enough wealth to pay the *stipendia* not only of the eleven legions that won them but those of an additional 20 legions besides. But against these 31 *stipendia* we need to set the fact that Rome's military presence in Spain during these years required the expenditure of funds to pay the annual *stipendia* of 62 legions. Even here, in other words, the conquest and pacification of the two Spanish provinces required a greater outlay for military pay than the victories won there returned to the treasury.

Spain of course possessed an abundance of mineral wealth, as Polybius attests when he notes that in his day the silver mines around New Carthage alone produced some 25,000 denarii each day (34.9.8–9). That there was plenty of booty for Roman armies to capture is not surprising therefore. But Italy was nothing like so rich in precious metals, as the rarity of spoils from second century victories there that equaled the wages of the legions that won them reflects. And that in turn makes it difficult to believe that victories in Italy prior to 218 paid for themselves, still less turned a profit for Rome. Certainly, some must have produced substantial booty. In 306 the consul Q. Marius Tremulus is reported to have forced the Samnites to pay a year's *stipendium* for his soldiers (Livy 9.43.21, cf. Plin. *HN* 34.23 and Livy 9.43.8). In 292, Livy reports, the consul Sp. Carvilius

Table 8.3 *Stipendium* vs spoils.

Year	Triumphing Commander	Booty (denarii)	*Stipendium* (denarii)
200	Lentulus	567,000	3,174,125
200	Purpurio	133,500	1,269,216
199	Acidinus	126,000	3,808,046
197	Cethegus	102,750	1,269,216
197	Minucius	78,400	1,269,216
196	Blasio	2,987,100	1,903,824
196	Stertinius	4,200,000	1,903,824
196	Marcellus	266,600	1,269,216
196	Helvius	1,373,950	0
196	Thermus	3,274,200	0
194	Cato	3,939,000	1,269,216
194	Flamininus	7,438,776	5,067,824
191	Nobilior	1,244,680	1,269,216
191	Nasica	638,040	1,269,216
190	Glabrio	1,451,000	1,269,216
189	Scipio	17,706,062	1,269,216
187	Nobilior	8,037,928	2,538,432
187	Vulso	21,896,200	2,538,432
185	Acidinus	2,387,280	2,538,432
184	Piso and Crispinus	2,016,000	5,076,864
183	Varro	851,760	2,538,432
181	Paullus	0	2,648,659
180	Flaccus	199,240	2,538,432
180	Cethegus	0	1,324,329
180	Tamphilius	0	1,324,329
179	Flaccus	0	1,269,216
178	Gracchus	3,360,000	2,538,432
178	Albinus	168,000	2,538,432
177	Pulcher	371,277	2,538,432
174	Centho	5,040,000	634,825
168	Marcellus	258,400	2,538,432
167	Gallus	127,276	1,269,216
167	Paullus	30,000,000	1,495,487

Maximus did the same and also deposited 380,000 pounds of bronze into the treasury (Livy 10.46.12–14). The consul of 282, C. Fabricius Luscinus, according to Dionysius of Halicarnassus, claimed in a speech that he repaid the *tributum* to the citizens and brought 400 talents into the treasury after his victories over the Samnites, Lucanians, and Bruttians (19.16.3). Fabius Pictor asserted that the Romans first knew wealth when they conquered the Sabines (c. 290; frag. 20

Peter = Strabo 5.3.1), while Florus claimed the spoils from Pyrrhus and Tarentum were like nothing the Romans had ever seen before (1.13.25–28). Yet, generals could pride themselves on such accomplishments and Romans could recall them years later precisely because they were rare and so something worth boasting about. It is hard to believe, therefore, that Rome's Italian victories prior to the Hannibalic war were on average significantly richer than those afterwards.

Not even the First Punic War forms an exception to the general impression that Roman victories rarely paid for themselves (Rosenstein 2016). As noted above, Carthage paid 4200 talents as the price of peace in 241 and 238 while Hiero's indemnity amounted to some portion of 100 talents. In addition, Roman armies won a number of major victories that produced significant spoils, including Duilius' mentioned earlier (cf. Polyb. 1.23.1–24.1), those taken after the captures of Agrigentum in 263 (Polyb. 1.19.15), and of Panormus in 254 (Diod. Sic. 28.18.5), in the raid on Africa in 255 (Polyb. 1.29.6–10), and in a variety of lesser successes (e.g. Polyb. 1.24.10–13). Still, taken all together it is difficult to imagine that all this wealth equaled what the Republic expended on *stipendia*. On the assumption that Rome mobilized four legions in each of the 23 years of the conflict, the cost of their *stipendia* would have been over 50 million post-211 denarii. The Carthaginian indemnity on the other hand was the equivalent of 29.6 million post-211 denarii. Even adding spoils from the other victories it seems very unlikely that what came into the treasury as a result equaled, much less surpassed, what it had paid out for *stipendium*. And this takes no account of the hundreds of ships and thousands of sailors Rome mobilized in these years (Thiel 1954, pp. 83–94). It is small wonder then that when the senators determined to make a final push against Carthage in 242 they found the treasury empty and were forced to borrow funds to launch a new fleet (Polyb. 1.59.6–7). The Carthaginian indemnity may have repaid those loans but certainly not the arrears in *tributum* levied previously.

War: Greed as a Cause

If the argument presented above is correct, then it is very difficult to believe that the Republic's conquests between the later decades of the fourth century and 167 almost always paid for themselves when all the other costs of waging war – food, equipment, transport, support personnel, the occasional fleets launched with their crews – are added in. That conclusion in turn raises serious doubts about claims that greed was one of the main driving forces – if not the principal one – behind Rome's war-making during the middle Republic. Of course some individual Romans expected to gain wealth from war. Polybius reports that voters in the *comitia centuriata* readily approved a bill to dispatch an army to aid the Mamertines in 264 after the consuls emphasized the great plunder they could expect to capture (Polyb. 1.11.2). Not much had changed nearly a century later when Livy recounts how the levy in 172 was flooded with volunteers eager to sign up to fight the Third Macedonian War because they had seen those who had gone east to wage earlier wars there come back rich (42.32.6). And without doubt, some of the commanders and officers who led these wars as well as others expected a victory to fill their purses. But the voters declared wars on the advice of the senators, and greed is a more difficult motive to ascribe to either group. The latter numbered about 300, only a few of whom would lead an army in any given year. A few more might accompany an army as a legate or military tribune or anticipate that a brother, son, or other relative might do so. But the overwhelming majority would derive no personal financial benefit from a victory, at least not immediately. Instead, they will have understood, as they weighed the costs and benefits of urging the citizens to vote to declare war, that in all likelihood the financial gains a victory would produce would not equal what the Republic had spent to win it. And yet the senate never to our knowledge hesitated to undertake a war because of its costs. Even in 200 when the Republic had incurred huge debts in its struggle with Hannibal, debts which the treasury was unable to repay when they came due that year (Livy 31.13.1–9), the senators elected to undertake a new war with Philip V of Macedon and were adamant that the voters ratify a declaration of war even after the assembly had rejected the bill when it was first presented to them (Livy 31.6.3–8.1).

Equally surprising, the assembly's defeat of the war declaration in 200 was unprecedented and would never be repeated as far as we know. The assembly obediently passed the bill after the consul had harangued the citizens about the threat Philip posed and ordered them to vote again. Yet the fact that the booty from Rome's wars so rarely equaled their costs meant that the burden of paying for them rested squarely on the shoulders of the *assidui*, the *tributum*-paying citizens who voted to declare every war Rome fought. Why did they do it, when they must have known that the "loans" they advanced to the treasury stood little chance of ever being repaid? In 200, Livy represents consul as telling the voters in essence that they could either fight Philip in Greece or fight him in Italy, and there is a strong probability that the speech the historian composed reflects more or less the argument actually presented on that occasion (Eckstein 2006, pp. 257–288). If so, then citizens who had recently experienced the terrors of Hannibal's invasion of Italy might understandably have been persuaded to part with their hard-earned cash to forestall a similar horror. But one might reasonable wonder what possible threat the citizens could have imagined the Ligurians posed, or the Brutti, or the Lucanians. Some scholars have claimed that the Romans felt a strong moral obligation to live up to the rhetoric of friendship with various smaller powers that had sought their protection, and this may have been true up to a point. But again, did the desire to protect Rome's *amici* or punish those who challenged Roman honor really weigh more heavily with the voters than the punishment going to war would inflict on their purses? We simply do not know. Of course Rome's wars led to a massive increase in the *ager publicus*, the Republic's public land, which was open to all citizens to cultivate. But unless we assume that an unorganized mass of Romans flocked to newly conquered territories to live among a potentially hostile population whose former lands they were going to occupy, for which there is little evidence, the main way most citizens would have benefited from newly won territory was by participating in a colony. But colonies contained typically between 4000 and 6000 adult male settlers together with their families, not all of whom were Roman citizens, and the senate dispatched them only every few years (Rosenstein 2004, p. 60). Again, it is difficult to imagine that many voters in the assembly had high hopes of being one of them. The number of citizens in the third and early second centuries ranged between 200,000 and 350,000, so the odds of being chosen to participate were slim to vanishing. *Assidui* already owned farms, and the richest of them, whose votes carried the greatest weight in the *comitia centuriata* and who bore the heaviest burden of *tributum*, were the least likely to seek an opportunity to join a colony. No *assiduus* can have relished paying *tributum* while those rare occasions when it was repaid contributed to the popularity of the commander whose victory had made it possible. That was the reason why, in 187, the friends of Manlius Vulso urged the senate to use the enormous booty he had brought back to Rome from his eastern conquests to pay off the arrears still owing in *tributum* (Livy 39.7.4–5). Even Megadorus' lament in Plautus' play, *Aulularia*, over having to fork over a soldier's pay tells us that the playwright and his audience understood and could joke about the grumbling that accompanied the levying of *tributum* (Plaut. *Aul.* 508–531).

Conclusion

Answering these questions would take the discussion well beyond the scope of this chapter, but I hope at least to have shown that the economic health of the Republic's *assidui* was a vital foundation of its military power in the third and early second centuries. That fact ought to have made the prosperity of the citizenry a matter of serious concern to the senators, a conclusion that raises a number of intriguing questions, none more critical than this one: how – if at all – did the relationship between the senate and the *assidui* change after 167, when the vast wealth Rome gained from the final conquest of Macedon enabled the senate to suspend collection of the *tributum* indefinitely and the senators thereafter no longer had to depend on the *assidui* to finance the Republic's wars?

Note

1 All dates BCE. This chapter summarizes an argument more fully presented in Rosenstein 2016, to which the reader is referred for a complete citation of ancient sources and modern scholarship.

References

Crawford, M. (1985). *Coinage and Money under the Roman Republic. Italy and the Mediterranean Economy*. London: Methuen.

Eckstein, A. (2006). *Mediterranean Anarchy, Interstate War, and the Rise of Rome*. Berkeley: University of California Press.

Erdkamp, P. (1998). *Hunger and the Sword. Warfare and Food Supply in Roman Republican Wars (268–30 B.C.)*. Amsterdam: J.C. Gieben.

Frank, T. (1933). *An Economic Survey of Ancient Rome*. Baltimore, MD: Johns Hopkins University Press.

Harris, W. (1979). *War and Imperialism in Republican Rome, 327-70 B.C.* Oxford: Oxford University Press.

Nicolet, C. (1980). *The World of the Citizen in Republican Rome*. Berkeley: University of California Press.

Rathbone, D. (1993). "The census qualifications of the *Assidui* and the *Prima Classis*." In: *De Agricultura. In Memoriam Pieter Willem de Neeve (1945–1990)* (eds. H. Sancisi-Weerdenburg and H.C. Teitler), 121–152. Amsterdam: J.C. Gieben.

Rosenstein, N. (2004). *Rome at War. Farms, Families, and Death in the Middle Republic*. Chapel Hill, NC: University of North Carolina Press.

Rosenstein, N. (2011). "War, wealth, and consuls." In: *Consuls and Res Publica. Holding High Office in Republican Rome* (eds. H. Beck, A. Duplá, M. Jehne and F. Pina Polo), 133–158. Cambridge: Cambridge University Press.

Rosenstein, N. (2016). "*Bellum se ipsum alet?* Financing mid-republican imperialism." In: *Money and Power in the Roman Republic* (eds. H. Beck, M. Jehne and J. Serrati), 114–130. Brussels: Collection Latomus.

Roth, J. (1999). *The Logistics of the Roman Army at War (264 B.C.–A.D. 234)*. Leiden: Brill.

Thiel, J. (1954). *A History of Roman Sea Power before the Second Punic War*. Amsterdam: North Holland Publishing Company.

Further Reading

Nicolet, C. (1980). *The World of the Citizen in Republican Rome* (trans. P.S. Falla). University of California Press, esp. 149–69 on assessment and collection of *tributum*.

Rosenstein, N. (2004). *Rome at War: Farms, Families, and Death in the Middle Republic*. The University of North Carolina Press.

Rosenstein, N. (2016). "*Tributum* in the middle republic." In: Circum Mare: *Themes in Ancient Warfare* (ed. J. Armstrong), 80–97. Leiden: Brill.

Rosenstein, N. (2016). "*Bellum se ipsum alet?* Financing mid-republican imperialism." In: *Money and Power in the Roman Republic* (eds. H. Beck and J. Serrati), 114–130. Brussels: Collection Latomus.

Tan, J. (2017). *Power and Public Finance at Rome, 246-49 BCE*. Oxford: Oxford University Press.

Tan, J. (2020). "The *dilectus-tributum* system and the settlement of fourth century Italy." In: *Romans at War: Soldiers, Citizens, and Society in the Roman Republic* (eds. M. Fronda and J. Armstrong) 52–75. London: Routledge.

9

Indiscipline in the Roman Army of the Late Republic and Principate
Lee L. Brice

Between 400 BCE and 212 CE the area under Rome's control swelled from a small area in central Italy to include the entire Mediterranean world, much of Europe, Anatolia, and parts of Mesopotamia. Roman legions played a significant role in acquiring and maintaining this empire. The legions were so successful that early-modern military planners sought to copy the Roman "recipe" and forged modern military institutions in the Roman form (Goldsworthy 1996, p. 8). Roman military discipline has long been recognized by modern planners and ancient authors as a key component of Rome's military success.

It has been common for modern authors to write about how well-disciplined the Roman legions were (Keegan 1976, p. 68; Le Bohec 1994, pp. 60–61; Keppie 1998, pp. 197–198), but historians have shown that this image of the Republican and early Imperial legions is imperfect (Messer 1920; Gabba 1975; Pekáry 1987; Chrissanthos 2001; Brice 2011, 2015a). Discipline undoubtedly contributed to the success of the Roman legions, but like every other institution in ancient Rome, the military was a human institution and therefore subject to human flaws: it is only as consistent as the people who served at all levels. The Roman military relied on consistent order and discipline on the part of soldiers and officers; there were formalized rules and laws to enforce it. Military behavior contrary to this formal order is called indiscipline or military disobedience.[1] Even when we can accept the presence of such military problems, our understanding of indiscipline has been superficial. However, recent studies demonstrate how approaches based in sociology contribute to better understanding military disobedience. This chapter shows how careful reading of the ancient sources with an awareness of these new approaches reveals specific details about indiscipline that permit us to discuss episodes with more certainty and clarity.

Military Discipline

Any army that requires discipline to maintain order and ensure its own effectiveness in combat will be susceptible to indiscipline. Every ancient army that fought in formations depended on discipline. When modern readers think of military discipline, they often think in terms of punishments, regulations, and obedience to orders, but it is more complex than that. Military discipline is a network of control with physical, mental, and social elements that are reinforced with a matrix of positive rewards and negative sanctions. Discipline is not just about victory. These components

New Approaches to Greek and Roman Warfare, First Edition. Edited by Lee L. Brice.
© 2020 John Wiley & Sons, Inc. Published 2020 by John Wiley & Sons, Inc.

of control make it possible to maintain military order, allowing officers and commanders to manage and direct soldiers at all times (Brice 2011, pp. 36–41, 2015b, pp. 69–70).

Since soldiers are trained to work together under stress and in the efficient use of weapons, outbreaks of indiscipline have the potential to become extremely violent. Organized violence outside of combat was to be avoided. Training soldiers to maintain ranks, maneuver collectively, and even remain in battle requires that soldiers learn and become accustomed to a level of discipline. Military discipline is acquired and reinforced through various aspects of service including drilling, learning how the unit works in battle, getting to know one's comrades in arms, and becoming accustomed to the society of the army (MacMullen 1984, pp. 440–456; Phang 2008, pp. 37–73).[2]

A combination of Roman institutional rules and circumstances made violations of discipline less likely. An important part of these was the *sacramentum* or oath. Because soldiers took the *sacramentum* to remain loyal and obedient to commands for the duration of the conflict, any violation of discipline carried religious and legal sanctions including the possibility of death (*Dig.* 49.16.6).[3] In practice officers often adjusted punishments to match the severity of the offense, though there were commanders (e.g. Crassus) known for harsh punishments (e.g. decimation, Plut. *Crass.* 10.2–3). Supplementing these sanctions were the cultural norms and mores of Roman society and especially of the military (Phang 2008; Brice 2011, pp. 36–39, 2020, pp. 249–250). The fact that measures like the oath tended to be accepted by soldiers as mores worked against outbreaks of severe indiscipline. And yet, sometimes soldiers or officers became alienated from these institutional norms. When that occurred, they could break from established discipline in a few ways.

Analytical Tools

Investigating indiscipline is made difficult not only by our limited sources, but also by our traditional tools for analyzing military disobedience. Traditional examinations of this topic have focused on large incidents and narratives. We can hardly blame historians for previously focusing exclusively on mutiny – their toolbox for analyzing disorder contained only a hammer, so every incident looked like a nail. In the past, historians of the Roman army have relied exclusively on ancient source narratives and an understanding of Roman history to discuss indiscipline. Narratives are useful for describing episodes, but explanation of indiscipline was limited and often incomplete (Chrissanthos 2001; Keaveney 2007). However, military sociology, organizational behavior, and collective action provide definitions, models, and vocabulary that, coupled with careful historical analysis, permit us to examine and discuss mutinies and other forms of indiscipline with more precision and authority.

Varieties of Indiscipline

A fundamental problem in traditional examinations of indiscipline has been the apparent lack of a broadly accepted language with which to discuss disobedience by soldiers. However, looking beyond ancient history, we find military sociologists and military historians have developed a varied and useful vocabulary for describing and analyzing indiscipline. Reflecting the varied scale of these incidents, there is a wide array of Greek and Latin terms (e.g. ἀταξία – disorder, indiscipline; *seditio* – mutiny, revolt, insubordination; ταράσσω – to cause a disturbance; *discordia* – discord) to describe military disobedience. Modern scholarship uses a similar diversity of terms to provide differentiation of scale, significance, and standardization.[4]

Table 9.1 Matrix of indiscipline.

Types of indiscipline	Aims	Participants	Collective	Violence
Military conspiracy	Removal or death (or both) of leader(s) or superior officer(s)	Officers – initiated from within the military	Initiated by a small nuclear group	Yes
Mutiny	Direct opposition to established military authority	Soldiers, and sometimes low-ranking officers	Always	Yes (actual or threatened)
Expression of grievances	Protest grievances (real and illusory)	Soldiers, and sometimes officers in support	Always	No
Insubordination	Disobedience, cowardice, defection, desertion, and dereliction of duty	Military personnel	Not necessarily	Not necessarily

Source: Adapted from Brice 2015b, p. 75.

Organizational behavior studies provide an additional level of nuance that is helpful in explaining indiscipline. Protest movements in organizations (e.g. strikes) are usually one of two types, *promotion of interests* or *secession/seizure* movements. A promotion of interest movement is exactly what the name implies – limited to promoting or protecting participants' interests. In these movements leaders tend to seek support *before* taking action. A secession or seizure of power movement is only interested in getting out of or overturning the organization. A small group of leaders in these movements usually recruits support in the organization *after* taking action. Either movement can be peaceful or violent (Lammers 1969, pp. 559–563). These categories make it easier to understand the goals of the soldiers protesting.

Incidents of indiscipline can be described as one of four types: military conspiracy, mutiny, expression of grievances, and insubordination. The first two categories are the more serious manifestations of indiscipline because of violence. The other categories are not necessarily threatening in and of themselves, thus are not as well attested in the sources. Listed in roughly descending order of size and seriousness, these terms permit a more nuanced and realistic discussion of indiscipline in any military context, including the ancient world. In keeping with the military context these categories are not determined by the protesters' goals or the results, but by the participants and their methods of expressing their indiscipline. We can visualize the types of indiscipline along a matrix (see Table 9.1).

Military Conspiracy

Conspiracy was, from a leader's perspective, the most dangerous type of indiscipline. Other forms of military disobedience threatened discipline in the camp or in battle in exchange for achieving a limited goal, but conspiracies were intended to result in a leader's (or other officer's) removal or death, or both. Walter Kaegi in his work on the Byzantine military defined "military conspiracy" as, "the conscious combination of [military] men, often generals or their subordinate officers, for a *coup d'état* or revolt in the field," (Kaegi 1981, p. 4). If one accepts that a revolt in the field could include a plot by subordinates to remove a superior officer below the rank of emperor, then Kaegi's definition is broad enough to encompass a broad range of plots. Military conspiracy is a form of *secession/seizure of power* type of protest movement (Lammers 1969; Pondy 1969, pp. 501–502).

The Roman army was conducive to conspiracies due to the hierarchical distribution of power among officers, the importance of military success in Roman politics and culture, and after 31 BCE, the autocratic nature of the Empire. Because of the societal connection between the military and politics it is often not appropriate to separate these conspiracies from politics. Just because a conspiracy among military officers has political aspects does not make it any less a military conspiracy; but when the conspiracy is initiated from outside the military (e.g. Scribonianus' revolt in 42 CE), it becomes a different kind of opposition and is excluded from this examination of indiscipline.

Military conspiracies were not common, but examples can be found during the Republic and the Empire. In one example, P. Tullius Albinovanus engaged in military conspiracy in 82 BCE when he murdered some of his fellow officers before defecting to Sulla (App. *B Civ.* 1.91). In the case of the *Fimbriani*, the quaestor, C. Flavius Fimbria, conspired in 86 with other officers to murder the commander, L. Valerius Flaccus. Flaccus dismissed Fimbria on account of "criminality and undermining the commander's authority," but Fimbria returned, murdered Flaccus, and took command without opposition (Livy *Per.* 82; Strabo 13.l.27; Vell. Pat. 2.24.1; App. *Mithr.* 51–52; de Blois 2000, pp. 18–19; Wolff 2013). Cassius Chaerea and Cornelius Sabinus, tribunes in the Praetorian Guard, successfully conspired in 40 CE to murder Gaius Caesar (Caligula). They included other officers and only then secured support outside the military (Suet. *Calig.* 56.1; Cass. Dio 59.29; Jos. *JA* 19.18-114; Barrett 1989, pp. 91–113, 77–81, and 154–61; Pagán 2004, pp. 98–108). Clearly, military conspiracy was often lethal and had immense potential for disruption. However, it did not result in political chaos during the Republic or the first two centuries of the Empire.

Mutiny

A "mutiny" is defined here as collective, violent (actual or threatened), direct opposition to established military authority (Brice 2015b, pp. 71–72). Events included in this variety of military unrest are riots, tumults, disturbances, and similar incidents, as well as their incitement. In this definition, "mutiny" is always a collective action and nearly always refers to protests by regular soldiers – although some officers might participate in special cases. Mutiny may include open refusal to follow orders, but it is not limited to this offense. Although mutinies were not the most common (i.e. insubordination) or most dangerous (i.e. conspiracy) variety of indiscipline, they tend to receive the most attention from historians because of their potential size. In some cases mutinies included five or more legions.

A mutiny is a form of promotion of interests movement, similar to a strike by workers (Lammers 1969; Pondy 1969, pp. 501–503). Unlike a strike, however, soldiers were trained to fight, were often armed, and were accustomed to working together under stress. Therefore, they represented a much greater threat to stability when they engaged in collective dissent than did typical crowds of non-soldiers. In addition to its potential for violence, a mutiny is a threat to military stability because it reflects damaged military order in the units where it occurs and it can undermine discipline among units that do not even participate.

Mutinies presented a threat to officers, campaigns, and peace. Several mutinies in the late Republic resulted in the death of officers. After he attempted to introduce more rigid discipline, A. Postumius Albinus faced a mutiny in camp; when he tried to respond, he was stoned to death by his soldiers (Livy *Per.* 75; Val. Max. 9.8.3; Plut. *Sull.* 6.9). In another incident, L. Cornelius Cinna was killed while attempting to restore discipline during a mutiny in 84 BCE. Cinna was trying to rally his new legions to cross the Adriatic and face Sulla's veteran legions, but his men were not confident in their commander (App. *B Civ.* 1.77-78; Plut. *Pomp.* 5.1-2; Livy *Per.* 83, 85; Lovano 2002, pp. 108–110; Brice 2020, pp. 254, 261–262).

Mutinies could erupt in any army. We tend to think of C. Julius Caesar as a great general, but in two incidents connected with doubts about his leadership Caesar encountered mutinies. During the civil war in 49 BCE, legion IX mutinied in Placentia (Caes. *BCiv.* 1.87, 2.22; App. *B Civ.* 2.47–48; Cass. Dio 41.26, 35–36; Brice 2015a, pp. 108–110), and in 47 BCE as many as eight legions mutinied in Campania (Caes. *BAfr.* 19.3, 28, 54; Cic. *Att.* 11.10, 16, and 20–22; App. *B Civ.* 2.92–4; Cass. Dio 42.52; Chrissanthos 2001). As with conspiracies, mutinies during the Republic and early Empire could have serious repercussions, but long-term problems were usually averted through commanders' response in restoring order (Brice 2015a and the case study below).

Expression of Grievances

Among lesser forms of collective military disobedience, an expression of grievances was the most peaceful. These less notorious varieties of indiscipline were often non-violent, vocal confrontations or communications in which soldiers, often acting collectively, sought to protest various grievances, real and illusory, and to protect their interests (Brice 2015b, pp. 72–73).

The expression of grievances was distinct from mutinies and insubordination, even if there were only shades of difference between this type of protest and some forms of indiscipline. Like a mutiny, an expression of grievances was collective, could include both soldiers and officers, and was a promotion of interests type of organizational protest. Also, in addition to being peaceful, an expression of grievances did not include a total resistance to authority through a refusal to follow orders or engage in combat. Peaceful forms of indiscipline were important because they could be broad and often more successful than other forms of indiscipline. They rarely resulted in punishment of participants (Kaegi 1981, p. 4; Brice 2015b, pp. 73).

There are good examples of expressions of grievances from the Republic and early Empire. In 40 BCE when M. Antonius returned to Brundisium and it looked like there would be war with Octavian, soldiers and veterans of both sides acted against their commanders' orders, refusing to serve or fight. They engaged in indiscipline to protect their benefits and worked peacefully with vigor to force a settlement (Plut. *Ant.* 30; App. *B Civ.* 5.55–64; Cass. Dio 48.27-28.2). Then in 47 CE, soldiers on the Rhine and Danube frontiers, tired of commanders who had them digging mines and building public works in hope of earning a triumph, sent a letter to emperor Claudius asking him to award triumphs to commanders when they were appointed, to save soldiers some toil (Tac. *Ann.* 11.20; Suet. *Claud.* 24.3). In both these peaceful protests, the soldiers successfully acted to protect their interests.

Insubordination

The most common type of indiscipline is insubordination which includes a variety of lesser offenses by individuals and groups. These were "lesser" offenses in that they were often individual acts and less likely to be broadly disruptive, although they could also be collective and serious. Officers and soldiers alike could take part in all these lesser forms of military disobedience. These incidents could be either promotion of interests or secession movements. Chief among these behaviors were defection, desertion, disobedience, or failure to follow orders (including cowardice and infighting), and dereliction of duty (Carney 2015, pp. 30–32; Brice 2015b, pp. 73–74).

Desertion was certainly indiscipline and was treated accordingly, but it provided soldiers an alternative to more serious forms of military disobedience. Soldiers could walk away from growing tensions, if they could get away unseen. Defection was a form of desertion, in which deserter(s) joined an enemy. Both desertion and defection could be an individual act or include entire units. In terms of organizational behavior, these desertions and defections were forms of secession movements since the soldiers sought to separate themselves from their established officers and commander. Sometimes defections occurred after an actual mutiny but, more typically, large numbers of soldiers changed sides without having mutinied beforehand. Defection usually occurred for one of three reasons: subornment (usually bribery), lack of cohesion with a commander, or because soldiers made a rational decision that changing sides was preferable to probable death in battle. Since ancient sources more readily report details of large-scale actions, defections dominate the record of lesser forms of indiscipline. We know of more than forty incidents of group defections during the late Republic, and several during the civil wars of 69 and 292. For example, Octavian used bounties and appeals to loyalty in enticing two of M. Antonius' legions to defect in 44 and the same tactics against Lepidus' army in Sicily in 36 BCE. The *Fimbriani* defected to Sulla in 84 rather than fight his numerous legions (Brice 2015a, pp. 110-112, 2020, pp.257–259).

Disobedience could include any act that was contrary to discipline. It could be as serious as disobeying orders or demonstrating cowardice in battle, or as simple as sleeping on duty. Cowardice was a regular problem especially among new recruits. This was a serious offense occurring during combat, putting the legion at risk. Examples of cowardice include soldiers serving under Sulla in 86 (Plut. *Sull.* 16.3, 5), Crassus in 71 (Plut. *Crass.* 10.2–3), Caesar in 48 and 45 (Caes. *BCiv.* 69, 74 and App. *B Civ.* 2.61–63, 103), Calvinus in 39 (Vell. Pat. 2.78.3 and Cass. Dio 48.42), Antonius in 36 (Plut. *Ant.* 39.7), Octavian in 34 (Cass. Dio 49.38.4 and Suet. *Aug.* 24), Agrippa in 19 BCE (Cass. Dio. 54.11.3 and Suet. *Aug.* 24), A. Caecina and S. Plautius in 7 CE (Vell. Pat. 2.112.4), Tiberius in 9 (Cass. Dio 56.13.1–2) and L. Apronius in 20 (Tac. *Ann.* 3.20–21). There were other incidents of disobedience that seldom survive in sources such as units disobeying orders, or pillaging communities they were to protect, or fighting among themselves. Commanders who encountered this kind of collective indiscipline include Cinna in 87 (App. *B Civ* 1.74 and Plut. *Ser.* 3), Pompey in 82 (Plut. *Pomp.* 10.7), Sertorius in 76 (App. *B Civ.* 1.109), and Antonius in 36 BCE (Plut. *Ant.* 48.2–5). While our sources stem from the Republic these kinds of insubordination must have been common in all periods.

Mixed Indiscipline

Organizational behavior studies draw attention to the fact that protest movements like collective indiscipline, are sometimes of mixed types and participants have mixed goals. For example, a mutiny may emerge as part of a military conspiracy, or a defection may lead to a mutiny (or vice versa). Similarly, protesting soldiers often have mixed goals that change over time, for example a protection of interest movement like a mutiny that eventually changes into a secession movement such as defection (Lammers 1969, pp. 561–563; Pondy 1969, p. 501). One of the best examples of this mixing occurred in the army of L. Valerius Flaccus, sometimes called the *Fimbriani*. As mentioned in the section "Military Conspiracy," Flaccus died in 86 BCE as a result of a *military conspiracy* by his quaestor, C. Flavius Fimbria. During the events that led to the murder, Flaccus' army *mutinied* after he dismissed Fimbria from service. Even though the soldiers were incited by their officers, this was still mutiny. After Fimbria had led the army successfully against Mithridates for more than a year these same soldiers were insubordinate and *defected* in 84 to Sulla. The soldiers' goals had changed from demanding Fimbria's restoration, a protection of interests protest in 86, to self-preservation through defection in 84, a secession movement (Livy *Per* 82–83; App. *Mithr.* 51–52; de Blois 2000, pp. 18–19; Wolff 2013). The episode of the *Fimbriani* is the best example of a variety of incidents where we can see mixed types of indiscipline and observe participants' goals change. On a related note, one of the most fascinating features of Roman mutinies is that, in most cases, soldiers did not use the mutiny to desert military service. They might end up defecting or being discharged legally, but they did not generally use mutiny as a means of covering desertion because in those cases they wanted their interests protected.

Causes of Indiscipline

In trying to understand why indiscipline occurred, several traditional explanations have been suggested. These included madness, idleness, political incitement, and conditions of service. Authors writing during the Republic and Empire sometimes describe mutineers as mad or irrational ("*eo furoris venere ut...*" Tac. *Ann.* 1.18), but such characterizations are simply bias on the part of elite authors (McPhail 1991; Woodman 2006; Connal 2012). Another cause commonly used in ancient sources is blaming indiscipline on "soldiers' idleness." Authors blame the commander, suggesting that because he let the soldiers have too much free time, discipline became lax and they mutinied (e.g. Tac. *Ann.* 2.55.5). The problem with idleness as an explanation is that authors confuse opportunity with cause. Idleness created the opportunity for joining indiscipline, it did not cause indiscipline. We should instead recognize that the charge of "idleness" is a criticism of officers, not soldiers, as incompetent.

Modern historians of Rome have generally preferred political instability and conditions of service as explanations for indiscipline. The unstable legitimacy of both commanders and the state during periods of political upheaval created a climate of uncertainty in which military discipline was more likely to break down. Also, the related competition among potential leaders for soldiers' political support provided a perfect climate for indiscipline. Examples of military disobedience during political instability are too numerous to list, but they can be found throughout Rome's civil wars in 88–82 BCE, in 49–45 and 43–31 BCE, and during the Empire in 69, 292–293, and 312–314 CE (e.g. App. *B Civ.* 3.86-88; and Cic. *Fam.* 10.23, 24, and 35). The other traditional explanation for indiscipline is conditions of service. Soldiers and sometimes officers initiated military disobedience when the conditions during which they served became so onerous they felt alienated and acted out. Typical complaints included late pay (Polyb. 11.29), corrupt officers (Tac. *Ann.* 1.17.2–6, 31.1, 44.7), terms of service (Tac. *Ann.* 1.17.2–6, 31.1), and combat exhaustion (e.g. App. *B Civ.* 2.92–94; Brice 2020, pp. 264–265). These potential causes of indiscipline, do not help us understand why some soldiers and officers joined in military disobedience while others in the same unit did not when the causes were often present for everyone.

Organizational behavior studies are helpful, having shown there are conditions that increase the likelihood soldiers would join in collective indiscipline such as mutinies and insubordination. These conditions include, in no particular order, group homogeneity, cohesive identity, lack of opportunities to report complaints, loss of faith in upper-level leadership, and the likelihood that authorities will not punish participants (Lammers 1969, pp. 564–566). These conditions can also be found in accounts of the Roman army. These conditions do not determine soldiers' participation in collective indiscipline; they help us understand why some soldiers joined and others did not. Participation in collective action rarely involved all members of a unit (as discussed in the section "Collective Action").

Roman legions were seldom homogeneous in their membership. This was especially true after the Social War when Italian allies became citizens. But citizenship was not, by itself, sufficient as a standard quality to encourage participation in disobedience. Sometimes legions were full of recruits from the same city or region, but more often soldiers were from diverse localities, with different backgrounds (Brunt 1971, 1988; Blois 2007, p. 166). Homogeneity was no guarantee of discipline, however, as ancient authors report consistently that legions raised entirely from urban recruits were unruly and disordered (e.g. App. *B Civ.* 1.85). Lack of homogeneity can contribute to individuals joining indiscipline, but since Roman legionaries were usually from mixed backgrounds, we cannot isolate this characteristic as a causative force.

Cohesive identity exists in military units (ancient and modern) in terms of vertical and horizontal forces. Vertical cohesion is the strength of links between individuals and others ranked above or below them, while horizontal cohesion was the bond among soldiers in a unit. Strong vertical cohesion was helpful in maintaining control and managing the legion in battle, but it was a problem when a commander wanted to lead his army against the state. Durable horizontal cohesion may have been helpful in combat but could also become a problem when there was potential indiscipline as soldiers might identify more strongly with fellow soldiers in opposition to officers and thus engage in collective indiscipline (MacMullen 1984; Hamby 2002; Armstrong 2016; Brice 2020, pp. 250–251). Strong horizontal cohesion was not necessarily a problem, but if combined with weak vertical cohesion, the odds increase for collective indiscipline. The legions of Albinus, Cinna, and Caesar (discussed in the section "Mutiny") were largely recruited from areas that made them more internally homogeneous than usual. This would have contributed to these units being more likely to develop strong bonds of horizontal cohesion. As it happens, these same units also had doubts about their respective commanders at the time of their mutinies.

Loss of confidence in superior officers is linked with weak vertical cohesion and military disobedience. Surveys of modern mutinies have corroborated a pattern observed in some Roman incidents of collective indiscipline. If members of a unit lack confidence in officers, this can contribute to soldiers' decisions to join in indiscipline (Lammers 1969, pp. 565–566). This pattern applies to officers, including centurions and tribunes, as well as soldiers. Because centurions and subalterns (e.g. *optiones*) were often drawn from the ranks, they were more likely than other officers to have strong horizontal and vertical cohesion with soldiers and so were liable to join soldiers in collective indiscipline; they might even take a leading role. When officers and soldiers suspected a commander's leadership would result in unnecessary losses they often acted out (e.g. Caes. *BGall.* 1.39–40). Even when they seemed aware commanders were usually winners, like Caesar, they were likely to act out if they thought leadership wavered, as they did in 47 (e.g. App. *B Civ.* 2.92–94). Caesar, for example, experienced indiscipline in his legions (Caes. *BGall.* 1.39–41) in part due to doubts about leadership (Brice 2015a, pp. 108–110, 2020, p. 252), and the mutinies in 14 CE may have reflected uncertainty about the leadership transition following Augustus' death (Vell. Pat. 2.124.1).

Avenues for soldiers to report complaints and seek change without breaking discipline were limited. Elections in Rome were a way to change some unpopular officers. This was of limited usefulness as soldiers needed to be present in Rome to vote or a commander might be prorogued by the senate. Roman citizens did have the customary right of free speech and were not afraid to use it with officers and commanders (Chrissanthos 2004). Soldiers presented complaints and demands through centurions, as when they clamored for permission to engage an enemy (e.g. Caes. *BCiv.* 1.64.2). They could also speak directly to the commander one-on-one, if he was present (e.g. Caes. *BGall.* 7.17). The commander's assembly (*contio*) was a public venue where soldiers occasionally shouted views (Pina Polo 1995, pp. 213–216; Chrissanthos 2004). Since we tend to hear only about incidents when soldiers' demands were not met, it is difficult to know how effective these avenues were, but if they were perceived by soldiers as ineffective then some might have been more likely to join in disobedience. Incidents where soldiers attacked their officers in assembly may stem from frustration with communication channels (e.g. Livy *Per.* 75; Val. Max. 9.8.3; Plut. *Sull.* 6.9; Polyaenus *Strat.* 8.9.1; Brice 2020, pp. 251–252).

The perceived unlikelihood of punishment is the last of the conditions found to increase participation in collective indiscipline. It has been correctly observed that during the late Republic most soldiers and officers who participated in military disobedience went unpunished regardless of their offense (Messer 1920, p. 159; Brice 2020, p. 253 n.22). During a time of internal conflict, when all sides needed support, it is not surprising that few punishments were imposed. For example, there were more than 40 incidents of group defections during the civil wars of the late Republic, but in only one case were the participants punished. In that case the commander left the unit in Asia when he returned to Rome (Livy *Per.* 83; App. *Mith.* 60; Plut. *Sull.* 25.1). Among all the possible contributors to soldiers' openness to indiscipline the perceived unlikelihood of punishment is most consistently present during all civil wars and even during times of political uncertainty.

The stresses that stimulated men to indiscipline were numerous and not limited to service conditions, or politics. Organizational behavior adds a suite of potential explanatory tools for studies of indiscipline. When our ancient sources provide sufficient evidence we can discern what contributed to the indiscipline regardless of the reasons our sources suggest (e.g. madness, idleness), as in the case of the mutinies of 14 CE (see the section "Indiscipline Case Study"). All these stimuli are the means to discuss such incidents with more precision. Understanding these behaviors also gives us a better way of explaining why some soldiers participated and others did not. The result is a more complete sense of how and why these incidents unfolded. Recognizing the wide variety of forces acting on men in the military helps us understand why so many soldiers could follow orders and fight hard much of the time but, sometimes, also join in collective indiscipline.

Collective Action

Most of the incidents discussed thus far are by groups of soldiers. When groups of soldiers engage together in an activity, it is called collective action or behavior, much like crowd behavior in other events such as concerts and sporting matches. Indiscipline by a group as in a mutiny, expression of grievance, or unit defection is a collective action. Studies in this field have contributed several significant observations to examinations of indiscipline in Roman armies. One well-supported observation is that participants in collective action, including indiscipline, are not temporarily insane or irrational, as our ancient authors would have us believe. Mutineers and defectors see their action as rational (McPhail 1991; Connal 2012). Given the alternative of putting up with the conditions that stimulated their alienation from the institution's norms, indiscipline seemed preferable. A second observation is that when a group or crowd engages in collective action it seldom does so unanimously. There are nearly always members of the crowd or unit who do not join in the action, choosing to watch the incident or engage in something else completely, such as remain disciplined and loyal to their commander (McPhail 1991, pp. 159–190, 1994). This observation helps explain why in some mutinies it is possible for the commander to recover control of the unit by relying on the soldiers and officers who did not participate.

Another way in which sociology has contributed to our understanding of military discipline and indiscipline is by demonstrating that we can understand collective action as unfolding in coherent stages. Just as any story has a beginning, middle, and end, collective action has stages. Elihu Rose suggested we should see a mutiny as having anatomy – it occurs in three parts: origin, act, and aftermath (1982, pp. 565–567). Collective action studies have used the labels *trigger*, *mobilization*, and *restoration of control* for these same phases. The latter three labels are more descriptive of what actually occurred. These terms work with ancient armies also because collective action of various kinds often unfolds in similar ways (McPhail 1991; Brice 2015a, pp. 107–108). That is why descriptions of indiscipline in different historical contexts often share many features across time and place. The actions unfold in similar ways, even though the way the group expresses itself is context specific.

Indiscipline Case Study: Mutinies of 14 CE

This case study of indiscipline illustrates how sociological approaches have improved our analysis and ability to explain indiscipline in the Roman army. In 14 CE, legions posted in Pannonia and along the Lower Rhine river mutinied simultaneously. The incidents are highly informative of how mutinies develop and of Roman responses to military unrest.[5]

Augustus died 19 August, 14 CE. The legions assigned to Pannonia (VIII, IX, and XV) were gathered together for summer duties such as building public works. The *trigger* phase of this mutiny began when the commander, Q. Junius Blaesus, declared a break of several days from standard camp duties in order for the soldiers to honor Augustus. During this break some of the soldiers began gathering to grumble about service conditions. This stage, where men had an opportunity to gather, complain among themselves, and plan action – "idleness" according to our sources – was the *trigger* of the mutiny. The free time provided the opportunity to gather. It was not the cause because, as we shall see, the causes had been present for years.

The *mobilization* phase began when the mutiny broke out and participants joined, and it continued until authorities could establish control. After several days of grumbling and coordinating plans, a mutiny erupted among the three legions. Although Blaesus was unable to stop the mutiny, he did get the mutineers to pause long enough to send envoys to Rome to present demands to the new emperor and await their return. While the envoys were gone, however, the mutiny flared up again and turned violent, resulting in the death of a centurion and some pillaging of the local area. Despite this violence the mutinous legions mostly remained in the camp, an indication that they did not seek to desert but wanted to secure legal discharge with the promised cash bonuses.

Nearly simultaneous with events in Pannonia, the four legions assigned to the Lower Rhine (I, V, XX, and XXI) mutinied. As with Pannonia, the four legions were assembled together in a summer camp. They were under the command of A. Caecina Severus, legate in the region. When he received news of Augustus' death, he also gave his men a couple days break from standard duties. During this rest-period the mutiny erupted. As with Pannonia, the *trigger* was the time off from normal duties. That no mutinies occurred among other legions in 14 CE is certainly a function of these commanders' decision to relax discipline for several days.

The *mobilization* phase of the Lower Rhine mutiny turned violent as soldiers attacked selected centurions, killing at least one, and expelling others from camp. Soldiers did not attack the commander, the higher-ranking officers, or civilians. They also did not pillage the local area but demanded to send envoys to Rome. As in Pannonia, the men who joined the mutiny were alienated from Rome by the failure of the military leadership (the emperor) to keep the promises made when they had joined. The superannuated legionaries wanted release from service after sixteen years, under the terms in effect when they had enlisted, and replacement of some centurions. The legions maintained order in camp and did not collectively desert. As with Pannonia, soldiers wanted release from the army by having their grievances met, not desertion.

Again, the release from normal duties was the *trigger*, but it was not the cause. Primarily, the mutineers sought restoration of the conditions under which they were enlisted, especially the honorable discharge after sixteen years with a cash bounty, as originally promised. Men joined the mutiny for various reasons once it began. The main reason was that in both cases, the soldiers were alienated from the administration in Rome because it was ignoring the terms of service it originally had offered them. It appears that men were not being discharged on schedule and this had been the primary cause of mutiny in both legionary camps. There was also a leadership issue that stimulated some men in Lower Germany to join. In the case of the Rhine mutiny, soldiers also demanded replacement of cruel or corrupt centurions. Some men in both mutinies may also have been concerned by doubts about future leadership of the empire given that this was the first leadership transition. The fact that a large number of the men serving in Lower Germany and some of those in Pannonia had been recruited in Rome during the emergency recruitments of 6 and 9 CE meant that there was some homogeneity in the groups of mutineers. As noted previously, this homogeneity may have contributed to cohesion among the urban recruits and the likelihood they would join in indiscipline.

The new emperor, Tiberius, was a seasoned commander, but had his hands full in Rome with the transition and ordered his sons to resolve the mutinies. This initiated the *restoration of control* phase of the mutinies. Germanicus, commander of the legions in Gaul and on the Rhine, was already in Gaul and went to the Rhine mutiny. Germanicus found the mutineers unsympathetic but peaceful. The soldiers were insistent about their demands and threatened to raid the countryside and march on Rome. After an initial botched effort that weakened perceptions of his leadership, Germanicus was able to conciliate the soldiers. He did so by promising to meet their reasonable demands for discharge, if they would return to service. The men took the oath to Tiberius and dispersed to two winter forts. Germanicus then went to make sure the Upper Rhine legions were settled.

Tiberius sent Drusus along with Aelius Sejanus and a couple cohorts of Praetorian guards from Rome to resolve the Pannonian mutiny. Drusus found the mutineers agitated and initial negotiations met with no luck. But a full lunar eclipse soon after he arrived frightened some soldiers, providing an opportunity for Drusus to recover control by swaying many over to his side. With the support of loyal men, Drusus had the Praetorian cavalry surround the camp as he moved against the ringleaders, and violently put down the mutiny in the *restoration of control* phase. Once he had restored order, he may have discharged the remaining superannuated soldiers and, after issuing a new military oath, dispersed the legions to separate winter quarters.

Events in Lower Germany, however, were less settled than Germanicus had thought. Despite earlier measures, the Lower Rhine legions remained agitated. They were not as confident in Germanicus' leadership as a result of his earlier weakness in negotiating with the mutineers. A new mutiny erupted in Germanicus' camp, *triggered* by senate representatives arriving to inform Germanicus that his authority had been extended. They had been sent out before news of the original Rhine mutiny had reached Rome. Members of Legion I, fearing that the envoys had arrived to rescind Germanicus' promises, rioted in camp during the *mobilization* phase of this mutiny. Because Germanicus had issued a new oath to the legions after the previous violence, this outburst was a new mutiny. Germanicus asserted leadership in an assembly the next day where he harangued his men. He also sent the non-combatants away; a clear signal that he intended to use violence to restore order. As a result, the mutineers lost heart and Germanicus was able to seize the initiative to restore control with support from loyal men. The recently mutinous legion then suffered a self-inflicted punishment similar to decimation, as they had to judge and execute their fellow soldiers.

Having restored order at camp, Germanicus turned attention to Vetera where yet another mutiny had erupted among the two legions (V and XXI) under the command of Caecina. The *trigger* of this mutiny seems to have been dissatisfaction with the previous resolution, connected with a lack of confidence in the commanders' leadership. Germanicus gathered auxilia with the legions and marched on the camp with a considerable force. Caecina, ordered to resolve the mutiny and restore control before Germanicus arrived, moved against the ringleaders violently with considerable casualties. The protest ended, but the *restoration of control* was not yet complete.

Afterward, Germanicus led the formerly mutinous legions on campaign across the Rhine. The campaign gave the survivors a chance to prove their valor and discipline while rebuilding group cohesion. It also reasserted Germanicus' leadership of the units and Caecina's role as a commander. After this campaign, order was fully restored and Germanicus returned the legions to their respective winter quarters. There were no further mutinies over length-of-service for more than a century, and there would not be another large-scale mutiny for more than 30 years. Despite the size of these incidents, they did not cause harm to the empire or the military because they were handled quickly and resolved completely.

Conclusion

Armies are more than battles, discipline, weapons, and wounds. They are made up of men who must work together as required before, during, and after battle or siege for the duration of their service. In many armies, discipline contributed to keeping men in good order during stressful circumstances, increasing unit efficiency, and lethality. Discipline was important in the success of Roman legions. But no matter how good their discipline, circumstances could reach a point where soldiers felt alienated and were prepared to "act out" against authority – engage in military disobedience – individually or collectively, in a variety of ways.

Incidents of indiscipline happened. They were not just *topoi* or literary devices. Certainly, elite authors used such military break-downs as vehicles to criticize officers and leaders. These episodes also provided a tool with which such authors could entertain readers and demonstrate their literary skills. But while we can acknowledge that authors used mutinies and other forms of indiscipline as literary devices, we can also acknowledge they were still real events. The reason so many of these incidents seem to develop along similar lines in narratives is not because of our authors, but because armies consist of humans who, under certain circumstances, can behave and act in similar ways (*contra* Fulkerson 2013, p. 166). The speeches and the like put into the mouths of the participants may be imagined by ancient authors, but collective indiscipline still occurred along a perceptible course. This pattern is revealed in studies of collective action and organizational behavior across time and place that provide us with better understanding of these phenomena.

Unlike traditional treatments of discipline, we now understand that both discipline and indiscipline were present in military institutions like that of Rome. Indiscipline was something that could happen in any unit and something every Roman commander might encounter. There were multiple varieties of military disobedience, some violent and some not. We can trace examples of it across the middle and late Republic and early Empire when our sources are sufficient to provide a window onto the society of the Roman army. And we know indiscipline was a common issue because disobedience and conflict are potential problems in every human institution.

In this brief chapter it is not possible to cover all examples or every facet of indiscipline. Much remains to be discussed elsewhere. But as with so many other aspects of studying warfare, we have made great strides. The result is a better understanding of not only the army, but also the society of which it was a part and the way both interacted at many levels.

Notes

1 The terms *indiscipline* and *military disobedience* are used synonymously in this chapter. The term *military unrest* still can be a synonym for indiscipline when it is violent and collective as in conspiracies, mutinies, and riots. See Brice 2020 for extended discussion of several aspects of indiscipline covered in this chapter.

2 On Roman military discipline generally, Phang 2008; Lendon 2005, pp. 177–231; Brice 2011, pp. 36–41.

3 See also Polyb. 6.38.2; Livy 8.7.16; Front. *Strat.* 4.1 *Dig.* 48.4, 48.19.8.2–3, 19.14, 19.38.1 and 11–12, and 49.16.

4 Lammers 1969; Kaegi 1981, pp. 4–6; Rose 1982; Brice 2015b, pp. 70–74. While much of military sociological research concerns itself with modern institutions, Kaegi (1981, pp. 4–6) refined a vocabulary for Byzantine armies that I have adjusted slightly by substituting the word "mutiny" for his "sedition."

5 Instead of citing them throughout, the ancient sources for these mutinies are: Pannonia: Vell. Pat. 2.125.1–6; Tac. *Ann.* 16–30; Suet. *Tib.* 25; Dio 57.4.1–3; and Lower Germany: Vell. Pat. 2.125.1–6; Tac. *Ann.* 31-49; Suet. *Tib.* 25; Dio 57.5.1–7.

References

Armstrong, J. (2016). "The ties that bind: military cohesion in archaic Rome." In: Circum Mare: *Themes in Ancient Warfare* (ed. J. Armstrong), 101–119. Leiden: Brill.

Barrett, A.A. (1989). *Caligula: The Corruption of Power*. New York: Simon and Schuster.

de Blois, L. (2000). "Army and society in the late Roman Republic: professionalism and the role of the military middle cadre." In: *Kaiser, Heer und Gesellschaft im der Römischen Kaiserzeit* (eds. G. Alföldy, B. Dobson and W. Eck), 11–31. Stuttgart: De Gruyter.

de Blois, L. (2007). "Army and general in the late Roman Republic." In: *A Companion to the Roman Army* (ed. P. Erdkamp), 164–179. Chichester, UK: Wiley Blackwell.

Brice, L.L. (2011). "Disciplining Octavian: a case study of Roman military culture, 44-30 BCE." In: *Warfare and Culture in World History* (ed. W. Lee), 35–60. New York: NYU Press.

Brice, L.L. (2015a). "Second chance for valor: restoration of order after mutinies and indiscipline." In: *Aspects of Ancient Institutions and Geography* (eds. L.L. Brice and D. Slootjes), 103–121. Leiden: Brill.

Brice, L.L. (2015b). "Military unrest in the age of Philip and Alexander of Macedon: defining the terms of debate." In: *Greece, Macedon, and Persia: Studies in Social, Political, and Military History in Honor of Waldemar Heckel* (eds. E. Garvin, T. Howe and G. Wrightson), 69–76. Oxford: Oxbow.

Brice, L.L. (2020). "SPQR SNAFU: indiscipline and internal conflict in the late Republic." In: *Romans at War: Soldiers, Citizens, and Society in the Roman Republic* (eds. J. Armstrong and M. Fronda), 247–66. New York: Routledge.

Brunt, P.A. (1971). *Italian Manpower*. Oxford: Clarendon Press.

Brunt, P.A. (1988). "The army and the land in the Roman revolution." *Journal of Roman Studies* 52 (1962): 69–86. Revised and reprinted in *The Fall of the Roman Republic and Related Essays*, edited by P.A. Brunt, 240–275. Oxford: Oxford University Press.

Carney, E. (2015). "Macedonians and mutiny: discipline and indiscipline in the army of Philip and Alexander." *Classical Philology* 91 1996: 19–44. Revised and reprinted in *King and Court in Ancient Macedonia: Rivalry, Treason, and Conspiracy*, edited by Elizabeth Carney, 27–59. Swansea: Classical Press of Whales.

Chrissanthos, S. (2001). "Caesar and the mutiny of 47 B.C." *Journal of Roman Studies* 91: 63–75.

Chrissanthos, S. (2004). "Freedom of speech and the Roman Republican army." In: *Free Speech in Classical Antiquity* (eds. I. Sluiter and R.M. Rosen), 341–368. Leiden: Brill.

Connal, R. (2012). "Rational mutiny in the year of four emperors." *Arctos* 46: 33–52.

Fulkerson, L. (2013). *No Regrets: Remorse in Classical Antiquity*. Oxford: Oxford University Press.

Gabba, E. (1975). *Le rivolte militari Romane dal IV secolo A.C. ad Augusto*. Florence: Sansoni.

Goldsworthy, A. (1996). *The Army at War, 100 BC – AD 200*. Oxford: Clarendon Press.

Hamby, J. (2002). "The mutiny wagon wheel: a leadership model for mutiny in combat." *Armed Forces and Society* 28: 575–600.

Kaegi, W.E. Jr. (1981). *Byzantine Military Unrest 471–843: An Interpretation*. Amsterdam: Adolf M. Hakkert.

Keaveney, A. (2007). *The Army in the Roman Revolution*. New York: Routledge.

Keegan, J. (1976). *The Face of Battle*. New York: Penguin.

Keppie, L.J.F. (1998). *The Making of the Roman Army, From Republic to Empire*. Updated ed. Norman, OK: University of Oklahoma Press.

Lammers, C. (1969). "Strikes and mutinies: a comparative study of organizational conflicts between rulers and ruled." *Administrative Science Quarterly* 14 (4): 558–572.

Le Bohec, Y. (1994). *The Roman Imperial Army*. New York: Routledge.

Lendon, J.E. (2005). *Soldiers and Ghosts: A History of Battle in Antiquity*. New Haven, CT: Yale University Press.

Lovano, M. (2002). *The Age of Cinna: Crucible of Late Republican Rome*. Stuttgart: Franz Steiner Verlag.

MacMullen, R. (1984). "The legion as a society." *Historia* 33 (4): 440–456.

McPhail, C. (1991). *The Myth of the Madding Crowd*. New York: Aldine de Gruyter.

McPhail, C. (1994). "The dark side of purpose. individual and collective violence in riots." *Sociological Quarterly* 35: 1–32.

Messer, W. (1920). "Mutiny in the Roman army. The Republic." *Classical Philology* 15 (2): 158–175.

Pagán, V. (2004). *Conspiracy Narratives in Roman History*. Austin, TX: University of Texas Press.

Pekary, T. (1987). "*Seditio*: Unruhen und Revolten im Römischen Reich von Augustus bis Commodus." *Ancient Society* 18: 133–150.

Phang, S. (2008). *Roman Military Service: Ideologies of Discipline in the Late Republic and Early Principate*. Cambridge.

Pina Polo, F. (1995). "Procedures and functions of civil and military *contiones* in Rome." *Klio* 77: 203–216.

Pondy, L. (1969). "Varieties of organizational behavior." *Administrative Science Quarterly* 14 (4): 449–509.

Rose, E. (1982). "The anatomy of mutiny." *Armed Forces and Society* 8 (4): 561–574.

Wolff, C. (2013). "Les légions de Fimbria." *Latomus* 72: 338–349.

Woodman, A. (2006). "Mutiny and madness: Tacitus *Annals* 1.16-49." *Arethusa* 39: 303–329.

Further Reading

Armstrong, J. (ed.) (2016). Circum Mare: *Themes in Ancient Warfare*. Leiden: Brill.

Brice, L.L. (2020). "SPQR SNAFU: indiscipline and internal conflict in the late Republic." In: *Romans at War: Soldiers, Citizens, and Society in the Roman Republic* (eds. M. Fronda and J. Armstrong) 247–266. New York: Routledge.

Hathaway, J. (2002). "Introduction." In: *Mutiny and Rebellion in the Ottoman Empire* (ed. J. Hathaway), 1–10. Madison, WI: University of Wisconsin Press.

Hechter, M., Pfaff, S., and Underwood, P. (2016). "Grievances and the genesis of rebellion: mutiny in the Royal Navy, 1740 to 1820." *American Sociological Review* 81 (1): 165–189.

Lammers, C. (2003). "Mutiny in comparative perspective." *International Review of Social History* 48 (3): 473–482. https://doi.org/10.1017/S0020859003001160.

Wolff, C. (2009). *Déserteurs et transfuges dans l'armée romaine à l'époque républicaine*. Naples: Jovene.

10

The Neurophysiology of Panic on the Ancient Battlefield

Susan M. Heidenreich and Jonathan P. Roth

Introduction

Since the publication of John Keegan's groundbreaking book, *The Face of Battle* (1976), military historians have focused more on the individual soldier's experience on the battlefield. Those who write on ancient warfare have followed suit (Lee 1996; Lendon 2005; Lynn 2003; Hanson 2009). Studies of the physical aspects of battle, such as the effectiveness of weapons, and the bodily effects of wounds, are quite sophisticated, drawing on the latest science. In general, however, much of the research on the role of the mind in battle has continued to rely on outdated theories, such as those of Freud and Jung (Grossman 2009). These older concepts are not deemed useful to modern researchers, who are studying the mind with increasingly powerful tools and models, with an approach known as neuroscience.

Neuroscience can be broadly defined as a multidisciplinary field that investigates the neurophysiological functions and the corresponding perceptual processes that underlie the actions and behaviors of humans in response to various conditions or types of stimulation. Modern research in neuroscience, which incorporates findings from diverse areas, such as chemistry, biology, neurophysiology, and psychology, allows scientists to describe these processes in great detail. In order to correlate this new information with descriptions of panic on the ancient battlefield, the military historian needs to familiarize him- or herself with the basics of how the human central nervous system (i.e. the CNS, which is composed of the brain and spinal cord) functions and how the resulting physiology affects perception and subsequent action.

One area where current advances in neurobiology have begun to have an impact on modern military history is the research concerning combat trauma, commonly called post-traumatic stress disorder (PTSD) (e.g. Koenigs et al. 2008; Vasterling and Verfaelle 2009; see also Tritle, Chapter 5). Although psychiatric casualties in war are as real as physical ones, there is much more to the role of mind in battle. Courage, fear, aggression, and other emotions affect the outcome of conflict, as does perception. Historians of ancient warfare have made virtually no use of recent advances in the understanding of the brain and its functions from the perspective of neuroscience. Recent works touch on the issue of military psychiatry, and psychological wounds, but without reference to neuroscience (Wheeler 1988; Gabriel 2012; Crowley 2012). Military historians can better understand ancient warfare with reference to recent advances in neuroscience. This chapter focuses on the nature of panic, an important factor in determining success or failure in battle.[1]

New Approaches to Greek and Roman Warfare, First Edition. Edited by Lee L. Brice.
© 2020 John Wiley & Sons, Inc. Published 2020 by John Wiley & Sons, Inc.

Philip Sabin noted recently (Sabin 2007, p. 431) that panicked flight was extremely dangerous and counterproductive:

> We need to explain why one side or the other eventually broke and fled, thereby exposing themselves to one-sided slaughter at the hands of pursuers .... Viewed from this perspective, flight...was a distinctly irrational act, since it placed the troops in far greater danger than they were in while they remained steady. Clearly something must have happened in the minds of individual soldiers...to make them give way to irrational panic.

That the state of panic often puts the soldier in more danger than standing and fighting was something of which the ancients were well aware. This is what Homer meant by "fatal flight," (*Il.* 11.70). Sabin's subsequent discussion of flight in battle does discuss various causes for an ancient army to run, including "psychological shock," but does not consider the nature of the panic that accompanies flight, that is, what is going on in the brain – and the body – of the panicked soldier.

The purpose of this study is to explore battlefield panic from a neuroscientific point of view. Neuroscience provides many tools that can aid the historian in judging the veracity of a particular account, for example, of a panicked soldier. Although current descriptions of the physiological properties of the underlying brain functions cannot explain every aspect of panic, such findings can provide some insight into and understanding of what happens to the soldier's biology and perception when panic occurs.

This approach raises a fundamental historiographical question: Did the basic properties of the brains of Greeks, Romans, Egyptians, or Carthaginians differ significantly from those of modern day humans? Much modern scholarship on antiquity is written with the tacit, or even explicit, belief that the minds of ancients were fundamentally different than our own (e.g. Wells 2012). Although it is certainly true that culture and language differ from time-to-time and place-to-place, there is no scientific evidence that ancient brains differed from modern ones. Virtually all contemporary scientists who study this issue would argue that such a difference is an unlikely possibility. Another point to make is that the traditional "mind/body" question is misleading. Most neuroscientists take the materialist viewpoint that two are not separable, in that the mind is an emergent property of brain activation (Koch 2004; LeDoux 2002).

The realization that ancient and modern brains function identically aids in a better understanding of the ancient battlefield. There is a caveat here: the stresses of ancient and modern war are not the same. Guns, and especially modern rapid-fire weapons and high-explosive shells, have created a set of stimuli that differ from those in wars before the late nineteenth century (Richardson 1978). Thus, the military historian must be careful and critical in drawing from modern works on morale and traumatic stress; this makes a basic understanding of neuroscience all the more important.

Definition of Panic in Military Terms

Certainly, soldiers feel fear constantly in war. The apprehension and anxiety that accompanies combat, however, is not the same as panic, which we define here as a specific instantiation of anxiety. Panic cannot be understood as a rational decision of the soldier to avoid danger – that is, in military terms "cowardice." In military contexts, the English language distinguishes fear, a normal anxiety associated with the dangers of war that can be overcome, from panic, understood as an uncontrollable reaction that overcomes training, discipline, and courage. Panicked flight, especially in a group, is called a "rout" and soldiers "flee" or are "in flight." On the other hand, movement away from the enemy, if based on a rational decision, is called a "withdrawal" or a "retreat" and corresponding verbs exist.

The distinction in terms existed in ancient Greek and Latin. The verb *phobeo* in the Homeric epics referred specifically to panicked flight in battle (e.g. *Il.* 5.232, 16.290, 17.667, 22.136), and the noun *phobos* to panic in a military context (15.327), though both verb and noun came to refer to fear in general in Classical Greek. The word *pheugo*, which is already present in Homer with this meaning, refers to flight in battle and was commonly used to describe panicked flight (e.g. Hdt. 4.125). In Homeric Greek, *anachazomai* (*Il.* 5.600, 16.818) meant to "fall back" and *antiphero*, which meant "to fight against," could also be used in the sense of "fighting withdrawal" (*Il.* 5.701.) The Greek term *choreo* appears in Homer with the meaning of a deliberate withdrawal. In Classical Greek it normally appears in the form *hypochoreo* (Thuc. 4.43.3; Polyb. 3.115.5). Xenophon (*Cyr.* 2.24.4) distinguishes withdrawal from the field (*hypochore tou pediou*), which is followed by further attacks, from a panicked flight (*pheuge*), which is followed by a slaughter. While it is rare, Josephus, writing about the Roman-Jewish War of the first century, does use the term *panikos* to refer to terrified soldiers (*BJ* 5.295). Latin military writing used *fugere* for panicked flight, and *se recipere* was used to indicate a planned withdrawal (Caes. *BGall.* 1.2.6, 2.12.2).

Of course, the difference between rout and withdrawal are not hard and fast, and especially on the individual level, this can be difficult to determine, even for someone watching the battle, as it involves the state of mind – and of the brain – of the soldier. Nevertheless, there certainly were, and are, cases in which participants in battle decided to run away, without experiencing panic. In addition, there are cases in which an officer or commander orders soldiers to move backward, away from the fighting, for tactical or strategic reasons.

Troops react differently to the circumstances, or rather their perception of the circumstances, that tend to induce panic. For example, Livy (22.48.5) writes that at Cannae an attack from the rear caused some Allied cavalry to flee, but led others to an "obstinate though hopeless struggle." Although behavior in battle has often been tied to somatic characteristics, for example, the so-called "heroic look," as Richardson pointed out "soldiers know from experience that it is...well-nigh impossible to foretell which men will do well in battle and which will fail" (Richardson 1978). This is true because the mechanisms and processes in the brain that inhibit panic can vary subtly for each person, producing what scientists refer to as individual differences. The variability in reactions is based on a number of factors, both related to the individual and the group. This was clear to the ancients, and is backed up by modern study.

Panic on the ancient battlefield resulted primarily from a participant's perception of the environment. Armies would sometimes panic and run immediately upon sighting an enemy (Sabin 2007). In other cases, they would keep fighting, despite evident mortal danger. One of the features of panic that was apparent to ancient observers was the remarkable way in which it rapidly spread, seemingly without any overt communication, through a unit or army. In a telling phrase, Livy (10.28.10) describes a *lymphaticus pavor*, panic seeming like water running from a spring. Homer uses several similes to describe a panicked army, stating it is like cows or sheep fleeing wild animals (*Il.* 15.320, 16.350, 630) or from a falcon (22.139–140). A classic description of panic is found in Livy (22.6.5–7). The historian describes the Roman panic at the battle of Trasimene (217), in which he uses the expression *inconsultus pavor* "unreasoning panic":

> A great part of the Romans now began to run; neither lake nor mountains could any longer check the panic; defiles and precipices were all alike to them, as they rushed blindly to escape, and arms and men came down pell-mell together. Many, having no room to flee, waded out into the shallow water at the margin of the lake, and kept on till only their heads

and shoulders were above the surface. Some were driven by their unreasoning panic even to attempt escape by swimming; but this was an endless, desperate undertaking, and either their hearts failed them and they sank in the deep water, or else, exhausted to no purpose, they struggled back with difficulty to the shoals, and were cut down on every hand by the horsemen, who rode into the water after them. (trans. B.O. Foster 1919)

Livy's geography may suffer from rhetorical devices, but his description of panic reflects the neurophysiology of human perception when in a condition of stress.

Neuroscientists usually consider the physiological and behavioral responses of the individual soldier, whereas military historians generally approach panic from the point of view of the group, that is, a unit or the army as a whole. Thus, panic in military discussions often refers to individual soldiers reacting in the same or similar ways. In one study, this is referred to a "military disintegration," a term that is used to express not only running from the enemy, but other instances of the loss of command and control (Watson 1997).

Definition of Panic in Neurophysiological Terms

In the context of neuroscience, panic can refer to a variety of behaviors. Here we define panic as one of many possible reactions to a fearful stimulus that occurs *during* battle. As such, it is an emotionally charged fear-response that usually evokes the concept of a fight, flight, or freeze pattern, often characterized as an adaptive or innate response to danger (LeDoux 1987, 2002).

Greek and Roman historical writing, however, usually took the commander's point of view, seeing combat in terms of units, rather than individual soldiers. This complicates the comparison between descriptions of the ancient battlefield and findings from modern neuroscience. There are some passages in ancient writing in which descriptions of individual panic do occur. Homer's *Iliad*, for example, has striking descriptions of panic and terror in battle: he compares terror in battle to a man's reaction to a poisonous snake "trembling and pale" (*Il.* 3.30), and elsewhere describes the panicked man's changing color, fast heartbeat, unsteadiness, and chattering teeth (*Il.* 13.277). The more personal lyrical poetry of Archilochus (seventh century) describes in fragment 5, his own panicked flight in a battle with the Thracians. A newly published fragment of Archilochus, reconstructed from Egyptian papyri, deals specifically with panic: "One doesn't have to call it weakness and cowardice, having to retreat, if it is under the compulsion of a god: no, we turned our backs to flee quickly: there exists a proper time for flight" (Obbink 2006). The complexity of description of an individual's psychological reactions in war makes the use of modern neuroscience more important as a historiographical tool.

An observer, such as an army's commander, may surmise that a soldier's panicked flight is the result of a rational, even calm, decision process; as such, the actions appear to be so deliberate that the observer might infer that the soldier is consciously aware of his or her decision to flee regardless of the consequences for doing so. That may or may not be the case (LeDoux 2002). Although the motor behaviors that can be empirically recorded might appear to be an instantaneous response to danger, they actually are a sequence of actions that result from the perception of what is happening on the battlefield over the course of time. That is, the soldier's perception of what occurs during confrontation is not a single event or outcome; rather, it is an awareness that results from an ongoing, dynamic process.

It is important to note that perceptual awareness of what is happening in the environment is not the same as conscious awareness of one's actions. Therefore, the actual flight response can be better characterized as one of several possibilities that fall along a continuum. On one end of the scale is a series of actions that result from one or more deliberate decisions to run from the confrontation, and on the other end is a pattern of behaviors resulting from perceptual processes that do not reach the level of the soldier's cognitive awareness. Thus, the soldier's experience can vary widely, depending on the degree to which the soldier can consciously control his or her motor behaviors. Viewing just the response pattern, the neutral observer mostly likely would not be able to distinguish the different sequences of actions and, consequently, may confuse motivations and responses.

Panic, therefore, is not a solitary outcome; rather, it is a series of actions that result from complex and integrated biological processes that develop throughout the body, over a finite time period. The body and mind have evolved to produce panic-type responses in order to improve the likelihood of an individual's survival. Such responses depend on both the anatomy and the physiology of the CNS, which are in direct correspondence in the sense that one constrains the other. When describing the functional characteristics of the brain, however, the discussion is determined by the level at which one approaches the topic. As an analogy, a description of a bridge could address the way it works within a system of highways, or it could describe the blueprints drawn for its construction, or the response properties of the materials used to build it (Marr 1982). To that end, we describe how perceptual processes lead to action, how the global properties of the brain determine the perception-to-action sequence, how activation of individual cells in the brain, referred to as neurons, and aggregates of neurons work in concert to control overall activity in the CNS.

Perception and Panic

Consider the example of a Roman legionary who has been stationed on the flank of his cohort. When our legionary spots approaching figures, he perceives the visual cues, such as the figures' size, speed, and direction of movement, as well as the auditory cues, such as the intensity and direction of the sound sources. The soldier forms a total percept that dictates whether the looming figures are perceived as enemies or comrades. The legionary does not have to engage in contemplative thought about the physical properties of the stimulus; nor does he need to consciously plan the exact amount of tension that must be exerted by the muscles in the arms and legs to make the appropriate movements. His responses are determined by his perceptions, which result from an extended pattern of signals processed by multiple components of the nervous system.

Continuing the example, perception begins when a physical stimulus occurs in the environment. Specifically, the light energy from the sun reflects off the surfaces of the objects and people in the field of vision, in the case of our soldier, advancing figures, and if cavalry, their mounts. The reflected array of light then projects onto the retina situated in the posterior portion of each eyeball. The rods and cones in the retina act as sensory receptors that transduce the physical energy, converting it to a series of electrical and chemical events that affect the next layer of neurons; this activation causes the affected neurons to generate rapid electrochemical signals, known as action potentials, that then travel down the optic nerve exiting the eyeball to multiple areas in the brain. The neuronal activation continues to spread to other neurons in the brain and spinal cord. The brain areas then transmit additional signals to subsequently activate the effectors. The effectors include system regulators, such as the circulatory system and the endocrine glands, which secrete hormones and other chemicals, as well as the nerves and muscles that control motor behaviors.

Action potentials that are transmitted to neighboring neurons form complex sequences across the vast neural network. Some neurons are activated while other neurons are inhibited, creating a specific pattern of activity over time. Note that inhibition of neurons is as critical as activation to the overall pattern of neuronal activity. The sequential pattern is analogous to a symphony, in which some instruments are activated and some are quieted during specified periods. The sequence of action potentials, known as the representation, acts as a code that is interpreted by the perceptual systems. Therefore, the perception of the event in the environment ignites the activation of action potentials across portions of the legionary's brain and spinal cord; the activated areas of the CNS, in turn, determine the soldier's behavioral responses.

This perceptual sequence is greatly modified by attention mechanisms. In neurophysiological terms, attention is a set of processes, rather than a single outcome or product. The initial activation occurs when the onset of a new stimulus in the environment activates a sudden change in attention and a behavioral sequence known as orienting. To return to our example, the legionary orients to the new stimulus, the approaching figures, by making eye and head movements that allow him to focus on them at a distance. The typical physiological responses that occur initially include dilation of the pupils, a temporary inhibition of gross motor activity, and a deceleration in heartbeat, followed by a change whereby the body is stimulated into action (Davis and Lang 2003). These biological responses are almost instantaneous, on the order of a few hundred milliseconds, and not under conscious control.

Our legionary's perception also can be modified by his thoughts and expectations. There is ample evidence that perceptual systems fill-in missing information, based on the context in which the visual or auditory stimulus occurs (Wolfe et al. 2019, for examples). Expectations combined with fear of uncertainty can further modify perceptions. This is pointed out by the Greek Onasander, author of a first century military treatise, "What a man has never seen he always expects will be greater than it really is," (*Strategicus* 14.4). One may question how accurate the soldier's perception of specific stimuli, such as shouted commands and aggressive grunts, would be during battle. The ancients recognized this problem. Asclepiodotus writes: "commands...given by the voice...may not carry at all times because of the clash of arms or heavy gusts of wind." (*Tactica* 12.10) Research studies concerning the cognitive aspects of human perception, however, indicate that perception of visual and auditory cues can be heightened during arousal. In fact, there is an entire body of literature, known as Signal Detection Theory (e.g. Green and Swets 1974), that describes how attention and motivation can affect an observer's ability to detect faint auditory and visual targets embedded in noisy environments. Therefore, it is not unreasonable to conclude that in the right circumstances a soldier could be aware of certain targeted stimuli in his or her surroundings, even when the environment includes a great deal of noise, dust, and other interference.

Perception is clearly the key element in the rise and spread of panic on the ancient battlefield. Although it seems self-evident, this is a point worth emphasizing. On one hand, an individual soldier may have responded to a threat perceived at the same time by the entire group; for example, a panic response, leading to rout was especially common in the case of the surprise appearance of an enemy force (Sabin 2007). Onasander notes on several occasions the importance of how things seemed to the soldiers, as opposed to how they actually were (*Strategicus*. 4.1, 4, 23.4). That a surprise attack or a sudden change in fortunes could induce panic was well known to ancient military writers (see Onasander *Strategicus* 21.9, 22.3; Frontin. *Str*. 1.5.22). The fact that in battle a soldier's perception is focused intensely in one direction, usually the front, makes a flank or rear attack all the more panic inducing. This is something that the ancients recognized. In his description of the battle of Cannae, Livy (22.48) describes an incident involving the Romans' Allied cavalry fighting Hannibal's Numidians. The Allies' "spirits and eyes were engaged in the struggle" and an attack from the rear causes "terror and confusion" and a panicked rout. If our legionary perceives the approaching figures as a sudden and unexpected threat, then his responses would be exacerbated.

General Neurophysiological Responses

If the approaching figures are perceived as threatening, the legionary's CNS and peripheral nervous system (i.e. the PNS, composed of all nerves outside of the CNS) are activated. The PNS has two major branches called the somatic and autonomic nervous systems. The somatic nerves control responses that can be consciously controlled, such as walking, talking, and sitting, whereas the autonomic nerves affect responses that cannot be brought under conscious control, such as heart rate, blood pressure, and digestion. When a general arousal is produced, one branch of the autonomic nervous system, called the sympathetic nervous system, increases the activation of nerves, especially those of the cardiovascular system, resulting in several changes: the legionary's nerves cause an acceleration in heart rate, a switch to shallow breathing, and a release of hormones from the adrenal glands. Simultaneously during arousal, a second branch of the autonomic nervous system, called the parasympathetic nervous system, works in an opposite manner, causing a deceleration in heart rate, a drop in blood pressure, and so on. That such physical reactions were associated with the feeling of fear is obvious to anyone who has been to war: Homer describes a fearful warrior in stark terms, "The coward will change color at every touch and turn; he is full of fears, and keeps shifting his weight first on one knee and then on the other; his heart beats fast as he thinks of death, and one can hear the chattering of his teeth..." (*Il.* 13.279ff, tr. Samuel Butler). In another passage, the Trojan Dolon is described as "stammering and pale with fear and the teeth chatter(ing) in his mouth," (*Il.* 10.374).

If our legionary perceives a threatening enemy force, multiple areas in his brain send signals to the spinal cord. The stimulation affects both branches of the autonomic nervous system, inducing classical symptoms such as sweating and agitation. Nerves that control the digestive tract stimulate muscle sphincters that can cause defecation and urination. Certain activated neurons change the heart rate and flow of oxygen in the blood, while other neurons in the spinal cord rapidly transmit signals to the limbs; the synergistic effects produce an increase in the speed and the intensity of the flexion of the soldier's arm and leg muscles. Homer refers in several passages to trembling warriors (*Il.* 3.34, 7.215, 14.506). One should note that the sympathetic and parasympathetic systems are not activated independently; rather, the two interact continuously, working in a complementary fashion, so that multiple bodily functions, such as body temperature, are kept within given ranges depending on the circumstances, in what neuroscientists refer to as allostatic processes. However, the sequence does not end there. The sum of these responses then modifies the soldier's perception of events in the environment. That, in turn, determines whether the soldier defensively fights, freezes, or flees from the aggressor.

Modular Characteristics of the Brain

All the physiological and behavioral actions that occur during panic are instantiated by a pattern of activity created by neurons that compose the central and peripheral nervous systems. To make sense of how this occurs, one can describe the brain as an extensive neuronal network that can be subdivided into smaller specialized networks, typically characterized as modules. Modules are subsets or aggregates of neurons that appear to respond in a quasi-independent manner, generating specific patterns of action potentials. Modules can refer to anatomically defined structures, such as the hippocampus, or to a subset of neurons within a given structure. Neurons within each module transmit electrochemical signals that stimulate the next level of neurons in an arrangement that is hierarchical. The transmission of action potentials from one layer to the next, however, is not strictly in one direction. A stimulated module can generate feedback signals to previously activated neurons and, therefore, modify the subsequent signaling. Just as a heat-sensing device in a thermostat determines whether the heater in a room is turned on or shut off, feedback signals to a given module determine whether specific clusters of neurons will be excited or inhibited, and which additional networks will be activated.

Although it is tempting to think of a given brain structure as the site that causes distinct behaviors and actions, such a description would be a false overgeneralization. Rather, each module is highly interconnected to multiple areas, so that no one portion of the brain acts in isolation. When our sample legionary views the approaching figures, for example, at least one neuronal aggregate in the visual cortex of the brain processes information about the color of the enemy's armament, while another distinct set of neurons processes information about the rate and direction in which the oncoming figures are moving. The combined signals create the representation, which directly corresponds to what is happening in the environment, in this case, the moving enemy. The representation is continually updated, so that the coded pattern changes spatially and temporally. The perceptual systems interpret the representation in an ongoing manner, affecting how the warrior responds. Thus, neuronal processing and perception are dynamic.

Likewise there is no one part of the brain that produces panic behaviors in soldiers. Rather, the activation of certain brain areas is correlated with the emotional response of fear, which can be instantiated by a panic response. For example, stimulation of a tiny structure called the amygdala appears to modulate violent or fearful (or both) behavior, but it would be an oversimplification to state that the amygdala is a "fear" center. Figure 10.1 shows the amygdala and surrounding structures situated in the left hemisphere of the brain; the right hemisphere contains the same components, in a mirror image (although there are two amygdalas, one in each hemisphere, the structures are referred to in the singular.) Furthermore, the amygdala actually is a conglomeration of multiple subsets of neurons that receive inputs from and send projections to different areas of the brain; when activated, these distinct subsets are associated with different behavioral responses (Davis and Lang 2003).

When our legionary views a fear-inducing stimulus such as aggressive attackers, neurons in his eyes and ears send signals, via multiple neuronal networks, that activate specific modules in cortex. One such area is a small section in the temporal lobe (i.e. the superior temporal sulcus, or STS) that responds when he views a moving person, but not when he sees a moving non-human object, indicating that perception of human motion is special and incorporates specific neuronal networks. Physiologically, this area of cortex is highly interconnected to the amygdala, suggesting that there is a direct link between visual and emotional signals that should affect perception (Shiffrar 2008). Shiffrar and colleagues have hypothesized that functionally this would mean that the perceptual system is primed to respond quickly to hostile human stimuli, to increase the likelihood of survival. This prediction is supported by recent research indicating that observers respond more quickly to angry body movements than neutral postures (Chouchourelou et al. 2006), an important point for military historians.

The amygdala also receives multiple inputs from an adjacent structure called the hippocampus, as shown in Figure 10.1 (as with the amygdala, the two hippocampi are discussed using the singular term). The hippocampus traditionally has been associated with memory formation. The current viewpoint in neuroscience is that neurons in the hippocampus and amygdala are highly interconnected via synapses with proximal sets of neurons; therefore, functions such as memory recall involve activation and inhibition across multiple, neighboring neuronal networks within and surrounding the medial temporal lobe (Baars and Gage 2010).

When neurons in our legionary's amygdala are activated, a cascading effect occurs, whereby excitatory signals are sent to multiple areas of the brain. One such output is to a subcortical structure called

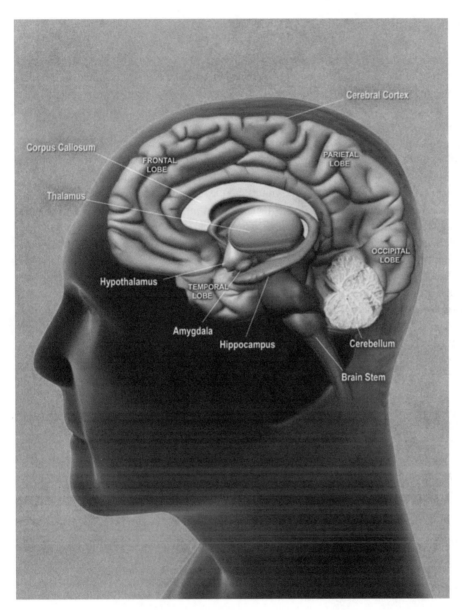

Figure 10.1   Image of normal brain physiology. *Source:* National Institute of Health, Public Domain.

the hypothalamus; when activated, it causes the pituitary gland to release hormones into the bloodstream. Hormones from the pituitary stimulate the adrenals, situated atop of the kidneys, to release epinephrine (referred to in Great Britain as adrenaline), a stimulating neurochemical that has widespread excitatory effects (Sapolsky 2004). Concurrently, other structures are activated, affecting responses controlled by the sympathetic nervous system, such as changes in heart rate, blood pressure, respiration, and incontinence, all associated with panicked soldiers. These brain modules then send signals to neurons in the brain stem that affect perception and awareness and to nerves in the spinal cord that subsequently activate muscles to coordinate movement patterns. Additionally, amygdalar neurons transmit signals to modules in the prefrontal cortex; this cortical area influences decision-making processes and conscious control of actions (Baars and Gage 2010; Davis and Lang 2003).

The Effects of Panic

Military panic is most commonly associated with soldiers running away from the battlefield. There are numerous descriptions of this; indeed, it is so common as to be a *topos*, of ancient historical writing. Despite the fact that the rhetoric of flight is often repetitive, running uncontrollably is indeed the most common reaction of soldiers seized with panic. Homer describes fleeing soldiers throwing themselves headlong into a trench and "fleeing this way and that," (*Il.* 15.344–345). In one case, Livy (22.9) describes Roman soldiers fleeing for nearly five miles, chased by Numidian cavalry. This seems like a remarkable distance for exhausted soldiers to run. Scientific research, however, suggests that individuals under stress can perform at levels far beyond the norm. When this occurs, high concentrations of neurotransmitters and neurochemicals, such as epinephrine (adrenaline), are released from neurons to cause excitatory effects, such as an increase in running speed, heart rate, and breathing. Simultaneously, other neurochemicals, can trigger a stress-induced analgesia that blunts the soldier's perception of pain (Butler and Finn 2009; Yamada and Nabeshima 1995).

Another fear response is evident when a soldier simply stops moving or freezes. In the *Iliad*, Homer sings that a Trojan warrior, Dolon, "stood still, seized with terror," (10.374). The military historian S.L.A. Marshall who accompanied World War Two soldiers into battle and recorded their experiences described a modern instance of response, "once the infantryman's mind is gripped with fear, his body is captured by inertia" (Marshall 1947, cited in Ondishko 1972). Soldiers, ancient and modern, sometimes throw themselves on the ground in panic. Although panic leads to the disintegration of formations, Keegan notes that panicked troops, when unable to run away, have a tendency to huddle together, even throwing themselves into heaps along with the wounded and killed (Keegan 1988).

Some of the actions associated with ancient panic are surprising, but can be better understood if the neurological state of fear is taken into consideration. For example, at Cannae, Livy (22.51.8) reports that after the battle, the Carthaginians found Romans "with their heads buried in holes dug in the ground. They had apparently made these pits for themselves, and heaping the dirt over their faces shut off their breath." This evidence was taken by those who found the bodies, or at least by our ancient sources, as attempts at suicide, but are better explained by the rational processes of thought being overwhelmed by an instinctual desire to dig oneself to safety. In another case, Herodotus (6.117.2) tells us that at the battle of Marathon, an unwounded Athenian soldier, Epizelus son of Couphagoras, was struck blind during the battle. If true then this may be an example of a neurological response to the stress of combat (Tritle 2000; Schoenfeld et al. 2011).

Conclusion

In discussing various panic reactions, we do not propose that describing neurological processes provides a complete explanation for why a given soldier exhibits panic responses. Neuroscientific evidence, however, can provide insight into behavior in battle. There is one caveat: although scientists can predict which areas in the brain are likely to be activated during a state of fear and anxiety, no one can definitively know why one person runs and another freezes. There would have been no way to predict if our legionary would have run, frozen in place, or fought more aggressively. One can generate the statistical probability of future outcomes, but one cannot predict with certainty that a specific behavior will occur, because of individual differences. Biological states and responses vary from moment to moment within the individual, as well as across people. Why certain soldiers react in what seem strange ways, such as trying to dig to safety on the battlefield, or why one might be struck with "hysterical blindness" is not clear.

In conclusion, when properly understood, scientific principles of neuroscience can be powerful tools in aiding the military historian. As Sabin (2007) noted, we need to delve into the mind of the ancient soldier, something we can now do with the help of neuroscience. Military historians need to educate themselves in the basics of the brain and its functions, and keep themselves aware of advances in neuroscience as they study the ancient battlefield.

Note

1 This chapter does not address *post-battle* behaviors, such as panic attacks, related to PTSD. See instead Tritle, Chapter 5.

References

Baars, B.J. and Gage, N.M. (2010). *Cognition, Brain and Consciousness*, 2e. Amsterdam: Elsevier.

Butler, R.K. and Finn, D.P. (2009). "Stress-induced analgesia." *Progress in Neurobiology* 88: 184–202. https://doi.org/10.1016/j.pneurobio.2009.04.003.

Chouchourelou, A., Matsuka, T., Harber, K., and Shiffrar, M. (2006). "The visual analysis of emotional actions." *Social Neuroscience* 1: 63–74. https://doi.org/10.1080/17470910600630599.

Crowley, J. (2012). *The Psychology of the Athenian Hoplite: The Culture of Combat in Classical Athens*. New York: Cambridge University Press.

Davis, M. and Lang, P.J. (2003). "Emotion." In: *Handbook of Psychology, Vol. 3: Biological Psychology* (eds. M. Gallagher and R.J. Nelson), 405–439. Hoboken, NJ: Wiley.

Foster, B.O. (1919). *Livy, with an English Translation*. London: Heinemann.

Gabriel, R.A. (2012). *Man and Wound in the Ancient World: A History of Military Medicine from Sumer to the Fall of Constantinople*. Washington, D.C.: Potomac Books.

Green, D.M. and Swets, J.A. (1974). *Signal Detection Theory and Psychophysics*. Huntington, NY: Krieger Publishing Co.

Grossman, D. (2009). *On Killing: The Psychological Cost of Learning to Kill in War and Society*. New York: Little, Brown and Company.

Hanson, V. (2009). *Western Way of War: Infantry Battle in Classical Greece*, 3e. Berkeley: University of California Press.

Keegan, J. (1976). *The Face of Battle*. New York: Penguin.

Keegan, J. (1988). *The Mask of Command*. New York: Penguin.

Koch, C. (2004). *The Quest for Consciousness: A Neurobiological Approach*. Englewood, CO: Roberts & Co. Publishers.

Koenigs, M., Huey, E.D., Raymont, V. et al. (2008). "Focal brain damage protects against post-traumatic stress disorder in combat veterans." *Nature Neuroscience* 11: 232–237.

LeDoux, J. (1987)." Emotion." In: *Handbook of Physiology. I. the Nervous System* (ed. F. Plum), 419–460. Bethesda, MD: American Physiological Society.

LeDoux, J.E. (2002). *The Synaptic Self*. New York: Penguin Group.

Lee, D. (1996). "Morale and the Roman experience of battle." In: *Battle in Antiquity* (ed. A.B. Lloyd), 199–238. London: Duckworth.

Lendon, J.E. (2005). *Soldiers & Ghosts: A History of Battle in Classical Antiquity*. New Haven, CT: Yale University Press.

Lynn, J.A. (2003). *Battle: A History of Combat and Culture*. New York: Basic Books.

Marr, D.C. (1982). *Vision: A Computational Investigation into the Human Representation and Processing of Visual Information*. New York: Freeman.

Obbink, D. (2006). "A new Archilochus poem." *Zeitschrift für Papyrologie und Epigraphik* 156: 1–9.

Ondishko, J.J. (1972). "A view of anxiety, fear and panic." *Military Affairs* 36: 58–60.

Richardson, F.M. (1978). *Fighting Spirit: A Study of Psychological Factors in War*. New York: Crane, Russak & Co.

Sabin, P. (2007). "Land battle." In: *CHGRW*, vol. 1, 399–433.

Sapolsky, R.M. (2004). *Why Zebras Don't Get Ulcers*, 3e. New York: W. H. Freeman and Co.

Schoenfeld, M.A., Hassa, T., Hopf, J.-M. et al. (2011). "Neural correlates of hysterical blindness." *Cerebral Cortex* 21 (10): 2394–2398.

Shiffrar, M. (2008). "Embodied motion perception: psychophysical studies of the factors defining visual sensitivity to self- and other-generated actions." In: *Embodiment, Ego-Space, and Action* (eds. R.L. Klatzky, B. MacWhinney and M. Behrman), 113–143. New York, NY: Psychology Press.

Tritle, L.A. (2000). *Melos to My Lai: War and Survival*. New York: Routledge.

Vasterling, J.J. and Verfaelle, M. (2009). "Introduction-posttraumatic stress disorder: a neurocognitive perspective." *Journal of the International Neuropsychological Society* 15: 826–829.

Watson, B.A. (1997). *When Soldiers Quit: Studies in Military Disintegration*. Westport: Praeger.

Wells, P.S. (2012). *How Ancient Europeans Saw the World: Vision, Patterns, and the Shaping of the Mind in Prehistoric Times*. Princeton: Princeton University Press.

Wheeler, E. (1988). "'Polla kena tou polemou': the history of a Greek proverb." *Greek, Roman, and Byzantine Studies* 29 (2): 153–184.

Wolfe, J.M., Kluender, K.R., and Levi, D.M. (2019). *Sensation & Perception*, 5e. Oxford: Oxford University Press.

Yamada, K. and Nabeshima, T. (1995). "Stress-induced behavioral responses and multiple opioid systems in the brain." *Behavioural Brain Research* 67: 133–145. https://doi.org/10.1016/0166-4328(94)00150-E.

Further Reading

Arkowitz, H. and Lilienfeld, S. (2008). "Why do we panic?" *Scientific American Mind*. 19 (5): 78–79.

Bardunias, P. and Ray, F.E. (2016). *Hoplites at War: A Comprehensive Analysis of Heavy Infantry Combat in the Greek World, 750–100 BCE*. Jefferson, NC: McFarland & Co.

Clark, J.H. and Turner, B. (eds.) (2018). *Brill's Companion to Military Defeat in Ancient Mediterranean Society*. Leiden: Brill.

Fricchione, G., Ivkovic, A., and Yeung, A.S. (eds.) (2016). *The Science of Stress: Living under Pressure*. University of Chicago.

Hamner, C. (2011). *Enduring Battle: American Soldiers in Three Wars, 1775–1945*. Lawrence: University Press of Kansas.

Leshan, L. (1992). *The Psychology of War: Comprehending its Mystique and Madness*. Chicago: The Noble Press.

Lawrence, C. (2017). *War by Numbers: Understanding Conventional Combat*. Dulles, VA: Potomac Books.

Sapolsky, R. (2017). *Behave: The Biology of Humans at our Best and Worst*. New York: Penguin.

Shorland, N. (2019). *Conflict: How Soldiers Make Impossible Decisions*. Oxford: Oxford University Press.

Ward, G. (2016). "The Roman battlefield: individual exploits in warfare of the Roman Republic." In: *The Topography of Violence in the Greco-Roman World* (eds. W. Riess and G. Fagan), 299–324. Ann Arbor: University of Michigan Press.

11

Roman Siege Warfare

Moral and Morale

Josh Levithan

Like a bodybuilder so enamored of his bulging pecs and biceps that his under-exercised back threatens to give out, military history has long suffered from the tendency to obsess over a few issues while neglecting the harmony of the whole. One preoccupation is with "decisive action," especially the set-piece battle, so exciting and so rare. With this fascination comes a neglect of the small actions that might take place out of view of the famous commander and yet nevertheless have more influence on the outcome. Another preoccupation is grand tactics, the troop movements directed by the commander which, if all goes impossibly smoothly, will vanquish his outwitted opponent and win the day. But combat is not chess, and describing it in a few paragraphs of stately tactical prose or flattening it onto a map, is inadequate. More important than the intentions of the commander are the perceptions of the fighters, and it is the moral intensity of their actions – the fears and motivations that play into their morale as well as the influence of cultural and ethical contexts – that lies at the root of military success. These neglected core muscles can be targeted to good effect with a close examination of Roman siege warfare.

Writing Battle

Long ago, words could be cleverly arranged so as to bring home all at once the physical intimacy and psychological intensity of combat. Short, sharp phrases could express something of the waves of fear and confidence and doubt and killing rage that swept over fighters, of how they recognized impossible strength or irresistible fury in their foe. Reading the *Iliad* can still have this effect. Ancient epic, however, attributes too much of this to the immediate intervention of the gods, who both inspire feats of superhuman valor and whisper discretion into other heroes' ears. One of the first things that Greek historians (Thucydides and his many followers) did was to sweep the gods out, leaving only the men behind. Less inevitably, ancient historiography – still much given to scenes of combat – swept the fighting men, too, nearly all of the way out of the picture.

By describing battle as a clash of masses rather than men, the standard battle piece cleared space for the heroic commander to stake his claim to a battle's authorship. Kings and statesmen, naturally, direct the course of wars, and generals are responsible both for the conduct of campaigns and for the dispositions of troops at the beginning of battles. Tactics – at its etymological root meaning the ordering of troops into battleline – was already a praiseworthy activity at the time of the *Iliad*

(2.360–368 or 4.294–309) and it certainly held the attention of Greek historians writing in the Hellenistic wake of Thucydides. By the time we arrive at Roman authors' accounts, several factors combined to further amplify the importance of tactics, and thus of the commander as dominant heroic actor in historical narrative.

The most important of these factors was the Roman Republican political system, in which the men of the senatorial families competed among themselves, seeking to rise to the highest magistracies by basking in the glory and profiting off the booty that came with a successful military command. Savvy senators soon came to realize the political benefits of controlling the representation of their victories. Writing a memoir, or commissioning (or otherwise influencing) the production of a narrative history, the commander could ensure a presentation of events that emphasized his own skill, good fortune, and courage. Fortune and courage, though important, were scattershot favors in that only a commanding general could make a plausible claim on the *intellectual* credit for a victory, and only by emphasizing the importance of tactical events. Polybius, who wrote the earliest (surviving) plausible descriptions of Roman battles, is a fairly hard-headed historian, but his portrayal of the Scipio clan – his patrons – is conspicuously heroic: not only are they brave and fortunate, they also win battles with their wits.[1] The historiographical habit of taking the point of view of the commanding general and giving him credit for whatever his troops accomplish was probably widespread, and it marks the influential battle narratives of Livy, who wrote over a century after Polybius. Livy was also influenced by Caesar, who both won many battles and wrote his own accounts of them. Bidding for supreme political power at Rome, Caesar took the time to transform the traditional "commentaries" (brief descriptions of campaigns) into artfully simple narratives that showed up his tactical genius, often at the expense of his subordinates. While Caesar's self-aggrandizement was always evident to any careful reader, his tendency to represent the confusion of battle as a performance that could be controlled by a few deft tugs on his puppeteer's strings has had an insidious influence on the "battle pieces" in historians' works, both ancient and modern.

The Caesarian operational style, too – relentless, fast-marching aggression – and the Caesarian depiction of combat as a tactical battle of wits have had many imitators. As a result of these several baleful influences we tend to expect far too much from the commander and to overlook the will of the participants. Not until Tolstoy's account of Borodino was there a serious attempt to describe battle as an agglomeration of myriad individual actions. Caesar's authority is great – he was there, in command, and he wrote the book – and this gave later writers *carte blanche* to obscure two important truths about large battles in the ancient world. First, that no one person can watch it all unfold, because battles are dusty, noisy, messy affairs (Thuc. 7.44.1). Second, that soon (if not immediately) after battle is joined, the commander possesses no "tactical" influence over the actions of engaged troops. He might run about encouraging those at the rear of the action, he might decide when to commit reserves, or he might grab a shield and try to personally shore up a faltering section of the line – but he is not in control.

One reason why this clever recasting of violent chaos as one man's stroke of genius went over as well as it did was that a Roman battle was actually relatively amenable to control. The Roman legion was divided into cohorts and centuries, and the cohort seems to have been expected to function independently, led by experienced junior officers. It could in theory carry out complicated tactical maneuvers and, in any case, every group of men could be expected to follow the lead of their centurion. This flexibility offered a new opportunity: where the commander of a hoplite phalanx might indulge in complex operational movements or play cat-and-mouse in the hours before battle, when the battle began he was among the heavy infantry and unable to influence its outcome (other than with his spear). Even Alexander, commanding mixed, multi-ethnic armies, contented himself with one basic tactical move and won by demonstrating his personal prowess, courage, and evident divine favor in the front line. Although Roman commanders were tantalized by this unreachable performance of heroic leadership, they realized both that Roman culture demanded a different mode of leadership and that its legions, capable of fighting with gaps in their ranks and moving with some precision, provided another opportunity for glory.

Drawing on the earlier Greek historians who had first worked up a version of this sort of intellectualized generalship, Caesar wrote himself into history as the very model of the commander as tactical genius (Lendon 1999). Even if Caesar dreamt of Alexander's cavalry charges (Suet. *Caes.* 7), the commanders who followed *him* imagined themselves as Caesarian paragons of command: gifted with foresight and instinct, able to lure the enemy into confidently accepting battle, to prepare his own men physically and psychologically, then to form a tactical plan which, when it was executed under his eyes, would smash the outwitted enemy and bring decisive victory.

Caesar's approach leads to the gripping, inaccurate sort of battle story we have preferred reading, but there are other, better, ways of telling these stories. Such alternatives may highlight such aspects as the ways in which the soldiers who chose either to move forward and engage or to hang back bear the responsibility for the battle's result (Tolstoy 2007; Keegan 1976). Yet there is something, too, to the popular belief that heroic actions by a few specially motivated fighters, combined with tactical acuity on the part of their commander, and perhaps some interesting deployment of weapons technology, should determine the course of combat. Can we have our cake and eat it too? Not when we are studying the ancient open-field battle. Squint though we may, there is no way to bring Tolstoy's roiling, aggregating masses of men into one binocular field of vision with the tidy curves of brightly colored arrows on maps, each showing a unit's united movement in accordance with the will of their commander.

From Battlefield to City Wall

Fortunately for the military historian, open-field battle was not the only form of major, decisive combat in the ancient world. Siege warfare provided a different venue in which the besieging commander found himself in firm control of the course of events even as the actual success of any tactic was likely to depend upon the voluntary actions of a handful of relatively low-ranking men.

The siege is made possible by the existence of fortifications – usually a wall – which not only defined the area of actual combat by limiting it to a shallow zone, but also contained the defenders, constrained the attackers, and set the distinction between attack and defense in stone. The goal of a siege could not be in doubt, and so neither could the outcome. If the attackers penetrated the fortifications and took the objective, they were the victors; if not, they lost. In another contradistinction to the fluidity of battle, the action of a siege was usually restricted even farther than the zone of the wall: either pre-existing weak points (a gap or gate) or points of weakness created by engineering (a breach in the walls, an infiltration tunnel, or a small area of wall made approachable by a siege ramp) were likely to be the focus of the action.

The ancient writers – and, in their footsteps, many recent, imaginatively illustrated books – lavish attention on the achievements of siege engineers, and ancient sources preserved lists both of machines and of a wide variety of ruses and stratagems. In addition to Caesar's asides on matters of engineering we have several technical treatises which give a good sense of the extent to which gadgetry occupied a portion of the ancient military mind (Caes. *B Gall.* 7.72–74; *B Civ.* 2.8–11; B. Campbell 1987; D. Campbell 2005). A largely unexamined tradition begins here, and we have tended to treat sieges as contests between the wily tacticians and innovative engineers on both sides. In many ways this is quite understandable, given that the commander's choice from among a handful of tactical approaches – general assaults, a passive blockade, stealth or surprise, intensive engineering – determined the course of the siege, and engineering was often essential to the eventual capture of the target. Yet, while Roman engineers certainly knew their business, they were not innovators on a grand scale. Instead, the ancient methods of reducing fortifications had been honed into a limited repertoire of approach techniques and supplemented by the use of accurate torsion artillery that could suppress fire from the walls as siege works approached. The Romans made much use of ladders when assaulting less imposing targets, but precipitous or high-walled sites were usually attacked by means of an embankment or "siege ramp," which neutralized the walls on a wide enough frontage to permit a powerful assault. Siege towers, rams, and (less frequently) tunnels dug to infiltrate or undermine were also used. This range of approaches enabled the Roman commander to choose the best technique for approaching any particular fortified site.

But practical or tactical considerations are not all there is to the story. Siege machinery draws our attention – a fascination that may lie, a millennium or more before the first Roman siege tower went up, behind the story of the Trojan horse. Siege ramps, too, are among the most photogenic archaeological remains of actual Roman military operations. The idea of looming siege machines even attracted ancient poets (Luc. 3.394), but these feats of engineering did not conquer cities any more than aerial bombing occupies contested territory: the engineers' task was only to refine the zone of the defenses into the point of the breach or the tunnel.

The engineers, in other words, fought the wall. Their task was to enable assault by opening access in the fortifications. This was a necessary preliminary to the action, but only an opening act. Victory or defeat took place not when the engineers made a breach but when it was actually assaulted. Moreover, since this point would always be known in advance, it would be intensely defended. If the defenders were willing to fight, the best engineering could only remove most of the huge tactical advantages of fortification and leave assault troops to funnel into a still-intensely dangerous area. Such an assault required no unusual physical abilities or technical skills but rather an extreme willingness to risk life and limb for collective military success. Call it combat motivation or morale, what remained was a matter of mind rather than matter.

This general sense that Roman sieges should be reread as stories that turned on matters motivational rather than physical or tactical is borne out by close examination of the Roman historians and the other important literary sources – Caesar above all. We will need the word "moral" to do double duty for us, now. In one sense, "moral" can describe the confidence and aggressive motivation of troops that is traditionally covered by the closely related word "morale." Yet when we apply it in this way to the psychological state of assault troops – to describe, for instance, the moral challenges of bringing oneself to climb a ladder all alone as stones and arrows rain down – we are usefully reminded of larger questions of morality. The tight focus and extreme danger of siege warfare cross into a moral sphere quite different from that of battle and other operations.

The Moral of the Battle Story

I have already touched on some of the reasons why open battle was generally, for a Roman commander, a desirable thing. Not only could he display tactical excellence and personal courage, but a battle often represented the best chance for a swift and satisfying decision to a military campaign. Along with these reasonably rational calculations ran a deep cultural affinity for battle as an event which would allow a man to test his mettle. An open-field battle provided an opportunity for any man in any unit that engaged the enemy to demonstrate his *virtus*, his killing courage and fundamental manliness, and quickly gain considerable prestige in the eyes of his comrades. Many of Rome's opponents felt similarly, and thus consensual battle was a relatively frequent occurrence in the years of Rome's imperial expansion.

But sometimes an invaded people would refuse battle, fearing defeat and preferring to defend only their strongly fortified places. Such behavior traded the inevitable ravaging of their country for the chance of living to fight another day by either discouraging or defeating any attempt at siege. This choice seems logical to us. Fighting from behind certain fortifications (a force-multiplier) makes more sense than embracing the uncertain risk of battle. Yet that old, lingering sense that battle – where the coward could run away, the brave seek the forefront, and the ordinary man earn respect in the mass of his fellows – was somehow a more proper form of contest, had great influence on the actual course of events.[2] Forcing the fight into a zone of fortification meant that missile weapons were more effective and that the foremost fighters could be killed by men (or even by a woman, which was considered an especially shameful death, see Loman 2004, p. 42 n. 49 and n. 51) running little personal risk. Those who offered battle showed an admirable courage, and those who killed brave men from positions of safety were craven. The "moral" choice and the tactical advantage of the defenders went hand in hand, and the fact that fighting took place around fortifications kept this moral disparity in clear view. This was no fencing match, no amoral duel of willing combatants, but rather an *unequal* fight, made more bitter because the more dangerous role fell to those who felt that they had been wronged – the attackers.

This cultural context undergirds the first of the three moral aspects of siege warfare that set it apart from battle and other operations. The defenders' choice to fight from a town or city wall meant that they would endanger Roman soldiers without suffering the same (initial) risks, and in the Roman view, this cowardice left them liable for the escalation in violence that took place during the siege.

This point of view explains the Roman sources' attention to the act of gate-closing. Throwing open the gates to an approaching army traditionally meant that the invaders would not harm the inhabitants, but closing the circle of resistance immediately inaugurated a different form of warfare in which "civilians" became legitimate targets for retributive violence.[3] This new sort of warfare, therefore, involved a new set of outcomes for each side. The attackers would spend much time and effort and were likely to suffer high casualties among their bravest men, and they were constrained to continue this costly form of warfare, since an army that dug in before a city but eventually raised the siege was acknowledging both a strategic error and a moral defeat. For the defenders, retreat or escape were usually impossible, and they bought the safety of their fortifications with the knowledge that violence might now grow and spread far beyond what could take place in open warfare. Having refused the test of open battle they were now liable to pay for it through the destruction of not just their bodies but of their homes and their families. This seems morally backward to us because the Romans, after all, were usually the aggressors, invaders, and oppressors. In the ancient view, by contrast, it was the defenders, however justified they might feel in their political cause or however much they might claim the right to be free, who were morally responsible for the suffering and destruction of siege warfare.

The second unique moral aspect of the siege also stems directly from the conditions of physical inequality, namely the particular challenge that fortifications posed to the combat motivation of the attackers. The vaunted tactical abilities of the Roman legion were of little moment here because coordinated movement was of no use in a siege assault. Neither was the motivational scheme that served for battle. Open-field combat typically involved some minutes or hours of jostling under formation discipline, the increasing tension of the approach into missile range (when tactical movement was still possible), and a final release into the rush to contact. Here various elements of

Roman training and military culture worked together. Those motivated more by the carrot of glory or the thrill of violence might lead the way, while habits of discipline, the desire to remain alongside one's comrades, and the example of such voluntary leadership might encourage others. For those tempted to hang too far back, the stick of shame (or even, rarely, of violent punishment) kept them close in support of their more valorous comrades, yet still relatively safe from the hand-held weapons of the enemy (see Lendon 2005, with Brice 2011, p. 36).

Siege warfare, by contrast, promised weeks or even months of hard labor, during which the psychological tension slowly ratcheted up as the works were brought closer to the target and missile fire from the walls became more dangerous. This tension required a sort of endurance morale – more typical of warfare in the twentieth century than the ancient world – that enabled progress on the siege works in all weather and under prolonged, if relatively slight, danger. Here a Roman commander might appeal to a soldier's pride in his occupation or his unit (e.g. Caes. *B Gall.* 7.17; Jos. *BJ* 6.142) or shore up their will to continue by displaying his own energy and willingness to see the task completed.

But exemplary behavior and appeals to any esprit de corps could do little to inspire motivation for the actual attack. Siege assaults had none of battle's push–pull tension, with a loose mass of men approaching another such group until the foremost fighters merged into a fluid zone of many individual or small-group fights. It was a matter, rather, of concentrated rushes by a few men who could come to grips with the enemy where ladder or tower met wall or in the narrow confines of a gateway or breach. These foremost fighters were subject to the focused attention of many more defenders while they negotiated obstacles, and they might be shot down, crushed, or knocked off a wall by a heavy object, or run through while they used a hand to climb instead of to defend themselves.

Josephus describes one such Roman assault during the siege of Jerusalem in 70 CE:

> The Romans set ladders up against the porticoes (of the Temple). The Jews did not hurry to stop this, but attacked violently when they had climbed up. Some they pushed back and threw down, others they attacked and killed, many they cut down with their swords as they stepped off the ladders, before they could protect themselves with their shields, and a few ladders laden with soldiers were pushed sideways at the top and toppled... the Jews slaughtered all who had mounted. The rest, intimidated by the fate of the fallen, retreated. (*BJ* 6.222-6, trans. adapted from Thackeray.)

This case was an assault from many ladders. In other situations, one man might have to go first – alone – and for this man the pressures of pride or loyalty or small-group shame were as irrelevant as any principle of tactical organization.

This sort of volunteer aggression was the only "moral" necessity of a successful siege assault, a fact that needs more emphasis than it has received. There is no clear example in the ancient sources of a formally constituted Roman unit being ordered to take the lead in a siege assault. In every instance that is described in some detail, these assaults are led by volunteers – sometimes formed into semiformal bands of "picked men," other times in seemingly unpremeditated actions. Without orders, a few men, even a single leader-of-the-moment, tap a sort of potentially self-sacrificing, heroic aggression. This is a completely different sort of combat motivation, requiring different moral preparation. In some sense Roman culture prepared young men from their youth: the spoils of old heroes were fixed to the gables of houses, and their deeds were remembered in popular song and history. The particular culture of the army, too, celebrated this extreme aggressive behavior, self-destructive in failure but tide-turning in success. There is no space here to delve into the scattered evidence for these practices (McDonnell 2006), but we can observe how the commanding general, his tactical choices having been effected by his engineers, sought to draw out this death-defying aggression in sufficient strength and numbers.

Following both literary convention and actual historical practice, commanders are often portrayed by their historians (or, in Caesar's case, portray themselves) as making speeches to their men just before siege assaults. These exhortations might include patriotic boilerplate or claims of divine sanction, but they also appeal directly to the soldiers' appetites for fame and fortune. It is only in the last century or two that we have turned against the idea that soldiers should profit from victory or that heroism can be unreservedly equated with courageous excellence in killing. Roman soldiers expected to reap the rewards of victory, and when exceptional acts were needed, exceptional rewards were offered. Self-sacrificing heroism could be bought at the right price. Roman commanders promised promotions and huge monetary rewards to successful assault troops, and they reminded their men of the rare opportunity to win the *corona muralis* – a military decoration that could only be awarded to a man who had been the first to reach the top of an enemy wall. The young Scipio (not yet Africanus) was praised by Polybius for his "shrewd combination of accurate calculation with the promise of gold crowns and the assurance of the help of Providence," which "created great enthusiasm among the young soldiers and raised their spirits" (Polyb. 10.11.8, trans. Scott-Kilvert). Caesar, too, made an assault into a contest, promising special "rewards" to those who were first on the wall (*B Gall.* 7.27; also Maxfield 1981; Goldsworthy 1996).

Those familiar with Roman culture are not likely to be surprised by the financial element, but Roman military historians have often overlooked the reliance on the *voluntary* commitment of the soldier. The fact that in the last extremity of a difficult campaign the Roman commander depended upon the will to extreme danger of a few ordinary soldiers should challenge – and change – the traditional view of Roman discipline and top-down tactical control. Even Josephus, the highly partisan historian who praises the young future emperor Titus throughout his narrative, lets his readers see the near-failure of combat motivation. When a new breach in formidable defenses reveals a makeshift wall that must now be assaulted through the breach and without the usual benefit of covering fire, Josephus adds, "none ventured to mount; for manifest destruction awaited the first assailants." This crisis triggers another long exhortation (composed by Josephus long after the fact) that discusses the likelihood of death for the assault leaders and their chance to win fame and immortality. Josephus gets carried away here, declaring that "souls released from the flesh by the sword on the battlefield are... placed among the stars" – a sentiment more inspiring to a Platonist Viking than a Roman soldier – but he rather tellingly ends the speech with yet another promise, blunt-yet-pointed, of reward and promotion for any volunteers who might survive the assault (*BJ* 6.23–53, trans. Thackeray, adapted). Siege assaults were too deadly to be combats of armies or even small units: they were an oddly epic stage for the men Homer calls the *promachoi*, those who earn fame and social prominence by choosing to fight in the front (Goldsworthy 1996).

In addition to the asymmetrical tactical situation and the different psychological pressures, there is a third distinct attribute of siege warfare that leads to its third, and most stark, "moral" quality. This is the presence in most, but not all, sieges of large numbers of non-combatants. The fact that non-combatants directly witnessed the behavior of combat soldiers changed the moral terms of close combat (e.g. Caes. *B Gall.* 7.26, 48). The defenders were not only fighting within the sight of their loved ones but they were vividly reminded of what would befall them should they fail. The idea that siege assaults are especially difficult due to the "desperate" intensity of the defenders' fighting is often invoked, and for good reason. It was well understood that once a siege had progressed to the point of an earnest assault on the walls, the symbolic beginning of which was the first use of a battering ram, (as both Caesar *B Gall.* 2.32 and Cicero *Off.* 1.35 mention) there would be no mercy for the city's inhabitants. Death was the usual outcome for males of fighting age, and rape and slavery were common fates for the non-combatants. But the sack of a long-resisting city might encompass any sort of violence at all: men of fighting age were slaughtered as a matter of course, even if they belatedly attempted to surrender; women were systematically raped; and, while survivors were often preserved for profitable sale into slavery, some particularly vicious sieges featured even the indiscriminate massacre of women and children (e.g. Caes. *B Gall.* 7.28; Jos. *BJ* 6.415-20; App. *Pun.* 15). A sack was an event outside of military discipline or social control, and the assault troops often seem to have gone well beyond any standard of human decency.

This understanding of siege and sack is also visible at the beginning of Greco-Roman culture. The *Iliad* takes place in the shadow not just of Troy's wall but of the fate that lies in store for its "civilian" inhabitants. Hector is repeatedly reminded – by his mother, by his father, and, most poignantly, by his wife as she holds their soon-to-be-murdered baby – that, after he is killed in open battle, the siege will close in on the walls of the city and, when they are penetrated, unbounded force will be released to wreak havoc on its people (*Iliad* bk. 6 and 22). The notion that the city wall is the dividing line between force and civilization, between open war and its contest of male courage and the slaughter of women and children, thus has foundations as solid in literature as in archaeology (Clay 2011, pp. 38–55). It is no accident, either, that Vergil included in the second book of the *Aeneid* a vivid and horrifying description of the destruction that was only foreshadowed in the *Iliad*. The plight of Hector and his family had been lived, in the interim, by countless thousands who had made the fateful decision to fight on after refusing, or losing, a battle.

This sort of violence was in some sense a penalty for that refusal, but it was also clearly a form of vengeance for the psychological strain and exhausting effort of attritional siege warfare. It was the pent-up rage and bloodlust of the frustrated besiegers, building during the months of prolonged danger and labor symbolized by the 10 years of Troy or Veii, that led to the transgressive violence of the sack. The sack of a city might well serve a grand strategic policy calling for exemplary punishment or the propagation of a reputation for ruthlessness that would serve to intimidate future foes into capitulation. But strategy came second: there is little evidence that a commander could, even if he wished, restrain his troops from pillage, rape, and murder as they broke into a city at the end of a long siege and a bloody assault.

Although there was no ancient equivalent to modern international law, the Roman world observed one general limitation on warfare: the circumscribing of its destructiveness through the preference for fighting consensual battles in the open. The transition from open fighting to the assault on a city most clearly demonstrates the alternate morality of siege warfare. The defenders have "forced" the invaders to carry violence from the open, where it operated only on adult males, in to the interior space of civilization. Therefore, following the logic of this alternate morality, the besieging army could exact payment for the effort of the siege in the form of violent plundering, and worse.

Sieges thus represented a breakdown of the preferred way of waging war, where courage might be tested in the open. Closing the gates forced a transition from what we might call the "warfare of acceptance" to the "warfare of refusal." A siege was conducted with an attitude of righteous valor forestalled, with a special motivational context in which the extreme measures demanded of the besiegers brought exceptional rewards. It has always been recognized that the sack serves a policy of aggrandizement by terror. The sack can also be seen as a counterbalancing of the practice of warfare after it has been knocked askew. When the defenders brought war home from its proper place in the open, they caused – or, at least, were complicit in causing – the amplification of violence and its extension to the non-combatant population.

Conclusion

Even the oft-tilled fields of Roman military history have new rows to hoe. The insights of new approaches to military history that include careful attention to cultural norms, their representation in the literary sources, and their impact on the actions of actual historical persons, can bring us further out from under the traditional biases of military history. This chapter should point the way toward those debatable borderlands of morale and morality, of reason, instinct, and cultural expectation. The study of combat is, in the end, less interesting when it concentrates on the whys and wherefores of command than when it recognizes the unusual interpenetration of fundamental aspects of human psychology and biology with culturally determined interpretations and actions. Reading for the interplay of these factors during the desperate moments of war might help us to understand ever-so-slightly better what the ancient world was really like.

Notes

1 A good example is the account of the tactics employed by Scipio in the Battle of Ilipa (Polyb. 11.20–24.9). Polybius repeatedly remarks on the foresight of his hero, who anticipates his opponent's tactics and rearranges the Roman line to counteract them. Scipio's complicated order of battle is lovingly described and given full credit for the Roman victory, while Polybius only mentioned high morale among the Roman troops as a derivative of their confidence in their commander's brilliant tactics.

2 Plato (*Leg.* 6.778e–779a) raised the idea that a good wall bred complacency, recalling the Spartan precept that dominant infantry do not need to fortify their city. Livy (e.g. 3.42.4, 3.60.8) imputed a similar disrespect for the act of defending fortifications to the early Romans. Cincinnatus (Val. Max. 2.7.7) was said to have punished a consul for waiting safely in his fortifications for relief, a shameful thing that showed a lack of manly courage. Later Romans were surely more pragmatic than these stories might suggest, and some of Caesar's legates are praised for their defense of fortified camps during Gallic rebellions (*B Gall.* 5.52).

3 In the Greco-Roman world in general it was in theory always possible to surrender (and receive good terms) simply by throwing open the gates to an approaching army, and thus it was considered bad form to treat people who had *not* closed their gates with the same severity earned by siege-resistors. Polyb. 3.86.11; Caes. *B Civ.* 1.18, 3.12, *B Afr.* 36; Sall. *Jug.* 91.7; Livy 2.17.6; App. *Pun.* 85, 92, *B Civ.* 5.56; Plut. *Aem.* 29; Tac. *Ann.* 13.41; Amm. Marc. 16.4.1–2.

References

Brice, L.L. (2011). "Disciplining Octavian: a case study of Roman military culture, 44-30 BCE." In: *Warfare and Culture in World History* (ed. W.E. Lee), 35–59. New York: New York University Press.

Campbell, B. (1987). "Teach yourself how to be a general." *Journal of Roman Studies* 77: 13–29.

Campbell, D. (2005). *Siege Warfare in the Roman World*. Oxford: Osprey.

Clay, J.S. (2011). *Homer's Trojan Theater*. Cambridge: Cambridge University Press.

Goldsworthy, A. (1996). *The Roman Army at War 100 BC–AD 200*. Oxford: Clarendon.

Keegan, J. (1976). *The Face of Battle*. New York: Viking.

Lendon, J.E. (1999). "The Rhetoric of combat: Greek military theory and Roman culture in Julius Caesar's battle descriptions." *Classical Antiquity* 18: 273–329.

Lendon, J.E. (2005). *Soldiers and Ghosts*. New Haven: Yale University Press.

Loman, P. (2004). "No woman no war: women's participation in ancient Greek warfare." *Greece and Rome* 51 (1): 34–54.

Maxfield, V. (1981). *The Military Decorations of the Roman Army*. Berkeley: University of California Press.

McDonnell, M. (2006). *Roman Manliness: Virtus and the Roman Republic*. Cambridge: Cambridge University Press.

Tolstoy, L. (2007). *War and Peace*. Trans. R. Pevear and L. Volokhansky. New York: Alfred Knopf.

Further Reading

Armstrong, J. and Trundle, M. (eds.) (2019). *Brill's Companion to Sieges in the Mediterranean World*. Leiden: Brill.

Davies, G. (2006). *Roman Siege Works*. Stroud: Tempus Publishing.

Davies, G. (2009). "Roman warfare and fortification." In: *The Oxford Handbook of Engineering and Technology in the Classical World* (ed. J. Oleson), 691–711. Oxford: Oxford University Press https://doi.org/10.1093/oxfordhb/9780199734856.013.0028.

Lendon, J.E. (2017). "Battle descriptions in the ancient historians, 2 pts." *Greece and Rome* 64: 39–64 and 145–167. doi:https://doi.org/10.1017/S0017383516000231 https://doi.org/10.1017/S0017383517000067.

Levithan, J. (2014). *Roman Siege Warfare*. Ann Arbor: University of Michigan Press.

Roth, J. (2009). *Roman Warfare*. Cambridge: Cambridge University Press.

Wheeler, E. (2011). "Greece: mad hatters and march hares." In: *Recent Directions in the Military History of the Ancient World* (eds. L.L. Brice and J.T. Roberts), 53–104. Claremont CA: Regina.

12

Roman Military Communities and the Families of Auxiliary Soldiers
Elizabeth M. Greene

Roman military studies have traditionally focused on state-level issues surrounding battle tactics, officer hierarchies, and the organization and placement of units. Although the New Military History of the 1960s made an impact in some fields of study, until the 1990s women, families, and non-combatants did not figure in Roman military history. Despite some work addressing these topics a lack of attention to these groups remains a problem in the field (Greene 2013b, n. 9). Since a typical soldier's life in the Roman army of the first and second centuries (all dates CE) was spent in camp more than in combat, it is imperative to understand the social side of Roman military life.

Introduction

The Roman army of the empire included legionary forces as its backbone, but these units were supported by auxiliary forces. Auxilia were traditionally non-citizens recruited from the empire and allies. These auxiliary forces were organized into smaller units, many of which were stationed in forts that tended to be near the frontier. These men committed the better part of their lives to military service as enlistment into the units was on average at around age twenty (Scheidel 1996), and both infantry and cavalry served twenty five years minimum. Auxiliary soldiers, therefore, spent in the military all the years during which men would typically marry and have families.

Before c.200 when Septimius Severus altered Augustus' law to permit soldiers to cohabit with women, Roman soldiers were not allowed to marry during active service and if they were married at the time of enlistment these unions were legally voided (Phang 2001). Social reality, however, differed from legal mandate. Describing the Roman column marching with Varus' legions in 9 before the German tribes attacked him near Kalkriese, Dio Cassius reports (56.20.1), "They had with them many wagons and many beasts of burden as in times of peace; moreover, not a few women and children and a large retinue of servants were following them."[1] Soldiers obviously continued or began relationships with women and had de facto wives during active service in the Roman military, which resulted in children and extended families living within military communities throughout the Roman empire. Such relationships are hardly surprising, but such de facto wives were often more than a relationship of conjugal convenience.

In other times and places the role of women in the daily routine of militaries has been crucial. Women were a fundamental part of the community, with the income and work contribution made by wives and family crucial for the subsistence of a military household (Hacker 1981; Ailes 2012;

New Approaches to Greek and Roman Warfare, First Edition. Edited by Lee L. Brice.
© 2020 John Wiley & Sons, Inc. Published 2020 by John Wiley & Sons, Inc.

Lynn 2012). Sources for modern armies show women in roles as traders and sellers of a variety of goods, cleaners, laundresses, spinning and sewing workers, midwives, nurses, and prostitutes. These are all positions that would have been necessary and vital for the Roman army also. The proximity of Roman forts and their extramural settlements and the number of military structures that are found outside the fort walls, indicate that the Roman army did not seek a strict separation of military and civilian. These lines were blurred because the Roman military community comprised a variety of individuals who all played a role in supporting a military unit.

Because of the legal ban on marriage, the role of family in the lives of soldiers did not form an important part of research agendas on the Roman army until the mid-1990s. Recent studies have made it clear that the legal certainty of the ban meant little for social reality and that military communities contained women and children.[2] At the same time as these studies have opened up our sense of the Roman military, certain obsolete paradigms as well as dogmatic and anecdotal assumptions about military life persist.

This chapter explores the veracity of Dio's report (56.20.1) through a close investigation of archaeological and historical evidence for families and non-combatants connected to the auxiliary soldiers in the imperial army. Contradicting the popular view that military spaces were exclusively masculine, evidence indicates the presence of women and children throughout the period of the legal ban on marriage (first and second centuries), even in the earliest phases of military occupation and in unsettled times and places (Greene 2013a). In combination with documentary evidence such as inscriptions and military diplomas (bronze discharge documents) that often list the wife and children of a veteran, it appears that in many cases we should interpret the material evidence for women and children as that of soldiers' families, rather than simply as prostitutes, slaves, or non-specific camp followers. As a result, it has become imperative that we also gain a sense of the dependents living within the military settlement and the use of space in and around the fort to fully understand life in the Roman army.

Military Families and the Fort Environment

At the same time that regular soldiers were banned from legal marriage, officers of a certain rank enjoyed legal marriage and could have brought their families with them into the military environment. Though a legal reality and well-represented in our documentary evidence (e.g. *RIB* 1482 and 1271), even the presence of officers' families in the military camp has not been properly incorporated into our vision of military life. It is still unclear exactly which ranks of officers were legally allowed to marry (Phang 2001, pp. 130–131). Most scholars assume that the centurion class and higher were given this privilege, including the centurions and decurions of auxiliary units, which is confirmed by epigraphic and archaeological evidence (Phang 2001, pp. 129–132; Hassall 1999, p. 36; Allason-Jones 2004, p. 274). Evidence for an officer's family in residence in the *praetorium* (commander's residence) should be expected, if not also the centurion's quarters within the fort.

Precisely where within the military environment families would have lived has been a point of some debate (Allison 2011, pp. 168–172, 2013). The families of at least some officers lived within the fort itself, as well as perhaps the wives or families of regular soldiers. Thriving extramural settlements that were dependent on the fort itself (*canabae* or *vicus*) often housed the family members of the soldiers. The military community altogether encompassed the fort and the settlement outside its walls, without a clear separation of military and civilian functions between the two spaces – there was no hard boundary where the fort's military function ended at the edge of the settlement, as will become clear in the case studies in this chapter. The entire settlement had its primary function as a military base, a community that included the families of soldiers and other non-combatants. Old paradigms juxtaposing the "military" fort with the "civilian" extramural settlement are obsolete and are being replaced with more flexible definitions (Birley 2010).

In Germany and Britain archaeological evidence suggests that the extramural settlement often was built contemporaneously with the fort, implying that the non-combatant population traveled with the unit and needed housing upon arrival at a new garrison location. Evidence of families should, therefore, be sought from the start of military occupation in a region and even in early military landscapes of the first century. At the same time, variation between forts and regional differences should be expected. Just as one would expect in any historical period, some soldiers may have chosen to marry informally during service, while others did not.

Early Military Communities in the German Provinces

Good evidence for the relationship between forts and their accompanying population in the early empire comes from the northern frontiers in Germany. The earliest forts on the German and Raetian frontiers were established in the first half of the first century. These sites provide evidence that suggests there was a meaningful non-combatant population present at many forts in the northwest from the earliest stages of military occupation, in both legionary and auxiliary contexts. This early evidence may support Dio's statement about the large number of non-combatants in the baggage train of Varus' three legions.

Some of the early first-century sites in southern Germany provide information about the residence of non-combatant populations in the military settlements just after the conquest period. The site at Kempten in southern Germany (Roman *Cambodunum*) suggests there was already a close relationship between garrison and non-combatant population in the earliest settlement phases. The site was an established town by 20, but grew out of a military garrison presumed to have been located here because of its strategic location and because of numerous finds of military equipment within the domestic spaces of the settlement (Kramer 1957, pp. 119–120). Burials at Kempten also suggest a close association between the military and civilian populations, especially children's graves that contain military graffiti (Mackensen 1978, No. 248 and 208; Faber 1995, p. 16). The burial sites of several females included items of personal adornment of northern European origin, which suggests the persistence of native forms of material culture in the first century, and points to a population consisting of both soldiers and civilians (Faber 1995, pp. 21–22). The mix of military and non-combatant material found at Kempten implies that the settlement may have been as military as it was civilian in its organization, thus providing a reminder that distinct categorization of sites is often unrealistic.

An auxiliary military settlement, especially in the first century, might exhibit native customs more readily than what one considers to be typically "Roman," with cultural traditions maintained on site, especially by the non-Roman populations. This may be particularly true with regard to tasks that were not associated with soldiers, but rather with the women that accompanied them (van Driel-Murray 1997, p. 55). In the first century in particular, ethnic units were raised and filled from the provincial populations of newly conquered areas. The finds, therefore, often reflect the auxiliary status of the unit, and do not imply that a local native group lived adjacent to the fort. Artifacts associated with female presence that have a non-Roman character strongly suggest the accompaniment of women with soldiers in the occupying garrison.

The progression of Roman conquest in first-century Germany moved north out of the Alps to the banks of the Danube. The Upper Danube frontier under Claudius was not an active war zone, nor was it a settled area confidently in Roman control. For this reason the evidence found here for extensive extramural settlement and occupation by women and children as early as the 40s is provocative because it contradicts our current expectations of military conquest and settlement. Scholars believed that we see the extensive growth of extramural settlements with the settled Roman army of the later second and third centuries, whereas the first-century army was considered too mobile to expect soldiers to have families with them. Nevertheless, first-century material from Germany contradicts this view.

The early Raetian frontier of the first half of the first century offers an interesting perspective on the relationship between forts and their settlements on a new frontier. A well-excavated fort on the eastern side of this frontier, at Oberstimm, was settled in c. 40 with an initial occupation phase until c. 70, and a second phase ending c. 120 (Schönberger 1978). Because Oberstimm has had extensive excavation with modern recovery techniques, the material remains have been analyzed with an eye toward understanding the gender balance in the garrison (Allison 2006, pp. 11–14; 2013). Artifact analysis, such as the location of certain beads and work implements, suggests that women appear to have had a presence in various contexts within the fort, as well as in all periods of occupation. There was a concentration of female and children's items in a first-century accommodation block for craftsmen and concentrations of material betrayed the presence of women and children in another barrack and a tavern (Allison 2006, pp. 13–14). Based on artifact evidence excavators hypothesized the presence of female occupants in the *praetorium* of phase two (c. 80–120) and in an open space with a probable commercial function (Schönberger 1978). The material at Oberstimm suggests a female presence from the earliest phases of occupation at this site throughout the first century and into the early second century. The specific locations of artifacts that had belonged to women and children point toward female participation in commercial activity at the fort. In the newly formed province of Raetia on a recently consolidated frontier, Oberstimm was likely already home to women and children in the earliest phases of its settlement.

Looking more broadly at the first-century frontier in Raetia to contextualize the material patterns at Oberstimm, evidence points to the simultaneous settlement by the military and non-combatants elsewhere. West of Oberstimm the forts at Aislingen and Burghöfe yielded brooches associated with female adornment dating to the earliest periods of occupation on the site in the mid-first century (Ulbert 1959). A substantial extramural settlement extended at least 200 m beyond the fort walls at Aislingen and grew contemporaneously with the fort from the beginning of military occupation (Kainrath 2008, pp. 126–128). Evidence from the site is primarily from the reign of Claudius, with some residual material from the late-Tiberian period. Such extensive extramural settlement constructed together with the fort suggests that a population connected to the garrison required housing within the military community immediately upon settlement. The fort at Burghöfe also had an extramural settlement contemporary with the fort and, like Aislingen, had its beginnings in the late-Tiberian period with its largest occupation in the Claudian-Neronian period (Ortisi 2002). In all cases there was an immediate need to house individuals outside the fort walls upon settlement.

Further west along this frontier the fort at Emerkingen exemplifies an interesting relationship between the fort and *vicus*. A granary dating to the earliest phase of the fort (c. 40) was located in the extramural settlement, rather than the more typical location within the fort (Wieland 1996, pp. 25–29). Extramural settlements always held buildings connected to the garrison such as bathhouses and temples; however, it is rare to find the granary outside the fort because of its importance to daily military needs. Its location in the *vicus* suggests there was not a substantial difference between the defined use of the two areas.

At the far western end of the Upper-Danubian frontier and at the confluence of several major traffic routes, the fort at Hüfingen rounds out this pattern. In addition to its location on the important southern Danube road that links the forts along this line, it is located directly north of the legionary fort at Vindonissa en route to the major Rhine forts. Thus, the settlement outside the fort was a potentially advantageous spot for any number of non-military activities including commercial business (Mayer-Reppert 1995, p. 37). The fort and extramural settlement at Hüfingen were constructed almost simultaneously in the late-Tiberian period (Mayer-Reppert 2005, p. 337). The need to accommodate non-combatants was present early, but the independent character of the *vicus* is evident in its location to the north further away from the fort than is typical. The cemeteries to the north and south of the *vicus*, however, contained burials of soldiers and civilians with no indication of separation or clustering, suggesting that the population formed a single community (Mayer-Reppert 1995, p. 40). Moreover, a large amount of equipment found within the *vicus* has been positively associated with soldiers, indicating that there was a mixed population in the extramural settlement as well.

Looking at the whole landscape of the Upper-Danube Raetian frontier in the early- to mid-first century it is clear that accommodation of non-combatant populations was characteristic from the earliest stages of military occupation. In all auxiliary forts along this early frontier there was an associated extramural settlement, usually constructed simultaneously with military occupation. The substantial growth of settlements and their extensive size by the mid-first century implies more than just a few "camp followers" were present. The extramural settlements were predominantly filled with domestic residences, often with a commercial space facing onto the street, indicating a possible commercial role for the inhabitants.

Early Military Communities in Britain

The frontier in Britain offers a good comparison to the German evidence. Some of the best evidence for women and children in the military environment at this time comes from Vindolanda. The site was first settled as part of the military occupation of northern Britain in the 80s and saw continual occupation throughout the Roman period (Birley 2009). The remarkable anaerobic environment of the first four settlement periods (c. 85–120) preserved unique evidence not typically visible in the archaeological record (Birley 2002). Leather shoes preserved within timber structures and fort ditches allow us to draw conclusions about the population of the fort in these earliest occupation periods. Even in the first period of settlement by the Roman army (c. 85–90) there appear to have been women and children associated with the garrison. Within the fort ditches of this period fifty-six shoes were found, 37% of which were worn by women and children. This is a significant number during the earliest stages of frontier consolidation in this region, when the garrison was living in a temporary fort that stood for only about five years in a still somewhat volatile region. The picture becomes clearer in periods two and three at Vindolanda (c. 90–105) when the footwear evidence places the family of the prefect living within the fort itself and other scattered footwear finds indicate habitation by women and children throughout the fort. By period four (c. 105–120) there is significant evidence for the habitation of women and children within a barrack block and all investigations of the internal structures of this fort have uncovered shoes belonging to women and children (van Driel-Murray 1993, 1998; Greene 2013a).

The archaeological material from Vindolanda is supported by a number of wooden writing tablets that elaborate the lives of the prefect's family living at the site in c. 97–105. The correspondence between Sulpicia Lepidina and Claudia Severa, the wives of the unit commanders at Vindolanda and Briga, shows that families enjoyed a relatively sophisticated lifestyle on the British frontier in the late first and early second centuries. The children of each are greeted and they invite each other to birthday parties and for other social visits (*Tab.Vindol.* 2, 291, 294). The Vindolanda tablets suggest also that within the military life of the fort there was a role for women. One tablet records supplies for the *Matronalia*, a Roman celebration in honor of wives and their fertility (*Tab.Vindol.* 3, 581). The letters further suggest that the families of prefects and perhaps other officers that lived within the fort were not hidden behind closed doors but were an active part of the community (Greene 2013b). A tablet from the prefect's subordinate confirms his attendance at a party in honor of Lepidina, the prefect's wife, suggesting that she was an important figure within the fort's social hierarchy (*Tab.Vindol.* 3, 629).

These clues to the social role of family members in the military community show the prominence of such individuals in the life of the fort. The *praetorium* was located in the central range of buildings in most standard auxiliary forts, next to the *principia* (headquarters building) and the granaries. Since this is the most public sector of any garrison, we must incorporate the presence of at least a wife and children into our reckoning of the function of some forts. This evidence does not take into account the dozens of female slaves who would also have been present, but further supports the conclusion that it is impossible to consider a Roman fort the masculine preserve it was thought to have been.

The material from Vindolanda is more extensive than that of any other site on the British frontier, but can be compared to artifacts from elsewhere in the region. This area was settled in the 70s and 80s, though there was not a consolidated frontier system before 105 (Hodgson 2000). The Stanegate frontier was a newly subjugated area, but was not yet the solid frontier it would become a half-century later with the construction of Hadrian's Wall. The best-understood fort in the north with archaeological data comparable to that of Vindolanda is Carlisle, about thirty miles to the west.

The earliest occupation at Carlisle is dated to 72/73, offering information on the military occupation of northern Britain about a decade before the occupation of Vindolanda. Carlisle also has phases contemporary to period one at Vindolanda, which facilitates further comparison (Zant 2009; Howard-Davis 2009; McCarthy 1991a). Carlisle has produced a small corpus of writing tablets that can be used to flesh out some social aspects of life in the fort (Tomlin 1998) and a modest assemblage of footwear helps to examine the population of the fort and the extramural settlements. The material from Carlisle, particularly from the period three fort (72/73–103/105), reflects a predominantly male population living here, with a few indications of female and adolescent presence. The extramural settlement dating to the Flavian period (c. 72–90) was an annex to the south of the garrison built about five years after the fort itself. There was a difference in the character of the finds and architecture between the fort and the annex, suggesting diverse activities took place in the two areas (Padley and Winterbottom 1991, p. 188). At the same time, there are striking planning differences between other extramural areas to the north and south of the fort and annex, indicative of two different zones of activity outside the official military area. These discrete spaces yielding unique artifact groups give even more depth to the character of early Carlisle. There appears to have been a structured demarcation of space as early as the 70s and certainly in the 80s and 90s. This, in turn, indicates that there was a need to accommodate different facets of a larger population with differing social identification at an early stage.

The character of the entire region changed in 105 when the establishment of the Stanegate Road solidified the frontier. At most sites, including Carlisle, a new fort was built and the character of the settlement changed. It is noteworthy that such extensive extramural occupation took place before the frontier was considered a settled landscape, and the complexity of the settlement at this early date is striking. There were in effect five zones of activity: the fort, the annex, and three separate areas of extramural occupation (McCarthy 2000, pp. 56–58). This complexity suggests the presence of a diverse community with various activities taking place in the early phases of settlement.

This may be due in part to Carlisle's possible status as a *civitas* capital (regional center) in this period (McCarthy 2003). Such status would draw a varied military and non-combatant population, and may have attracted more than just those individuals who had a direct association with the Roman army. This possibility may ultimately hinder our ability to interpret the military community, but it may provide an answer to the extensive variety of extramural occupation found at such an early phase. At military sites such as Carnuntum in Pannonia and Xanten on the Rhine, the extramural occupation of the legionary and auxiliary forts is distinct from that of the truly civilian *colonia* nearby. It is possible that the discrete settlements at Carlisle show this phenomenon on a much smaller scale. The proximity of the extramural occupation to the fort at Carlisle is too close to have been entirely unrelated to the military and it should be understood as a different facet of the early military settlement.

The footwear from the early periods at Carlisle is less abundant but still offers a similar picture as was seen at Vindolanda. The shoe sizes rendered from complete insoles reflect the presence of some women or adolescents within the fort in the late first and early second centuries (Mould 2009, p. 840). A single shoe reminiscent of the high-end female shoes found in the Vindolanda *praetorium* also indicates the presence of similar individuals at Carlisle. At least the family of the prefect and a few other non-adult male individuals were present within the early military settlement of the late first century. The annex to the south of the fort has been interpreted as a primarily military space because of the armor and military equipment found there (McCarthy 1991b, pp. 19–21) and the footwear from this area associates non-adult male individuals with the space. Of the complete shoes from this area, those having belonged to children or adolescents come from late-first and early second-century contexts (Padley and Winterbottom 1991, pp. 228–243). It is interesting to find evidence of children in this space because the annex was most likely used for light industrial work, storage, and workshops, so this evidence perhaps indicates the presence of slaves, another group within the military community which is difficult to assess.

The picture of the early military settlement at Carlisle reflects a largely male population, with the presence of at least some women and children from the earliest stages of occupation. Some material is reminiscent of the Vindolanda evidence from the period three *praetorium* such as the high-quality women's shoe and a writing tablet greeting the prefect's family (Tomlin 1998). The few glimpses of the presence of women or adolescents in the fort itself are intriguing, as are the few shoes reflecting children concentrated in the annex to the south of the fort. This is especially noteworthy in light of the interpretation of the annex as a direct extension of the fort with military-related activities taking place from c. 72–125.

These dates correspond well with the Vindolanda material from period one (85–90) that suggested a clear presence of women and children in this initial occupation phase. The shoes were found in communal spaces within the ditches to the west of the fort, which were active only during a short period in the second half of the 80s. We might see in the Carlisle and Vindolanda material a general reflection of a growing non-combatant population in the 70s and 80s throughout this new military landscape. The construction of the annex at Carlisle and the need to provide further occupation spaces outside the fort throughout the decade after initial settlement indicates a growing population, but one that did not strictly comprise soldiers who would be housed within the fort. Moreover, extramural settlement was needed even outside the annex in these early phases, as evidenced in the small excavations outside the fort. The need to provide moderate extramural living space is suggestive of a growing non-combatant population, unexpected in the last quarter of the first century in an unsettled period on the frontier.

Documentary Evidence and the Identification of Soldier's Families

A combination of archaeological, epigraphic, and literary sources brings together a more complete understanding of military communities, particularly as each body of evidence sheds light on a different aspect of this community. Documentary material such as funerary inscriptions and military diplomas contextualizes the archaeological evidence and helps to give social meaning to the material. Names of soldiers' wives and children found in epitaphs and diplomas confirm that in many cases the material evidence for the presence of women and children should be interpreted as items having belonged to the families of soldiers (Greene 2015, 2017). The formulaic content of all diplomas gives the right of citizenship to the soldier as well as *conubium* (legal marriage), indicating that the creation of family was an important issue for soldiers. The bottom of each diploma contained the personal information of the individual receiving the certificate (name, father's name, native tribe, or province) and in many cases the soldier also named the woman who was his de facto wife during service, solidifying that relationship. The children of soldiers are also named in this section and were given citizenship until 140 when policy concerning this grant changed. With at least 18 examples naming more than four children (e.g. *CIL* 16, 78; *RMD* 235), the diplomas show clearly that soldiers formed families well before retirement. The diplomas also challenge the commonly held belief that soldiers formed unions with local women from around the garrison (Watson 1969, p. 135). Diplomas that name a specific woman with whom *conubium* will be shared also name her origin and the name of her father. In the majority of cases where this information is supplied, the soldier and his wife originated from the same tribe; or the soldier probably married the sister or daughter of a comrade, a relationship originating from within the military community (Greene 2015, 2017).

From the corpus of diplomas that have this section of personal information preserved (c. 400), 43% name either a wife or children. Family is included as early as the mid-first century and is on diplomas for soldiers of different ranks from foot soldiers to centurions and decurions. The number of documents naming family rises steadily through the first century until a dramatic change takes place in the early second century. Between 105 and 140, after which children are no longer named on diplomas, 70% of the corpus name some form of family. The soldiers who retired in the early second century were probably recruited around 80, so we might look to the end of the first century as the start of this dramatic change in the social relationships of soldiers. Given the evidence discussed above for the presence of women and children in military communities through the first century and the relationship between forts and extramural occupancy, this evidence may be interpreted as the culmination of a steadily growing trend in military life. The diplomas allow us to begin to appreciate the depth of familial organization in military communities, even as early as the second half of the first century.

Conclusion

Different types of evidence come together to form a picture of a varied population living in military settlements in the first two centuries of the principate. Though old paradigms supported the notion that the military sphere was an exclusively masculine domain, new excavation and approaches from the past two decades have significantly changed our vision of Roman military life. Women and children were an important part of military settlements even in the two centuries during which marriage was illegal for soldiers. Documentary evidence indicates that in many cases these individuals were the wives and children of soldiers, not simply the obligatory group of prostitutes and camp followers to which any female-owned artifact was once assigned if found in a military setting. The spaces outside forts were a vital part of military communities and should be highlighted further in treatments of military space. Even within the fort itself the daily presence of the prefect's family was of great importance and their central location suggests that they could have played an important role in the social hierarchy of the fort. With reconsiderations of old material and new evidence emerging every year, a more nuanced vision of military life and the daily functioning of Roman forts emerges.

Notes

1 Compare Dio with a 1622 description of a military column on the move, "Such a small army with so many carts, baggage, horses, nags, sutlers, lackeys, women, children, and a rabble which numbered far more than the Army itself" (Parker 1972, p. 176). Other sources for women in camp, Greene 2013b.

2 See van Driel-Murray 1995, 1997, 1998; Goldsworthy and Haynes 1999; Allason-Jones 1999, 2004; Phang 2001, 2002; Allison 2006, 2007, 2013; Stoll 2006; Brandl 2008; and Greene 2013a, b.

References

Ailes, M.E. (2012). "Camp followers, sutlers, and soldiers' wives: women in early modern armies (1450–1650)." In: *A Companion to Women's Military History* (eds. B. Hacker and M. Vining), 61–91. Leiden: Brill.

Allason-Jones, L. (1999). "Women and the Roman army in Britain." In: *The Roman Army as a Community* (eds. A. Goldsworthy and I. Haynes), 41–51. Portsmouth, RI: Journal of Roman Archaeology.

Allason-Jones, L. (2004). "The family in Roman Britain." In: *A Companion to Roman Britain* (ed. M. Todd), 273–287. Oxford: University Press.

Allison, P. (2006). "Mapping for gender. Interpreting artefact distribution inside 1st- and 2nd-century A.D. forts in Roman Germany." *Archaeological Dialogues* 13 (1): 1–20.

Allison, P. (2007). "Artefact distribution within the auxiliary fort at Ellingen: evidence for building use and for the presence of women and children." *Bericht der Römische-Germanischen Kommission* 87: 387–452.

Allison, P. (2011). "Soldiers' families in the early Roman empire." In: *A Companion to Families in the Greek and Roman Worlds* (ed. B. Rawson), 161–182. Malden, MA: Wiley Blackwell.

Allison, P. (2013). *People and Spaces in Military Bases*. Cambridge: Cambridge University Press.

Birley, Andrew. (2010). "The nature and significance of extramural settlement at Vindolanda and other selected sites on the northern frontier of Roman Britain." Dissertation. University of Leicester.

Birley, Anthony R. (2002). *Garrison Life at Vindolanda: A Band of Brothers*. Gloucestershire: Tempus.

Birley, R. (2009). *Vindolanda: A Roman Frontier Fort on Hadrian's Wall*. Stroud: Amberley.

Brandl, U. (ed.) (2008). *'Frauen und Römisches Militär': Beträge eines Rundes Tisches in Xanten vom 7. Bis 9. Juli 2005*. Oxford: Archaeopress.

van Driel-Murray, C. (1993). "The leather." In: *Vindolanda Research Reports. Volume III, The Early Wooden Forts* (ed. R. Birley), 1–75. Hexham, UK: The Vindolanda Trust.

van Driel-Murray, C. (1995). "Gender in question." *TRAC* 2: 3–21.

van Driel-Murray, C. (1997). "Women in forts?" *Jahresbericht–Gesellschaft Pro Vindonissa* 1997: 55–61.

van Driel-Murray, C. (1998). "A question of gender in a military context." *Helinium* 34: 342–362.

Faber, A. (1995). "Zur Bevölkerung von Cambodunum-Kempten im 1. Jahrhundert. Archäologische Quellen aus der Siedlung auf dem Lindenberg und dem Gräberfeld auf der Keckwiese." In: *Provinzialrömische Forschungen* (eds. W. Czysz, C.-M. Hüssen, H.-P. Kuhnen, et al.), 13–23. Espelkamp: Leidorf.

Goldsworthy, A. and Haynes, I. (eds.) (1999). *The Roman Army as a Community*. Portsmouth, RI: Journal of Roman Archaeology.

Greene, E.M. (2013a). "Before Hadrian's Wall: early military communities on the Roman frontier in Britain." In: *Breaking Down Boundaries: Hadrian's Wall in the 21st Century* (eds. R. Collins and M.F.A. Symonds), 17–32. Portsmouth, RI: Journal of Roman Archaeology.

Greene, E.M. (2013b). "Female networks in the military communities of the Roman west." In: *Gender and the City: Women and Civic Life in Italy and the Western Provinces* (eds. E. Hemelrijk and G. Woolf), 369–390. Leiden: Brill.

Greene, E.M. (2015). "*Conubium cum uxoribus:* wives and children in the Roman military diplomas." *Journal of Roman Archaeology* 28: 125–159.

Greene, E.M. (2017). "The families of Roman auxiliary soldiers in military diplomas." In: *Proceedings of the XXI International Limes Congress 2009* (eds. N. Hodgson and P. Bidwell), 23–25. Oxford: Archaeopress.

Hacker, B. (1981). "Women and military institutions in early modern Europe: a reconnaissance." *Signs* 6 (4): 643–671.

Hassall, M. (1999). "Homes for heroes: married quarters for soldiers and veterans." In: *The Roman Army as a Community* (eds. A. Goldsworthy and I. Haynes), 35–40. Portsmouth, RI: Journal of Roman Archaeology.

Hodgson, N. (2000). "The Stanegate: a frontier rehabilitated." *Britannia* 31: 11–22.

Howard-Davis, C. (2009). *The Carlisle Millennium Project. Excavations in Carlisle, 1998–2001. Volume II: The Finds*, Lancaster Imprints, vol. 15. Lancaster: Oxford Archaeology.

Kainrath, B. (2008). *Der Vicus des frührömischen Kastells Aislingen*. Kallmünz/Opf: Lassleben.

Krämer, W. (1957). *Cambodunumforschung I. Die Ausgrabung von Holzhäusern zwischen der 1. und 2. Querstrasse*. Kallmünz/Opf: Lassleben.

Lynn, J. (2012). "Essential women, necessary wives, and exemplary soldiers: the military reality and cultural representation of women's military participation (1600–1815)." In: *A Companion to Women's Military History* (eds. B. Hacker and M. Vining), 93–136. Leiden: Brill.

Mackensen, M. (1978). *Das Römische Gräberfeld auf der Keckwiese in Kempten. I. Gräber und Grabanlagen des 1. und 4. Jahrhunderts. Text. II. Tafeln*. Kallmünz/Opf: Lassleben.

Mayer-Reppert, P. (1995). *Brigobannis—Das römische Hüfingen*. Stuttgart: Theiss.

Mayer-Reppert, P. (2005). "Zivilisten an der Oberen Donau–Die 'Canabenses' von Brigobannis/Hüfingen (Schwarzwals-Baar-Kries, Baden-Württemberg, D)." In: *Limes XIX. Proceedings of the XIXth International Congress of Roman Frontier Studies* (ed. Z. Visy), 337–349. Pécs: University of Pécs Press.

McCarthy, M. (1991a). *The Structural Sequence and Environmental Remains from Castle Street, Carlisle: Excavations 1981–2*. Kendall, UK: Cumberland and Westmorland Antiquarian and Archaeological Society.

McCarthy, M. (1991b). *The Roman Waterlogged Remains and Later Features at Castle Street, Carlisle: Excavations 1981–2*. Kendall, UK: Cumberland and Westmorland Antiquarian and Archaeological Society.

McCarthy, M. (2000). *Roman and Medieval Carlisle: The Southern Lanes. Excavations 1981–2*. Carlisle: Carlisle Archaeology Limited.

McCarthy, M. (2003). "*Luguvalium* (Carlisle). A civitas capital on the northern frontier." In: *The Archaeology of Roman Towns: Studies in Honour of John S. Wacher* (ed. P. Wilson), 145–155. Oxford: Oxbow.

Mould, Q. (2009). "The Roman shoes." In: *The Carlisle Millennium Project Excavations in Carlisle, 1998-2001, Volume 2: The Finds* (ed. C. Howard-Davis), 831–841. Oxford: Oxford Archaeology North.

Ortisi, S. (2002). *Römische Kleinfunde aus Burghöfe. 2, Die früh- und mittelkaiserzeitlichen Fibeln.* Rahden/Westf: Leidorf.

Padley, T.G. and Winterbottom, S. (1991). *The Wooden, Leather and Bone Objects from Castle Street, Carlisle: Excavations 1981-2.* Kendall, UK: Cumberland and Westmorland Antiquarian and Archaeological Society.

Parker, G. (1972). *The Army of Flanders and the Spanish Road, 1567–1659.* Cambridge: Cambridge University Press.

Phang, S. (2001). *The Marriage of Roman Soldiers (13 BC–AD 235): Law and Family in the Imperial Army.* Leiden: Brill.

Phang, S. (2002). "The families of Roman soldiers (first and second centuries A.D.): culture, law and practice." *Journal of Family History* 27: 352–373.

Scheidel, W. (1996). *Measuring Sex, Age, and Death in the Roman Empire: Exploration in Ancient Demography.* Portsmouth, RI: Journal of Roman Archaeology.

Schönberger, H. (1978). *Kastell Oberstimm. Die Grabungen von 1968 bis 1971.* Berlin: Gebr. Mann.

Stoll, O. (2006). "Legionäre, Frauen, Militärfamilien. Untersuchungen zur Bevölkerungsstruktur und Bevölkerungsentwicklung in den Grenzprovinzen des Imperium Romanum." *Jahrbuch des Römisch-Germanischen Zentralmuseums Mainz* 53 (1): 217–344.

Tomlin, R. (1998). "Roman manuscripts from Carlisle: the ink-written tablets." *Britannia* 29: 31–84.

Ulbert, G. (1959). *Die römischen Donau-Kastelle Aislingen und Burghöfe. Limesforschungen Band 1.* Berlin: Gebr. Mann.

Watson, G.R. (1969). *The Roman Soldier.* Bristol: Thames and Hudson.

Wieland, G. (1996). "Das Donaukastell Emerkingen und sein Umland." In: *Römer an Donau und Iller. Neue Forschungen und Funde* (eds. B. Reinhardt and U. Museum), 23–29. Sigmaringen: Thorbecke.

Zant, J. (2009). *The Carlisle Millennium Project: Excavations in Carlisle, 1998–2001.* Lancaster: Oxford Archaeology North.

Further Reading

Brice, L.L. and Greene, E.M. (eds.) (forthcoming). *Present But Not Accounted For: Women and the Roman Army.* Cambridge: Cambridge University Press.

Greene, E.M. (2016). "Identities and social roles of women in military communities of the Roman west." In: *Women in Antiquity: Real Women Across the Ancient World* (eds. S. Budin and J. Turfa), 942–953. London: Routledge.

Maxfield, V. (2002). "Soldier and civilian: life beyond the ramparts." In: *The Second Augustan Legion and the Roman Military Machine* (ed. R.J. Brewer), 145–163. Cardiff: National Museum Wales.

Phang, S. (2001). *The Marriage of Roman Soldiers (13 BC–AD 235): Law and Family in the Imperial Army.* Leiden: Brill.

13

Approaching "Ethnic" Communities in the Roman Auxilia
Alexander Meyer

Introduction

This chapter focuses on the identification of "ethnic" communities in the epigraphic record of the Roman auxilia and on the treatment of these groups by their commanding officers and the military administration. It has long been argued that auxiliary units lost their initial "ethnic" character by the end of the first century CE (all dates CE), as local recruitment became the norm and units were rarely stationed where they had been initially recruited (Cheesman 1914, pp. 67–82; Holder 1980, p. 123; Kraft 1951, pp. 62–63). However, detailed examination reveals that tribally and geographically based groups persisted among Roman auxiliary soldiers who had been removed from their homelands and were faced with contrasting social groups into the third century at least. Furthermore, these groups were maintained as distinct elements of the military by the command structure of the Roman army. These conclusions contribute to a growing skepticism of the traditional assessment of "ethnicity" in the Roman auxilia (Driel-Murray 2012, pp. 115–117; Haynes 2013, pp. 122–129; A. Meyer 2013, pp. 31–52).

The examples used as evidence in this case study are drawn mostly from the epigraphy of Roman Britain, but examination of sources from elsewhere in the empire yields similarly interesting results. While this chapter is concerned only with "ethnic" communities in the auxiliary units, the subject fits into a broader dialogue about the mobility of various groups within the Roman empire, of which the movement and travel of soldiers is only a part.

While epigraphic and literary studies occasionally reveal the ethnic bonds that connected mobile members of wealthy subsets of the population (Syme 1988), the evidence for groups formed by auxiliary soldiers, who found themselves far from home, often involuntarily, allows a glimpse of the experiences of displaced members of the humbler populations of the empire. This chapter explores some of the more notable evidence of the ways in which communities were defined among low-ranking soldiers in the Roman auxilia and the implications of these interactions within military studies. It is necessary, however, before examining the evidence to understand its limits and to define what is meant in this context by "ethnicity."

Epigraphy, Inscriptions, and the Epigraphic Habit

Epigraphy is the study of texts inscribed, scratched, or otherwise written on any surface. It includes all ancient texts except those (especially literary texts) that have been passed down to us through the manuscript tradition and those that are preserved on papyrus and similar perishable materials

New Approaches to Greek and Roman Warfare, First Edition. Edited by Lee L. Brice.
© 2020 John Wiley & Sons, Inc. Published 2020 by John Wiley & Sons, Inc.

(though those are the focus of disciplines intimately related to and often overlapping with epigraphy). Epigraphic texts include, most prominently, inscriptions on stone. Over 300,000 inscriptions survive from the Roman world (Beltrán 2015, p. 132). Epigraphy does not, however, provide a complete or even a truly representative record of the population of the empire or of the army; not all inscriptions from antiquity have survived or been recovered. Furthermore, surviving inscriptions are not evenly distributed through time; most were created in the first three centuries, and production reached its height in the second (Beltrán 2015; MacMullen 1982; E. Meyer 1990; Woolf 1996). Therefore, these periods are more fully represented in the epigraphic record. More significantly, only a small, self-selecting segment of the population chose and could afford to record information in inscriptions. Inscribing on stone is also a particular cultural practice of the Romans and Greeks, but not of many of the societies with which Rome came into contact (Robert 1961).

The desire to record information on stone and other durable material is often referred to as the "epigraphic habit" (Beltrán 2015; MacMullen 1982). Although the epigraphic habit was generally strong in the Roman army, Roman auxiliary soldiers were often recruited from communities that did not engage in the epigraphic habit. Nevertheless, after being exposed to it for many years, some auxiliary soldiers used epigraphy to record their lives and accomplishments individually, as members of their units, or as smaller groups defined by various criteria. Among this last group are some groups that are defined by their association with a culture or geographical area. We might, for lack of a better term, refer to these groups and "ethnic." This is not, however, unproblematic. We must, in fact, be especially careful to define what criteria define "ethnic" groups in this context.

Ethnicity and Ancient History

This article uses the term "ethnic" guardedly because its relationship to one's identity or to the material culture left by an individual in the archaeological record is at the center of a considerable amount of academic debate (e.g. Ivleva 2011; Jones 1998; McInerney 2014).[1]

Despite the Greek origins of the word, ethnicity is a decidedly modern concept rooted in colonial ideologies that sought to define populations according to essentially arbitrary criteria including race, religion, language and "culture" (another term which is often used without careful definition) (Jones 1998, pp. 18–83; McInerney 2014, pp. 1–8). We can trace the use of ethnic groups in archaeology back to the nineteenth century at least and it was at the heart of Gustaf Kossinna's attempts to trace the foundations of the Germanic people before the First World War (Kossinna 1911; cf. Diaz-Andreu 2015; Jones 1998, pp. 15–16). Kossinna's work, which was controversial even in its own time, was then taken up by the National Socialists and, consequently, the study of ethnicity fell completely out of favor. Ethnicity has, however, reemerged in the last 30 years as a fundamental topic in archaeology and ancient history.

There is no clear consensus about the definition of ethnic or what qualifies as an ethnic group. This is largely a result of the fact that classicists and ancient historians do not operate in a vacuum and ethnicity is also a focus of great concern to scholars in other fields including anthropology, sociology, and political science. Furthermore, scholars in those fields, especially those working in a modern context, have the luxury, or perhaps the curse, of much more robust information. This allows them to be far more specific about their definitions. For example, Anthony Smith defined six requisites to identifying an ethnic group: a collective name, a common myth of descent, a shared history, a distinct shared culture, an association with a specific territory, and a sense of solidarity (Smith 1986, pp. 21–31). Jonathan Hall pared down this definition in his examination of Hellenic identity, writing "Ultimately, the definitional *criteria* or 'core elements' which determine membership in an ethnic group – and distinguish the ethnic group from other social collectives – are a putative subscription to a myth of common descent and kinship, an association with a specific territory and a sense of shared history" (Hall 2002, p. 9). He also notes that "biological features, language, religion, or cultural traits may appear to be highly visible markers of identification but they do not ultimately define the ethnic group" (Hall 2002, p. 9). Indeed, many of the criteria that modern scholars, and especially scholars of modernity, have used to define ethnicity are subjective and depend almost entirely on circumstantial and context-dependent perceptions rather than on objective criteria (Jones 1998, pp. 18–83; McInerney 2014, pp. 1–8). While some of the more abstract aspects of ethnicity, such as shared culture, are visible only to ancient historians in isolated archaeological contexts (largely religious) and some literary sources, the epigraphic record can provide clear insight into the nomenclature of communities. These names, in turn, sometimes suggest geographical and tribal aspects of potential ethnic communities, fulfilling Smith's demands for a collective name and association with a geographical area. Moreover, in much of the evidence of the auxilia group identifications appear to be self-identified (emic), rather than being imposed on the group from outside (etic). It is on these groups that this chapter focuses.

The Roman Auxilia and the Roman Army

The Roman auxilia provide an ideal context in which to study geographically and tribally defined groups because their soldiers were drawn from communities all over the empire and they are relatively well documented in the epigraphic record. The auxilia comprised about half of the Roman army. They were made up of infantry and cavalry units called cohorts and alae, respectively, and were populated initially by non-citizen soldiers, generally from the peoples of the frontiers and less well-integrated portions of the empire. These soldiers were required to serve 25 years in the army in exchange for steady pay and grants of citizenship and *conubium* upon their discharge (legal marriage by which their children would hold Roman citizenship; Cheesman 1914; see Greene, Chapter 12 on auxilia families).

When the individual units of the auxilia were raised (and there are over 400 of these) they were given a name that reflected the tribal or geographical origin of the soldiers enlisted in them. For example, from the Iberian Peninsula there are units Aravacorum (raised from the Aravaci in the northwestern Spain) and units Hispanorum (raised from the broader population of the Spanish provinces). These units were usually posted far from the areas in which they were originally recruited. Soon after their formation, certainly after the first 25 years of their existence, they started to take on recruits from other parts of the empire. These new recruits were often natives of the areas in which the units were posted and by the Hadrianic period it is generally accepted that so-called "local" recruitment was the norm, although this generalization has come under acute scrutiny recently (Driel-Murray 2003, pp. 115–117; Haynes 2013, pp. 122–129; A. Meyer 2013, pp. 31–52). Thus, by the second century, the units of the auxilia had lost the original ethnic character that defined them in their early years. This led Simon James and Ian Haynes, among others, to stress the importance of a unifying "military" identity among auxiliary soldiers (Haynes 1993, 1999; James 1999, 2001).

It is not the case, however, that all the cohorts and alae of the auxilia simply traded one homogeneous collective background for another or that they abandoned native or tribal identities in favor of a military identity. Indeed, some units with specialist skills, such as archers and slingers, continued to recruit from specific peoples (Kennedy 1980), while other groups known for their martial qualities, such as the Batavians from the lower Rhine, continued to contribute soldiers to units that bore their names (Derks and Roymans 2006, pp. 122–123; Driel-Murray 2003, pp. 115–117; Haynes 1999, p. 166, 2013, p. 116). Such units seem to have retained at least some of their homogeneity for a considerable time. These high-profile units appear in many case studies, but there is evidence that other less obvious groups, defined by tribal and geographical criteria, existed early in the history of the auxilia and persisted within the units with heterogeneous bodies of soldiers into the third century.

What follows explores a few of the more notable examples of geographically and tribally based communities in the epigraphic record of the Roman auxilia. These communities betray a wider tendency of auxiliary soldiers to preserve some aspects of their native identity when they are displaced from their homelands and when placed within a wider heterogeneous group, and further, that this process was endorsed and perhaps supported by military commanders. While some of the communities documented in these inscriptions may be associated with times of transition, in which the composition of individual units was affected by the influx of new soldiers, this need not be a prerequisite for the formation and maintenance of geographically and tribally based communities.

The communities identified here do not fulfill all of Smith's or even Hall's criteria for ethnic communities, but they meet some important ones. Groups identified by geographical and tribal origins have explicit relationships with a specific territory, they have an implicit sense of community, and their persistence in foreign territories and in the Roman army provides a sense of shared history. These groups have the potential to illuminate some aspects of our understanding of Roman auxiliary recruitment, but more importantly, recognition of the significance of these communities within the army and their presence throughout the empire can illuminate important aspects of identity formation, code-switching, and acculturation within the auxilia. These communities, based on the relatively well-documented military sphere, may also serve as a proxy in exploration of similar issues of identity formation, mobility and sociopolitical interaction in civilian contexts.

The Epigraphic Evidence of Geographically and Tribally Based Groups in the Auxilia

One may identify these groups by two primary methods. There are those that are named on inscriptions and those that must be inferred from the origins of the individuals named and the circumstances that surrounded them. The first category is, of course, much easier to deal with. Several of these groups are named in inscriptions from the frontiers of Roman Britain. For example, exploration of the Roman fort at Birrens, northwest of modern Carlisle, in 1812 produced an altar dedicated to Mars and the emperor's victory by the citizens of Raetia serving in the second cohort of Tungrians (*RIB* 2100). These soldiers were probably recruited into a vexillation of *cohors II Tungrorum* that is recorded in Raetia from 121 to 153 and rejoined its unit before 157 at which time it no longer appears in Raetia (Holder 1982, p. 52). The identification of the *cives Raeti* in this inscription indicates that these soldiers comprised a distinct group within the cohort after the vexillation returned to its unit. It is not surprising that it would take some time for members of this vexillation to be reintegrated fully into their cohort and that the men recruited in Raetia while the vexillation was there would be identifiable as a distinct entity. Two additional inscriptions from Birrens (*RIB* 2107 and 2108) record the presence of men of the *pagus Vela(v)us* and *pagus Condrustis* in *cohors II Tungrorum*.

These inscriptions and the groups they mention are particularly significant because two of these stones, *RIB* 2100 and 2108, mention the same commanding officer, Gaius Silvius Auspex. They were, therefore, erected within a few years of each other and indicate that the *cives Raeti* and *pagani Condrusi* served together in the second half of the second century. It is also reasonable to assume that the Vellavi served in the same period. Thus there were likely to have been at least three distinct tribal/geographic groups in this unit at the same time and perhaps, more importantly, they or someone else defined these groups by their origins, rather than by some other characteristic.

We can see evidence of another geographically based group in an inscription recovered from Vindolanda. This inscription, *RIB* 3332, is a dedication to the *Dea Gallia* by the *cives Galli concordesque Britanni*, "the citizens of Gaul and the Britons in agreement" (Birley 2008). This stone was discovered in secondary construction and therefore provides no clear indication of its original context. Nevertheless, it may reasonably be associated with *cohors IV Gallorum* which inhabited the site from the early third century and was responsible for the construction of the second stone fort at Vindolanda (Birley and Birley 2012; Birley 2008, p. 176; Birley 2009, pp. 18, 118, 155–157, 183; Tomlin 2010, pp. 444 and 467). This is particularly significant because *cohors IV Gallorum* had been in Britain since at least the reign of Trajan (Birley 2008, p. 175). Thus, it had more than sufficient time to lose whatever Gallic character it may have had before it entered the province. Nevertheless, this inscription clearly identifies two distinct geographically defined groups. It may be suggested that the contrast highlighted in this inscription is between soldiers (the *Galli*) and civilians (the *Britanni*) but this is unlikely. Local inhabitants around Vindolanda are elsewhere attested as *vicani* (*RIB* 1700) and it is more likely that this was the customary term for the civilian population (Birley 2008, p. 172). Furthermore, it is significant that the inscription names the *cives Galli* rather than the *cohors Gallorum* and the *Britanni* (whether or not we should understand them to be *cives*) rather than the *vicani Vindolandenses*. This seems to indicate that the distinction here is between subdivisions of the *cohors IV Gallorum*. Unfortunately, there is no way to know exactly how these groups were defined; the Gauls may have been recruited from Gaul itself and posted to the frontier or they may have been descendants of soldiers displaced from their original homeland a generation or more before this inscription was composed. Either way they comprised a distinct body in their own perception and/or that of others.

Similar groups can also be identified in other units, in different parts of the empire, and in other chronological periods. For example, *ILS* 9132 from Samaria in Syria Palaestina dating probably to the second century, identifies soldiers from a vexillation from Pannonia Superior as *cives Sisciani*, *Varciani*, and *Latobici*. These three communities were located on the banks of the Sava River in Pannonia (Wilkes 1992, pp. 213, 217–218). Unfortunately, it is impossible to say how many men from these communities were serving in this vexillation. However, whether this vexillation was large or small it seems clear that they comprised the entirety of the detachment and that they were differentiated from their colleagues by their origins, which were used to construct a defined body. Although the men responsible for this inscription were from three different communities, the proximity of their homelands and their shared service allowed them to be perceived, either in their own eyes or those of others, as geographically or culturally distinct groups and as a single military entity. The exact criteria that led to the composition of this group are unclear but they may have shared a language with which others were unfamiliar, peculiar cultural habits, or distinct physical features or clothing. Regardless, this inscription vividly demonstrates the potential for situational identity formation and code-switching in the Roman auxilia.

Discussion: Ethnic Groups and Military Administration

These inscriptions have interesting implications in regard to the recruitment of auxiliary soldiers and the administration of the Roman army. The inscriptions associated with the Condrusi, Vellavi, and Raeti serving in *cohors II Tungrorum* indicate a variety of recruitment practices not normally ascribed to the auxilia in the second century. Based on Tacitus' statement that two cohorts of Tungrians had participated in the battle of Mons Graupius in 83 (*Agr.* 36.1), the bulk of *cohors II Tungrorum* had probably been stationed in Britain since the campaigns of Agricola. Thus it had been in Britain for over 60 years when it was posted at Birrens and these inscriptions were erected. Nevertheless, these inscriptions show no indication of strictly local recruitment, which is generally accepted as the norm in this period. Rather, there is evidence of recruitment from three distinct peoples in three separate provinces, none of which is Britannia. The homeland of the Condrusi lay in Germania, the Vellavi inhabited land in Gallia Belgica, and the Raeti were, predictably, in Raetia. As already noted, the Raeti were probably enlisted into the vexillation of *cohors II Tungrorum* that is recorded in Raetia in the middle of the second century, but the presence of Condrusi and Vellavi are harder to explain. The Vellavi were from Gallia Belgica, the province in which the Tungri lived, but at a significant distance from them (Caes. *BGall.* 7.75), while the Condrusi lived in Germania (Caes. *BGall.* 6.32.1). These are not insurmountable obstacles to recruitment but previous studies have argued that recruitment was the responsibility of provincial administrators as part of an over-arching military apparatus (Haynes 2013, pp. 98, 125, 129; Speidel 1977, p. 169). If this was the case it is remarkable that these soldiers were then assigned to the same unit in a foreign province. It would seem to indicate a coordinated effort to keep Germanic tribesmen together during their service, at least to a certain degree.

This has logical advantages, including the possibility that they spoke the same language or similar languages and that bonds fostered in this manner would improve horizontal cohesion and lead to a stronger fighting force (Lendon 2005, pp. 254–259; see also Brice, Chapter 9 on mutiny). However, it is clear that this cohort could at times be subdivided by more specific criteria than service in the unit, language, or Germanic origin. When it came time to erect a votive statue, the two tribes are identified separately. Although we cannot say whether this was the result of a decision by the soldiers themselves or their commanding officer, there is a clear maintenance of tribal identity.

However, one must not forget about the Raeti. If we are correct to assign their recruitment to the vexillation in Raetia, they represent so-called "local" or provincial recruitment. Nevertheless, the men characterized as Raeti were probably recruited from a number of smaller tribes. Yet, they are referred to, or refer to themselves (again we cannot be sure) by a collective name. This is common among displaced persons and Speidel has even argued that it was the norm for soldiers to refer to their origins by their home province when removed from that province (Speidel 1986, p. 467). In that case then it seems noteworthy that tribal appellatives are used for the Condrusi and Velavi, when they could easily be grouped together as Germani.

Terminological choices like these were likely a function of the numbers of men involved and the changing conditions within *cohors II Tungrorum*. It is reasonable to presume that the Condrusi and Velavi differentiated themselves in the years before the vexillation of this cohort returned to Britain. In the absence of other evidence, one might suppose that they were the only two groups present in the unit. The Raeti then defined themselves, or others defined them, by their difference from these two groups. In order to comprise a roughly equal population, men of different back-grounds, but collectively from Raetia, came together as the "Raeti." Thus there came to be at least three groups in this cohort, each defined by tribal or geographical criteria.

Similar group definitions are visible in the inscription from Vindolanda that contrasts Gauls and Britons (Birley 2008). There is also a similar contrast in the recruitment practices visible in this unit. If we accept that both the *cives Galli* and the *Britanni* refer to soldiers and that they are to be associated with *cohors IV Gallorum*, the former must represent homeland recruitment and the latter local recruitment. This suggests the continuation of homeland recruitment 100 years after local recruitment supposedly became the norm and does so in a unit with no known special relationship with Rome or special skills, such as those that characterized the Batavians or Syrian archers (Derks and Roymans 2006, pp. 122–123; Driel-Murray 2003, pp. 115–117; Haynes 1999, p. 166, 2013, p. 116; Kennedy 1980).

It is clear from the Birrens inscriptions, which include reference to the commanding officer of *cohors II Tungrorum*, that the tribal groups they mention were an accepted reality. The use of the unit's name and that of its commander lend the inscriptions an official or semi-official air, but how these groups were treated within their unit may be a separate matter. The fact that they were recruited from different provinces certainly suggests that they entered service at different times, but comparison with the inscription of the vexillation of the Pannonian unit in Samaria further suggests that these groups were differentiated in their service (*ILS* 9132).

The wording of this inscription is particularly significant. The text seems to imply that the Sisciani, Varciani, and Latobici comprised the entirety of this vexillation. It seems that the soldiers from these tribes were consciously selected from a large population, including men of different tribes, to serve in this detachment. Furthermore, it is logical to suppose they constituted one century or perhaps three centuries of the cohort as a whole. This is also a logical assumption to make about the Condrusi, Velavi, and Raeti in *cohors II Tungrorum*. It is, after all, reasonable to assume that the Raeti, who themselves constituted a vexillation of this unit at one time, had been formed into centuries that were well established when they returned to the larger unit.

This evidence implies an administrative recognition and perhaps exploitation of the utility of these tribal and geographical groups within the auxilia. One need not search any further than Britain to find more evidence of the use of tribal and geographic groups to create distinct components of the military. Two inscriptions from Old Penrith in the English Lake District record two more vexillations of the third century comprised of soldiers drawn from the Marsaci, another Germanic tribe (*RIB* 919) and the *Germani Voredensium* (*RIB* 920) (Voreda was the Roman name of this fort). However, there is no record of the existence of a *cohors Marsacorum* and the reference to the *Germani* is unlikely to be a generic reference to a cohort or ala. This suggests that these soldiers, like those of the other units mentioned, represent distinct populations within their units, though their names are not preserved. Furthermore, the specific terms by which they are described indicate the real or imagined geographical and tribal background that defined them.

The inscriptions related to *cohors II Tung*rorum, *cohors IV Gallorum*, the Pannonian vexillation, and the vexillations at Old Penrith give clear evidence of communities within auxiliary units. There are, however, more subtle indications of geographically defined groups within other auxiliary units that suggest these groups were more widespread than is readily apparent in the epigraphic record. In Britain, further evidence of a much smaller group defined along similar lines and without evidence of official recognition comes from Brampton, on Hadrian's Wall. *RIB* 2063 is a votive altar dedicated to the Celtic god Maponos and the *numen* of the emperor by four men who identify themselves as *Germani*. This inscription stands apart from the others in that it names individuals and that there is no indication of any official element to the dedication; it mentions neither a military unit nor a commanding officer. This lack of information makes it impossible to assign these men to a specific auxiliary unit. However, one must assume, given the general location of the stone and the origin of the four men, that they were soldiers. Furthermore, their origins seem to be a crucial aspect of their relationship since they chose to include them on the inscription. One may also infer that these four Germans comprised a discrete social unit of some kind.

While this is just one isolated inscription and can hardly be used to determine the frequency of similarly defined groups of this size, it stands as a clear indication that small groups of men of similar backgrounds did exist in and around the military. In fact, a wider search reveals an inscription that highlights the chronological and geographical spread of these groups and touches upon the potential systematic exploitation of them by the Roman military administration among auxiliary soldiers of Iberian origins.

CIL III 4227 records personal relationships between three Spaniards in an ala Pannoniorum in the first century. This inscription was found at Gyalóka, Hungary and reads:

> Abilus, son of Turancus, from Lucocadia, horseman of the ala Pannoniorum, having lived 43 years and served 23, lies here. In accordance with his will, his heirs, Bovegius, son of Veminus, of Lancia, and Pentius, son of Doviderus, of Aligantia set this up.

Although Lucocadia is not otherwise directly attested in literature or epigraphy, appearances of the name Apilus (with a P) and its variants are concentrated in the valley of the Durius (the modern Douro River in Spain), and south of Asturica. This strongly suggests that Abilus originated in this part of the Iberian Peninsula (Le Roux 2007). Of Bovegius' origins there is no question. Lancia (modern Villasbariego) is in the territory of the Astures. Since the exact location of Aligantia is unclear, one is forced to rely on onomastic evidence in order to track Pentius' origins. Fortunately, occurrences of the name "Pentius" are restricted almost entirely to the territory of the Cantabri and Vettones, making it quite likely that Aligantia lay in the northwest of the peninsula.

Abilus, Bovegius, and Pintius were probably sent to Dalmatia and then Pannonia during the Pannonian revolt of 6–9. It took at least 10 legions, 70 auxiliary cohorts, and 14 alae to suppress the Pannonians and Dalmatians and many of these troops, including three legions, likely came from the garrison of Spain (Vell. Pat. 2.113). Legion IX Hispana certainly came to the Balkans from Spain, where it had fought in the Cantabrian war, and served in Pannonia before the invasion of Britain (Pollard and Berry 2012, p. 95). It has also been suggested that Legion XV Apollinaris and Legion XX were in Spain before serving in Pannonia and Dalmatia, respectively (Pollard and Berry 2012, p. 99; Wheeler 2000, pp. 270, 306–308). Any one of these legions could have arrived on the Adriatic coast with a complement of associated auxilia, many of whom would have been levied in Spain. The Pannonian revolt also provides the most likely opportunity for Abilus and his countrymen to have been integrated into this ala Pannoniorum. The gravity of the situation would have highlighted the need to ensure the loyalty of Rome's Pannonian soldiers (Suet. *Tib.* 16). This could be accomplished by introducing soldiers from other backgrounds. Roman concern about the loyalty of Abilus' ala Pannoniorum may also explain the discovery in Salona of another tombstone related to this unit (*CIL* III 2016 = 8577). The coastal regions of Pannonia and Dalmatia were least affected by the rebellion of 6–9 and were a logical place to post units whose loyalty was, perhaps, suspect. Indeed Cloutius, son of Clutamus from Curunda, who died at the age of 35 after serving at least 11 years in the army may also be traced back to Northwestern Spain through the names Cloutius, Clutamus, Susarra, and Curunda. Thus Cloutius may be another of the soldiers transferred to the ala Pannoniorum in order to secure its loyalty.

It appears that these three men were recruited in Spain at roughly the same time. One might even suggest, based on the relative proximity of their homelands, known and inferred, that they were assigned to the same unit, perhaps ala III Asturum which is attested in Pannonia in 61, immediately upon their recruitment. These circumstances, in turn, suggest that Abilus, Bovegius, and Pintius had served together for the entirety of their military careers. These men do not seem, however, to have been from the same tribe or to have been connected by any familial relationship. Their affinity for one another must have been defined by broader geographic, linguistic or cultural criteria.

Nevertheless, it is clear that Abilus, after 23 years in the Roman military, chose as his heirs two fellow Iberians. A soldier in a unit that was raised in his homeland might expect to be surrounded by men of a similar origin to his own, especially within the first 25 or 30 years of its existence.

However, the ala Pannoniorum was likely comprised mostly of Balkan natives while Abilus served in it. It seems that Abilus made a conscious decision to nurture his relationships with his country-men, although their native ties may have seemed tenuous in an Iberian context. Abilus chose as his heirs, two of the men with whom he was in contact that most resembled him from a cultural and geographical perspective. In fact, their relationship may have been based as much on the fact that they were not Pannonian as on any concrete shared characteristics associated with their origins in Spain. In this regard, these three men seem to represent a community based on the similarity of the backgrounds, although we have no record of a collective name applied to them. While the absence of a collective name prohibits this group from being called an ethnic unit according to Smith's criteria (1986, pp. 21–31), these soldiers may represent a community as valid as those for whom a collective name has been preserved.

The location of Abilus' inscription is also worthy of discussion. The ala Pannoniorum in which Abilus and his commemorators served was stationed in Arrabona (modern Gyor), about 50 miles east of Gyaloka, where this inscription was found. This has caused Spaul to suggest that Abilus and his comrades represent a detachment of the ala sent to patrol the western approach to the area (Spaul 1994, p. 170). If Spaul is correct, one might suggest that it was the Iberian soldiers of the unit who were selected for this assignment. This use of geographic origins as the criterion by which auxiliary commanders in first-century Pannonia formed smaller corps of soldiers within their regiments suggests a continuity of practice with the vexillations in Britain and Syria, and the importance of geographical and tribal bonds in the administration of the auxilia.

The circumstances surrounding the creation of the inscriptions discussed here also deserve some attention. Three of these inscriptions may be attributed to times of transition. *Cohors II Tungrorum* at Birrens may have been newly reunited with its vexillation from Raetia when the inscriptions naming the Raeti, Vellavi, and Condrusi were erected in Britain. Likewise, the vexillation from Pannonia Superior may have been newly formed when the Siciani, Varciani, and Latobici erected their altar to Jupiter Optimus Maximus and the Spaniards may have been recently transferred when they were recorded in the ala Pannoniorum. It need not, however, be the case that these groups retained their unique character for only a short time. *Cohors IV Gallorum*'s presence in Britain for perhaps more than a century indicates that the distinction between Gauls and Britons on the Dea Gallia stone from Vindolanda was not the result of recent exposure to a new population. While some of the soldiers referred to may have been recent recruits, *cohors IV Gallorum* had probably been receiving British recruits for some time (Dobson and Mann 1973). This suggests that there was a consciously maintained differentiation between Gauls and Britons long after the two groups were exposed to each other. The persistence of these groups is significant because it allows us to posit the existence of geographically and tribally defined groups in a broad spectrum of auxiliary units over an extended period of time, rather than only in the immediate aftermath of troop transfers. This then opens up further lines of inquiry into the ways these groups interacted and were defined over time.

Conclusions

Despite the small sample from which to draw conclusions and the fact that few scholars would deny the existence of subordinate identities among the auxilia of the Roman army, these inscriptions have important implications. Primarily, they show the wide distribution and chronological breadth of geographically and tribally based groups in the Roman army and the potential of epigraphy to identify communities that have gone unnoticed. Furthermore, the Dea Gallia inscription from Vindolanda may indicate that although these subordinate identities are most visible in times of transition, when soldiers from different backgrounds are thrust together in their service, they were not confined to the years immediately following punctuated changes of circumstance. This suggests that a reassessment of the generally held belief that the auxilia lost their "ethnic" character in the second century is in order. Rather, it may be the case that auxiliary units included several ethnic groups at once, rather than a single homogenous ethnic identity.

The evidence of vexillations in Syria, Britannia, and, perhaps, Pannonia show that tribal and geographical origins were used as criteria in the formation of centuries and turmae, the next smallest regular divisions in cohorts and alae, respectively. However, this can only be determined in cases in which the origins of individual soldiers and their position within their units and subunits can be determined. The evidence presented here has highlighted the potential of this line of inquiry and the importance of further investigation of the issue.

Finally, this evidence and its interpretation have important implications concerning "ethnicity" in the Roman world. In these inscriptions we have seen a small sample of the ways in which groups of shared origin were defined in the Roman army. The reliance on tribal and geographical criteria of varying specificity, ranging from single tribes to whole provinces, stresses the flexibility of identity. This and the apparent use of these criteria by the soldiers themselves and their commanders also highlight the instrumentalist use of "ethnicity" in the army. This utilitarian approach to ethnicity is remarkable and has important ramifications in our understanding of similar civilian populations.

Note

1 From this point on "ethnic" will appear without quotation marks for ease of reading, but these caveats ought still to be understood.

References

Beltrán, F. (2015). "The 'epigraphic habit' in the Roman world." In: *The Oxford Handbook of Roman Epigraphy* (eds. C. Bruun and J. Edmondson), 131–148. Oxford: Oxford University Press.

Birley, A. (2008). "*Cives Galli De(ae) Galliae Concordesque Britanni:* a dedication at Vindolanda." *L'antiquité classique* 77: 171–187.

Birley, A. and Birley, A. (2012). "A new Dolichenum, inside the third-century fort at Vindolanda." In: *Jupiter Dolichenus* (eds. M. Blömer and E. Winter), 231–257. Tübingen: Mohr Siebeck.

Birley, R. (2009). *Vindolanda: A Roman Frontier Fort of Hadrian's Wall.* Stroud: Amberly Publishing.

Cheesman, G.L. (1914). *The Auxilia of the Roman Imperial Army.* Oxford: Clarendon Press.

Derks, T. and Roymans, N. (2006). "Returning auxiliary veterans." *Journal of Roman Archaeology* 19 (1): 121–135.

Diaz-Andreu, M. (2015). "Ethnic identity and ethnicity in archaeology." In: *International Encyclopedia of the Social & Behavioral Sciences*, vol. 8, 102–105.

Dobson, B. and Mann, J.C. (1973). "The Roman army in Britain and Britons in the Roman army." *Britannia* 4: 191–205.

Driel-Murray, C.v. (2003). "Ethnic soldiers. The experience of the Lower Rhine tribes." In: *Kontinuität und Diskontinuität. Germania Inferior am Beginn und am Ende der römischen Herrschaft. Beiträge des deutsch-niederländischen Kolloquiums in der Katholieke Universiteit Nijmegen, (27. bis 30.6.2001)* (eds. T. Grünewald and S. Seibel), 200–217. Berlin: De Gruyter.

van Driel-Murray, C. (2012). "Batavians on the move: emigrants, immigrants and returnees." In: *TRAC* 21: 115–122.

Hall, J.M. (2002). *Hellenicity: Between Ethnicity and Culture*. Chicago: University of Chicago Press.

Haynes, I. (1993). "The Romanization of religion in the 'auxilia' of the Roman Imperial Army from Augustus to Septimius Severus." *Britannia* 24: 141–157.

Haynes, I. (1999). "Military service and cultural identity in the *auxilia*." In: *The Roman Army as a Community* (eds. I.P. Haynes and A.K. Goldsworthy), 165–174. Portsmouth, RI: Journal of Roman Archaeology.

Haynes, I. (2013). *Blood of the Provinces*. Oxford: Oxford University Press.

Holder, P. (1980). *Studies in the Auxilia of the Roman Army from Augustus to Trajan*. Oxford: British Archaeological Reports.

Holder, P. (1982). *The Roman Army in Britain*. London: B. T. Batsford.

Ivleva, T. (2011). "British emigrants in the Roman empire: complexities and symbols of ethnic identities." In: *TRAC 2010: Proceedings of the Twentieth Annual Theoretical Roman Archaeology Conference* (eds. D. Mladenović and B. Russell), 132–153. Oxford: Oxbow.

James, S. (1999). "The community of soldiers: a major identity and centre of power in the Roman Empire." In: *TRAC 1998* (eds. P. Barker, C. Forcey, S. Jundi and R. Witcher), 14–25. Oxford: Oxbow.

James, S. (2001). "'Romanization' and the peoples of Britain." In: *Italy and the West. Comparative Issues in Romanization* (eds. S. Keay and N. Terrenato), 187–209. Oxford: Oxford University Press.

Jones, S. (1998). *The Archaeology of Ethnicity: Constructing Identities in the Past and Present*. London: Routledge.

Kennedy, David. (1980). "The auxilia and numeri raised in the Roman province of Syria." PhD dissertation. University of Oxford.

Kossinna, G. (1911). *Die Herkunft der Germanen: zur Methode die Siedlungsarchäologie*. Würzburg: C. Kabitzsch.

Kraft, K. (1951). *Zur Rekrutierung der Alen und Kohorten an Rhein und Donau*. Bernae: Aedibus A. Francke.

Le Roux, P. (2007). "Géographie péninsulaire et épigraphie romaine." In: *La invención de una geografía de la Península Ibérica* (eds. G.C. Andreotti, P. Le Roux and P. Moret), 197–217. Madrid: Centro de Ediciones de la Diputación de Málaga.

Lendon, J.E. (2005). *Soldiers & Ghosts: A History of Battle in Classical Antiquity*. New Haven, CT: Yale University Press.

MacMullen, R. (1982). "The epigraphic habit in the Roman empire." *American Journal of Philology* 103 (3): 233–246.

McInerney, J. (2014). "Ethnicity: an introduction." In: *A Companion to Ethnicity in the Ancient Mediterranean* (ed. J. McInerney), 1–16. Malden, MA: Wiley-Blackwell.

Meyer, A. (2013). *The Creation, Composition, Service and Settlement of Roman Auxiliary Units Raised on the Iberian Peninsula*. Oxford: Archaeopress.

Meyer, E. (1990). "Explaining the epigraphic habit in the Roman Empire: the evidence of epitaphs." *Journal of Roman Studies* 80: 74–96.

Pollard, N. and Berry, J. (2012). *The Complete Roman Legions*. London: Thames & Hudson.

Robert, L. (1961). "Épigraphie." In: *L'histoire et ses méthodes: recherche, conservation et critique de témoignages* (ed. C. Samaran), 453–497. Paris: Bibliothéque de la Pléiade.

Smith, A. (1986). *The Ethnic Origins of Nations*. Oxford: Oxford University Press.

Spaul, J. (1994). *Ala 2.: the Auxiliary Cavalry Units of the Pre-Diocletianic Imperial Roman Army*. Andover: Nectoreca.

Speidel, M.P. (1977). "A thousand Thracia recruits for Mauretania Tingitana." *Antiquités africaines* 11: 161–173.

Speidel, M.P. (1986). "The soldiers' homes." In: *Heer und Integrationspolitik. Die römischen Militärdiplome als historische Quelle* (eds. W. Eck and H. Wolff), 467–481. Köln-Wien: Böhlau Verlag.

Syme, R. (1988). "Spaniards at Tivoli." In: *Roman Papers IV* (ed. A.R. Birley), 94–114. Oxford: Oxford University Press.

Tomlin, R.S.O. (2010). "Inscriptions." *Britannia* 41: 441–469.

Wheeler, E. (2000). "*Legio XV Apollinaris*: from Carnuntum to Satala—and beyond." In: *Les Légions de Rome sous le haut-empire*, vol. 3 (eds. Y. Le Bohec and C. Wolff), 259–308. Lyon: Éditions de Boccard.

Wilkes, J.J. (1992). *The Illyrians*. Cambridge: Blackwell.

Woolf, G. (1996). "Monumental writing and the expansion of Roman society in the Early Empire." *Journal of Roman Studies* 86: 22–39.

Further Reading

van Driel-Murray, C. (2003). "Ethnic soldiers. The experience of the Lower Rhine Tribes." In: *Kontinuität und Diskontinuität. Germania Inferior am Beginn und am Ende der römischen Herrschaft. Beiträge des deutsch-niederländischen Kolloquiums in der Katholieke Universiteit Nijmegen, (27. bis 30.6.2001)* (eds. T. Grünewald and S. Seibel), 200–217. Berlin: De Gruyter.

Gilliver, K. (2011). "The Augustan reform and the structure of the Imperial army." In: *A Companion to the Roman Army* (ed. P. Erdkamp), 183–200. Malden, MA: Blackwell.

McInerney, J. (ed.) (2014). *Companion to Ethnicity in the Ancient Mediterranean*. Malden, MA: Wiley-Blackwell.

14

Health, Wounds, and Medicine in the Late Roman Army (250–600 CE)
Philip Rance

The Roman army created the most extensive and advanced medical services of any institution in the pre-industrial era. Following the establishment of a standing army by Augustus, the Roman state sanctioned and funded empire-wide, if not necessarily uniform, organizational structures and facilities for safeguarding the health of servicemen and treating those who were sick, injured, or wounded. Provision of medical care recognized long-service professional soldiers as a financial investment and reinforced bonds of loyalty between armies and emperors. The history of this institutional approach to health, which embraces developments in medicine, sanitation, hygiene, diet, logistics, and weaponry, reflects changes in the nature and expectations of military service and cultural attitudes to soldiers, and supplies criteria for judging the relative sophistication and effectiveness of the Roman armed forces.

Scholarship has succeeded in delineating the medical personnel, facilities, and practices of the Roman army, though significant obscurities persist (Wilmanns 1995; Salazar 2000, pp. 74–83; Baker 2004; Bader 2014). All previous studies terminate around the mid/late third century,[1] partly a reflection of conventional periodizations of Roman military studies, but primarily in response to a drastic diminution in the quantity and quality of source material. Knowledge of medical provision in the army of the Principate relies predominantly on two categories of evidence. First, epigraphy, particularly funerary inscriptions, provides information on the terminology, organization, status, and expertise of medical personnel and sometimes elucidates individual careers. Second, archaeology, principally excavations of buildings identified as hospitals (*valetudinaria*) at selected legionary and auxiliary forts, with associated finds of medical/surgical instruments and *materia medica* (medicinal plants, foodstuffs, pharmaceutics), permits conjectural reconstruction of the layout and functions of medical amenities (Davies 1970, pp. 89–98; Wilmanns 1995, pp. 103–116; Baker 2004, pp. 83–114; Peters 2011; Bader 2012). Literary, legal, and documentary sources can supplement this evidence, but the epigraphic and archaeological data are valuable, over and above their quantity, insofar as they cast light on practices usually too mundane or technical to attract the interest of contemporary historical writers.

In Late Antiquity, these two sources of information dry up almost completely. An overall decline in the "epigraphic habit," which severely reduces documentation of army personnel from the late third century, means that physicians are just one of several military grades or posts that are not thereafter attested epigraphically, but whose continued existence is corroborated in other sources. Similarly, the dearth of securely dated structural evidence for the continued functioning of *valetudinaria* into the fourth century (Vetters 1976, pp. 365–366; Baker 2004, p. 92) is consistent with the

New Approaches to Greek and Roman Warfare, First Edition. Edited by Lee L. Brice.
© 2020 John Wiley & Sons, Inc. Published 2020 by John Wiley & Sons, Inc.

broader difficulties of tracing the late Roman army archaeologically, largely owing to changes in its strategic deployment, organizational structure and accommodation. With their apparent resemblances to modern hospitals, *valetudinaria* have come to be seen as the acme of Roman military medicine, but they were a relatively short-lived product of particular circumstances. The archaeological evidence mainly relates to certain first- and second-century legionary bases along the Rhine and Danube frontiers, where construction of purpose-built army hospitals was chiefly necessitated by a lack of existing urbanism and infrastructure, as well as shifting strategic priorities. The demise of *valetudinaria* correspondingly mirrors the changing shape, location and significance of legions and the evolution of legionary bases into fortified towns (Dyczek 2005). From c.300, frontier troops (*limitanei*) became smaller operational units dispersed in numerous garrisons, while higher-grade "mobile" forces (*comitatenses*) were typically quartered in cities of the interior, often in temporary civilian billets. These interrelated developments not only diminished (or eliminated) the need for large-scale *valetudinaria* but also complicate the excavation and identification of military structures on urban sites.

This study collects and evaluates evidence from the late third to early seventh centuries, with a view to investigating medical provision in the late Roman army.[2] No alternative category of evidence fills the lacunae in the epigraphic and archaeological records, but diverse sources, in some cases superior to those for the Principate, partly ameliorate these deficiencies, including literary histories, law codes, juristic writings, documentary papyri, and military and medical treatises. Where possible, analysis will extend beyond personnel and facilities to examine perceptions of and attitudes to soldiers' health, especially battle-wounds, and official arrangements for invalided servicemen. Such medico-historical perspectives of ancient combat originate from nineteenth-century scholarly interest in descriptions of wounds in Homer's *Iliad*, but in recent decades "traumatology," more broadly construed, has furnished valuable insights into Greco-Roman culture (Leigh 1995; Evans 1999; Salazar 2000, pp. 126–227; Baroin 2002; Neal 2006, 2008). While late Roman sources pose specific interpretative problems, certain general considerations caution against crude comparisons with the better-documented army of the Principate. Despite a current scholarly inclination toward more positive assessments of the operational capabilities of the late Roman army, emotive preconceptions of "decline and fall" continue to inspire simplistic interpretations of the evidence for its medical care (e.g. Gabriel 2012, pp. 185–204). In contrast, there is a danger of overstating the monolithic perfection of the Roman "military machine" during the Principate. Older studies assumed a high degree of institutional uniformity throughout the empire, but recent reevaluation of the evidence infers variations in medical personnel and facilities according to region and unit-type and/or ethnicity (Baker 2004, 2009). Given the greater diversity of units, troop-types, and terms of service in the late Roman army, we should be all the more wary of generalizing on the basis of much scantier source material.

Health, Disease, and Wounds

Keeping soldiers fit and healthy was a priority for the late Roman army, as for any military institution. At a day-to-day level, this was understood to be a question of diet, exercise, and hygiene (Veg. 3.2.6–12; 4.7.5), complemented by treatment of diverse ailments, infections, and injuries to which servicemen are prone, on and off duty. Even minor conditions, if left untreated, could become debilitating or fatal. As historians with literary ambitions rarely deemed such matters worthy of record, and late Roman military medicine is untraceable archaeologically, the dearth of period-specific data permits only general remarks. Military manuals warn against routine hazards to soldiers' health: noxious locations for encampments, sunstroke, cold weather, contaminated water (Veg. 3.2.1–5, 12; Maur. 12.B.22.59–68, 23.28–36). In certain regions, especially the Near East and Africa, inhospitable frontier environments exacerbated vulnerabilities. Troops transferred from European provinces were particularly susceptible to heat and thirst in northern Mesopotamia, one of the principal combat zones of Late Antiquity (e.g. ps.-Zach. 9.1; Procop. *Wars* 2.18.18, 19.31–33). Legislation governed soldiers' bathing and the watering of horses, especially when large troop-concentrations threatened to pollute civilian water-supplies, and similar procedures were pre-scribed on campaign (*CTh* 7.1.13 [391] > *CJ* 12.35.12; Maur. 12.B.22.71–75). Nevertheless, thirsty men and horses could quickly foul streams and oases, and even in temperate regions campaigning armies might struggle to locate adequate sources of potable water (e.g. Coripp. *Ioh.* 6.292–390; 7.333-350; Theoph. Sim. 7.5.6–8).

The prevalent infectious diseases were gastroentric – notably typhoid fever and dysentery – or endemic to wetlands – principally malaria (Scheidel 2001, pp. 51–117, 2003, 2007; Stathakopoulos 2004, pp. 88–103; Hirt Raj 2006). Although the Romans lacked true understanding of pathogens, the occurrence and nature of these maladies had long signaled the importance of hygiene and sanita-tion (bathhouses, latrines, sewerage), varying in design and sophistication according to circum-stances, which provided basic protection against infections and, overall, were probably more significant in keeping soldiers healthy than medical intervention. Even so, the long-term distribu-tion of garrisons along the Rhine and Danube, until the early fifth and late sixth centuries respec-tively, and reliance on riverine supply lines, inevitably exposed soldiers to seasonally malarial marshland. Infectious diseases could ravage troops in high-density communal quarters or during prolonged static operations such as sieges, but reports of epidemics are rare and it is difficult to gauge their incidence or virulence (e.g. Amm. Marc. 19.4.1–8, 30.6.4; Procop. *Wars* 6.3.1–2, 4.16, 6.1; Stathakopoulos 2004, pp. 46–48, 99, 108–109, 164–165, 189–190). The only new contagion to emerge in this period was the recurring pandemic of bubonic plague in Justinian's reign (Stathakopoulos 2004, pp. 110–154; Little 2006). Whatever its broader and much-disputed demographic impact, there is no evidence of outbreaks afflicting Roman armies in the field, although fear of the plague induced Persian forces to abandon offensive operations in 542 (Procop. *Wars* 2.24; Kislinger and Stathakopoulos 1999, pp. 94–95). More telling is the far higher frequency of epidemics reported in Hunnic and Germanic armies, which affirms Roman superiority in sanitary measures and logistics (e.g. *Pan. Lat.* 10.5.2; Claud. *De IV cons. Hon.* 467; *De VI cons. Hon.* 238–249; Soc. *HE* 7.43.3; Procop. *Wars* 6.25.16–18; Agath. 2.3.4–8; Greg. Tur. *HF* 3.32; Paul. Diac. 3.31; Stathakopoulos 2004, pp. 100–103, 231–232, 236, 275–276, 301–302). This is not to say that Germanic peoples neglected their wounded (e.g. Procop. *Wars* 5.23.27, 7.24.15). While infectious diseases were doubtless the most pervasive threat to soldiers' health in peacetime and possibly, as in most modern conflicts, accounted for the highest proportion of combatant fatalities (Seibert 1983; Scheidel 2007; modern comparanda in Prinzing 1916), casualties sustained in combat, especially large-scale battles and sieges, sharply increased demand for acute medical care, and these usually brief but intensive episodes are the aspect of military medicine most frequently documented in historical narratives.

Late Roman sources acknowledge the importance of caring for wounded soldiers on fiscal, psy-chological, and moral grounds. The provision of effective medical services identified trained sol-diers as a valuable and hard-to-replace resource and, in simplest terms, reduced wastage of manpower. Access to or expectation of medical treatment also reinforced morale, especially during combat operations. The knowledge that wounded comrades had been properly cared for reassured soldiers that they likewise would not be neglected (Maur. 7.B.6). Similar concerns, heightened by religious obligations, demanded proper burial of the fallen, insofar as circumstances allowed (Amm. Marc. 17.1.1, 19.2.14, 4.1, 25.6.4, 31.7.16; Procop. *Wars* 4.4.22–24; Agath. 2.10.7, 3.28.4).

Wounds sustained in combat acquired moral and remunerative dimensions. Sixth-century disciplinary regulations exempted wounded men from penalties meted out to units that had performed badly in battle (Maur. 1.8§17–18). Some commanders disbursed exemplary rewards of money, property and/or promotions to wounded combatants (Procop. *Wars* 7.1.8; Theoph. Sim. 2.6.10–11). More generally, wounds were the most conspicuous and emotive statement of the debt of gratitude owed to soldiers for their services to the state. Fourth-century legislation regulating the privileges accorded to discharged soldiers invokes "the praiseworthy justification of wounds" and "the scars of glorious wounds" (*CTh* 7.20.12.1 [400], 21.3.2 [396]). Rehearsing a topos of classical literature, historians relate how soldiers "displayed their wounds" when pressing a claim to reward, recompense, and gratitude (Procop. *Wars* 6.27.31, 7.1.33; Theoph. Sim. 2.16.2–6; also P'awstos Buzand, *The Epic Histories* 5.44). In the overwrought imagery of late antique rhetoric, wounds become "founts of triumphs" and "trophies are purchased with wounds" (Theoph. Sim. 3.13.9–10, 5.4.7–8, also 2.14.4; Whitby 1988, pp. 226, 343–344).

Attentiveness to the well-being of soldiers, including care of and visits to the sick and wounded, and sharing their privations in the field, were conventional themes of imperial panegyric (Davies 1970, p. 98; Campbell 1984, pp. 32–59). This rhetorical tradition continued to shape idealized portrayals of emperors in fourth-century literature (Ausonius, *Gratiarum actio* 17; *SHA Hadr.* 10.6, *Alex. Sev.* 47.2–3, *Aurel.* 7.8). Military treatises make senior officers responsible for the medical care of men under their command. Vegetius assigns oversight of physicians (*medici*) and facilities in the camp to the commander-in chief and regimental officers (3.2.6; cf. *Dig.* 49.16.12§2), observing that this function was previously performed by *praefecti castrorum* (2.10.3), though his report of ancient practice may entail misconception. Similarly Maurice, in part reproducing older sources, requires commanders to make adequate provision for the wounded on the day of battle (2.9, 7.B.6, 8.B.43; Rance forthcoming). Historical narratives report instances of Roman commanders taking steps to fulfill this obligation to their men (Mal. 12.36; Procop. *Wars* 2.19.45; Theoph. Sim. 2.6.12).

Medical Personnel

A brief outline of what is known of medical personnel in the army of the Principate will assist in clarifying the character and limitations of the late antique evidence. Army physicians, broadly termed *medici*, varied in background, rank, and expertise. Many were professional soldiers (*milites*). Some of these were ordinary servicemen, who probably received medical instruction in the army. As soldiers assigned to special duties, they were classed as *immunes* and excused menial tasks. Others attained more senior grades, though questions of hierarchy and remuneration remain unresolved. In addition, civilian *medici* administered to the army, apparently in accordance with shorter-term contractual arrangements, varying in length and conditions. Others offered their services whenever local medical or military exigencies required. These different recruitment mechanisms responded to the difficulties of procuring enough physicians to meet fluctuating numerical and geographical need. There was no independent medical corps; rather *medici* were enrolled in individual units of all types. Conservative assessments estimate one *medicus* per c.500-man unit (*cohors, ala, numerus*) or 200/250-man warship, though recent scholarship has challenged assumptions of organizational standardization. Categories of specialist are documented, including surgeon (*medicus chirurg(ic)us*), ward doctor or internist (*clinicus*), and oculist (*ocularius*). An *optio valetudinarii* exercised administrative supervision of a hospital; *capsarii* are conjecturally identified as orderlies or paramedics (Davies 1969, 1970, pp. 86–89, 1972; Wilmanns 1995, pp. 61–102, 117–132; Baker 2004, pp. 41–53, 128–131).

The late Roman evidence, though more meager and ambiguous, shows that various circumstances continue to account for the presence of doctors in the army. At the highest level, as in previous centuries, medical practitioners attended emperors and perhaps commanders on campaign. Most famously, Oribasius accompanied Julian on his Persian expedition in 363 and reportedly tended the wounded emperor on his death-bed (Philostorg. 7.15; J. Lyd. *De mens.* 4.118; Baldwin 1975; Lascaratos and Voros 2000). Besides treating the wounds and ailments of the commander-in-chief and his staff, a body of senior medical expertise could advise on matters relating to the health of the army, such as outbreaks of epidemic disease (e.g. Amm. Marc. 30.6.4–5). Possible candidates for this role were *archiatri sacri palatii*, "chief physicians" who from the mid-fourth century, if not earlier, were appointed to "serve within the palace" (*intra palatium militantes*), though their number and responsibilities are uncertain (Hoffmann 1969–1970, I 100 n.391; Blockley 1980).

Beyond the privileged circle of a commander's entourage, the evidence for *medici* in the late Roman army encompasses narrative histories, legal codes, and papyri. Given the likelihood that civilian doctors periodically treated army personnel, determination of an individual's status is sometimes unclear even in military contexts. Ambiguity surrounds Ammianus' circumlocutory references to "carers" (*curantes*) and "men experienced in healing" (*mederi periti*) who tended the defenders of Amida in 359, an event the historian witnessed (19.2.15). Even if these physicians were civilian Amidan residents, however, Ammianus' gory tableau of the plight of the wounded during this siege does not justify crude assumptions of a general disintegration of the army's medical services by this date (thus Gabriel 2012, pp. 188–189). Nor can an overall shortage of army doctors be inferred from Ammianus' report that he himself, in the thick of a mounted skirmish, was asked to assist a comrade by pulling an arrow from his thigh (18.8.11; Salazar 2000, pp. 47, 83, 92–93). Ammianus subsequently (30.6.4–5) relates that when Valentinian I suffered a fatal apoplectic fit at Brigetio in 375, while campaigning against the Quadi, initially "no physician could be found owing to the fact that [Valentinian] had dispatched them to various places to tend soldiers beset by plague. Eventually, however, one was located." Again it is uncertain whether these *medici* were army personnel, imperial physicians and/or local civilians. Similarly indeterminable is the status of the doctor (*iatros*) named Theodore who treated the commander Bonus when wounded during the Avars' siege of Sirmium in 568 (Men. Prot. frag. 12.5; *PLRE* III, Bonus[4]; Theodorus[28]). Allusions to doctors in military manuals likewise lack specificity (Veg. 2.10.3, 3.2.6; Maur. 7.B.6, 8.B.43).

As previously observed, epigraphic evidence for army physicians terminates in the late third century. Once doubtful cases are excluded (*CIL* V 8741 = *ILCV* 833 = *ILS* 7797; Hoffmann 1969–1970, I 63, 100, 111; Lettich 1984, pp. 52–53; Schulze 2005, p. 100), the remaining evidence is thin but instructive. In particular, it attests to the existence of army medical personnel up to the late sixth century, and potentially beyond, and their continuing organization on a regimental basis. Furthermore, the implication of different grades or categories of *medicus* suggests that, as during the Principate, the army continued to acquire medical expertise by various means. The record supplies three examples of named army physicians, whose careers can be elucidated by legal and circumstantial evidence. Ammianus mentions a certain Dorus, a "former physician" (*ex medico*) in a *schola palatina*, one of the elite mounted guard units attached to the imperial household. The historian remarks that, during the reign of the usurper Magnentius (350–353), this Dorus was promoted to the post of *centurio nitentium rerum* at Rome, apparently a superintendent of public works of art. Dorus' elevation from regimental *medicus*, albeit in a palatine unit, to an unrelated urban magistracy, with the rank of *centurio*, is without parallel and interpretation is fraught with difficulty, but it seems likely that as *medicus* he already held an officer-grade consistent with this promotion (Amm. Marc. 16.6.2; *PLRE* I, Dorus). Of potential relevance is a near-contemporary bilingual Latin/Greek funerary stele erected by Flavius Maximinus, a *senator* (senior officer) in another *schola palatina* based at Nicomedia in Bithynia, in memory of his five-year-old son, "who, cut by the doctor, has taken his place among the martyrs." The unnamed *medicus/iatros* may, like Dorus, have been the regimental physician of a *schola palatina*, although employment of a local civilian doctor cannot be ruled out. In any case, the epitaph underlines the dangers of surgery, for both the patient's life and the surgeon's reputation (*CIL* III 14188 = *ILCV* 2180 = *SEG* XXXVII 1081; Schulze 2009, pp. 19–20).

Sixth-century papyrological evidence testifies to another regimental physician. The documentary dossier of Patermouthis, a soldier in the legion based at Syene in Upper Egypt, contains a record of a property transaction in 585. Collectively the signatory, scribe, and witnesses comprise eight men of the same regiment, including "Fl(avius) Joseph (son of?) Victor, physician (*iatros*) and soldier (*stratiōtēs*) of the legion of Syene" (*P. Münch.* 9.106). Among Joseph's comrades, three are termed simply "soldier," three are centurions, and one a former *vicarius* (acting unit commander). This mixture of ordinary soldiers and the highest-ranking regimental officers leaves the physician's relative seniority unclear, and in any case literacy and/or acquaintance rather than hierarchy probably determined this selection. The conjunction "*iatros* and *stratiōtēs*," however, recalls the expression *miles medicus*, "soldier physician," documented in legions of the Principate and interpreted as a *medicus* with the grade of *immunis* (*CIL* III 14347; XIII 7943; Davies 1969, pp. 84–87; 1972, pp. 9–10; Wilmanns 1995, pp. 77–78). As legionary grades and posts remained largely unchanged in the late Roman period, it is legitimate to conclude that Joseph the "physician and soldier" had the same status in 585. This interpretation is supported by the *Digest* (50.6.7), compiled 530–533, which cites a late second-century juristic definition of those specialists in a military unit who should be classed as *immunes* and thus exempted from menial duties: the list includes *optio valetudinarii, medici, capsarii* (Davies 1969, p. 87; Wilmanns 1995, pp. 185–186, 217–219). The reiteration of this passage, presumably on account of its continued relevance, likewise points to the persistence of the grade of "soldier physician" in the sixth-century army.

Finally, the sixth-century papyrological archive from Nessana, a small fortress town in the southwestern Negev, contains a record of official payments, which in some way relate to the garrison. The schedule lists groups and individuals, many bearing administrative and military titles, and includes "John, physician (*iatros*)" (*P. Ness* 36.15). In the absence of additional distinctions, there can be no certainty that John was a member of the unidentified unit stationed in the fort (Rubin 1997). His inclusion in this document, however, suggests that, if not an enlisted soldier, he was at least a civilian physician providing services or temporarily contracted to the army, perhaps attracted to this remote garrison town by favorable terms, including regular pay and immunity from civic obligations. Again, this interpretation finds support in contemporary legislation (*CJ* 10.53.1), which reiterates an earlier legal ruling (dated 212–217) concerning the privileges of civilian *medici* employed by the army (Davies 1969, pp. 93–94; Wilmanns 1995, pp. 91, 208–209), with the implication that these circumstances persisted in the sixth century.

For most of Roman history almost nothing is known about personnel or procedures for retrieving casualties from the battlefield during and after combat. Incidental reports hint at the use of improvised "stretchers," at least for commanding officers, but their regularity and character are uncertain. One account of the fatal wounding of Julian in 363 relates that his attendants laid the emperor on a shield and quickly bore him to his tent (Philostorg. 7.15). A Roman officer wounded in a cavalry action in 556 was extricated from the fighting by his entourage and brought back to camp "on a litter" (*epi klinēs*); as all his troops were mounted, this was presumably a makeshift structure slung from or drawn behind a horse (Agath. 4.14.1-5; *PLRE* III, Maxentius[2]). It is only toward the end of the period that personnel dedicated to the retrieval of the wounded are attested. In his prescription for large-scale cavalry deployment in the *Strategicon*, Maurice defines the organization and duties of medical orderlies whom he terms *deputati* (1.3.30–32, 2.9, 3.7–8, 5.2.7–8, 7.B.17.17–19). Late Latin *deputatus* is not specific to this function but rather a generic label applied to soldiers "seconded" to diverse special or technical assignments (*CTh* 6.24.5 [393]; *CJ* 12.37.17 [491–518]; *Nov.* 85.1, 3 [539]; J. Lyd. *De mag.* 1.46; Philipsborn 1950). The term is not attested elsewhere in connection with the army's medical personnel, though in some documents its meaning is unspecified (e.g. *P. Masp.* 67321.B.10 [533/4 or 548/9]). Maurice states that eight to 10 poorer-quality men, unarmed, and lightly equipped, should be selected from each regiment as ad hoc ambulanciers; no paramedical competence or specialist kit is stipulated other than a water flask. Their primary function was to ride in the rear of the battle-line, rescuing troopers wounded or unhorsed in action and transferring them to medical assistance or a fresh mount. Stirrups, a recent innovation, facilitated this task – Maurice specifies that both stirrups should be affixed to the left side of the saddle, one at the pommel, the other at the cantle, to assist in hoisting an injured passenger on to the horse. For each man rescued a *deputatus* was to receive one *solidus* from regimental funds. These measures are not otherwise documented and it remains unclear whether *deputati* were an older institution or the author's innovation, whose implementation cannot be demonstrated (Rance forthcoming).

Wounds and Their Treatment (Literary and Medical)

Soldiers sustained injuries on and off the battlefield. Training posed diverse hazards, typically from projectiles, sword-cuts, or equestrian collisions (Maur. 3.5.105–109; *Mirac. S. Anast. Persae* 8; Rance 2000). Special legal provisions governed cases of men accidentally wounded or killed on the exercise-ground (Just. *Instit.* 4.3.4). Combat not only intensified casualties but also proved of greatest interest to historical writers. Their accounts, augmented by the known capabilities of weaponry and protective equipment, indicate that likely wounds encompassed incisions, lacerations, abrasions, penetrations, and broken bones (Salazar 2000, pp. 9–53; Golubović et al. 2009; James 2009; Laskaris 2015). While the evidence permits identification of broad trends, notably the increasing importance of archery, any attempt at quantitative analysis rests on multiple conjectures that would be insecure even in better-documented periods and cultures. In addition, literary considerations call for careful handling of historical sources. Episodes of precision marksmanship by elite warriors aimed to thrill contemporary readers (Procop. *Wars* 1.1.6–16, 4.13.14–16, 24.11, 5.22.1–7; Agath. 1.9.3–4; 2.14.1–4), but the realities of archery training and combat affirm a long-standing Roman tactical doctrine prioritizing volume and continuity of missile-fire over accuracy (Wheeler 2001), while the empire's primary eastern opponent, the Persians, customarily practiced rapid, massed high-trajectory archery. Furthermore, some contemporary Latin and Greek histories indulge a taste for graphic accounts of remarkable or grotesque wounds. Around the mid-160s Lucian's satirical essay on how to write history had ridiculed the kind of historian who dwells upon "altogether incredible wounds and bizarre deaths" (*Hist. conscr.* 20; D'Huys 1987, pp. 245–248), but in late antique classicizing historiography the wounded soldier becomes an occasion for purple prose and/or displays of technical expertise. Ammianus regales his audience with grisly and sensationalized descriptions of heads severed or hacked apart, for which he alleges eyewitness testimony: "the corpses of the slain, kept upright by the throng, could find no space to fall, and before me one soldier, his head cleft asunder and split into two equal parts by a powerful sword stroke, was so pressed from all sides that he stood upright like a tree trunk" (18.8.12; also 16.12.52–53, 19.2.7, 31.7.13–14, 13.3–4). In some instances, Vergilian allusion is discerned (*Aen.* 9.749–756; with Kelly 2008, pp. 22, 34).

Procopius reports in greater detail (*Wars* 6.2.14–18) astounding head wounds sustained by members of Belisarius' retinue outside Rome in 537:

> Cutilas, though struck in the middle of the head by a javelin, set off in pursuit, with the projectile still embedded there. Once the rout was completed, he galloped into the city around sunset together with the survivors, the javelin in his head swaying back and forth, a most outlandish sight. In this action also a Gothic bowman hit Arzes ... between the nose and the right eye. And the tip of the arrow penetrated as far as the back of the neck, but did not in fact show through, while the rest of the shaft protruded from his face and shook as the man rode. And on seeing him with Cutilas, the Romans reacted with great astonishment to the fact that they continued to ride, paying no heed to their injuries.

Procopius stands out among late antique historians for the anatomical precision of his accounts of combat-wounds, both mortal and minor, in terms of muscles, arteries, and tendons (e.g. *Wars* 2.3.24–25, 3.23.18, 5.18.29–33, 6.1.26, 2.22–23, 32, 4.15, 5.24–27, 27.14–15, 7.4.23–29). This trait has been variously explained in terms of his medical interest or knowledge, his fondness for extraordinary phenomena and desire to cater to readers' curiosity, and/or a self-conscious echoing of the gruesome anatomism of battle-wounds in Homer's *Iliad*, in tune with Procopius' penchant for heroic episodes of monomachy, though the absence of obvious Homeric parallels, in language or substance, would make this an oblique form of Homerizing (Salazar 2000, pp. 13, 34–35, 120–121, 220–122; Hornblower 2007, pp. 48–49; Rance 2005, pp. 428–429; Whately 2016, pp. 161–169). Similarly sensational in tone and objective is Theophylact's baroque vignette of a much-wounded soldier found on the battlefield of Solachon in 586, pierced with four missiles in his face, arm, and flank. These included two arrows, one penetrating his upper lip from above, the other piercing his lower lip from below, "so that owing to such opposing projectiles his tongue was marked with a cross by the counterposed conjunction of their points, and hence the hero was not able to close his lips." Theophylact's melodramatic narration of the physicians' attempts to save this paladin and his ultimate demise is clearly modeled on a well-known story of the death of Epaminondas in 362 BCE (Theoph. Sim. 2.6.1–9; cf. Diod. Sic. 15.87.5–6). This phenomenon is not restricted to historical prose writing. The peculiarly gory esthetic that emerges in some portrayals of combat in epic poetry between the later fourth/fifth and sixth centuries may similarly reflect a contemporary taste for the macabre, most evidently in Corippus' Vergilian verse narrative of recent campaigns against the Moors (546-548), whose unrelenting sequences of severed limbs, rolling heads and fountains of blood are not precedented in Vergil or his previous imitators (e.g. Coripp. *Ioh.* 5.104–133, 280–290; 8.479–488; also e.g. *Blemyomachia* frag. 11 [*P. Berol.* 5003 A^r], ll. 8–15 [ed. Steinrück]; Nonnus, *Dion.* 22.168–246, 293–372; 23.18–116; 28.27–172).

Diverse considerations determined access to medical assistance, including severity of wounds, troop-type, and rank. A wounded cavalryman, assuming his mount was unharmed, could more easily make his way to the rear of the battle-line (Procop. *Wars* 6.2.21–24, 7.4.21–30). In the fifth and sixth centuries, senior officers were often attended by personal retinues (*bucellarii*), who in emergencies could carry or drag them to safety (Procop. *Wars* 4.21.27–28, 8.11.39–52; Agath. 4.14.4–5; Evagr. 6.15). A crucial factor was the outcome of the engagement: victors were able to tend their wounded and bury their dead; defeat ordinarily precluded both practices. Furthermore, discounting hyperbole, starkly asymmetrical losses indicate the high proportion of casualties suffered by the defeated side in the final phase of battle. For example, at Strasbourg in 357 the Romans lost 243 men and four senior officers killed, and the Alemanni 6–8000; near Châtlons-sur-Marne in 364 the Romans lost 1200 killed and 200 wounded, and the Alemanni 6000 and 4000 respectively.

Outside Ctesiphon in 363, 2500 Persians fell in flight compared to c.70 Romans, and similarly 800 Vandals to 50 Romans at Tricamerum in 533. In contrast, the Roman army routed at Adrianople in 378, perhaps 20,000 strong, reportedly lost two-thirds of its strength (Amm. Marc. 16.12.63, 24.6.15, 27.2.7, 31.13.18; Lib. *Or.* 18.60; Zos. 3.25; Procop. *Wars* 4.3.18). If circumstances permitted, treatment of casualties took place on the battlefield, in the army's encampment, and/or after evacuation from the combat zone. Historical narratives indicate that on campaign, and particularly after engagements, commanders took steps to evacuate the wounded by wagon-train to secure locations, usually cities or fortresses in friendly territory, where they could be treated and recuperate. Convalescents might be billeted in civilian households (*SHA Sev. Alex.* 47.2; Mal. 12.36; Procop. *Wars* 2.19.45; Theoph. Sim. 2.6.12).

Procopius supplies the only contemporary report of surgical procedures (*Wars* 6.2.25–31). Continuing his account of Belisarius' wounded retainers:

> In the case of Arzes, though the physicians wished to extract the missile from his face, they were for some time reluctant to do so, not on account of the eye, which they surmised could not possibly be saved, but for fear that, by piercing any of the numerous membranes and sinews in this region, they might cause the death of a man who was one of the best in Belisarius' household. Subsequently one of the physicians, Theoctistus by name, pressing on the back of the man's neck, inquired whether he felt much pain. When he said that he did feel pain, he declared, "Then both you yourself shall be saved and your sight shall suffer no damage." And he made this assertion, having inferred that the tip of the missile had penetrated to a point not far from the skin. So he cut off and discarded the part of the shaft that was externally visible, and making an incision in the skin at the back of the head, at the point where the man felt the greatest pain, without difficulty he extracted the tip, which had three sharp barbs projecting backwards and brought with it the remaining section of the missile. Thus Arzes remained altogether unharmed by his injury, and no trace of his wound was left on his face. As for Cutilas, however, when the javelin was extracted more forcefully from his head – for it was very deeply embedded – he fell into unconsciousness. Since the membranes in that region began to be inflamed, he was seized by phrenetis and died not long afterward.

If Procopius was not actually present in the "operating theater," as a member of Belisarius' retinue he was well placed to consult physicians or staff-officers, and this section of his narrative is especially informed by medical opinion (also *Wars* 6.2.22–23, 32). It is not known whether Theoctistus, apparently a Greek, and the other unnamed physicians were military personnel or inhabitants of Rome. Although the typicality of such surgical expertise is questionable, Theoctistus applied age-old techniques recommended in Greco-Roman medical literature, both ancient and near-contemporary: Celsus prescribed similar procedures in the early first century (*De med.* 7.5.1–3), while the medical compendium compiled by Paul of Aegina (fl. 640s) contains a more systematic analysis of missile extraction (6.88; Salazar 1998, 2000, pp. 47–51).

Medical Discharge

Following convalescence, successfully treated soldiers returned to their units. Men disabled in action or rendered unfit by illness or infirmity were typically discharged. Selective reiteration of earlier imperial judgments and juristic opinions in Justinianic legislative compilations suggests continuity of practices and principles. The *Codex Iustinianus* incorporates a rescript of Gordian III (238–244) to a former soldier who sought re-admittance into the army, having previously received a medical discharge (*causaria missio*): "Once soldiers have been discharged on medical grounds, it is not usual for them to be reinstated on the pretext of recovered health, since there is no chance that they would have been discharged, unless it was established by reports from physicians (*medicis denuntiantibus*) and also careful inspection by a competent official that they had sustained an impairment" (12.35.6). This ruling implies that army doctors had to certify that a soldier's disability or infirmity was irremediable and permanent (Davies 1969, p. 92; Campbell 1984, pp. 311–314). A number of paragraphs in the *Digest*, drawing on the writings of third-century jurists, clarify aspects of medical discharge (*Dig.* 3.2.2§2, 29.1.4, 26, 49.16.13§2–3). Another rescript issued c.244–247 had affirmed that anyone "discharged on medical grounds" should suffer no stain on his reputation (*CJ* 12.35.8). Nevertheless, in specific circumstances, later legislation had deemed a medical discharge on account of combat-wounds to be more deserving than one arising from illness or infirmity (*CTh* 7.20.4.3 [325]). Subsequent laws promulgated throughout the fourth century nuanced the privileges and immunities granted to soldiers discharged on medical grounds, depending on length of service, class of regiment and/or nature of invalidity (*CTh* 7.18.9.2 [396], 20.4 [325], 8 [364], 12.1 [400]; *CJ.* 10.55.3 [293–305]). Late fifth- and sixth-century sources allege that some injured or infirm soldiers, presumably with their officers' connivance, remained on regimental muster-rolls by fraudulent means in order to retain the pay, rations, and legal security of their profession. Successive emperors, notably Anastasius and Justinian, sought to suppress or delimit this recurrent abuse (*SEG* IX 356§7 [501]; Proc. Gaz. *Pan. Anast.* 7; Procop. *Anecd.* 24.2–8). In 594, Maurice's improvement of privileges accorded to men disabled in action, including pensions and rights of urban residence (Theoph. Sim. 7.1.7), though ostensibly popular measures, probably also sought to address the continuing problem of "non-effectives" on the muster-rolls.

Conclusion

This chapter has sought to assemble and contextualize the written evidence relating to health and medicine, broadly construed, in the late Roman army. Beyond the overarching constraints imposed by the dwindling source material for all aspects of the army in this period, individual genres present particular interpretative challenges, especially the literary priorities of late antique historiography. The evidence points to substantial continuity in institutional attitudes to soldiers' health, including treatment of combat-wounds, which is apparent at both a procedural and organizational level. Prescriptions in military treatises and descriptions in historical narratives concur that late Roman commanders, with good reason, endeavored to care for sick and wounded soldiers on campaign. While information about structures and personnel is slim, some soldiers clearly enjoyed access to medical treatment and regimental *medici* continue to be documented in units of different type, class, and history, ranging from a new-style palatine cavalry unit in Rome to an old-style legion in Upper Egypt. Even so, as during the Principate, generalizations are hazardous and uniformity through time and place cannot be assumed. Much remains obscure, particularly with regard to routine healthcare of soldiers in peacetime. Avenues for future inquiry include the location of health and medicine within the larger picture of late Roman military culture and society, and specifically the shifting nature and proximity of soldier–civilian relations, changes to soldiers' family life and residence, and the spread of Christian beliefs.

Notes

1 All dates CE unless otherwise indicated.
2 I plan to pursue aspects of this study in greater detail elsewhere.

References

Bader, P. (2012). "L'implantation des espaces de soins dans les camps permanents de l'armée romaine." In: *Conserver la santé ou la rétablir. Le rôle de l'environnement dans la médecine antique et médiévale* (ed. N. Palmieri), 227–247. Saint-Etienne.

Bader, P. (2014). "The identity, legal status and origin of the Roman army's medical staff in the Imperial Age." In: *In 'Greek' and 'Roman' in Latin Medical Texts* (ed. B. Maire), 43–59. Leiden: Brill.

Baker, P. (2004). *Medical Care for the Roman Army on the Rhine, Danube and British Frontiers in the First, Second and Early Third Centuries AD (BAR int. ser. 1286).* Oxford: Archaeopress.

Baker, P. (2009). "Medicine, death and military virtues." In: *Formae mortis: el tránsito de la vida a la muerte en las sociedades antiguas* (eds. F.M. Simón, F.P. Polo and J.R. Rodríguez), 25–37. Barcelona: Universitat de Barcelona.

Baldwin, B. (1975). "The career of Oribasius." *Acta Classica* 18: 85–97.

Baroin, C. (2002). "Les cicatrices ou la mémoire du corps." In: *Corps romains* (ed. P. Moreau), 27–46. Grenoble: Millon.

Blockley, R. (1980). "Doctors as diplomats in the sixth century A.D." *Florilegium* 2: 89–100.

Campbell, J.B. (1984). *The Emperor and the Roman Army 31 BC–AD 235.* Oxford: Clarendon.

Davies, R. (1969). "The *medici.* of the Roman armed forces." *Epigraphische Studien* 8: 83–99.

Davies, R. (1970). "The Roman military medical service." *Saalburg Jahrbuch* 27: 84–104.

Davies, R. (1972). "Some more military *medici.*" *Epigraphische Studien* 9: 1–11.

D'Huys, V. (1987). "How to describe violence in historical narrative. Reflections of the ancient Greek historians and their ancient critics." *Ancient Society* 18: 209–250.

Dyczek, P. (2005). "The site of the *valetudinarium* in Novae in the third century AD: remodelling the architecture." In: *Römische Städte und Festungen an der Donau (Akten der regionalen Konferenz, Beograd, 16–19 Oktober 2003)* (ed. M. Mirković), 231–238. Belgrade: Filozofski Fakultet.

Evans, R. (1999). "Displaying honourable scars: a Roman gimmick." *Acta Classica* 42: 77–94.

Gabriel, R. (2012). *Man and Wound in the Ancient World. A History of Military Medicine from Sumer to the Fall of Constantinople.* Washington DC: Potomac Books.

Golubović, S., Mrdjić, N., and Scott Speal, C. (2009). "Killed by the arrow: grave no. 152 from Viminacium." In: *Waffen in Aktion (ROMEC XVI)* (eds. A. Busch and H.-J. Schalles), 55–63. Mainz: Philipp von Zabern.

Hirt Raj, M. (2006). *Médecins et malades de l'Égypte romaine.* Leiden: Brill.

Hoffmann, D. (1969–1970). *Das spätrömische Bewegungsheer und die Notitia Dignitatum.* Dusseldorf: Rheinland-Verlag.

Hornblower, S. (2007). "Warfare in ancient literature." In: *CHGRW*, vol. 1, 22–53.

James, S. (2009). "The point of the sword: what Roman-era weapons could do to bodies – and why they often didn't." In: *Waffen in Aktion (ROMEC XVI)* (eds. A. Busch and H.-J. Schalles), 41–54. Mainz: Philipp von Zabern.

Kelly, G. (2008). *Ammianus Marcellinus. The Allusive Historian.* Cambridge: CUP.

Kislinger, E. and Stathakopoulos, D. (1999). "Pest und Perserkriege bei Prokop. Chronologische Überlegungen zum Geschehen 540-545." *Byzantion* 69: 76–98.

Lascaratos, J. and Voros, D. (2000). "Fatal wounding of the Byzantine Emperor Julian the Apostate (361-363 A.D.)." *World Journal of Surgery* 24: 615–619.

Laskaris, J. (2015). "Treating hemorrhage in Greek and Roman militaries." In: *Ancient Warfare: Introducing Current Research*, vol. I (eds. G. Lee, H. Whittaker and G. Wrightson), 273–290. Newcastle: Cambridge Scholars Publishing.

Leigh, M. (1995). "Wounding and popular rhetoric at Rome." *Bulletin of the Institute of Classical Studies* 40: 195–215.

Lettich, G. (1984). *Le iscrizioni sepolcrali tardoantiche di Concordia*. Trieste: Centro studi storico-religiosi Friuli-Venezia Giulia.

Little, L. (ed.) (2006). *Plague and the End of Antiquity: The Pandemic of 541–750*. Cambridge: Cambridge University Press.

Neal, T. (2006). *The Wounded Hero. Non-Fatal Injury in Homer's* Iliad. Bern: Lang.

Neal, T. (2008). "Blood and hunger in the *Iliad*." *Classical Philology* 101: 15–33.

Peters, S. (2011). "Hygieneaspekte im *valetudinarium* an der römischen Rheinfront." In: *Medizingeschichte in Schlaglichtern. Beiträge des "Rheinischen Kreises der Medizinhistoriker"* (eds. D.G.A. Karenberg, S. Kaiser and W. Antweiler), 15–32. Kassel: Kassel University Press.

Philipsborn, A. (1950). "La compagnie d'ambulanciers "parabalani" d'Alexandrie." *Byzantion* 20: 185–190.

Prinzing, F. (1916). *Epidemics Resulting from Wars*. Oxford: Clarendon.

Rance, P. (2000). "*Simulacra pugnae*: the literary and historical tradition of mock battles in the Roman and Early Byzantine army." *Greek Roman and Byzantine Studies* 41: 223–275.

Rance, P. (2005). "Narses and the Battle of Taginae (Busta Gallorum) 552: Procopius and Sixth-Century Warfare." *Historia* 54: 424–472.

Rance, P. (forthcoming). *The Roman Art of War in Late Antiquity: The Strategikon of the Emperor Maurice. A Translation with Commentary and Textual and Historical Studies*, 2 vols. London: Routledge.

Rubin, R. (1997). "Priests, soldiers and administrators: society and institutions in the Byzantine Negev." *Mediterranean Historical Review* 12 (1): 56–74.

Salazar, C. (1998). "Getting the point: Paul of Aegina on arrow wounds." *Sudhoffs Archiv* 82 (2): 170–187.

Salazar, C. (2000). *The Treatment of War Wounds in Graeco-Roman Antiquity*. Leiden: Brill.

Scheidel, W. (2001). *Death on the Nile: Disease and the Demography of Roman Egypt*. Leiden: Brill.

Scheidel, W. (2003). "Germs for Rome." In: *Rome the Cosmopolis* (eds. C. Edwards and G. Woolf), 158–176. Cambridge: Cambridge University Press.

Scheidel, W. (2007). "Marriage, families, and survival: demographic aspects." In: *A Companion to the Roman Army* (ed. P. Erdkamp), 417–434. Oxford: Wiley-Blackwell.

Schulze, C. (2005). *Medizin und Christentum in Spätantike und frühem Mittelalter*. Tubingen: Mohr Siebeck.

Schulze, C. (2009). "Angst um die eigene Gesundheit – Patientenzeugnisse aus der Antike." In: *Gesundheit – Geisteswissenschaftliche und Medizinische Aspekte* (eds. W. Geerlings and A. Mügge), 11–24. Berlin: Lit-Verlag.

Seibert, J. (1983). "Heeresseuchen und Kriegsverlauf." In: *Althistorische Studien. Festschrift Hermann Bengtson* (eds. H. Heinen, K. Stroheker and G. Walser), 78–91. Wiesbaden: Steiner.

Stathakopoulos, D. (2004). *Famine and Pestilence in the Late Roman and Early Byzantine Empire: A Systematic Survey of Subsistence Crises and Epidemics*. Aldershot: Ashgate.

Vetters, H. (1976). "Lauriacum." In: *Aufstieg und Niedergang der römischen Welt* II.6: 355–379.

Whately, C. (2016). *Battles and Generals. Combat, Culture, and Didacticism in Procopius'* Wars. Leiden: Brill.

Wheeler, E.L. (2001). "Firepower: missile weapons and the "face of battle"." In: *Roman Military Studies* (ed. E. Dąbrowa), 169–184. Cracow: Jagiellonian University Press.

Whitby, M. (1988). *The Emperor Maurice and his Historian, Theophylact Simocatta on Persian and Balkan Warfare.* Oxford: Clarendon Press.

Wilmanns, J. (1995). *Der Sanitätsdienst im römischen Reich: Ein sozialgeschichtliche Studie zum römischen Militärsanitätswesen nebst einer Prosopographie des Sanitätspersonals.* Hildesheim: Olms-Wiedemann.

Further Reading

In addition to studies of Roman military medicine during the Principate cited in the References, and in light of the comparatively limited evidence for and research into Late Antiquity, some recent investigations of other pre-modern periods and cultures offer potential historical comparanda and novel methodologies.

Harris, W.V. (ed.) (2016). *Popular Medicine in Graeco-Roman Antiquity: Explorations.* Leiden: Brill.

Kirkham, A. and Warr, C. (2014). *Wounds in the Middle Ages.* Aldershot: Ashgate.

Nutton, V. (2004). *Ancient Medicine.* London: Routledge.

Petridou, G. and Thumiger, C. (eds.) (2016). *Homo Patiens: Approaches to the Patient in the Ancient World.* Leiden: Brill.

Samama, E. (2017). *La médecine de guerre en Grèce ancienne.* Turnhout: Brepols.

Smith, M. (2017). *Mortal Wounds: the Human Skeleton as Evidence for Conflict in the Past.* Barnsley: Pen and Sword Military.

Tracy, L. and DeVries, K. (2015). *Wounds and Wound Repair in Medieval Culture.* Leiden: Brill.

Index

Note: Locators followed by 'n' refer to notes.

a

Achaea/Achaeans   24, 62
Achaean League   68–69, 71
Aegesilaos   24, 44
Aemilius Lepidus M. (younger)   118
Aemilius Paulus, L.   76, 106–107
Aitolia/Aitolians   23, 71, 73
Aitolian League   69–70, 103, 106
Agrigentum   108
Ala, *see* Units, Roman
Ala Pannoniorum   168, 169
Alcibiades   42, 54
Alexander III, the Great   2–4, 21, 48, 56, 67–68,
   71–74, 76, 81, 91, 140–141
   Mosaic   74
   Sarcophagus   74
Ammianus Marcellinus   82, 177, 179
Amygdala   57, 134–135
Antigonid Dynasty   68–70, 76
Antigonus Monaphthalmus   68, 70
Antiochus III, the Great   68–73, 102–103, 106
Antiochus IV   73
Antonius, M.   117–118
Archers/Arrows   47, 70–71, 83, 142, 144, 163,
   166–167, 179–180
archiatrisacripalatii   177
Argos/Argives   18, 23, 34–35
Aristophanes   18, 21, 57
Armenia/Armenians   73
Armor   1–2, 9, 22, 41, 47, 58, 61, 65, 67, 92, 155,
   see also Cavalry, Armor

Asia, Central   47, 56
Asia Minor/Anatolia   24, 45, 68, 76, 81, 101,
   106, 121
Assassination   116, 118, *see also* Conspiracy,
   Military
Assembly
   Greek   23, 35–36
   Military (*contio*)   120, 123
   Roman   108–109
assidui   101, 109–110
Athens/Athenians   18–24, 29–36, 42–43, 45–46, 53,
   55–62, 65, 67, 69–71, 73, 76–77, 81–84, 88–89,
   91, 136, *see also* Cavalry, Athenian
   Agora   65, 70–71, 77, 82–84, 88–89, 91
   Commanders/Generals   19, 23, 32, 35, 73
   Navy   20–21, 24, 45
Attica   18–20, 65, 71
Augustus (C. Iulius Caesar [Octavianus] and
   Imp. Caesar Augustus)   56–57, 117–118,
   120, 122, 149, 173
Auxilia, Roman   61, 123, 132, 149–151,
   153–155, 161, 163–170, 173 *see also* Forts,
   Roman; Units, Roman

b

Bakers   19, 46
Barley   19, 102
Barracks
   Greek   40, 46
   Roman   152–153
Batavi (Batavians)   163, 167

New Approaches to Greek and Roman Warfare, First Edition. Edited by Lee L. Brice.
© 2020 John Wiley & Sons, Inc. Published 2020 by John Wiley & Sons, Inc.

Battle(s)
  Greek   3, 18, 21–22, 30–32, 35, 40, 45, 48,
    54–55, 60–61, 67–69, 73, 76–77, 81, 83,
    91–92
  Roman   100, 114, 118, 127–130, 132, 136–137,
    139–143, 146, 174, 180
Belisarius   180–181
Birrens   164, 166–167, 169
Blockade, see Siege: methods
Booty, *see* Plunder
Bravery   22, 43, 53–54, 69, 143–145
Bribery   118
Britain   151, 153–155, 161, 164–170
Britanni (Britons)   165–166, 169

c

Caligula, *see* Gaius
Callicratidas   19
Camps, *see also* Forts
  Greek   43–46, 68
  Roman   116, 122–123, 149, 153, 176, 178
Camp Followers
  Greek   39, 43
  Roman   101, 149–150, 153, 157
canabae, *see vicus*
Cannae, Battle of   56, 129, 132, 136
capsarius   176, *see also* Medical personnel
Carthage/Carthaginians   19, 100, 102–103, 106,
    108, 136
Carvilius Maximus, Sp.   106–107
Cataphracts   68, 72–73, 77
Cavalry   65–77, 91, *see also* Cataphracts; *sarissa*
  armor   65, 67, 72–73, 75–77
  Athenian   65–67, 70–72, 77
  Macedonian   67–68, 73–75, 91
  shields   73, 75–77
  weapons   67, 70–75, 91
Central Nervous System (CNS)   57, 127, 131–133
Centurion   103, 120, 122, 140, 150, 156, 178
Chaerea, C.   116
Chaironeia, Battle of   55, 67, 81, 83–88, 91–92
Children   29, 43, 58–59, 84, 89, 91–92, 100, 146,
    149–157n1, 163, 182
Cimon   21
Civil War
  Roman   117–119, 121
  United States   40, 54, 60–61

Claudius Centho, Ap.   106–107
Claudius (Tib. Claudius CaesarAugustus
    Germanicus)   116–117, 151–152
Clearchus   61
Cleidemus   21
Cleisthenes   21, 23
Cognition   131–132
Cohesion, Unit   40, 42–43, 48, 118–120,
    123–124, 144, 166
Cohorts, *see also* Units, Roman
  cohors IV Gallorum.   165–167, 169
  cohors Marsacorum.   167
  cohors II Tungrorum.   164–167, 169
Coins/Coinage   17–21, 23–25, 29, 33, 35–36, 44,
    47, 57, 70, 74, 77, 99, 101–108, 176
Combat   40, 113–114, 117–120, 128, 130, 136,
    139–147, 149, 174–176, 178–182
comitia centuriata, *see* Assembly, Roman
Commander/General   1–2, 18–19, 24–25, 36,
    39–43, 45, 48–49, 56, 61, 69, 73, 100–102,
    107–109, 115–124, 128–130, 139–147, 150,
    161, 164, 166–167, 176–178, *see also*
    Commanders, Athenian; Leadership
Condrusi   164–167, 169
Conspiracy, Military   115–116, 118
Consul   69, 100, 106–109, 147n2
contio, *see* Assembly
conubium   156, 163
Corinth   18, 23, 31–32, 35
Cornelius Cinna, L.   116–118, 120
Cornelius Scipio Aemilianus Africanus, P.
    101, 140
Cornelius Scipio Africanus, P.   100–101, 140,
    145, 147n1
Cornelius Scipio, L.   100–101, 106–107, 140
Cornelius Sulla Felix, L.   116–118
Cowardice   54–58, 67–68, 115, 117–118,
    128–133, 136, 143–144
Croton   32
Cynoscephalae, Battle of   69, 103
Cyrean, *see* Ten Thousand
Cyrus II, the Great   47
Cyrus (the Younger)   18, 22, 43–45, 61

d

Danube Frontier   117, 151–153, 174–175
Dea Gallia   165, 169

Decimation   114, 123

Defeat   23–24, 30, 43, 46, 53, 60–61, 67–69, 73,
       91–92, 99–100, 103–106, 142–143, 180

Defect/Defection   116–118, 121

Delian League   34–36, *see also* Empire, Athenian

Delium, Battle of   55, 60

Delphi   22–24, 31, 69, 76

Demetrius Poliorcetes   68, 70

Demosthenes   19, 23–24

deputatus   179, *see also* Medical personnel

Desert/Desertion   44, 117–119, 122

Dionsysius I of Syracuse   19, 24

Diplomas, Military   150, 156

Discharge
   honorable   119, 122–123, 150, 163, 176
   medical   176, 178, 181–182

Discipline   41, 43, 47–48, 69, 100, 113–125, 128,
       143–146, 176

Disease   44, 58, 174–175, 177

Doctor (*medicus, iatros*)   173, 176–178, 180–182

Drums and Trumpets history   2–3, 9

Drusus (Drusus Julius Tib. *f.*Caesar)   123

Duilius, C.   102, 108

e

Egypt   2, 47–48, 58, 68, 77, 128, 178, 182

Elis   18, 24, 70–71

Elite authors   1, 119, 124, 140–141, 179–180

Elite status   43, 47–48, 177, 179

Empire
   Athenian   21, 24, 29, 33
   Persian, Achaemenid   21, 30, 39, 41, 47–48, 74
   Persian, Sassanid   73, 175, 177, 179, 181
   Roman   56, 102, 106, 113, 116–117, 119,
       123–124, 149, 151, 161–165, 173–174

Engineers, Combat   141–142, 145

Epaminondas   23–24, 67, 180

ephodia (Travel Money)   19–20

Epigraphy, *see* Inscriptions

Epigraphic Habit   162, 173

Epinephrine/Adrenaline   135–136

Eretria   20, 31

Ethnicity   161–163, 170

Euripides   53, 58–61

Eurymedon River, Battle of   23

Expression of Grievances   115, 117, 120

Extramural settlement, *see vicus*

f

Face of Battle School   12–13, 9, 40, 127, 141

Family/Families   21, 43, 53, 55–56, 58–61,
       99–100, 109, 140, 143, 146, 149–157, 163,
       182, *see also* Children; Women

Fear, *see* Cowardice; Panic

Fimbriani   116, 118–119

Flavius Fimbria, C.   116, 118

Fleeing/Flight, *see* Cowardice; Panic

Fortifications, see also Walls, City; Forts
   Greek   29–31, 44, 82, 84
   Roman   141–143, 147

Forts, Greek   30, 46

Forts, Roman (*castra*)
   auxilia   149, 150–157, 173
   frontier
       Aislingen   152
       Burghöfe   152
       Carlisle   154–155
       Carnuntum   155
       Castra Vetera   123
       Emerkingen   152
       Hüfingen   153
       Kempten   151
       Oberstimm   152
       Vindolanda   153–155
       Vindonissa   153
       Xanten   155
   legionary   46, 123, 150–152, 155–157, 174

Fulvius Nobilior, M.   107

g

Gaius (C. Iulius Caesar Augustus
       Germanicus)   116

Galatians   68, 76

Galli   61, 99, 106, 165–166, 169

Gaul   147, 165–166, 169

Generalship, *see* Leadership

Germani   166–167, 175

Germanicus (Germanicus Iulius Caesar)
       123–124

h

Hadrian (Imp. Caesar Traianus Hadrianus
       Augustus)   163

Hadrian's Wall   105, 153–154, 167

Hannibal   69, 99–100, 102, 108–109, 132

Hanson, V.D.   3, 6, 17, 29, 40
Helots, *see* Messenia
Herodotus   1, 22–24, 32–35, 47–48, 55, 57, 136
Heroic behavior, *see* Bravery
Herulians   81–84, 88–91
Hiero   102–103, 108
Homer   22, 30, 40, 53, 55, 60, 91, 128–130, 133, 136, 145, 174, 180
Hospital, Military   173–174, 176
Hygiene (sanitation)   39, 45–46, 173–175
Hysterical blindness   53, 55–58, 136

i

iatros, *see* Doctor
Identity   162–166, 170
Iliad   30, 45, 130, 133, 136, 139–140, 142, 146, 174, 180
immunis   176, 178
Immunity   178, 182
Indemnity   102–103, 105–106, 108
Indiscipline   42, 47, 113–124
Inscriptions (Epigraphy)   9, 19–20, 48, 56, 65, 70–71, 76–77, 102, 150, 156, 161–170, 173–174, 177
Instinct   136, 141, 147
Insubordination   42, 114–118, *see also* Desert/ Desertion; Defect/Defection
Ipsos, Battle of   68

j

Jason of Pherae   22
Jerusalem   144–145
Jewish Revolts   129
Josephus   129, 144–145
Julius Caesar, C. (C. Iulius Caesar)   2–4, 103, 117–118, 120, 140–142, 145, 147n2

k

Kalkriese (Teutoburg Forest)   2, 149, 151
Keegan, John   2–3, 40, 127, 136, *see also* Face of Battle School
Kerameikos Cemetery   60–61, 65, 67

l

Lancia   168
laphuropoloi   23
Latobici   165, 167, 169

Law   57, 62n3, 113–114, 119, 122, 146, 149–150, 156, 163, 173–174, 177–179, 182
Leadership   1, 56, 115, 117, 119–120, 122–123, 141, 144–145
Legate   102, 108, 122, 147n2
Legion, *see also* Units, Roman
   Legion I   122–123
   Legion V   122–123
   Legion IX Hispana   117, 122, 168
   Legion XV Apollinaris   168
   Legion XX   122, 168
   Legion XXI   122–123
Legionary   56–57, 61, 101–103, 120, 122, 131–134, 136 *see also* units, Roman
Livy   56, 103, 106, 108–109, 129, 132, 136, 140, 147n2
Logistics   17–20, 25, 31–32, 39–41, 43–48, 101, 173, 175
Lucocadia   168

m

Macedon/Macedonia/Macedonians   34, 48, 59, 67–70, 73–77, 81, 91–92, 101, 108–110
Magna Graecia   67, 75, *see also* Croton; Sybaris; Taras/Tarantines
Magnesia, Battle of   68, 70, 103
Mamertines   108
Manlius Vulso, Cn.   101, 106–107, 109
Manpower
   Greek   17, 30, 62
   Persian   47
   Roman   99–101, 175
Mantineia, Battle of   18, 23, 69, 71–72
Marathon, Battle of   3, 32, 55–57, 60, 136
Marriage   48, 55, 57, 73, 99–101, 149–150, 156, 163
Marsaci   167
Matronalia   154
Marshall, S.L.A.   40, 136
Medical personnel   173–174, 176–179, 181–182
Medical services   41, 173–182
Medicines (*res medica*)   173–175, 183n3
medicus   176–178, *see also* Doctor; Medical personnel
Memorials
   Greek   60–61, 81, 83, 87
   Modern   60–61
   Roman   60–61

Mercenaries   19, 21–24, 42–48, 56, 62, 69–73, 75–77

Messenia/Messenians   23, 30, 34–35, 42

Military Community/Society
  Greek   39–40, 42–45, 48
  Roman   114, 120, 124, 144, 149–157, 161, 163–165, 167, 169, 182

Military Sociology   4, 114, 125n4

Miltiades   20, 32–33, 35, 55

Mind/Body Question   128

Mithridates VI   73, 118

Morale   56, 69, 128, 139, 142, 144, 147, 175

Motivation   142–145

Mutiny   19, 114–124, 125n4

n

Nero (Nero Claudius Caesar Augustus Germanicus)   152

Nessana   178

Neurophysiology   127–137

Nicias   19, 61

Non-Combatants (incl. Civilians)   24, 42–43, 81, 84, 89–92, 101, 122–123, 143, 145–146, 149–153, 155, 164–165, 176–178

o

Octavian (C. Julius Caesar Octavianus), *see* Augustus

Officers, *see also* Commander; Centurion
  Greek   23, 41, 47
  Modern   2, 41, 43
  Persian   47
  Roman   61, 108, 113–122, 124, 129, 140, 150, 154, 176–178, 180–182

Onasander   132

optio/valetudinarii   176, 178

p

Panic   56, 58, 74, 127–137, 143, 180, *see also* Cowardice

Pannonia   122–123, 125n5, 155, 165, 167–170

Panormus   108

Paros   24, 32–33, 35

Peloponnesian War   18–19, 21, 29, 33–36, 46, 54, 57–59, 61

Peloponnesus   18, 24, 30, 62, 67, 69, 81

Perception   127–136

Pericles   18–19, 21, 34–35, 37n4

Peripheral Nervous System   133

Persia, *see* Empire, Persian

Persian War   3, 17, 20, 22–23, 25n1, 32–34, 36n2, 48, 54–55, 57, 60, 136

Phalanx
  hoplite   55, 67, 91–92, 140
  Macedonian   48, 67–68, 73, 91

Philip II   48, 67, 69, 71, 73, 75, 81, 91

Philip V   69, 76, 103, 109

Philopoemen   69, 72

Philosophers   1, 32, 42–43, 53–54, 57–58, 62, 147n2

Physicians, *see* Doctor; Medical personnel

phobos   129

Plataea   22, 36n2, 48, 54

Plato   42–43, 54–55, 147n2

Plunder   17–25, 40, 44, 73, 101–103, 105–109, 140, 144, 146

Plutarch   21, 35, 53, 56, 81, 91

Polybius   69, 73, 99, 103, 106, 108, 140, 145, 147n1

Pompeius Magnus, Cn.   118

Porcius Cato, M., (the elder)   5, 102–103, 106–107

Post-Traumatic Stress Disorder (PTSD)   57–58, 127–128, 137n1

Postumius Albinus, A.   116, 120

Postumius Albinus, L.   106–107

Potidaia   35–36, 42, 54–55, 71

Praetorian Guard   116, 123

Prisoners of war   21

Pritchett, W.K.   21–24, 29, 46

Procopius   180–181

prodromoi   68, 70–72

Ptolemy IV   68

Ptolemy V   69

Punishment   32, 47, 55, 109, 113–114, 117, 119–121, 123, 144, 146

Pydna   34

q

Quinctilius Flamininus, T.   69, 73, 106–107

Quinctilius Varus, P.   149, 151

r

Raetia/Raeti   151–153, 164–167, 169
Rape   47, 146 *see also* Sack
Raphia, Battle of   68, 72
Recruit/Recruitment   43, 69–71, 99–101, 118–120, 123, 149, 156, 161–169, 176
Reenactment, Reenactors   41, 73–74
Religion, Greek   19, 22–24, 31, 44, 48, 55–56, 69, 73, *see also* Sanctuaries
Religion, Roman   152, 154, 164–167, 169
Revolt
  Greek   55
  Helot   34–35
  Roman   114–116, 168
Rewards   20–24, 122, 145–146, 176, *see also* Plunder
Rhine Frontier   117, 122, 163, 175
  forts   123, 153, 155, 174
  legions   122–123
Rome (city)   61, 102, 109, 120–123, 140, 177, 180–182, *see also* Empire, Roman
Rout, *see* Cowardice; Panic

s

Sack   23–24, 29–32, 34, 36, 71, 81–84, 88–91, 100, 143, 145–146
sacramentum (oath)   114
Sacred Band, Theban   43, 81, 85, 87, 91
Sacred Wars   24, 31
Samaria   165, 167
Samos/Samians   31–33, 35–36, 37n3
Sanctuary/Sanctuaries, Greek   19, 22–24, 31, 44, 69, 73
sarissa   67, 71–75, 91
schola palatine   177–178, 180, 182
Sempronius Gracchus, Ti. (the elder)   106–107
Senate   101–103, 108–110, 120, 123, 140
Sertorius, Q.   118
Service Conditions
  Greek   20–21, 24, 47, 71
  Persian   47–48
  Roman   99–100, 114, 119–122, 149, 163, 173–174, 182
Shoes, Roman   153–155
Sicily   19, 21, 24, 32, 34, 36, 37n2, 48, 60–61, 102–103, 108, 118

Siege   17–18, 24, 29–37, 42–43, 100, 124, 139–147, 175, 177
  methods/tactics
    assault   35, 45, 100, 142–146
    battering   142, 145
    blockade   24, 30, 36, 45, 142, 144–145
    circumvallation   29–30, 34–36, 37n2
    escalade (ladders)   142, 144
    mining/sapping   30, 141–142
    machines   141–142
    passive, *see* blockade
    ramp   141–142
    stealth   142
    tower   142, 144
Siscani   165, 167
sitêresion (grain money)   19–20, 24
Slaves   18, 21, 24–25, 29, 34, 36, 39, 42–44, 71, 84, 101, 146, 150, 154–155
Slingers/sling stones   29, 56, 83, 163, 166–167
Socrates   42, 54–55
Sophocles   59–61
Spain/Spaniards   99–103, 106, 163, 168–169
Sparta   18–19, 22–23, 30–32, 34–35, 41–47, 53–57, 61, 67, 69, 71, 76, 103
Spear (incl. Javelin)   55–56, 67, 70, 73–76, 83, 85, 91, 180–181
  Butt Spike   83, 85
Spoils, *see* Plunder
Stimulus   130–132, 134
stipendium   101, 103–108
Stanegate   154
Strategy   2–3, 39–40, 100, 129, 143, 146, 151, 174
Stretcher   178
Sulpicia Lepidina   153–154
Supplies, *see* Logistics
Surgery   178, 181, *see also* Wounds: healing
Surrender   18, 30, 32–36, 100, 103, 143, 146, 147n3
Sword   21, 56, 83, 85, 88, 91–92, 144
Sybaris   32–33, 35–36
Syene   178

t

Tactics   2, 39–40, 46, 68, 118, 129, 139–145, 147n1, 149, 179
Taras/Tarantines   70–72, 75–76
Ten Thousand, The (Cyreans)   18–19, 22, 24, 42–46, 61

Thasos 34–35, 37n3, 75
Thebes/Thebans 22–24, 30, 35, 43, 46, 55, 60, 67, 81, 85, 87, 91, 180
Themistocles 22, 24, 32
Thermopylae, Battle of 3, 54, 57
Thucydides 1, 17–19, 21–25, 29, 31–36n2, 41, 139–140
Tiberius (Tiberius Iulius Caesar Augustus) 118, 123, 152–153
Timotheus 19
Training 1–2
   Greek 18, 21, 48, 67, 69, 71, 81
   Roman 100, 114, 116, 128, 143–144, 175, 179
Trajan (Imp. Caesar Nerva Traianus Augustus) 165
Tribute 19, 21, 24, 35, 102
tributum 101–102, 107–110
Triumphs (Military Parade) 102–103, 106, 117
Trophy 23, 30, 92, 176
Troy 17, 30, 58, 61, 133, 136, 142, 146
Tungri 164, 166

u

Units, Roman
   ala 163, 167–170, 176
   century 140, 167–168, 170
   cohorts 123, 131, 140, 163–168, 170
   elite guards 116, 123, 177–178, 180, 182
   legions 8, 100–106, 108, 113, 116–120, 122–124, 131–134, 136, 140–141, 143–144, 149, 151, 153, 155, 168, 173–174, 178, 182
   turmae 170
   vexillation 164–167, 169–170

v

Valerius Flaccus, L. 116, 118
valetudinarium, see Hospital, Military
Varciani 165, 167, 169
Vegetius 176
Vellavi 165–166, 169
Veterans
   Greek 53–62

Modern 53–57, 59–62
Roman 53–62
vicus (Extramural Settlement) 150–157
Vietnam War 40, 54, 60–61
Vindolanda 153–155, 165–166, 169
Vipsanius Agrippa, M. 118
Vordenses (Voreda) 167

w

Wages, military 17, 19–21, 23–25, 36, 56, 101–103, 106, 109, 119, 163, 178, 182, *see also stipendium*
Walls, City 23, 30, 82, 84, 100, 102, 141–146, *see also* Fortifications
Weapons 3, 21, 40, 46–47, 56, 58, 67, 73, 76–77, 83–85, 89, 91–92, 114, 127–128, 141, 143–144, 179, *see also* Cavalry, weapons
Wheat (grain) 18–20, 23, 25, 36, 44–45, 60, 101–103, *see also sitêresion* (grain money)
Wives 48, 53, 58–59, 100, 146, 149–150, 153–154, 156
Women 4, 21, 29, 42–43, 45, 47–48, 53, 55–56, 58–61, 84, 89–92, 99–100, 109, 143, 146, 149–157n1, 163, 182, *see also* Family/Families
World War I 53–55, 57, 61
World War II 40, 55, 57, 61
Wounds/Wounded
   attitudes to 55–57, 175–176, 179–182
   blunt force trauma 56, 83, 85, 89–92
   discharge due to 55–56, 82–85, 87–92, 174, 176–177, 179–180, 182
   healing/treatment 56, 82, 84, 88–89, 174–182
   physical trauma 54, 82–92, 174–175, 180–181
   projectile/puncture 56, 83, 85, 177, 179–181
   psychological trauma 54–59, 127–128
   sharp force or blade trauma 56, 83–92, 179
Writing tablets 65, 71, 76–77

x

Xenophon 19, 22, 24, 42–48, 61–62, 67, 69, 71, 75, 129